BAR

Civil and Criminal Procedure

18th edition

Edited by Martin Hannibal
BA, LLM, Barrister

HLT Publications

HLT PUBLICATIONS
200 Greyhound Road, London W14 9RY

First published 1979
18th edition 1996

© The HLT Group Ltd 1996

All HLT publications enjoy copyright protection and the copyright belongs to The HLT Group Ltd.

All rights reserved. No part of this publication may be reproduced or transmitted in any form or by any means, electronic, mechanical, photocopying, recording or otherwise, or stored in any retrieval system of any nature without either the written permission of the copyright holder, application for which should be made to The HLT Group Ltd, or a licence permitting restricted copying in the United Kingdom issued by the Copyright Licensing Agency.

Any person who infringes the above in relation to this publication may be liable to criminal prosecution and civil claims for damages.

ISBN 0 7510 0710 2

British Library Cataloguing-in-Publication.
A CIP Catalogue record for this book is available from the British Library.

Acknowledgement

The publishers and author would like to thank the Incorporated Council of Law Reporting for England and Wales for kind permission to reproduce extracts from the Weekly Law Reports, and Butterworths for their kind permission to reproduce extracts from the All England Law Reports.

Printed and bound in Great Britain

Contents

Preface *ix*

Sources of the Law of Procedure *xi*

Abbreviations *xiii*

Table of Cases:

   Civil Procedure *xv*

   Criminal Procedure *xxv*

Part I Civil Procedure

1 The Choice of Court *3*

Introduction – English or foreign – Court or tribunal – High Court or County Court – The High Court – High Court Masters

2 Rules of the Supreme Court *10*

Origin of the Rules – Function of the Rules – Non-compliance with the Rules

3 The Issue of Proceedings *13*

Originating process – Writ – Originating Summons – Originating Motion – Petition – Issue of proceedings

4 Parties *19*

Introduction – Companies and corporate persons – Persons under a disability – Partnerships and sole traders – Foreign States – Trusts – Deceased defendants and parties who die during the action – Bankruptcy and liquidation – The Crown – Unincorporated associations – Joinder of parties – Representative actions – Test cases – Joinder of causes of action – Misjoinder and non-joinder of parties – Case management

5 Service of Proceedings *30*

Introduction – Duration of the Writ – Service of Writ and Originating Summons – Personal service – Postal service – Service by agreement – Substituted service – Service outside the jurisdiction – Defective service – Statement of claim – Compelling the service of proceedings

6 Defending the Action *37*

Introduction – Acknowledgement of Service – The defence – Judgment in default against particular defendants – The importance of time limits – Counterclaim and set-off – Disputes as to service or jurisdiction – Security for costs – Security on appeal

7 Summary Judgment 47

Introduction – Practice where the action is on a cheque – Practice in other cases – Personal injury cases – Powers of the Master – Judgment for the plaintiff – Unconditional leave to defend – Conditional leave to defend – Dismissal of summons – Directions – Costs – Appeals – 'There ought for some other reason to be a trial' – Determination of questions of law or construction; RSC O.14A – General principles of summary judgment – Other matters

8 Contribution and Indemnity 56

Introduction – Rights between co-defendants – Rights where not all potential defendants are joined – Rights where the plaintiff cannot sue the third party – Other cases – Third party proceedings – Nature of third party proceedings – Restrictions on third party proceedings – Joinder of the third party as a defendant

9 Pleadings 63

The purpose and types of pleadings – Time for service – Trial without pleadings – Formal contents of pleadings – Material contents of pleadings – Special pleading – Pleading the defence – Inconsistent defences – Judgments on admissions – Further and better particulars – Reply and Defence to Counterclaim – Close of pleadings – Amendment and striking out

10 Amendment and Striking Out of Pleadings 73

Introduction – Amendment of the Writ – Amendment of the pleadings – The practice of amendment – Amendment in third party proceedings – Striking out the Writ and pleadings – Striking out for failure to comply with the Rules – No cause of action or defence – Scandalous, frivolous and vexatious pleadings – Pleadings which may embarrass, prejudice or delay a fair trial – Pleadings which are an abuse of the process of the court – Powers on striking out pleadings – Inherent jurisdiction

11 Discovery and Inspection of Documents 82

Introduction – Pre-action inspection – Pre-action discovery and inspection in personal injury and death cases – Discovery and inspection against non-parties in personal injury cases – Discovery and inspection against other non-parties – Discovery between parties to the action – Discovery and inspection in actions begun by Writ – Discovery in other actions – Failure to make discovery – Discovery in personal injury actions – Use of discovered documents – Interrogatories – Discovery of expert evidence – Expert reports in non-personal injury cases – Expert reports in personal injury and fatal accident cases – Mutual disclosure of expert evidence – Medical examination of injured plaintiffs – Disclosure by agreement of the parties – Agreement of expert evidence – Witness statements

12 Preserving Evidence and Assets 98

Introduction – Anton Piller orders – Mareva injunctions – Finding the assets – The risk of disposal – Justice and convenience – Making the application – Other matters – Extension of Mareva

13 Interlocutory Injunctions and Interim Payments 110

Introduction – Interlocutory injunctions – Defamation cases – Secondary picketing – Interlocutory injunction in effect whole relief – Facts and law clear – Plaintiff or defendant certain to succeed – The survival of *Cyanamid* – Undertakings on damages – Undertakings in lieu of injunctions – *Quia timet* injunctions – Mandatory injunctions – Procedure – Interim payments – Interim payments for debt – Contributory negligence – Manner of payment – Additional matters – Procedure for interim payment

14 The Effect of Delay *121*

Introduction – Limitation periods – Contract – Tort – Fraud and mistake – Trespassers and land – Limitation periods in personal injury actions – 'Significant' – Identity of the defendant – Disapplying the limitation period – Limitation in claims for death – Claimants under a disability – Amendment of proceedings after expiry of limitation – Delay after service of proceedings – Effect of dismissal – Dismissal and limitation – Delay by agreement

15 Payment into Court *135*

Introduction – Procedure – Acceptance of the payment – Other matters – Acceptance with leave of the court – Disclosure of the payment in – Miscellaneous points

16 Arrangement for and Conduct of a High Court Trial *142*

Introduction – Summons for Directions – Additional directions – Arranging for trial – Adjournment before trial – Exchange of evidence and other pre-trial matters – Trial – Submissions of no case to answer – Defendant's case – Judgment – Form of judgments and orders – Interest – Family Division Practice Direction

17 Costs *153*

Introduction – General principles – Judicial discretion – Successful plaintiffs – Successful defendants – Trustees – Legally-aided parties – Wasted costs – Bases of taxation – Costs on appeal – Appeals from costs orders – Interlocutory orders for costs

18 Enforcement of Judgments *167*

Introduction – Fieri Facias – Garnishee proceedings – Charging orders – Appointment of a receiver – Bankruptcy and liquidation – Liquidation of limited companies – Enforcement in the County Court – Attachment of earnings – Writ of Delivery – Writ of Sequestration – Writ of Possession – Committal for contempt of court – Foreign judgments – The importance of insurance

19 Miscellaneous Proceedings *178*

Introduction – Withdrawal and discontinuance – Interpleader proceedings – Proceedings in the Chancery Division – Summary possession of land – Judicial review – References to the European Court of Justice – Confiscation orders under the Drug Trafficking Offences Act 1986

20 Appeals *185*

Introduction – Appeal from Master's orders – Appeals from orders of High Court Judges – Appeals direct to the House of Lords – Procedure on appeal to the Court of Appeal – Hearing of the appeal – Fresh evidence – Judgment – Appeal to the House of Lords – Other matters

21 County Court Procedure *193*

Introduction – Transfer of proceedings – Transfer to the High Court – Commencing proceedings – Issue and service of proceedings – Parties – Pre-trial review and automatic directions – Summary judgment – Pleadings – Interlocutory proceedings – Trial – Enforcement of judgments – Small claims procedure – Costs – Appeals – Nonsuit

Appendix: Rules of the Supreme Court *204*

Part II Criminal Procedure

22 Introduction *211*

23 Arrest and Prosecution *213*

Introduction – Arrest with warrant – Arrest without warrant – Procedure on arrest – Detention and police bail – Decision to prosecute – Director of Public Prosecutions – Attorney-General – Government departments – Private individuals – Caution – Time limits – Motoring offences

24 Prosecuting a Summary Offence *224*

Introduction – Summary offences – Commencing proceedings – Issue of the Summons – Form of the information in the Summons – Course of the trial – Pleading guilty by post – Adjournment – Proceeding in the absence of the parties – Acceptance and change of plea – The magistrates' clerk – Conflicts of interest – Composition of the court – Powers of sentencing for summary offences – Variation of findings and sentences – Defects in information and variance with evidence

25 Committal Proceedings *237*

Introduction – Committal with consideration of the evidence – Submission of no case to answer – Procedural points – Committal without consideration of the evidence – Ancillary orders – Place of trial – Witness orders – Bail – Alibi warning – Legal aid – Costs of the committal proceedings – Publicity at committal proceedings – Additional evidence – Voluntary bill of indictment – Committal of summary offences – Transfer for trial

26 The Bill of Indictment *249*

Introduction – Form of indictment – Time for and procedure on drafting – The rule against duplicity – Duplicity in the Particulars of Offence – Reasons for the duplicity rule – Joinder of accused in the same count – Joinder of counts in an indictment – Joinder of defendants in one indictment – Combination of defendants and counts – Severance: separate trials of defendants and counts – Amendment of the indictment – Comparison with Summons in summary trial

27 Arraignment and Plea *262*

Introduction – Place of trial and composition of court – Time for trial – Arraignment – Standing mute – Answers less than proper pleas – Equivocal plea – Not guilty plea – Guilty plea – Plea bargaining – Other pleas on arraignment – Presence of the accused

28 Trial by Jury *273*

Introduction – Absence of the accused – Choosing the jury panel – Choosing from the panel – Excusing jurors – Challenging individual jurors – Peremptory challenges – Challenges for cause – Challenges to the array – 'Challenges' by the prosecution – Praying a tales – Time for making challenges – Interfering with the process of selection – Questioning potential jurors – Providing a 'balanced' jury – Investigating the background of jurors – Swearing in the jury – Appeals on the ground of improperly constituted juries – Course of the trial – Prosecution case – Defence case – Closing speeches – Summing-up – Other procedural points – Considering the verdict – Returning the verdict – Failure to agree on a verdict – Judicial pressure on the jury – Rejecting the verdict – Alternative offences and verdicts – Lesser offences under s6(3) Criminal Law Act 1967 – Sentencing

29 Offences Triable Either Way *292*

Introduction – Summary offences – Indictable offences – Triable either way offences – Beginning the prosecution – Determining the mode of trial – Absence of the accused – Change to and from summary trial – Criminal damage charges – Committal for sentence to the Crown Court – Committing on offences triable either way – Committing with summary offences – Committing for other offences or orders – Breach of orders made by the Crown Court

30 Sentencing of Adult Offenders *302*

Introduction – Sentencing procedure – Deferring sentence – Absolute discharge – Conditional discharge – Community sentences – Probation orders – Effect of and breach of probation and revocation of community orders – Community service orders – Combination orders – Curfew orders – Fines – Young offender institutions – Imprisonment – Justifying the imposition of custody – Suspended sentences – Breach of the suspended sentence – Detention in a young offender institution – Life imprisonment – Early release and parole – Determining the length of the sentence – Offences taken into consideration – Other orders

31 Trial and Sentence of Juveniles *317*

Introduction – Mode of trial – Trial on indictment – Summary trial in the magistrates' court – Critical date for determining the mode of trial – Trial procedure on indictment or trial in the magistrates' court – Trial procedure in the youth court – Sentencing of juveniles tried in the magistrates' court – Sentencing following conviction on indictment – Sentencing in the youth court – Attendance centre order – Detention in a young offender institution – Community sentences – Supervision orders – Recognisance by parent or guardian – Sentencing policy – Table of orders and sentences with age limits

32 Orders Other Than Sentences *325*

Introduction – Binding over – Compensation orders – Restitution orders – Costs – Forfeiture orders – Recommendation for deportation – Criminal bankruptcy orders – Criminal Injuries Compensation Board

33 Appeals *332*

Introduction – 'Appeal' from committal proceedings – Appeal from acquittal on indictment – Appeal against conviction on indictment – Appeal against sentence on indictment – Procedure on appeal to the Court of Appeal – Grounds of appeal – Application for leave to appeal – Direction for loss of time – Hearing appeals against conviction – Powers of the Court of Appeal – The conviction is 'unsafe' – Powers of the Court of Appeal in determining appeals – Fresh evidence – Additional powers of the Court of Appeal – Appeals against sentence – Composition and judgment – Other hearings by the Court of Appeal from trial on indictment – Appeal to the House of Lords – Judicial review of the Crown Court – Appeal from summary trial in the magistrates' court – Appeal to the Crown Court – Appeal from the Crown Court to the Court of Appeal – Appeal from the magistrates' court to the Divisional Court – Appeal from the Divisional Court to the House of Lords – Appeal from the Crown Court to the Divisional Court – Judicial review of the magistrates' court and Crown Court – Appeals from youth courts – Appeal to the European Court of Justice – Diagram of appeals in criminal cases

34 Miscellaneous Proceedings *351*

Introduction – Legal aid – Legal aid as of right – Legal aid in the court's discretion – Application for legal aid – Amount of aid and contributions – Choice of representative – Remands – The duty of counsel

35 Bail 358

Introduction – The presumption of bail – Grounds for denial of bail – Factors material to a bail application – Procedure at a bail hearing – Renewed applications to the magistrates – Application to the Crown Court – Application to the High Court – Bail conditions – Bail following conviction – The prosecution's right of appeal

36 Recent Cases 366

Service of proceedings – Discovery and inspection of documents – The effect of delay – County court procedure – Prosecuting a summary offence – Trial by jury – Offences triable either way – Sentencing of adult offenders

Preface

HLT textbooks are written specifically for students. Whatever their course, they will find our books clear and concise, providing comprehensive and up-to-date coverage. Written by specialists in their field, our textbooks are reviewed and updated on an annual basis.

As last year, we have included a chapter called 'Recent Cases'. This chapter includes the most significant cases that have occurred in the last year. In order to assist the student, extracts from the judgments and commentary, where appropriate, have been included. In many instances these cases highlight new interpretations of particular facets of existing law.

Knowledge of recent cases is extremely important for those studying for their examinations. It demonstrates not only an active interest in the law as it develops, but also the dynamic nature of the law which is constantly adapting to changing social and economic trends.

Though written for students of the Bar Finals course this *Civil and Criminal Procedure* textbook is intended to carry further than the doors of the examination hall. It is often a considerable shock for newly-qualified Barristers to enter pupillage and to find that the courts apply the rules of procedure in quite a different way from the way in which the theory of those rules has been taught. If this textbook can, in even some small degree, help to lessen that feeling of surprise, then its writing will have been justified.

This textbook describes the procedure of the principal English courts – the High Court, County Court, Crown Court, magistrates' court, Court of Appeal, and House of Lords. It is divided into two main sections, one each dealing with civil and criminal procedure. The intention in each is the same: to describe the workings of the law stage by stage, from the decision to commence proceedings, through their issue, preparation for trial, trial, judgment and verdict, enforcement and sentence, to appeal and conclusion. At each stage the rules of procedure are discussed, and the practical use of the rules outlined. Topics of particular interest or complexity are considered in detail. The emphasis throughout is upon practice rather than upon theory.

In the section on Civil Procedure, emphasis is given to High Court procedure but the equivalent County Court provisions are noted and any differences explained. Chapter 21 is also devoted to the County Court and concentrates on those procedural stages which are markedly different in the lower jurisdiction. Students for the Bar Finals examinations should note that the two jurisdictions are of equal importance in the examination.

As well as covering recent cases, this edition incorporates the relevant changes made by new legislation, the most important being the Criminal Appeal Act 1995.

Developments in this edition represent the law at 1 January 1996, although it has been possible to include some later material.

Sources of the Law of Procedure

The courts whose workings this textbook describes are all creatures of statute. Similarly, the rules of procedure have their origin in Acts of Parliament, though a very few stem from the common law. On to the statutory framework is engrafted a large body of case law, the great majority of which concerns interpretation of the rules. Any study of procedural law must involve first an understanding of the rules themselves, followed by a knowledge of the meaning given to them by the courts. The use of judicial precedent in this area should, however, be treated with care, for many of the rules, especially those of the civil courts, confer upon the court a discretion to act in a particular way, and the width of language used by the draftsmen means that the facts of one case will rarely, if ever, fall squarely within those of a previous one. Just as the *ratio decidendi* of a precedent on substantive law must be sorted from the obiter dicta, so in the law of procedure precedents are the servants and not the masters of the rules they interpret.

In each of the civil and criminal courts, there are works of reference which the courts recognise and which are of persuasive authority on the interpretation of the law. The practitioner must equip him or herself with these, and learn to employ their valuable commentaries. Each is comprehensive in its own field, and is regularly supplemented by new material.

Civil procedure

The Supreme Court Practice: commonly known as the 'White Book', published in new editions every three years. About 4,000 pages. Procedure for the High Court, Court of Appeal (Civil Division) and House of Lords.

The County Court Practice: the 'Green Book', published annually. About 2,500 pages. Procedure for the County Court.

Criminal procedure

Archbold Criminal Pleading & Practice: a work which contains not only the procedure of the Crown Court and Court of Appeal (Criminal Division), but also large sections devoted to the law of Evidence and the substantive law of crime. About 4,000 pages, in two volumes, one of which is replaced annually.

Stone's Justices' Manual: the comprehensive reference work for the magistrates' court comprising, like *Archbold*, substantive law, evidence and procedure. Published annually, it runs to 8,500 pages in three volumes.

Blackstone's Criminal Practice: the alternative to *Archbold*. This work is in one volume, published annually.

The standard works contain much reference to decided cases, often with a brief summary of the facts and principle of precedents. The original source of case law is, however, the several series of law reports. The same case may be reported in more than one series, and the order of precedence of each series differs according to the court. In civil cases, reports are normally cited in the following descending order: Law Reports, Weekly Law Reports, All England Law Reports, Lloyd's Law Reports, Times Law Reports; other series have no recognised order, for example, Fleet Street Reports, Solicitors' Journal, Estates Gazette, New Law Journal and the private series of older reports. Some judges refuse to pay attention to a report in one series if it is contained in a series they consider more reliable, but there is no set rule of citation.

In the criminal courts, greatest heed is paid to the Criminal Appeal Reports, the contents of which are checked and approved by judges involved in a case before the report is published. This series should therefore be used in preference to the others, though the LR, WLR, All ER, Criminal Law Review and others are on occasion accepted.

Very many cases never find their way into the official or any series of reports. This may be because of pressure of space, or because their importance is not recognised by the reporter. It is therefore useful to know of the existence, in the Supreme Court Library in the Royal Courts of Justice, Strand, of unedited transcripts of cases decided by the Court of Appeal, referred to by number and year, copies of which must, however, be purchased from the court's shorthand writers' department at a high cost (though they may be inspected free of charge).

Abbreviations

In this textbook, the following abbreviations are used:

CLSA	Courts and Legal Services Act 1990
CCA	County Courts Act 1984
MCA	Magistrates' Courts Act 1980
SCA	Supreme Court Act 1981
CCR	County Court Rules
AJA	Administration of Justice Act (year as appropriate)
CJA	Criminal Justice Act (year as appropriate)
CLA	Criminal Law Act (year as appropriate)
CJPOA	Criminal Justice and Public Order Act 1994
PACE	Police and Criminal Evidence Act 1984
All ER	All England Law Reports
Ch	The Law Reports, Chancery Division
CL	Current Law
CLY	Current Law Yearbook
Com LR	Commercial law Reports
Cr App R	Criminal Appeal Reports
Crim LR	Criminal Law Review
Eur LR	European Law Reports
Fam	The Law Reports, Family Division
FSR	Fleet Street Reports
Lloyd's Rep	Lloyd's Law Reports
NLJ	New Law Journal
QB	The Law Reports, Queen's Bench Division
Sol Jo	Solicitors' Journal
TLR	Times Law Reports
WLR	The Weekly Law Reports
WR	Weekly Reporter

Table of Cases: Civil Procedure

Abouchalache v Hilton Hotels (1982) The Times 15 November   *132*
Adams v Riley [1988] 1 All ER 88   *162*
Afzal and Others v Ford Motor Co Ltd [1994] 4 All ER 720   *201*
Akhtar v Harbottle (1982) The Times 4 August   *131*
Alexander v Rayson [1936] 1 KB 169   *148*
Ali v Moneim [1989] 2 All ER 404   *107*
Allen v Jambo Holdings [1980] 1 WLR 1252   *102, 106*
Allertext v Advanced Data Communications [1985] 1 All ER 395   *100*
Allied Arab Bank Ltd v Hajjar [1987] 3 All ER 739   *108*
Alltrans Express v CVA Holdings [1984] 1 WLR 394   *165*
Amercian Cyanamid v Ethicon [1975] AC 396   *111, 112, 113, 114*
American Cyanamid v Upjohn [1970] 1 WLR 1507   *187*
An Bord Baine v Milk Marketing Cooperative (1984) The Times 26 May   *184*
Anderson v Hill [1965] 1 WLR 745   *161*
Andrew v Grove [1902] 1 KB 620   *159*
Antcliffe v Gloucester Health Authority (1992) The Times 6 May   *127*
Arab Monetary Fund v Hashim (1989) The Times 16 January   *109*
Argyll v Argyll [1967] Ch 302   *92*
Ashmore v British Coal Corporation [1990] 2 WLR 1437   *80*
Associated British Ports v TGWU (1989) The Times 9 June   *190*
Austin Rover Group v Crouch Butler Savage (1986) The Times 1 April   *33*

Babanaft International v Bassatne (1988) The Independent 30 June   *107*
Bailey v Bailey [1983] 3 All ER 495   *133*
Bankamerica Finance Ltd v Nock [1988] 1 All ER 81   *160*
Bankers Trust v Shapira [1980] 1 WLR 1274   *103*
Bank fur GA v City of London Garages [1971] 1 WLR 149   *53*
Barclays Bank of Swaziland Ltd v Hahn [1989] 1 All ER 193   *33*
Barraclough, Re [1965] 3 WLR 1023   *148*
Bayer v Winter [1986] 1 All ER 733   *108*
Bayer v Winter (No 2) [1986] 2 All ER 43 Ch D   *103*
Behbehani v Salem [1989] 2 All ER 143   *108*
Bekhor v Bilton [1981] 2 WLR 601   *103*
Berkeley Administration Inc v McClelland [1990] 2 WLR 1021   *90*
Bernstein v Jackson [1982] 2 All ER 806   *12, 31*
Bestobell v Bigg [1975] FSR 421   *113*

Billington v Billington [1974] Fam 24   *174*
Birkett v James [1978] AC 297   *131, 132*
Biss v Lambeth [1978] 1 WLR 382   *132*
Black King Shipping Corporation v Massie (1984) The Times 9 July   *25*
Bloomfield v BTC [1960] 2 QB 86   *161*
Bolvinter Oil v Chase Manhattan [1984] 1 All ER 351   *48*
Bowen-Jones v Bowen-Jones [1986] 3 All ER 163   *164*
Brady v Group Lotus plc [1987] 2 All ER 674   *191*
Breeze v McKennon (1985) The Times 23 November   *117*
Briamore Manufacturing, Re [1986] 3 All ER 132   *88*
Bridge v Deacons (1984) The Times 28 March   *114*
Brink's-Mat v Elcombe [1988] 3 All ER 188   *107*
British Frame v McGregor [1943] AC 197   *190*
British Steel v Granada [1980] 3 WLR 774   *86*
Brooks v Coates [1983] 3 All ER 702   *127*
Bullock v London General Omnibus [1907] 1 KB 264   *159*

CBS v Lambert [1983] Ch 37   *102, 104*
CSI v Archway [1980] 2 All ER 215   *55*
Cable, Re [1976] 3 All ER 417   *114*
Cambridge Nutrition Ltd v BBC [1990] 3 All ER 523   *113*
Castanho v Brown & Root [1980] 3 WLR 991   *119*
Cayne v Global Resources [1984] 1 All ER 225   *113*
Chapman v Chief Constable of South Yorkshire and Others,
    Rimmer v Same (1990) The Times 20 March   *29*
Chilton v Saga Holidays [1986] 1 All ER 841   *200*
Chrzanowska v Glaxo Laboratories Ltd (1990) The Times 16 March   *29*
Clarapede v Commercial Union (1883) 32 WR 262   *76*
Claremont v GCT (1983) The Times 17 June   *131*
Clark v Forbes Stuart [1964] 2 All ER 282   *126*
Clipper Maritime v Mineralimportexport [1981] 1 WLR 1262   *105*
Clovertogs v Jean Scene [1982] Com LR 88   *49*
Coast Lines Ltd v Hudig Charrering [1972] 1 All ER 451   *368*
Colchester v Carlton (1984) The Times 9 April   *17*
Columbia Pictures v Robinson [1986] 3 All ER 338   *100*
Company, a, In re (1983) The Times 10 May   *80*
Conry v Simpson [1983] 3 All ER 369   *126, 127, 190*
Corby v Holst [1985] 1 All ER 321   *157*
Costellow v Somerset County Council (1992) The Times 25 November   *133*
Cowan, ex parte [1983] 3 All ER 58   *183*
Crest Homes v Ascott (1975) The Times 4 Febuary   *113*
Crest Homes v Marks [1987] 2 All ER 1074   *101*
Cropper v Smith (1884) 26 Ch D 700   *76*

Curwen v James [1963] 1 WLR 748   *190*
Cutts v Head [1984] 2 WLR 349   *157*

Deerness v Keeble [1983] 2 Lloyd's Rep 260   *126, 134*
Department of Transport v Chris Smaller (Transport) Ltd
    [1989] 1 All ER 897   *132*
Derby & Co v Weldon (No 1) [1990] Ch 48   *107*
Derby & Co v Weldon (No 4) [1990] Ch 65   *107*
Dexter v Courtaulds [1984] 1 All ER 70   *151*
Distributori v Holford [1985] 3 All ER 750   *101*
Donoghue v Stevenson [1932] AC 562   *59, 68*
Donovan v Gwentoys Ltd [1990] 1 All ER 1018   *126*
Dormeuil Freres SA v Nicolian International Ltd [1988] 3 All ER 197   *99*
Dove v Banham Locks [1983] 3 WLR 1436   *123*
Drennan v Brooke Marine (1983) The Times 20 June   *88*
Dubai Bank Ltd v Galadari (No 2) (1989) The Times 11 October   *115*
Dummer v Brown [1953] 1 QB 710   *50*
Dunning v United Liverpool Hospital [1973] 1 WLR 586   *84*

EMI v Ian Cameron Wallace [1983] Ch 59   *163*
EMI Records v Riley [1981] 2 All ER 838   *27*
Edmeades v Thames Board Mills [1969] 2 QB 67   *95*
Evans v Bartlam [1937] AC 473   *39, 190*
Evans v BBC (1974) The Times 26 February   *113*
Evans v Charrington & Co [1983] 2 WLR 117   *76, 129*
Evans v London Hospital [1981] 1 WLR 184   *78*

Fawcett v Johnson's [1939] 3 All ER 377   *190*
Fellowes v Fisher [1975] 3 WLR 184   *114*
Fellows v Barrett (1830) 1 Keen 119   *45*
Femis-Bank (Anguilla) Ltd v Lazar [1991] 2 All ER 865   *113*
Fielding & Platt v Selim Najjar [1969] 1 WLR 357   *49*
Firman v Ellis [1978] All ER 851   *133, 134*
First National Security v Hegarty [1983] 1 WLR 865   *171*
Forward v West Sussex County Council and Others [1995] 1 WLR 1469   *33, 366*
Foster v Great Western Railway (1882) 8 QBD 515   *159*
Fredericks v Wilkins [1971] 1 WLR 1197   *180*
Fryer v London Transport (1982) The Times 4 December   *140*

Galaxia v Mineralimportexport [1982] 1 WLR 539   *105*
Garvin v Domus Publishing (1988) 132 Sol Jo 1091   *101*
Gascoigne v Haringey Health Authority (1992) The Times 21 January   *133*
Gaskins v British Aluminium [1976] QB 524   *140*

General Accident v Foster [1973] 1 QB 50   *162*
Gloria v Solokoff [1969] 1 All ER 204   *131*
Golden Ocean Assurance Ltd and World Mariner Shipping SA v Martin [1990] 2 Lloyd's Rep 215   *12*
Goldstraw, ex parte [1983] 3 All ER 257   *183*
Goldsworthy v Brickell [1987] 1 All ER 853   *160*
Grewal v National Hospital (1982) The Times 15 October   *76*
Guinness plc v Saunders (1987) The Independent 16 April   *104*
Gurtner v Circuit [1968] 2 QB 587   *34*

Hadmor v Hamilton [1982] 2 WLR 322   *190*
Halford v Brookes and Another [1990] 1 WLR 428   *125*
Hallam-Eames and Others v Merrett and Others (1995) The Times 25 January   *123*
Hall v Avon [1980] 1 All ER 516   *95*
Halls v O'Dell (1991) The Times 5 November   *132*
Hanning v Maitland [1970] 1 QB 580   *162*
Haras v Baltic Mercantile [1982] 1 WLR 959   *113*
Hargreaves v Limeside (1982) The Times 3 July   *139*
Haron Zaid v Central Securities [1982] 3 WLR 134   *186*
Harper v Gray [1985] 2 All ER 507   *58*
Harrington v North London Polytechnic [1984] 3 All ER 666   *87*
Harris v Newcastle Area Health Authority [1989] 2 All ER 273   *84*
Hayes v Bowman [1989] 1 WLR 456   *132*
Heath (CE) plc v Ceram Holding Co [1989] 1 All ER 203   *55*
Heaton's Transport v TGWU [1973] AC 15   *177*
Heaven v Road & Rail Wagons [1965] 2 QB 355   *31*
Heer v Tutton and Another (1995) The Times 5 June   *197, 371*
Heyes v Lord Derby [1984] The Times 19 January   *61*
Heyes v Lord Derby [1989] 1 WLR 777   *54*
Hobbs v Marlow [1977] 2 WLR 777   *158*
Hodgson v Hart (1985) The Times 25 November   *33*
Hoffman La Roche v S of S [1975] AC 295   *115*
Hollis v Jenkins (1984) The Times 31 January   *188*
Home Office v Harman [1982] 2 WLR 338   *92*
House of Spring Gardens v Waite (1984) The Times 12 November   *103*
House of Spring Gardens v Waite [1990] 2 All ER 990   *80*
House of Troy v OMC Group (1987) The Independent 2 February   *49*
Howe v David Brown Tractors (Retail) Ltd [1991] 4 All ER 30   *76*
Howell v Montey (1990) The Independent 28 March   *171*
Hubbard v Pitt [1975] 2 WLR 254   *114*
Hudson v Elmbridge Borough Council [1991] 1 WLR 880   *139*
Hultquist v Universal Pattern [1960] 2 All ER 266   *157*
Humber Asphalt v Squire W Swift Ltd (1987) The Independent 6 April   *136*

Hunt v R M Douglas (Roofing) Ltd [1988] 3 All ER 823   *164*
Hunter v Chief Constable of West Midlands [1982] AC 529   *80*
Hyland v Lamont [1950] 1 KB 585   *48*

Jackson, ex parte [1985] 3 All ER 769   *183*
Janov v Morris [1981] 1 WLR 606   *133*
Jefford v Gee [1970] 2 QB 130   *151*
Jeffrey Rogers Knitwear v Vinola Manufacturing (1984) The Times 5 December   *100*
John Michael Design plc v Cooke [1987] 2 All ER 332   *114*

Kenning v Eve Construction [1989] 1 WLR 1189   *93*
Ketteman v Hansel [1985] 1 All ER 352   *123*
Kierson v Thompson [1913] 1 KB 587   *158*
Kim Barker Ltd v Aegon Insurance Co (UK) Ltd (1989) The Times 9 October   *45*
King v Weston-Howell (1989) The Times 28 March   *138*
Kinnear v Falconfilms NV and Others [1994] 3 All ER 42   *62*
Kirkup v BRB [1983] 3 All ER 147   *95*
Kleinwort Benson v Barbrak Ltd [1987] 2 WLR 1053 HL   *31*

Ladd v Marshall [1954] 3 All ER 745   *191*
Langdale v Danby [1982] 1 WLR 1123   *53*
Law v National Greyhound Club [1983] 3 All ER 300   *183*
Leal v Dunlop Bio-Process [1984] 2 All ER 207   *12*
Liddell v Middleton (1995) The Times 17 July   *94, 368*
Lister v Romford Ice [1957] AC 555   *58*
Little Olympian Each Ways Ltd, Re [1994] 4 All ER 561   *45*
Lloyds Bank v Ellis [1983] 1 WLR 569   *53*
Lloyds Bowmaker v Britannia Arrow Holdings [1988] 3 All ER 178   *106–107*
London Congregational v Harris [1985] 1 All ER 335   *123*

McCafferty v Metropolitan Police District Receiver [1977] 1 WLR 1073   *125*
Mackay v Essex Health Authority [1982] QB 1166   *78*
Maclaine Watson & Co v International Tin Council [1987] 3 All ER 787   *171*
Maclaine Watson & Co v International Tin Council (No 2) [1987] 3 All ER 886   *168*
Manuel v Attorney-General [1982] 3 WLR 821   *79*
Maynard v Osmond [1979] 1 WLR 31   *162*
Megarity v Ryan [1980] 2 All ER 832   *96*
Mercury Communications v Stanley (1983) The Times 10 November   *113*
Midland Bank v Hett, Stubbs & Kemp [1979] Ch 384   *123*
Midland Bank v Phillips (1986) The Times 28 March   *50*

Miles *v* Bull [1969] 1 QB 258   *53*
Moore (DW) & Co Ltd *v* Ferrier [1988] 1 All ER 400   *122*

NWL *v* Woods [1979] 3 All ER 614   *114*
Nimmo *v* Alexander Cowan [1968] AC 107   *67*
Ninemia *v* Trave [1983] 1 WLR 1420   *104*
Norwich Pharmacal *v* Commisioners of Customs & Excise [1973] 3 WLR 164   *86, 87*
Nova Jersey Knit *v* Kammgarn Spinnerei [1977] 2 All ER 463   *49*

O'Brien *v* Robinson [1973] 2 WLR 393   *187*
O'Connor *v* Amos Bridgman Abbatoirs Ltd (1990) The Times 13 April   *51*
Oceania *v* Mineralimportexport [1983] 1 WLR 1294   *105*
Office Overload *v* Gunn [1977] FSR 39   *114*
Oriental Credit Bank, Re [1988] 2 WLR 172   *109*
Orwell Steel *v* Asphalt & Tarmac [1984] 1 WLR 1097   *102, 168*
Owen (t/a Max Owen Associates) *v* Pugh; Beamish and Another *v* Owen (t/a Max Owen Associates) [1995] 3 All ER 345   *132, 369*

PCW *v* Dixon [1983] 2 All ER 158   *106*
Paclantic *v* Moscow Narodny Bank [1983] 1 WLR 1063   *51*
Palata Investments *v* Burt & Sinfield [1985] 3 All ER 517   *188*
Palmer *v* Birks [1985] NLJ 1256   *133*
Paragon Group Ltd *v* Burnell [1991] 2 WLR 854   *34*
Parker *v* Camden London BC [1985] 2 All ER 680   *116*
Parkinson (Sir Lindsay) *v* Triplan [1973] QB 609   *46*
Parry *v* Phoenix Assurance plc [1988] 3 All ER 60   *171*
Pearson *v* Naydler [1977] 1 WLR 899   *46*
Peco *v* Hazlitt Galleries [1983] 3 All ER 193   *124*
Pepper *v* Hart [1993] AC 593   *147*
Pepper *v* Healey (1982) The Times 9 March   *201*
Peruvian Guano Case (1882) 11 QBD 55   *88*
Pickin *v* BRB [1974] AC 765   *79*
Pirelli *v* Oscar Faber & Partners [1983] 2 WLR 6   *123*
Pocock *v* ADC [1952] 1 TLR 29   *52*
Portico Housing *v* Moorhead (1985) The Times 5 February   *31*
Porzelack KG *v* Porzelack (UK) Ltd [1987] 1 All ER 1074 Ch D   *45*
Power Curber *v* Bank of Kuwait [1981] 1 WLR 1233   *48*
Powney *v* Coxage (1988) The Times 8 March   *119*
Practice Direction (Judgment: Foreign Currency) [1976] 1 WLR 83   *15, 138*
Practice Direction [1979] 1 WLR 290   *96*
Practice Direction (Interpleader Proceedings) [1982] 1 WLR 2   *180*
Practice Direction (Claims for Interest) [1983] 1 WLR 377   *15*

Practice Direction (Writ: Service Abroad) [1987] 1 All ER 160   *35*
Practice Direction [1988] 3 All ER 896   *139*
Practice Direction (Chancery: Transfer of Business) [1988] 3 All ER 96   *195*
Practice Direction (County Court: Transfer) [1988] 2 All ER 64   *194*
Practice Direction (County Court: Transfer) [1988] 3 All ER 95   *194*
Practice Direction (Trial Out of London) [1988] 1 WLR 1322   *146*
Practice Direction (Mareva Injunctions and Anton Piller Orders) [1994] 4 All ER 52   *99, 100, 106*
Practice Direction [1995] 1 FLR 456   *143, 151*
Practice Direction [1995] 1 WLR 1096   *148*
Practice Direction (Civil Litigation: Case Management) [1995] 1 WLR 262   *143, 368*
Practice Direction (Court of Appeal Handed Down Judgments) [1995] 1 WLR 1055   *149*
Practice Direction (Reference to Extracts from Hansard) (1995) The Independent 11 January   *147*
Practice Note (Chambers Proceedings) [1989] 1 All ER 1120   *186*
Practice Note (Civil Appeals) [1982] 1 WLR 1312   *189*
Practice Note (Claims for Interest) [1983] 1 WLR 377   *67, 150*
Practice Note (County Court: Transfer of Jury Cases) [1989] 2 All ER 128   *195*
Practice Note (Court of Appeal: Appeals: Timetable) [1987] 3 All ER 434   *189*
Practice Note (Skeleton Argument) [1989] 1 All ER 891   *189*
Prescott v Bulldog Tools [1981] 3 All ER 869   *96*
Procon (GB) Ltd v Provincial Building Co Ltd [1974] 1 WLR 557   *46*
Prudential Assurance v Newman Industries [1979] 3 All ER 507   *26, 27*
Pumfrey Construction v Childs (1985) The Times 12 July   *53*

RHM v Bovril [1982] 1 WLR 661   *91*
R v BBC, ex parte Lavelle [1983] 1 WLR 23   *183*
R v Civil Service Appeal Board, ex parte Bruce [1988] 3 All ER 686   *183*
R v Inland Revenue, ex parte National Federation of Self-Employed [1981] 2 WLR 722   *183*
Rafidain Bank v Agom Universal Sugar Trading Co Ltd [1987] 3 All ER 859   *90*
Rahman v Abu-Taha [1980] 1 WLR 1268   *104*
Ramsey v Hartley [1977] 1 WLR 686   *45*
Randolph Fields v Watts (1984) The Times 22 November   *100*
Rapley v P & O European Ferries (Dover) Ltd (1991) 21 February Court of Appeal transcript 91/0132   *53*
Rastin v British Steel [1994] 1 WLR 732   *198*
Rasu Maritima v Pertimina [1977] 3 WLR 518   *105*
Rawlinson v Westbrook and Another (1995) The Times 25 January   *94, 368*
Raymond v Attorney-General [1982] QB 839   *78*
Redland Brick v Morris [1970] AC 652   *115*
Ricci v Chow [1987] 3 All ER 534   *86*

Ricci Burns Ltd v Toole and Covey [1988] 1 WLR 993   *117*
Ridehalgh v Horsefield [1994] 3 All ER 848   *163*
Roberts Petroleum v Kenny [1982] 1 WLR 301   *170*
Rolph v Zolan [1993] 1 WLR 1305   *31*
Rome v Punjab National Bank (No 2) (1989) 5 British Company Law Cases 785   *32*
Roth v CS Lawrence (P J Cook & Co (A firm) (3rd Party)) [1991] 1 WLR 399   *122*
Rowe v Glenister and Others (1995) The Times 7 August   *132, 370*

SCF v Masri [1985] 2 All ER 747   *106*
Sanders Lead v Entores (1983) The Times 1 December   *108*
Sanderson v Blyth Theatre [1903] 2 KB 533   *159*
Seacroft Hotel v Goble [1984] 1 WLR 939   *202*
Secretary of State v Essex, Goodman Suggitt [1986] 2 All ER 69   *123*
Secretary of State v Guardian Newspapers [1984] 2 WLR 268   *87*
Shanning International Ltd v George Wimpey Ltd [1988] 3 All ER 475   *117, 118*
Shell Pensions Trust v Pell Frischmann [1986] 2 All ER 911   *93*
Shepherd v Sandham [1971] Ch 340   *116*
Sherratt v John Bromley [1985] 1 All ER 216   *138*
Simpson v Norwest Holst [1978] 1 WLR 863   *126*
Sincroflash v Trusthouse Forte (1983) The Times 7 January   *191*
Singh v Atombrook Ltd [1989] 1 All ER 385   *36, 75*
Siskina, The [1977] 3 WLR 803   *107*
Skrzypkowski v Silvan [1963] 1 WLR 525   *191*
Slazengers Ltd v Seaspeed Ferries [1987] 3 All ER 967   *45*
Smith v Baron (1991) The Times 1 February   *76*
Smith v Cardiff Corporation [1954] 1 QB 210   *26*
Steamship Mutual v Trollope & Colls (1986) The Times 31 March   *80*
Stockler v Fourways Estate [1984] 1 WLR 25   *108*
Stubbings v Webb [1992] 1 WLR 782   *125*
Sullivan v West Yorkshire PTE [1985] 2 All ER 134   *94*
Sybron v Barclays Bank (1984) The Times 9 March   *92*

TDK v Videochoice [1985] 3 All ER 345   *103*
Tabata v Hetherington (1983) The Times 15 December   *131*
Talamba, The [1965] P 433   *136*
Tate & Lyle v GLC [1983] 1 WLR 65   *151*
Taylor v Remploy [1995] 3 CL 434   *198, 371*
Third Chandris v Unimarine [1979] QB 645   *103, 104, 105*
Thompson v Brown [1981] 2 All ER 296   *126*
Thompson-Houston v British Insulated [1924] 1 Ch 203   *69*
Thorpe v Alexander [1975] 1 WLR 1459   *131*
Tolley v Morris [1979] 1 WLR 205   *131*

Trade Indemnity plc and Others *v* Forsakringsaktiebolaget Njord (in liquidation)
   [1995] 1 All ER 796   *35, 367*
Trafalgar Tours Ltd *v* Henry (1990) The Times 8 June   *74*
Trow *v* Ind Coope [1967] 2 QB 899   *31*
Tsai *v* Woodworth (1983) The Times 30 November   *10*
Turner *v* Ford Motors [1965] 2 All ER 583   *130*
Twentieth Century Fox *v* Tryare Ltd [1991] FSR 58   *101*

Unigate Dairies *v* Bruce (1988) The Times 2 March   *112*
Unilever plc *v* Chefaro Proprietaries Ltd [1994] NLJ 1660   *189*
Universal Thermosensors *v* Hibben (1992) The Times 12 February   *100*
University of Essex *v* Djemal [1980] 1 WLR 1301   *182*

Valor *v* Application de Gaz [1977] Eur LR 308   *81*
Varnazza, Re [1959] 1 WLR 622   *17*

Waddon *v* Whitecroft Scovill Ltd [1988] 1 All ER 996   *31*
Walkley *v* Precision Forgings [1979] 1 WLR 606; [1979] 1 All ER 102   *126, 133, 134*
Ward *v* Chief Constable of Avon (1985) The Times 17 July   *67*
Ward-Lee *v* Lineham [1993] 2 All ER 1006   *12*
Welling Private Hospital *v* Baum (1988) 10 CL 268   *55*
Welsh Development Agency *v* Redpath Dorman Long [1994] 1 WLR 1409   *129*
Wilkinson *v* Ancliff [1986] 3 All ER 427 CA   *31, 125*
Woodford *v* Smith [1970] 1 WLR 806   *113*

Yorke Motors *v* Edwards [1982] 1 WLR 444   *51, 190*
Yorkshire Regional Health Authority *v* Fairclough Building Ltd (1995) The Times
   16 November   *129–130, 370*

Table of Cases: Criminal Procedure

An Bord Bainne v Milk Marketing Board (1984) The Times 26 May   *349*

Boulding, ex parte [1984] 2 WLR 321   *326*
Brownlow, ex parte [1980] 2 WLR 892   *282*
Bulmer v Bollinger [1974] 1 WLR 1107   *349*

Chief Constable of Norfolk v Clayton [1983] 2 WLR 555   *227*
Christie v Leachinsky [1947] AC 573   *216*
Connelly v DPP [1964] AC 1254   *271*

DPP v Boardman [1975] AC 421   *258*
DPP v Merriman [1973] AC 584   *255*
DPP v Porthouse [1989] Crim LR 224   *271*
DPP v Richards [1988] 3 All ER 406   *364*

Foster Haulage v Roberts [1978] 2 All ER 751   *231*

Garfield v Maddocks [1974] QB 7   *235*
Gibbons, ex parte [1983] 3 All ER 523   *227*
Gillard, ex parte [1985] 3 All ER 634   *297*
Gouriet v Union of Post Office Workers [1978] AC 435   *220*

Heaton v Costello (1984) The Times 10 May   *253*
Hill, ex parte (1984) The Times 2 November   *345*

Jemmison v Priddle [1972] 1 QB 489   *254*
John Lewis v Tims [1952] AC 676   *216*

Kinnear v Falconfilms NV and Others [1994] 3 All ER 42   *357*

Lamb, ex parte [1983] 3 All ER 29   *305*
Ludlow v MPC [1971] AC 29   *256, 258*

MacKenzie v MacKenzie [1970] 3 All ER 1034   *228*
Massarro, ex parte [1973] 1 QB 433   *246*

Nanan v The State [1986] 3 All ER 248   *288*

Osman, ex parte [1971] 1 WLR 1109   *348*

Pennington, ex parte [1975] 1 QB 459   *233*
Percy v DPP (1994) The Times 13 December   *326*
Poh, Re [1983] 1 WLR 2   *343*
Practice Direction [1953] 1 WLR 1416   *372*
Practice Direction [1967] 1 WLR 1198   *287*
Practice Direction [1974] 1 WLR 441   *305*
Practice Direction [1981] 1 WLR 1163   *232*
Practice Direction (Crime: Jury Oath) [1984] 1 WLR 1217   *283*
Practice Direction (Crown Court: Plea and Directions Hearings) (1995) The Times 31 July   *264*
Practice Direction on Classification and Allocation of Crown Court Business (1995) The Independent 31 May   *263*
Practice Note [1980] 1 All ER 555   *336*
Practice Note (Court of Appeal: Service) [1988] 1 All ER 244   *335*
Practice Note [1988] 3 All ER 1086   *279, 282*
Procedure Directions [1988] 2 All ER 819 and 831   *343*

R v Amey (1982) The Times 21 December   *327*
R v Andrews (1985) The Times 11 October   *290*
R v Armstrong [1995] Crim LR 831   *284, 373*
R v Assim [1966] 2 QB 881   *257*
R v Avon Magistrates' Courts Committee, ex parte Bath Law Society [1988] 2 WLR 137   *357*
R v Baird (1993) The Times 12 January   *256*
R v Balls (1871) 1 CCR 328   *254*
R v Ballysingh (1953) 37 Cr App R 28   *253*
R v Barnes (1970) 55 Cr App R 100   *268*
R v Barrell (1979) 69 Cr App R 250   *255*
R v Bellman [1989] 1 All ER 32   *255*
R v Bettaney [1985] Crim LR 104   *282*
R v Bills (1995) The Times 1 March   *290, 374*
R v Birmingham Magistrates' Court, ex parte Ahmed [1995] Crim LR 503   *232, 372*
R v Birmingham JJ, ex parte Lamb [1983] 3 All ER 29   *348*
R v Bonner [1974] Crim LR 479   *260*
R v Bow Street Magistrates' Court, ex parte Welcombe (1992) The Times 7 May   *297*
R v Brentwood Justices, ex parte Nichols [1992] 1 AC 1   *294*
R v Brooks (1991) 92 Cr App R 36   *258*
R v Cain [1976] Crim LR 464   *269*
R v Cain [1983] Crim LR 802   *255*
R v Central Criminal Court, ex parte Randle and Pottle (1991) 92 Cr App R 323   *343*

Table of Cases: Criminal Procedure

R v Chapman (1976) 63 Cr App R 75   *283*
R v Chappell (1984) The Times 26 May   *328*
R v Chard [1983] 3 All ER 637   *342*
R v Clinton (1993) The Independent 18 March   *269*
R v Coventry City Magistrates, ex parte M (1992) The Times 13 April   *318*
R v Coward [1980] Crim LR 117   *269*
R v Croydon Crown Court, ex parte Clair [1986] 2 All ER 716   *345*
R v Cullen [1985] Crim LR 107   *269*
R v Danga (1991) The Times 1 November   *320*
R v Deakin [1972] 1 WLR 1618   *252*
R v Dixon (1991) 92 Cr App R 43   *258*
R v Dodd (1982) 74 Cr App R 50   *286*
R v Dorking JJ, ex parte Harrington [1984] 3 WLR 142   *348*
R v Drew [1985] 2 All ER 1061   *268*
R v Eccles Justices, ex parte Fitzpatrick (1989) 89 Cr App R 324   *372*
R v Elliott (1984) The Times 13 December   *220*
R v Ellis (1973) 57 Cr App R 571   *268*
R v Flack (1984) The Times 20 October   *286*
R v Follett [1989] 1 All ER 995 CA   *256*
R v Foster [1984] 3 WLR 401   *339*
R v Francis [1988] Crim LR 250   *285*
R v George [1984] 1 WLR 1082   *304*
R v Gorman [1987] 2 All ER 435; [1987] 1 WLR 545   *286*
R v Gough [1993] AC 646   *375, 376*
R v Gould [1968] 2 QB 65   *342*
R v Governor of Pentonville Prison, ex parte Bone (1994) The Times 15 November   *365*
R v Gregory [1972] 1 WLR 991   *260*
R v Hamberry [1977] QB 924   *285*
R v Hogan [1960] 2 QB 513   *272*
R v Hoggins [1967] 1 WLR 1233   *259*
R v Ipswich Justices, ex parte Callaghan (1995) The Times 3 April   *294, 376*
R v Johal and Ram [1973] 1 QB 475   *260*
R v Jones [1990] Crim LR 815   *269*
R v Jones, Platter and Pengelly [1991] Crim LR 856   *275*
R v K (1995) The Times 14 April   *282, 283, 374, 376*
R v Knightsbridge Crown Court, ex parte Goonatilleke [1985] 2 All ER 498   *348*
R v Kray (1969) 53 Cr App R 412   *281*
R v Lake (1977) 64 Cr App R 72   *259*
R v Lee [1984] 1 All ER 1080   *269, 339*
R v Leyland JJ, ex parte Hawthorn [1978] Crim LR 627   *348*
R v Lombardi [1989] 1 All ER 992 CA   *260*
R v McCluskey (1993) 98 Cr App R 216   *375*

R v McGlinchey [1983] Crim LR 808   *256, 258*
R v McKenna [1960] 1 QB 411   *289*
R v Maidstone County Court, ex parte Lever (1994) The Times 7 November   *364*
R v Maidstone Crown Court, ex parte Gill [1987] 1 All ER 129 DC   *330*
R v Maloney [1985] Crim LR 49   *259*
R v Mansfield [1977] 1 WLR 1102   *255, 258*
R v Mason [1980] 3 WLR 617   *282*
R v Moghal (1977) 65 Cr App R 56   *259*
R v Morais [1988] 3 All ER 161   *250*
R v Morley [1988] 2 WLR 963   *285*
R v Morley (1995) The Times 25 January   *337*
R v Moylan [1970] 1 QB 43   *312*
R v Mudd [1988] Crim LR 326   *303*
R v Newcastle Justices, ex parte Skinner [1987] 1 All ER 349   *346*
R v Newham Juvenile Court, ex parte F [1986] 3 All ER 17   *297*
R v Newland [1988] 2 WLR 382   *256*
R v Newton (1982) 4 Cr App R (S) 388   *303*
R v Nugent [1977] 1 WLR 789   *373*
R v O'Coigley (1798) 26 St Tr 1191   *278*
R v Oliva [1965] 3 All ER 116   *373*
R v Peace [1976] Crim LR 119   *269*
R v Pigg [1983] 1 WLR 6   *288*
R v Pitman [1991] 1 All ER 468   *269*
R v Plymouth Justices, ex parte Hart [1986] 2 All ER 452   *231*
R v Radley (1973) 58 Cr App R 394   *260*
R v Rose [1982] 3 WLR 192   *286, 339, 341*
R v Russell (1984) The Times 25 March   *289*
R v Russell-Jones [1995] 3 All ER 239   *284, 373, 375*
R v Secretary of State for the Home Department, ex parte Thornton [1986] 2 All ER 641   *305*
R v Sheerin (1976) 64 Cr App R 68   *250*
R v Silcott, Braithwaite, Raghip (1991) The Times 9 December   *340*
R v Smithers [1973] Crim LR 65   *312*
R v Southampton Justices, ex parte Green [1976] QB 11   *364*
R v Spencer [1986] 2 All ER 928; [1985] 1 All ER 673; [1985] 2 WLR 197   *286, 342*
R v Stanton [1983] Crim LR 190   *258*
R v Sutton Justices, ex parte DPP (1992) The Times 6 February   *230*
R v Sweeting [1988] Crim LR 131   *303*
R v Teong Sun Chuah and Teong Tatt Chuah [1991] Crim LR 463   *251*
R v Thames Magistrates' Court, ex parte Polemis [1974] 2 All ER 1219   *348*
R v Thomas (1983) The Times 19 August   *288*
R v Thorne (1978) 66 Cr App R 6   *259*
R v Towers (1984) The Times 16 October   *335*

R v Turner [1970] 2 QB 321   *268*
R v Viola [1965] 3 All ER 116   *375*
R v Walhein (1952) 36 Cr App R 167   *289*
R v Wanklyn (1984) The Times 14 November   *336*
R v Ward [1988] Crim LR 57   *254*
R v Watson [1988] 1 All ER 897   *289*
R v Wells [1989] Crim LR 67 CA   *258*
R v West [1898] 1 QB 174   *223*
R v Weston-super-Mare Justices, ex parte Shaw [1987] 1 All ER 255   *233*
R v Whitting (1987) The Independent 2 February   *291*
R v Williams [1977] 2 WLR 400   *268*
R v Wilmot (1933) 24 Cr App R 63   *252*
R v Wilson (1979) 69 Cr App R 83   *251*
R v Wilson [1983] 3 All ER 448   *291*
R v Wilson [1995] Crim LR 510   *303, 377*
R v Wilson; R v Sproson (1995) The Times 24 February   *283, 376*
R v Woods [1988] Crim LR 52   *287*
R v Yates (1872) 12 Cox CC 233   *261*

Radcliffe v Bartholomew [1892] 1 QB 161   *223*
Raymond v Attorney-General [1982] QB 839   *220*
Richards, ex parte [1985] 2 All ER 1114   *328*
Robinson, ex parte (1985) The Times 11 October   *233*
Rowland, ex parte [1983] 3 All ER 689   *232*

Sawyers, ex parte [1988] Crim LR 754   *232*
Seneviratne v R [1936] 3 All ER 36   *373*
Shah v Swallow [1984] 2 All ER 528   *227*
Sharma, ex parte [1988] Crim LR 741   *344*

T, ex parte (1984) The Times 28 July   *320*
Tesco Stores, ex parte [1981] 2 WLR 419   *348*
Thompson v Knights [1947] KB 336   *252*
Three Rivers District Council and Others v Governor and Company of the Bank of England (No 2) (1996) The Times 8 January   *338*

Vernon v Paddon [1973] QB 663   *252*

Walters v W H Smith [1914] 1 KB 595   *215*
Westminster City Council v Wingrove (1990) The Times 13 August   *329*
Wheatley v Lodge [1971] 1 WLR 29   *216*
White v WP Brown [1983] CLY 972   *215*
Williams v DPP (1991) The Times 26 March   *272*
Wright v Nicholson [1970] 1 WLR 142   *235*

PART I
CIVIL PROCEDURE

1

The Choice of Court

1.1 Introduction

1.2 English or foreign

1.3 Court or tribunal

1.4 High Court or County Court

1.5 The High Court

1.6 High Court Masters

1.1 Introduction

The High Court was set up in its present form by the Judicature Acts of 1873 and 1875. Its composition is now regulated by the Supreme Court Act 1981, its procedure by the Rules of the Supreme Court (the RSC) which are regularly amended. The County Court was established in 1846 and now draws its jurisdiction from the County Courts Act 1984, its procedure from the County Court Rules (the CCR) which in many respects are the same as those of the High Court. This part of the textbook will describe the High Court rules, and in closing chapters the procedure of the County Court will be compared and, where necessary, contrasted with them. The Courts and Legal Services Act (CLSA) 1990 substantially alters much of the provision relating to High Court and County Court practice.

1.2 English or foreign

Whatever the nature of the claim, the first decision facing a potential litigant is that of forum: in what country should he bring his action? In some cases he will have no choice. If he wishes to sue the government of a State, he must usually sue in that State unless the State consents to the action being tried elsewhere. His choice may be restricted by contract: most commercial agreements contain clauses specifying where disputes are to be tried. He may start his action in one country, but the court of that country may dismiss it on the ground of *Forum Non Conveniens*, that is, that the action is more appropriately tried elsewhere because of the availability of evidence, or for some other procedural reason. The choice may be decided by application of the rules of private international law, conflict of laws. In all these and other events, the English courts cannot or will not hear the action.

An action may be started in England, subject to the matters discussed above, even though the facts giving rise to the claim have no connection whatever with England or with English law. For example, a shipping charter made between the owner of a ship resident in Germany and a carrier resident in Brazil concerning hire of a ship registered in France, the charter governed by Spanish law, may perhaps be commenced in the High Court. Or a Nigerian employee of an American company injured in an accident on board a North Sea oil platform owned by a Dutch company may sue in England or in the United States. Where the claimant has a choice, he will have to consider the advantages of suing in one country rather than another. The ease of proof, or the availability of evidence, may affect choice, as may the remedies he can expect. In the United States, for instance, awards of damages for personal injury are far higher than in the United Kingdom, for different rules of assessment apply and the American action will be tried usually by jury; also discovery (see Chapter 11) may be more liberal than in the United Kingdom. Where there is a choice of forum, a claimant's legal advisors must know that there is a choice, and point out these material differences to their client.

1.3 Court or tribunal

Once a claimant has decided that he must or will bring his claim in England, he must be advised which 'court' to use. The High Court and County Court have a wide jurisdiction in all areas, but in many cases statute prescribes an alternative proceeding, in a specially constituted tribunal. Advisors must therefore know when a claim cannot be brought in the ordinary civil courts. Detailed discussion of the alternatives is outside the scope of this book, but a few examples will help to identify what should be considered. An employee who is dismissed may have a claim for breach of contract; this he must pursue in the High Court or County Court, in an action for damages. He may also have a separate but concurrent claim for unfair dismissal; this he can only establish in proceedings before an industrial tribunal, for the ordinary courts have no jurisdiction to hear the claim. The owner of a restaurant who desires to sell intoxicating drinks to his customers must apply to the magistrates' court for the area in which he carries on business; he cannot use the High Court or County Court to begin his claim. People who have been denied Social Security benefits, or Civil Service pensions, or whose land has been compulsorily purchased by local authorities, must make their claims before the tribunals set up to hear them, and cannot in the first instance bring the claim before the ordinary courts. Parties to commercial agreements may have stipulated for arbitration of disputes, in which case the claim comes before an arbitrator rather than a judge of the High Court or County Court.

In deciding whether a claim must or may be brought before some tribunal other than the High Court or County Court, advisors must consult the appropriate statute or agreement between the parties. That statute, or instruments made under it, will also lay down the procedure to be followed, and the remedies available. In some cases, an appeal will be possible to the ordinary courts, in others to the Secretary of State, in others to a second tribunal, while in some there is no right of appeal at all.

1.4 High Court or County Court

The claimant having been advised that his claim lies in one of the ordinary civil courts, he must then decide which to use. Statute may require the claim to be brought in one or other, or there may be a choice; in the latter event, the factors influencing choice should be considered. In general, an action commenced in the High Court may be transferred to the County Court, and vice versa; transfer is described in detail in Chapter 21.

By s3 CLSA 1990, the County Court has jurisdiction to make any order which could be made by the High Court, including conditional, final and interlocutory orders. There is now no jurisdictional limit to damages actions, except that personal injury claims over £50,000 must be commenced in the High Court. As claims under £25,000 are normally tried in the County Court, it is sensible to commence them there. Claims between £25,000 and £50,000 should be commenced wherever is tactically sensible. Detailed provisions as to jurisdiction, as well as factors to consider where there is a choice, are contained in the High Court and County Courts Jurisdiction Order 1991 (SI 1991/724).

There are, however, still some actions which must be commenced in the High Court, such as:

1. claims in defamation;
2. applications for judicial review (see Chapter 19).

The County Court has jurisdiction only where granted by statute, and this is of two kinds, *general* and *special*. General jurisdiction covers the most common types of claim in contract and tort, and other fields of equity and common law, subject to financial limits. Special jurisdiction is that given by particular Acts in particular fields, for example, admiralty, adoption, housing, race relations and mental health. To determine what, if any, of these special claims may be brought in the County Court, the relevant statute must be consulted (see Part 2 of the 'Green Book'). In the following cases, among others, proceedings *must* be commenced in the County Court and not the High Court:

1. proceedings under the Rent Acts for possession of premises within them;

2. claims by creditors to enforce instalment payments agreements regulated under the Consumer Credit Act 1974;
3. proceedings under the Race Relations Act 1976 (except where the discrimination is in relation to employment);
4. claims for the possession of property by a mortgagee where the property is outside Greater London, is a dwelling-house, and the net annual value for rating does not exceed £1,000 (s21 CCA 1984).

In cases where neither the High Court nor County Court has a sole and exclusive jurisdiction over claims, a claimant has a free choice of court. It must also be remembered that he may be able to bring his action in the County Court, even though that court has at first sight no jurisdiction, in the following cases:

1. if his claim is for personal injury, by limiting the amount to £50,000. This may be done in the Particulars of Claim (the formal document by which the action is begun).
2. where the proceedings are transferred to the County Court from the High Court, by consent of the parties, application by one of them, or by the High Court of its own motion (see Chapter 21).

Once a claimant is told he has a choice of High Court or County Court, whether by statute or by agreement of his opponent, he must choose which to proceed in. He should consider all the circumstances but in particular the following:

1. If the action is brought in the High Court unnecessarily (in the court's view), the party bringing the action may be penalised in costs (s51(8) SCA 1981).
2. *Time*: High Court litigation is notoriously slow, even if the time limits fixed by the Rules of the Supreme Court are followed strictly. To a trader seeking to recover the price of goods delay may mean bankruptcy or irrecoverable loss of goodwill. To the victim of personal injuries delay will cause mental suffering and anxiety.
3. *Convenience*: County Courts are more numerous and accessible than High Court locations. Parties and witnesses have less far to travel, the procedure is less cumbersome and may remove the need for barristers and even solicitors. Proceedings are less formal, especially if the claim is for a small amount.
4. *Complexity*: claims involving difficult questions of fact or law are more suited to the High Court, where the greater experience of judges tells heavily. The greater the value of the claim, the greater the need for a careful trial.

1.5 The High Court

The High Court is a single court which for convenience and the proper despatch of judicial business is divided into three divisions and sits at many locations. Having decided that he must or will commence a claim in the High Court, the claimant now decides which division and which location will hear his action. Just as there is separation of jurisdiction between High Court and County Court, so the choice of division is sometimes restricted by statute, and sometimes lies with the claimant. By combination of statute and practice, the divisions hear the following types of claim:

1. *Queen's Bench Division*: most actions in contract and tort. Within the division there are special lists for commercial and admiralty matters which are heard by judges experienced in those fields.
2. *Chancery Division*: actions concerning title to and rights over land, administration of estates of deceased persons, execution of trusts, mortgage actions, liquidation of companies (in the Companies Court) patent and passing off actions, the affairs of mentally disordered persons (in the Court of Protection), and revenue matters.
3. *Family Division*: defended matrimonial causes, decrees of death, legitimacy and nullity, actions involving the rights of children such as adoption, wardship, and actions between spouses for the ownership of property and occupation of the matrimonial home.

If an action is brought in the County Court for which the County Court has no jurisdiction, it is likely to be dismissed. In the High Court, however, actions may be transferred at any stage to another division, or the 'wrong' division may deal with the matter.

This emphasises that there is only one High Court; judges of each division have all the powers of all the divisions. Nonetheless, it is advisable to begin proceedings in the correct division, if one is prescribed, for defective procedure may lead to delay through adjournment, liability in costs for the extra delay and any necessary amendments to the claim and trial of the claim before a judge unfamiliar with the particular field of substantive law. No reasonable counsel would commence an action for personal injuries in the Chancery Division, for the judges of that division have little if any knowledge of the principles of liability or the level of awards of damages. Likewise, a claim for the application of charitable funds cy-près would not be advised in the Queen's Bench Division.

Whatever division is chosen, a claimant can choose whether to begin and maintain his action out of the Central Registry of the High Court, in London, or at the District Registry where his cause of action arose; in each case the procedure is the same, and the choice will be influenced by the following factors:

1. *Speed*: actions begun in District Registries tend to take longer to come to trial than those begun in London. High Court judges travel on circuit infrequently.
2. *Cost*: in proceedings before trial (interlocutory proceedings) there is need to attend court on several occasions. If the claimant's own solicitors cannot easily attend in London, other London-based firms (London agents) must be instructed, and this will add to the costs and probably also to the delay.
3. *Practice*: it is rare for actions suitable to the Chancery Division to be started outside London; the specialised nature of claims usually makes London more appropriate.

1.6 High Court Masters

After proceedings have been issued and served, there are several distinct stages to an action before it reaches the trial judge. Each of these stages is described in the chapters which follow, but it may help to understand the procedure by which each is brought before the court on an interlocutory hearing.

In the Queen's Bench Division, interlocutory applications are made by one party taking out (issuing and serving) a *Summons in Action*, requiring the other party to attend before a *Master of the Supreme Court* (in the Queen's Bench Division Masters are barristers). The Master is in effect the equivalent of a High Court judge, and exercises in general the same powers (with the important exception that a Master cannot generally grant injunctions). It is to the Master that parties apply for discovery, dismissal, summary judgment, interim payment, directions on expert evidence, orders for the enforcement of judgments, and other pre-trial matters. In some cases the application will be made *ex parte*, that is, without notice to the other side, but that procedure is confined to cases where urgency requires or secrecy is needed to prevent the other side from defeating the aims of the order to be made by the Master; in most cases the summons will be *inter partes*, both sides having advance notice of the date and time of the hearing, and having the right to appear and present argument before the Master makes his order. Where proceedings are extant out of a District Registry, the District Judge exercises the powers of the Master.

Hearings on interlocutory applications before Masters are invariably brief. They are arranged either as 'private room appointments' at a fixed time and before a named Master, or are left to be dealt with by one of the two or more Masters in Chambers; in the latter case the hearing takes about five minutes, and the Master remains seated while advocates stand at a bench in front of him (there are no seats for counsel); the Master will deal brusquely with each side's argument, and endorse his order in manuscript on the original of the Summons. There is little or no time for citation of authorities or involved discussion of the case. Where a private room appointment is made, the the hearing will be longer (15–30 minutes), and counsel sit even when addressing the Master. There is more time for outlining the claim and for a right of reply to the other side's argument. Nonetheless, counsel are expected to be concise, and if the hearing lasts longer than the time stated to the court office when the summons was taken out the Master will comment adversely and may deprive a party of his costs. It is rare for Masters to hear oral evidence on interlocutory matters; they read statements sworn by a party or his solicitor (affidavits) and hear argument on the facts and law.

It is common for all the principal interlocutory stages of an action in the High Court to be heard by the same Master. This ensures consistency, for although the Master may not remember a case when next it comes before him, he is likely to act in a way consistent with his own previous orders, and the parties know in advance the style of hearing they will receive and the manner in which it should be conducted to persuade the Master to their view.

In the Chancery Division, Masters exercise rather more extensive functions than in the Queen's Bench Division. They handle complicated details of accounts and enquiries, for Chancery actions have fewer of the minor procedural stages than those of the Queen's Bench. There are slightly different powers of appeal from orders. Chancery Masters are qualified solicitors.

2
Rules of the Supreme Court

2.1 Origin of the Rules

2.2 Function of the Rules

2.3 Non-compliance with the Rules

2.1 Origin of the Rules

The organisation and function of the High Court is regulated by the Supreme Court Act 1981. That Act empowers the making of rules for the procedure of the court; the rules are drafted and kept up-to-date by a Rules Committee, and are brought into effect as statutory instruments, a form of delegated legislation. As subordinate legislation, they are liable to be struck down as *ultra vires* if they purport to create new rights or to take away rights and remedies afforded by the substantive law. The law of procedure concerns the means by which rights are enforced and established, and not the means by which they are conferred. The present Rules of the Supreme Court ('RSC') date from 1965, and are the subject of constant revision, amendment and interpretation.

The RSC are contained in 115 Orders, each of which is devoted to a specific topic, and is sub-divided into Rules and sub-Rules. The standard mode of citation is by abbreviation, where 'O.' corresponds to the number of the Order, 'r' to the number of the Rule, and sub-Rules are given in parentheses, so that, for example, Order 14, Rule 1, sub-Rule 3 appears as O.14 r1(3). This mode will be adopted in the text which follows.

2.2 Function of the Rules

The function of the RSC has been succinctly and firmly stated by May LJ in *Tsai* v *Woodworth* (1983) The Times 30 November:

> 'The Rules of the Supreme Court are not to be treated as the rules of a game ... The object of the Rules is to ensure that justice is done between the parties and that the proceedings are dealt with expeditiously.'

The Rules prescribe all aspects of procedure: the mode of proceeding, time for compliance, forms of documents and mode of filing, service, trial, hearing, summons, judgment, costs and enforcement. It is for a party upon whom the Rules place a duty of compliance to comply with them. So long as the English system of civil procedure remains adversarial, the court has no part to play in modifying the rules; but it can grant relief against the effects of non-compliance, so as to produce the results stated by May LJ.

2.3 Non-compliance with the Rules

O.2 r1 provides:

> 'Where there has been a failure to comply with any requirement of these rules, the failure shall be treated as an irregularity and shall not nullify the proceedings, but the court may set aside the proceedings wholly or in part or exercise its powers under these rules to allow any such amendments and to give any such directions as it thinks fit ... no application to set aside any proceedings for irregularity shall be granted unless made within a reasonable time ...'

O.2 r1 confers a discretionary power upon the court, but does not of course allow it to alter the rules of substantive law. The power is most commonly used to correct defects where an action has been commenced in the wrong division of the High Court, or has been wrongly served, or a party has been late in complying with his obligation to serve a list of documents, or to allow their inspection, or in disclosing his expert evidence, or has used an incorrect form of originating process, for example, Writ when he should have proceeded by Originating Summons. The practice is that unless the opposing party has been prejudiced by the non-compliance in a way that cannot be adequately compensated for by an award of costs in his favour, the action will be allowed to continue; and if he does not object to the defect within a reasonable time, he is bound to allow it to continue, for then the prejudice to him is of his own making.

Notwithstanding the power in O.2 r1, a party is well advised to comply strictly with the Rules. If he does so, there is no risk that he may later have to persuade the court to exercise its discretionary relieving power in his favour. Even if persuasion works, it may be at the cost of the party applying for it, for he could be ordered to pay the costs of any adjournments or amendments made necessary by the failure to comply, even if he eventually wins the action at a full trial.

There are some failures to comply with the Rules which are too fundamental to be cured by the application of O.2 r1. For instance, a Writ is valid for four months after the date of its issue; if it is to be validly served after the expiry of that period, the plaintiff must first obtain leave of the court to renew the Writ. If the Writ is served after the four months have expired, and without the necessary leave to renew, such a non-compliance cannot be remedied, and if the defendant objects to the validity of the Writ it must be set aside, and the plaintiff must commence a fresh action, the law of limitation of actions permitting; *Bernstein v Jackson* [1982] 2 All ER 806. In *Ward-Lee v Linehan* [1993] 2 All ER 1006 CA, it was held that the court can use its discretion here, as elsewhere, if the particular facts justify it. The tendency of the courts is however to find that failures to comply are mere 'irregularities' rather than fundamental to the validity of the action, and so to retain their curative power: *Leal v Dunlop Bio-Process* [1984] 2 All ER 207.

The court will look at the effect of the irregularity on the other parties to the action so that, for instance, defective service or even non-service of proceedings may be cured if the party to be served is aware of the proceedings: *Golden Ocean Assurance Ltd and World Mariner Shipping SA v Martin* [1990] 2 Lloyd's Rep 215.

3

The Issue of Proceedings

3.1 Originating process

3.2 Writ

3.3 Originating Summons

3.4 Originating Motion

3.5 Petition

3.6 Issue of proceedings

3.1 Originating process

When a claimant has decided in which division of the High Court he must or will proceed, he must decide what form of proceeding to use, who will be the parties to it, and how it must be served. The choice of form of proceeding is sometimes prescribed by the Rules, sometimes a matter of free choice.

There are four principal modes of commencing High Court proceedings. In order of importance they are *Writ, Originating Summons, Originating Motion* and *Petition*. The circumstances of their use are regulated by O.5 rr1–4.

The issue of proceedings in the County Court is dealt with in Chapter 21, section 21.5.

3.2 Writ

If the claim is to be brought in the Queen's Bench Division, O.5 r2 prescribes that the following types of action must be begun by Writ rather than any other mode:

1. a claim for any relief or remedy for any tort, other than trespass to land;
2. a claim based upon an allegation of fraud;
3. a claim for damages for breach of duty where the damages claimed consist of or include damages in respect of the death of any person or in respect of personal injuries to any person or in respect of damage to any property.

In the Chancery Division, any action concerning a patent must be commenced by

Writ, and will be heard in the Patents Court established by the Patents Act 1977. A claim for trespass to land can be begun by Writ, but if the claim is for possession against squatters a speedier procedure is available by way of Originating Summons under O.113 (see Chapter 19).

The form and contents of a Writ are governed by O.6. It must bear the Royal Arms at its head, identify the Division of the High Court in which the action is proceeding, identify the parties to it, inform the party against whom it is issued (the defendant) of the nature of the claimant's (the plaintiff's) claim, and identify the capacity in which the plaintiff sues if he is not suing on his own behalf, for example, if he is a trustee, or nominal plaintiff, or next friend of a claimant who is not yet 18 years old. Forms of Writ are prescribed in Appendix A of the White Book, but may be adapted as the nature of the case requires. The Writ also bears the address of the plaintiff's solicitors, if any, and the number of the action.

Where the claim is for a *liquidated* sum, that is, a debt or specific sum payable under a contract, the Writ also bears an indorsement for *fixed* or 'fourteen day' costs; if the defendant pays the amount of the demand within 14 days of service of the Writ, together with the stated amount of costs, the action will proceed no further. The amounts of the fixed costs are regulated by the Rules and vary according to the value of the claim: O.62 Appendix 3. Damages in tort are always *unliquidated* even though they may be easily calculable as specific sums of lost earnings or cost of repair to property, and the fixed costs rule applies in practice only to claims in contract for, for example, the price of goods sold and delivered, or money due under a loan or guarantee, and to claims to a *Quantum Meruit*.

Whatever the basis of the claim, the defendant must, in the Writ, be notified of its nature. The plaintiff may do this by a *special indorsement* on the Writ, a *Statement of Claim* which gives the defendant the fullest particulars to which he is entitled of the plaintiff's claim and which complies with the rules of pleading laid down in O.18 (see Chapter 19). As will be seen, a Statement of Claim must be served within 14 days of the defendant giving notice that he will defend the action, and indorsement on the Writ itself saves time in the action. Alternatively, the Writ may bear a *general indorsement*, a brief description of the nature of the claim, for example, 'the plaintiff's claim is for damages for personal injuries and consequential loss sustained as a result of the defendant's negligent driving of a motor vehicle at Fleet Street, London on 1 June 1995' or 'the plaintiff's claim is for £5,000 being the price of goods sold and delivered to the defendant full particulars of which the defendant has had notice'. General indorsements are made under O.6 r2(1)(a) and where used they must be followed by a full Statement of Claim within 14 days of acknowledgement of service. General indorsements are used either when the Writ must for some reason be issued speedily, perhaps because a relevant limitation period is about to expire, and there is insufficient time to send the papers to counsel to draft a Statement of Claim, or when the plaintiff does not expect the defendant to dispute the claim and has no wish to incur the extra costs of counsel in drafting a pleading that will be superfluous.

In appropriate cases the Writ will contain additional matters. If the claim is liquidated and payable in foreign currency, the foreign currency equivalent may be stated as rates stand at the date of issue of the Writ: *Practice Direction (Judgment: Foreign Currency)* [1976] 1 WLR 83. It may contain a claim for interest, due either under a contract or by s35A Supreme Court Act 1981, and if the demand is liquidated the rate claimed will be stated together with a calculation of the total interest claimed to the date of issue of the Writ and the daily or weekly amount of interest payable thereafter: *Practice Direction (Claims for Interest)* [1983] 1 WLR 377. If a claim is made for possession of a dwelling house, the Writ must state whether the property falls outside the rateable value of the Rent Acts: O.6 r2(1)(c).

3.3 Originating Summons

An Originating Summons is a summons which begins an action, and in the main a party may choose to sue by it or by Writ. Three factors, however, may make its use imperative or inappropriate: cases where statute prescribes it as the sole available proceeding; cases where the Rules suggest its use; and practical considerations of remedies.

Originating Summons procedure will only be required where statute says so: O.5 r3. In the following examples it is the only available mode:

1. applications for pre-action discovery under s33 Supreme Court Act 1981 (see Chapter 11);
2. application under the Married Women's Property Act 1882, for the determination of spouses' respective interests in matrimonial property.

Where there is a choice of proceeding by Originating Summons or by Writ, the Rules suggest that an Originating Summons will be appropriate in the following cases, by O.5 r4:

1. in which the sole or principal question at issue is, or is likely to be, one of the construction of an Act, or of any instrument made under an Act, or of any deed, will, contract or other document, or some other question of law; or
2. in which there is unlikely to be any substantial dispute of fact.

The terms of O.5 r4 are directory and not mandatory, and illustrate that originating summons procedure is not suitable where the basic facts of a claim are in dispute; this is because there are no pleadings where an Originating Summons is used. It would be unthinkable that a claim for damages for breach of contract would be brought by way of Originating Summons if, for instance, the defendant denies having signed the alleged agreement, or asserts that his signature was obtained by misrepresentation. The most common use of the procedure is by trustees who are unsure of the meaning of a trust document, or of their powers under it, and apply to the court for directions under O.85 r2.

The availability of interlocutory remedies will also influence the choice between Writ and Originating Summons. As will be seen, the defendant may file a defence to the claim which the plaintiff regards as spurious or hopeless. If the action is begun by Writ, the plaintiff may apply for summary judgment under O.14 (see Chapter 7). If the action has been started by Originating Summons, summary judgment is not available, and the plaintiff must wait until full trial to obtain his remedy (though he may in the meantime be able to obtain an interlocutory injunction). Similarly, interim payments on account of debt or damages can be given in a Writ action, under O.29 r9, but not where the Originating Summons is used (see Chapter 13).

The form and contents of an Originating Summons are governed by O.7. There are three forms; the *general* form (the usual one), the *expedited* form (available only where the Rules allow, for urgent applications), and the *ex parte* form (where the defendant does not have notice of the first hearing). Whichever is used, it should be in one of the forms suggested in Appendix A, and must, by O.7 r2:

> '... include a statement of the questions on which the Plaintiff seeks the determination or direction of the High Court or, as the case may be, a concise statement of the relief or remedy claimed ... with sufficient particularity to identify the cause or causes of action in respect of which the plaintiff claims that relief or remedy'.

An Originating Summons is not a 'pleading' within the meaning of O.18, but in many respects the court has the same power to allow amendment, to strike out and to deal with it as if it were an action with pleadings begun by Writ. The differences are mentioned in their proper place in later chapters.

3.4 Originating Motion

Commencement by Originating Motion is possible only where statute or the Rules permit, and is quite rare. The most important types of action in which it is used are:

1. applications for leave for judicial review for one of the prerogative orders of *certiorari*, *mandamus* or prohibition: O.53 (see Chapter 19);
2. applications for an order directing a Minister or tribunal to state a case for consideration by the High Court;
3. appeals from awards of an arbitrator to the Commercial Court, under the Arbitration Act 1979;
4. applications for committal for contempt of court where there are no other pending proceedings in which the committal can be made: O.52 r3.

The form and contents of an Originating Motion are governed by O.8. The motion, which is an order to a party to attend court on the hearing of the claim, must include a concise statement of the nature of the claim made or the relief or remedy required: O.8 r3.

3.5 Petition

As with Originating Motions, the Petition can be used only where statute or the Rules permit, and its use is equally rare. The principal occasions of its use are:

1. applications for divorce and dissolution of marriage;
2. applications to declare an individual bankrupt;
3. applications to wind-up a company compulsorily;
4. claims to set aside the result of elections of Members of Parliament and local government representatives.

The form and contents of a Petition are governed by O.9, but may be further subject to other statutes and instruments, for example, the Insolvency Rules 1986. They are generally in a far greater standard form than the other modes, and contain less detail of the facts of the case.

3.6 Issue of proceedings

When the plaintiff has decided upon the correct mode of beginning his action, and has chosen the parties to it (see Chapter 4), he must issue process through the court. This involves the court allotting a number to the action, sealing the process with the court stamp, and where appropriate fixing a hearing date.

The plaintiff must consider whether he needs the leave of the court to issue his action against the defendant. In general any High Court action may be started without leave, but in the following cases the plaintiff must first apply for leave:

1. Where the proposed defendant resides outside England, Wales, Scotland, Northern Ireland and countries covered by the Civil Jurisdiction and Judgments Acts 1982 and 1991, and the Writ is to be served outside one of those territories, application for leave to issue is usually combined with application for leave to serve the Writ under RSC O.11 (see Chapter 5, section 5.8).
2. Where the plaintiff has been declared a vexatious litigant by order of the court under s42 Supreme Court Act 1981. This order is made rarely, and in practice only where the plaintiff has made a thorough nuisance of himself by issuing many hopeless or frivolous actions against a defendant or class of defendants, and is not truly litigating to establish rights. Since it deprives a plaintiff of his right to sue, it is made only in outrageous cases: *Re Varnazza* [1959] 1 WLR 622.
3. Proceedings in respect of the breach of a covenant to repair property within the Leasehold Property (Repairs) Act 1938: *Colchester* v *Carlton* (1984) The Times 9 April.
4. Certain proceedings under the Mental Health Act 1983.

5. Proceedings under s30(5) the Post Office Act 1969 by someone other than the sender and addressee of a postal packet against the Post Office in respect of the loss of the mail.

Where leave is not necessary or has been granted, the plaintiff drafts his originating process and, in the case of a Writ and Originating Summons, takes three copies to the Central Office or District Registry, pays the court fee for issue and has returned to him the original and one copy of the Writ duly sealed and numbered; the other copy is retained in the court records.

Where proceedings are begun by Originating Summons, the court may at the time of issue fix a hearing date for the claim, a *return day*; this is only done in practice when the expedited form is used, and a speedy trial is desirable, for example, where trustees need to know quickly what to do with trust funds before the end of a fiscal year.

4
Parties

4.1 Introduction

4.2 Companies and corporate persons

4.3 Persons under a disability

4.4 Partnerships and sole traders

4.5 Foreign States

4.6 Trusts

4.7 Deceased defendants and parties who die during the action

4.8 Bankruptcy and liquidation

4.9 The Crown

4.10 Unincorporated associations

4.11 Joinder of parties

4.12 Representative actions

4.13 Test cases

4.14 Joinder of causes of action

4.15 Misjoinder and non-joinder of parties

4.16 Case management

4.1 Introduction

Before issuing proceedings a plaintiff must consider carefully who is to be in the action with him, either as a co-plaintiff or as a defendant. He should sue with and against all individuals concerned with his 'cause of action' (his claim), for it is in general only those named as parties who are bound by any order and judgment given in the action. In the great majority of cases there will be only one plaintiff, one defendant, and one cause of action; but even there statute or rule may lay down special procedures. Matters take on complexity when there are multiple plaintiffs and defendants, and several causes of action. The claims that may be raised by defendants in actions brought against them (*counterclaims*) are considered in Chapter 6; the procedure for adding and removing parties after the issue of proceedings is dealt with in Chapter 10, under the headings of amendment of Writ and pleadings. O.15 regulates parties in actions (CCR O.5).

Where no special rules apply, each party is described in the heading of the Writ, and on every pleading, Summons and other document in the action, by his full name or, if the plaintiff does not know it, by such name or parts of name as is known. If a party is a married woman, the words 'married woman' appear in parentheses after her name: the capacity 'spinster' is now rarely used. Procedures where the name of the defendant is unknown arise in practice only in claims for possession of land against squatters, and are considered in Chapter 19, section 19.5.

4.2 Companies and corporate persons

Limited companies incorporated by charter, or under the Companies Act 1985, or some earlier legislation, and other legal persons such as Industrial and Provident Societies and Friendly Societies, together with certain unincorporated associations which are by statute so allowed, for example, Trade Unions, sue and are sued in their own name. It is important to ascertain the full registered name of the corporation, and searches should be made at the appropriate registry.

Local authorities and statutory utilities such as Area Electricity Boards are similarly sued in their own name, as are nationalised industries. Central government departments are divisions of the Crown, and other rules govern actions by and against them.

Where a limited company fails to disclose on any order for goods or request for money the fact that it is a limited company, then in certain circumstances a claim may lie both against it in its corporate role and against its individual directors personally: s349(4) Companies Act 1985.

4.3 Persons under a disability

Minors, that is, persons under the age of 18 at the date of commencement of proceedings, and persons who are the subject of orders under the Mental Health Act 1983 or earlier, similar, Acts cannot sue or be sued without the intervention of an adult 'assistant' to protect their interest. Where the minor is plaintiff, this is the *next friend*, where he is a defendant the *guardian ad litem*: O.80 r2(1) (CCR O.10 r1). These will usually be the minor's father or guardian, but in exceptional cases, where they are unable or unwilling to act, or it is against them that the action is being brought by the minor, or vice versa, then an independent assistant is needed, and will usually be the Official Solicitor. A minor must act through a solicitor, and cannot conduct proceedings himself; the solicitor must obtain the next friend's written consent to act before the Writ is issued. A next friend becomes personally liable for the costs of the action though he may have a right to be indemnified by the minor against costs properly incurred. A guardian *ad litem* is not so personally liable unless he is guilty of misconduct in protecting the minor's interests. These rules are contained in O.80 rr2 and 3 (CCR O.10 rr2 and 3). The next friend and guardian *ad litem* do not become, in strict law, parties to the action; the minor remains plaintiff or defendant as the case may be.

Mental patients sue and defend actions in much the same way as minors. The next friend or guardian *ad litem* is usually the Receiver appointed by the court to manage the patient's estate, though if the action is by or against the Receiver and the patient is the opposing party, an independent person, usually the Official Solicitor, will act instead.

4.4 Partnerships and sole traders

A partnership is a group of individuals trading together either under their own names or under a collective name which may or may not be their own, usually with a view to profit. A sole trader is an individual trading either under his own name or some other name. Neither business is a corporate entity, and must sue or be sued either by all its constituent partners or in its trade name; the plaintiff has an option whether to sue the partners individually or to sue the firm: O.81 r1 (CCR O.5 r9). If the action is brought against the firm in the firm's name, the partners must each acknowledge service individually (see Chapter 6). It will usually be advantageous to sue the firm rather than its individual partners, for any judgment can be executed against the property of the firm and against the personal assets of any partner who acknowledged service and has been adjudged a partner. If the action is against the individual partners alone, it is only against their own assets not used in the business that a judgment can be executed without leave of the court: O.81 r5.

Where an individual carries on business on his own account, and not in partnership, he may be sued in his own name, or in the name under which he trades. There is little to choose between the alternatives, since a judgment may be executed against his property without leave, whether or not it is property forming part of his business assets.

When the action is by or against the firm in its business name, the words 'a firm' appear after the name in the title of the action. Where it is against an individual sole trader in his own name, it is common to add after the name 'trading as ...'.

4.5 Foreign States

A foreign sovereign State is usually immune from being sued in the English courts unless it agrees and 'submits to the jurisdiction': State Immunity Act 1978. The immunity extends to heads of state and their governments, but is subject to important exceptions. Most commercial contracts to which the State is a party, and other contracts out of which claims for personal injury and damage to property arise, carry no immunity: ss2–11.

Special rules of procedure apply to the service of documents, the availability of privilege, the availability of remedies, and the enforcement of judgments against foreign States, all of which are outside the purview of this book but which can be found in the Act itself. No further consideration of this special position will be made in the chapters which follow.

4.6 Trusts

Where trustees are suing in respect of trust property, or are being sued, all should be joined as parties; if some refuse to be joined as plaintiffs together with others, they should be joined as defendants (no-one can be compelled to be plaintiff in an action against his will). Beneficiaries of trust funds are not normally parties to an action unless of course they are suing the trustees, or are being sued themselves.

Where the trustees are the personal representatives of a deceased, and the action concerns the deceased's estate, all should be joined as parties in the same way as trustees of other trust funds. If there are no personal representatives at the time the proceedings are issued, the court on the plaintiff's application may order that the action proceed without them, or may appoint an *administrator ad litem* to represent the estate until probate or letters of administration are granted: O.15 r15 (CCR O.5 r7). The administrator will usually be the Official Solicitor.

4.7 Deceased defendants and parties who die during the action

Most rights of action and most liabilities, with the exception of defamation and exemplary damages, survive after death for and against the person who would have sued or been sued had he lived: s1 Law Reform (Miscellaneous Provisions) Act 1934 as amended by s4 Administration of Justice Act 1982. Upon death, the estate will be administered by personal representatives either under a grant of probate (if the deceased made a valid will) or of letters of administration (if he died intestate). Where there are such representatives, the action should be brought by or against all as discussed in section 4.6.

It is sometimes the case, however, that the plaintiff does not know at the time of issuing proceedings that the defendant has died, or that there have been no personal representatives yet appointed. In this case he may begin his action against the deceased in his own name (if he does not know of the death), or against 'the personal representative of AB deceased' if there are no representatives. In both cases the action will have been validly commenced: O.15 rr6, 6A (CCR O.5 r8). In the latter case the plaintiff must, before serving proceedings and during the period of validity of the proceedings for service (usually four months, though it may be extended by order of the court: see Chapter 5), apply to the court for an order appointing some person or persons to represent the estate; if a grant of probate or administration has been taken out between the issue of proceedings and the date of the application, it will be that appointed personal representative that the court orders be made a party.

If a party, whether plaintiff or defendant, dies during the action, and the cause of action is one which survives for or against his estate, then on application to the Master the Writ and pleadings or other process will usually be amended to substitute the personal representatives as parties in place of the deceased: O.15 r7 (CCR O.5 r11).

4.8 Bankruptcy and liquidation

If a potential plaintiff or defendant is made bankrupt or (if a limited company) goes into liquidation, before the issue of proceedings then, if the cause of action survives the bankruptcy or winding-up order, it passes to the trustee in bankruptcy or to the liquidator. Special rules apply to the commencement of actions by and against the bankrupt or the wound-up company. In general, actions may be brought and maintained as in the normal case of a solvent party, but if the bankruptcy or liquidation begins after proceedings have been issued, the trustee or liquidator must obtain leave from the court to carry on the action, if a plaintiff; and the action will generally be stayed, that is, held in abeyance, pending the completion of the assessment of the liabilities of the individual or company, if defendant.

4.9 The Crown

By the Crown Proceedings Act 1947 the Crown is made generally liable to actions in the High Court both in tort and contract, though there are exceptions, such as injuries sustained on active service where the victim will receive a disability pension: s10. Where the Crown is to be made a party, as plaintiff or defendant, the action is brought in the name of the appropriate department, for example, Inland Revenue, Department of Health and Social Security, Home Office, as stated in a list issued by the Treasury. If no department is specified, proceedings are brought by or against the Attorney-General.

4.10 Unincorporated associations

A collection of individuals may not have corporate status; partnerships have already been mentioned, and have their own rules for suing and being sued. Other examples are members' clubs, tenants' associations, youth clubs, trade guilds and the like. It must be remembered that some may be corporate by reason of a special charter, or may sue and be sued in their own name notwithstanding their non-corporate nature: see section 4.2. In the case of a true unincorporated association, such as a club, it is usual for a small number of individuals, probably the club committee or trustees, to sue or be sued 'on behalf of themselves and all the members of the ... club'. This does away with the need to name every club member in the title to the action. Representative actions are considered in more detail below.

4.11 Joinder of parties

There is probably no subject in the law of civil procedure which gives students so much difficulty as the rules relating to the joinder of parties and causes of action; when can more than one plaintiff sue, when can more than one defendant be sued in the same action; when can a plaintiff make more than one claim against a defendant or defendants in the same action? Joinder of causes of action is discussed in section 4.14, counterclaims in Chapter 6. In this section joinder of parties will be examined. The general rules are contained in O.15 (CCR O.5).

In the following cases, the parties should be those stated:

1. All parties to a contract must sue in an action on the contract. If one or more does not consent to be joined as a plaintiff, he must be joined as a defendant with the true defendant. Similarly, joint contractors should all be sued as defendants, though the plaintiff may choose to sue one or only some of them.
2. In an action founded upon a tort, the plaintiff may but not must join all tortfeasors whether joint or several; for example, a passenger injured in a road crash may sue both the driver of the car in which he was travelling and the driver of the car into which his car crashed, in the same action. He is well advised to sue all tortfeasors in one action, so as to have only one trial and to avoid the risk of inconsistent findings of fact in separate trials.
3. Where there is more than one victim of a tort committed by the same defendant or defendants, all may sue as plaintiffs provided their rights arise out of 'the same transaction or series of transactions'. Where the passengers of a coach are all injured when the coach overturns, or there is a pile-up on the motorway in which many passengers in separate vehicles are injured, all may sue as plaintiffs against all the drivers of all the vehicles. Each *may* bring separate actions against each of the drivers, but that would be both costly and time-consuming, and the court would probably exercise its power to consolidate the actions so that all evidence relevant to liability is heard in a single trial.

4. In an action for recovery of land the parties should be all persons entitled to possession of it, that is, all landlords or all tenants holding immediately beneath the plaintiff landlord or above the plaintiff tenant.
5. Where the plaintiff is not certain which of two possible defendants is liable to him whether in contract or tort, for example, agent or principal, then he may sue both as defendants in the same action, in the alternative.
6. Where there is doubt as to which of two possible plaintiffs is entitled to sue, for example, agent or principal, or landlord or tenant of premises in respect of a nuisance caused by a third party, both may sue as plaintiffs, together or in the alternative.

Although the rules may permit joinder of parties in one action, the practice of joinder needs to be understood. First, the court has power of its own motion to disallow joinder otherwise permitted by the rules, if it appears that joinder may embarrass or delay the trial or is otherwise inconvenient, and may order that the claim of each plaintiff or against each defendant be tried separately, or that there be a single trial of some issues and separate trials of others (for example, a joint trial on liability, separate trials on quantum), or make any other order it thinks expedient: O.15 r1 (CCR O.5 r3). In addition, the plaintiff must bear in mind that if he sues jointly with others as co-plaintiffs, the court will require that all be represented by the same solicitor, and that he might thus not be in the strongest position to impose his choice of legal adviser upon those co-plaintiffs: *Black King Shipping Corporation v Massie* (1984) The Times 9 July QBD.

Secondly, a plaintiff may elect to sue some rather than all of the defendants he could sue in one action; some may be insolvent or untraceable, or he may think he has a better chance of success against some only. He may be able to bring separate actions against the others at a later date.

Where a plaintiff sues one or less than all the parties he could, it is very likely that the defendant(s) sued will seek to issue third party proceedings against those not joined. This will be both to claim contribution or indemnity from them, or to persuade the plaintiff to join the third party as a full defendant in the action. This is more fully considered in Chapter 8.

4.12 Representative actions

The rules often permit joinder of plaintiffs and defendants, in the interests of avoiding a multiplicity of proceedings, unnecessary costs, wasted time and the danger, already mentioned, of inconsistent findings of fact by different judges at different trials, on the same evidence. It must now be considered when claimants can obtain the relief of the court without needing to be joined as plaintiffs, and when relief can be obtained against persons liable without their being joined as defendants. The general rule is that every person who has a cause of action, or against whom relief is claimed, must be joined as a party if the court is to make an order enforceable by or against him. In some circumstances, however, claimants and defendants are permitted to be represented in the action by others. The rules of representative actions concern therefore this question: in what circumstances may a claimant obtain relief or a person liable be bound by a judgment without his being named as a party on the face of the proceedings?

Judicial precedent has put a gloss on O.15 r12 (CCR O.5 r5), which authorises representative actions. If a person is to be represented in proceedings brought or defended by another on his behalf:

1. he must have an interest in the subject-matter of the action common with the other persons being represented;
2. he must have a grievance common with those others;
3. the nature of the relief claimed must be beneficial to him as it is all those others.

These obscure rules are best described through example. In the leading case, *Smith v Cardiff Corporation* [1954] 1 QB 210, the Corporation had sought to alter the basis upon which council house rents were calculated. This would have had the effect of raising S's rent, and he brought an action to reverse the decision to amend the basis. He sued 'on behalf of himself and all tenants of the Corporation'. The court held the action misconceived. All the tenants had an interest in the way their rent was calculated, but it could not be said that *all* had a common grievance or that all had something to gain from S winning the action; the new basis of calculation had actually *reduced* the rents payable by some tenants, so that a return to the old system would, far from being beneficial to them, have caused them prejudice. This is just another way of saying that no action can be brought to represent someone who would not consent to being joined as a plaintiff in the action. S should have brought his action in his own name alone, as a 'test case' (see section 4.13), or all those who wished to overturn the Corporation's decision should have been joined as plaintiffs and named in the Writ.

The most common types of case in which representative actions are allowed are, in the case of both plaintiff and defendant, actions involving unincorporated associations (members' clubs, trade unions: see section 4.10). The action, if brought by the club against a third party, or defended by it in such an action against it, names 'AB and CD the trustees (or "committee") of the XYZ. Club suing (or "sued") on behalf of themselves and all members for the time being of the said club'. Where the action is by the members against the trustees, the trustees will usually all be joined as parties, while the members sue by a representative: 'EF on behalf of himself and all other members for the time being of the XYZ Club'. Such actions will almost always be to sue for the return of club property appropriated by the trustees, or for negligence or breach of duty in their running of the club's affairs.

A representative action may also be brought by one or more shareholders of a limited company against the directors, for a declaration that an act done or proposed to be done will be outside the powers of the company: *Prudential Assurance* v

Newman Industries [1979] 3 All ER 507. Syndicates of insurance underwriters in the Lloyd's market trade as unincorporated associations, and actions are usually brought against one member of the syndicate who represents all the others.

A species of representative action about which there can be no dispute is an action by or against trustees of a trust fund on behalf of the beneficiaries (but not of course where the beneficiaries are the other parties to the action). Specific provision is made for such actions in O.15 r14 (applicable to the County Court by virtue of CCA s76), and judgments given for and against trustees bind the beneficiaries unless the court otherwise orders.

It now seems clear that where the persons represented are claimants but not members of a club or beneficiaries under a trust, it will only be in the rarest cases that damages can be claimed and recovered in a representative action; since each claimant may be entitled to a different amount of damages, so that inquiries into damages must be held, each must bring his own action or all must be named in the proceedings and joined as parties: *Prudential Assurance* (above). The only types of relief available are therefore restricted to declarations and injunctions. However, in *EMI Records* v *Riley* [1981] 2 All ER 838, EMI sued on its own behalf and on behalf of all the members of British Phonographic Industry for damages against R for infringement of copyright in musical records and tapes. The action was allowed to proceed without the need to join as parties all the many dozens of members of BPI, but the court seems to have been swayed by two factors: (1) that the organisation of BPI resembled very closely a members' club and (2) that the members of BPI had made it clear that they would assign all their rights to damages to BPI if they won the action. In essence, the claim was not one for damages for each of the members.

Where a claim could be brought by representative action, but instead all the claimants are named in the proceedings as parties (perhaps out of an abundance of caution by counsel), the court may order that some be appointed to represent the others, and that the others cease to be parties; all will be bound by the judgment however, as is the case in all representative actions: O.15 r12 (CCR O.5 r5). This will usually be done where one side applies for it to be done, though the court can order it of its own motion. It should be noted that representative actions are only permitted where the number of persons who are to be represented is 'numerous': five has been held not to be 'numerous', and there is no fixed rule. If there is doubt, all should be joined as parties and named in the proceedings, leaving the other side or the court to apply for or make an order for representation.

4.13 Test cases

Where several persons have individual claims arising out of the same transaction or series of transactions, or based upon the same interpretation of a statute or document, they may usually be joined as co-plaintiffs in a single action. For instance, the injured passengers mentioned in section 4.11. Instead of bringing a single action to which they are all parties, they may decide that one will bring his action on his own and that, depending upon the outcome of that, the others may bring their own separate actions later. Although the outcome of the first action will or may be binding so far as it concerns any question of law, it will not be binding as to the facts. Thus, in the example given, the first passenger may win or lose his action on the issue of negligence; but the court's finding of negligence or absence of negligence in that trial will not bind the judge who tries later actions brought by passengers on the same coach. He is entitled to come to a different conclusion on precisely the same evidence. Thus a 'test case' binds only the parties to it and only in respect of the claim of the particular plaintiff. In practice, however, the remaining claims will be settled on the basis of the result of the test case. If the first passenger to bring his action against the coach driver succeeds, the driver's insurers will not seriously defend claims brought by other passengers injured in the same incident, but will settle out of court for very nearly the full value of the injuries.

4.14 Joinder of causes of action

A plaintiff may join any two or more causes of action he has against the same defendant, even if the claims are totally unrelated in nature or amount: O.15 r1 (CCR O.5 r1). Thus a plaintiff may sue a defendant for breach of contract to deliver goods in the same action as he sues for personal injuries caused by the defendant on a different occasion when the defendant ran him down. The rule exists to reduce the multiplicity of actions and to reduce costs. The court has the same power to order the causes of action severed or tried separately as it does with joinder of parties: see section 4.11. It is rare for causes of action to be joined, since complications are caused in pleading each and in giving discovery and preparing the case.

Generally the plaintiff must be suing, and the defendant sued, in the same capacity in all causes of action. A defendant sued as trustee by a plaintiff claiming damages for breach of contract can be sued in the same action by the same plaintiff for a claim in negligence against the defendant in his personal capacity (that is, not as trustee) provided that the trusteeship arises in the case of a personal representative of a deceased's estate (as administrator or executor) but not where the trusteeship arises in some other way. The rule applies in reverse where the trustee is plaintiff, and applies to all causes of action and not just the examples given. It is within the court's power to order that a claim by or against a trustee not a personal representative be joined with one by or against him in his personal capacity, but application must be made *ex parte* by affidavit before the proceedings are issued. Leave is rarely given, the court preferring that claims involving the interests of beneficiaries be brought and defended separately from those involving the trustee in his own right.

4.15 Misjoinder and non-joinder of parties

The proceedings are valid notwithstanding that some parties may have been joined who should not have been or that some have been omitted who should have been joined. The court will usually correct the mistakes under its general power to add or subtract parties at any stage of the proceedings, but will often order the costs of the amendment to be paid by the party who made the error: see O.15 r6 (CCR O.5 r4) and also Chapter 10 below.

4.16 Case management

Consistency in the management of multi-party litigation is viewed as an uppermost consideration: *Chrzanowska* v *Glaxo Laboratories Ltd* (1990) The Times 16 March. This was also the basis of the decision in *Chapman* v *Chief Constable of South Yorkshire and Others, Rimmer* v *Same* (1990) The Times 20 March. The case involved litigation which could affect some 900 claims arising from the Hillsborough disaster in 1989. Initially, claims had been issued against the Chief Constable and the football club. The Chief Constable had issued contribution proceedings against the club and a firm employed in respect of work at the stadium. The Chief Constable then sought to issue notices of discontinuance of the contribution notices. It was held that, in the public interest, the concept of *dominus litis* ought, as far as possible, to be subordinated in case management techniques controlled by the court. Subject to preserving the protections offered by the adversarial system, the court ought to control the pace of the litigation.

An important aspect of the management of these cases has been held to be the setting of a cut-off date for parties to join the action. Joining after this date does not automatically destroy the claim, however, and plaintiffs are not prevented from commencing new causes (unless statute-barred).

5

Service of Proceedings

5.1 Introduction

5.2 Duration of the Writ

5.3 Service of Writ and Originating Summons

5.4 Personal service

5.5 Postal service

5.6 Service by agreement

5.7 Substituted service

5.8 Service outside the jurisdiction

5.9 Defective service

5.10 Statement of claim

5.11 Compelling the service of proceedings

5.1 Introduction

Once the plaintiff has formulated his claim and issued his Writ or Originating Summons, he must serve it on the defendant. In the exceptional case of an *ex parte* Originating Summons no service is needed, but all other proceedings must be served by one of the methods given in the Rules. If service is not made within the first four months after the issue of the Writ it can be validly served only after being renewed by order of the court. If service is made by a method not permitted by the Rules, it will be invalid. Service can be made by agreement of the parties, in which case it need not be in accordance with the Rules. And a defendant who does not take objection to defective service may be bound to accept it as valid.

Issue and service of a County Court summons are dealt with in Chapter 21, section 21.5.

5.2 Duration of the Writ

A Writ is valid for service for four months after (and including) the date of issue: O.6 r8(1). The time runs from the date of issue, so that a Writ issued on 6 June 1995 must be served on or before 5 October 1995: cf. *Trow* v *Ind Coope* [1967] 2 QB 899. If four months have expired without service the Writ is said to have expired, and if it is served after expiry, and the defendant objects to service, the action it begins fails: *Bernstein* v *Jackson* [1982] 2 All ER 806. The plaintiff must begin a fresh action by new proceedings.

Exceptionally, a Writ for service outside England and Wales is valid for six months instead of four months.

The court has power to extend the time for service, by 'renewing' the Writ, on application *ex parte* by Summons in the action supported by affidavit explaining why the Writ has not been served. If the defendant has been avoiding service, or is untraceable, the Master will normally renew the Writ, but the following excuses have failed to persuade the court to exercise its discretionary power: that there was a delay in obtaining legal aid, or that service was delayed so as not to prejudice continuing negotiations for a settlement of the claim, or that there was a mistake in the instructions the plaintiff gave his solicitors. While there is a greater chance of being allowed to renew the writ during the period of its validity, the power to renew can be exercised up to eight months after issue. There is no justification to order an extension after that: *Rolph* v *Zolan* [1993] 1 WLR 1305. The Writ may be renewed only for periods of up to four months at a time. Where the plaintiff postpones service despite having sufficient evidence to justify immediate service, renewal should not be allowed: *Portico Housing* v *Moorhead* (1985) The Times 5 February.

Where an application for renewal is made after the four months have elapsed, and if the plaintiff were to take out fresh proceedings the defendant could rely upon a Limitation Act defence (that the claim is statute barred), renewal will not be granted: *Heaven* v *Road & Rail Wagons* [1965] 2 QB 355. This principle seems not to have been affected by the power, created in 1975, to override the limitation period in actions for personal injury: see Chapter 14. Where the court cannot be certain, at the interlocutory stage, whether the defendant's limitation defence will succeed, it is most unlikely to renew a writ for service: *Wilkinson* v *Ancliff* [1986] 3 All ER 427 CA. The House of Lords has however denied that a plaintiff must show 'exceptional circumstances' to justify renewal of his Writ if both it and the limitation period have expired. It is enough if he demonstrates some 'good reason' for renewal, and the court's power to extend the Writ's validity is not limited to cases where the defendant has been evading service: *Kleinwort Benson* v *Barbrak Ltd* [1987] 2 WLR 1053 HL. The House of Lords has further confirmed that the principles upon which renewal will be granted, whether before or after expiration of a Writ, are the same in personal injury cases as in commercial actions: *Waddon* v *Whitecroft Scovill Ltd* [1988] 1 All ER 996.

The duration of an Originating Summons, and the powers and procedure for its renewal, are the same as those in a Writ action. It is however far less common for a plaintiff to have to use them.

5.3 Service of Writ and Originating Summons

There are three principal ways of serving a Writ or Originating Summons on a defendant who is within the jurisdiction of the High Court: personal service, postal service and substituted service. Where the defendant is outside England and Wales, leave is needed to serve him, and there is a special procedure for service.

5.4 Personal service

This is governed by O.65 rr1 and 2. The plaintiff or his agent (usually his solicitor's clerk or a professional process server) leaves the originating process with the defendant, and shows it to him if the defendant so requests. So long as the defendant is told that the document contains a claim against him, it is not necessary that he actually accept it into his possession; if he refuses to accept service, there is no need for the server to go to extraordinary lengths to thrust the Writ into his hands or to touch him with it; he need only leave it as close as possible to him.

Personal service on limited companies is effected by service on a suitable officer, for example, the company secretary, or leaving it at the company's registered office: s725 Companies Act 1985. If an overseas company no longer has (but formerly had) a place of business in England and Wales, service is still good if effected on persons nominated to accept service on its behalf under s695(1) Companies Act 1985: *Rome v Punjab National Bank (No 2)* (1989) 5 British Company Law Cases 785, CA. Service on partnerships may be upon any partner or upon any person having or appearing to have management and control of the firm's business at its principal place of business where the action is in the firm's name: O.81 r3. In the case of the Crown, personal service consists in leaving the process at the office of the person nominated in the Treasury list of proper defendants (O.77 r4), or upon the Treasury Solicitor if none is nominated. Persons under a disability are served personally by service upon the defendant's father (if the defendant is a minor) or his receiver or the person with whom the defendant resides or who cares for him (if the defendant is a mental patient): O.80 r16.

Personal service is only necessary when required by the rules, and has been largely replaced by postal service of originating process, much to the distress of process servers. It has however one advantage over postal service; where process is served by post other than on a limited company, it is not deemed to be served until seven days after the day of posting unless the plaintiff can prove that the defendant actually received it within the seven days. If the Writ is about to expire, and no renewal has been obtained or seems likely, then personal service may be the only way of ensuring that it is properly served in time.

5.5 Postal service

Postal service of originating process is a convenient form of 'personal' service, governed by O.10. A Writ or Originating Summons may be served on an individual defendant (that is, other than a company or other non-natural person) either by sending a copy of the Writ by first-class post to his usual or last-known address, or if there is a letter-box at the address, by inserting a copy of the Writ through the letter-box in a sealed envelope addressed to the defendant: O.10 r1. It is not necessary to use the Recorded Delivery service of the Post Office. Whichever mode is used, service is deemed to occur, unless the contrary is shown, seven days after the posting or insertion. If either party can prove on a balance of probabilities that the Writ in fact arrived with the defendant on some earlier or later day, the presumption of 'seven-day service' does not apply, and the actual date of receipt is taken as the date of service: *Hodgson v Hart* (1985) The Times 25 November.

Postal service is valid even though the defendant is not physically present within England and Wales at the moment the Writ is consigned to the mail or inserted through the letter box at the defendant's usual or last-known address, provided the plaintiff believes that the Writ will come to the defendant's attention, and it does come to his attention, within seven days of posting: *Barclays Bank of Swaziland Ltd v Hahn* [1989] 1 All ER 193. The Court of Appeal's recent decision in *Forward v West Sussex County Council and Others* [1995] 1 WLR 1469 emphasised the need for proceedings to come to the defendant's notice: on a true construction of O.10 r1(2), service was effected when the proceedings were brought to the attention of the defendant and not on the delivery of the Writ to his last known address. For further details see Chapter 36, section 36.1.

Postal service on a limited company is effected in either of the two stated ways, but service is deemed to occur, somewhat optimistically, the day following posting, that is, the presumed date of delivery. Postal service on a partnership where sued as a firm is effected in the same way as service on an individual. Even though the Writ is addressed to premises which are not the principal place of business of a partnership, if it is in fact delivered at that place of business (having been redirected there by the Post Office) it is deemed served validly: *Austin Rover Group v Crouch Butler Savage* (1986) The Times 1 April. Where a Writ for service on a limited company is properly consigned to the mail, the court will presume that it is delivered in the ordinary course of post, and a defendant who claims that delivery was delayed and only occurred on a date subsequent to the Writ's expiration must prove those facts on a balance of probabilities.

Where both parties are subscribers to a recognised document exchange system which bypasses the Post Office, service of the Acknowledgement of Service and subsequent documents through the medium of that exchange will now generally be valid provided the plaintiff has by his solicitor endorsed upon the Writ his box number at such an exchange: RSC O.6 r5(5); O.12 r3 and O.65 r5.

Service on a defendant firm cannot be effected by the insertion of a copy of the

Writ through the firm's own letter box but must be served at the partner's own address: O.81 r3 RSC.

5.6 Service by agreement

The rules so far discussed exist to increase the chances that a defendant will have notice of proceedings being taken against him, and will have the opportunity to defend them. Where a defendant agrees to be served in a manner not authorised by the Rules, he will be held to his agreement, for then he cannot complain that service is defective. Agreements may be made far in advance of the issue of proceedings, for example, on making a contract the parties may specify a mode of and address for service, and service in compliance with that agreement will be valid. Or a defendant may authorise his solicitors to accept service on his behalf; this he will do if he knows proceedings are about to be served, for in any event if he received the Writ personally he would merely pass it to his solicitors to allow them to acknowledge service and defend the claim. If service is made upon a defendant's solicitors, they must indorse on the Writ a statement that they accept service on his behalf: O.10 r1(4). Service by agreement on solicitors is by far the most common mode of service for claims where one or both of the parties is insured, or where the parties have been in negotiation with each other through their advisors for some time before proceedings are issued.

5.7 Substituted service

It will sometimes be very difficult to serve proceedings by any of the methods so far described. The defendant may be untraceable, or have no address for service and be unwilling to stay long enough in one place for personal service to be made. If, after due attempts to serve him by post or in person, the plaintiff has been unable to do so, he may apply *ex parte* to the Master for an order that service be allowed in some other way. The application must be made by an affidavit setting out the attempts which have been made to effect service; the White Book suggests several visits to his last-known address, inquiry of his solicitors, and reasonable steps to locate him. If satisfied that the Writ will not come to the attention of the defendant by ordinary postal or personal service, the Master will usually make an order for substituted service; this may be by means of an advertisement in newspapers circulating nationally, or in the area where the defendant was last known to reside, or by registered or recorded delivery mail, or in the case of a defendant insured against the claim made, upon his insurers: *Gurtner* v *Circuit* [1968] 2 QB 587. The Master has power to order any form of substituted service: O.65 r4. On an application for substituted service in a case to which O.10 r1 applies, the court must have evidence showing how and why service of the document in the manner prescribed by O.10 r1 was impracticable: *Paragon Group Ltd* v *Burnell* [1991] 2 WLR 854.

Orders for substituted service are appropriate in practice only when a defendant is insured in cases where, if judgment is given against him and he fails to satisfy it, the plaintiff has rights against the insurer directly. This is so in personal injury claims arising from motor vehicle accidents, and in some claims for personal injury against employers, when the employer is subsequently bankrupted. In other cases, there will be little point in 'serving' a defendant who cannot be found, for the plaintiff will be unable to enforce any judgment or recover the costs of the proceedings. However, where the plaintiff fears that the limitation period for bringing his claim may expire before the defendant can be traced, he is well advised to issue and serve his proceedings even if the defendant is not immediately available; he may later reappear, and have sufficient assets to meet the claim.

5.8 Service outside the jurisdiction

It has been noted above that, where proceedings are to be served outside England and Wales (and outside Scotland, Northern Ireland and countries not covered by the Civil Jurisdiction and Judgments Acts 1982 and 1991), leave of the court is needed to issue them: Chapter 3, section 3.6. Service outside these territories also requires leave: O.11. There are more than a dozen cases in which leave may be granted, and the common theme of all is that either the cause of action, the defendant, or the subject-matter of the action, have some connection with the jurisdiction. They are listed in O.11 rr1 and 2 and include actions founded upon a tort committed within the jurisdiction, actions concerning land situate within it, or against a defendant who is ordinarily resident within it though abroad at the time proceedings are desired to be served.

The grant of leave is discretionary. Not only must the plaintiff show that the case falls within one of the classes in O.11 rr1 or 2, but also that the case is a proper one where leave should be given. If the court considers that England would not be the convenient forum for trial, leave will usually be refused. A recent example of this is *Trade Indemnity plc and Others* v *Forsakringsaktiebolaget Njord (in liquidation)* [1995] 1 All ER 796. See Chapter 36, section 36.1 for further details.

Where the defendant resides within Scotland, Northern Ireland, or one of the countries covered by the Civil Jurisdiction and Judgments Acts 1982 and 1991, no leave is required to issue and serve proceedings within one of those territories provided the Writ is endorsed with a statement that the High Court of England and Wales has power under the Civil Jurisdiction and Judgments Act 1982 to hear and determine the claim and that no proceedings are pending between the parties in those territories: *Practice Direction (Writ: Service Abroad)* [1987] 1 All ER 160 and O.11 r1.

5.9 Defective service

Service which does not comply with the rules, or with any court order for substituted service or service abroad, is *prima facie* irregular, and may be objected to by the defendant. The court has power under O.2 r1 to cure the defect in most cases, and to declare the service valid. It is for the plaintiff to show that the power should be exercised, but if the defendant cannot show he has been prejudiced by the irregularity he has little chance of having service set aside: see Chapter 2, section 2.3.

For many years it was thought that the court had no power to declare valid the purported service of a Writ upon a limited company at an address other than its registered office (see section 5.5). It is now clear that such defective service does not render the proceedings null and void, and that the court has its general power to uphold service if the defendant has not been prejudiced: *Singh* v *Atombrook Ltd* [1989] 1 All ER 385 CA.

5.10 Statement of claim

The Writ will usually be indorsed 'specially'. If it is indorsed 'generally', a full statement of the nature of the plaintiff's claim must be served on the defendant within 14 days of notice of intention to defend being given: O.18 r1. If not so served, the defendant may apply to strike out the plaintiff's action: O.19 r1. That application is unlikely to be successful unless the delay has gone very far beyond the 14 day period and the court considers that it amounts to delay risking serious prejudice to the defendant's preparation or presentation of his case: see further Chapter 14. The time may be extended by agreement of the parties or by order of the court, even after it has expired.

5.11 Compelling the service of proceedings

O.12 r8A provides that a defendant who knows that a Writ had been issued against him and fears prejudice from the threat of proceedings and of financial liability has to decide whether to force the plaintiff's hand by delivering to him a notice requiring that the Writ be served or the action discontinued within not less than 14 days following receipt of that notice, failing which service or discontinuance the defendant may apply to the court to have the Writ struck out. This procedure was only rarely used when the expiry period for all Writs was one year and it may become even rarer with the new, shorter periods.

6

Defending the Action

6.1 Introduction

6.2 Acknowledgement of Service

6.3 The defence

6.4 Judgment in default against particular defendants

6.5 The importance of time limits

6.6 Counterclaim and set-off

6.7 Disputes as to service or jurisdiction

6.8 Security for costs

6.9 Security on appeal

6.1 Introduction

A defendant who has been served with proceedings must decide whether to admit the plaintiff's claim in full or in part. If he fails to informs the court of his intention to defend, he may have judgment given against him; if, having given notice of his intention to defend, he does not serve his full defence, judgment may likewise be entered against him. He may wish to dispute the validity of service of the proceedings, or argue that England is not the proper forum for trial. He may want to set up his own claim against the plaintiff in answer to the plaintiff's claim or to bring his own claim against the plaintiff before the court without having to begin separate proceedings. He may want the plaintiff to provide some security for costs before pursuing the action further. Or he may consider the claim against him is so ill-founded that it must fail.

6.2 Acknowledgement of Service

With every Writ must be served an Acknowledgement of Service in the prescribed form: O.12 r1 and Appendix A of the White Book. The form contains boxes in which the defendant can either admit the claim or give 'notice of intention to defend' it. If he admits it, he is given the opportunity in the form to state whether he will apply for a stay of execution, to prevent judgment being levied against his property without court order. He must send the form to the court office out of which the Writ was issued within 14 days of the Writ being served upon him; where the Writ is served out of the jurisdiction, extra time is allowed depending on the place of service. The form must arrive at the court office within 14 days, and may be sent by post.

If the defendant fails to return the form of acknowledgement within the time allowed, or returns it not having stated in it that he intends to contest the plaintiff's claim, the plaintiff is entitled to enter judgment against him *in default*, if the claim falls within one of the four cases set out in O.13.

1. A claim for debt or liquidated damages, for example, the price of goods sold and delivered, or monies due under a loan or guarantee or a liquidated damages clause in a contract. The plaintiff proves that the Writ was served by producing either a sworn statement by the person who served it (an affidavit of service) or by a sworn statement that it was served by post and has not been returned to him by the Post Office, or by producing the Acknowledgement of Service on which no intention to defend the claim appears. The court checks the documents produced against its own copies of the Writ and (if any) the Acknowledgement, and enters judgment for the plaintiff, giving him a form of judgment which he uses in enforcing the judgment: O.13 r1.
2. A claim for the recovery of land. The plaintiff must show that the premises fall outside the Rent Acts (this should appear on the face of the Writ itself). Service is proved in one of the ways described in (1) above, but the affidavit must, if made personally by the plaintiff, contain in addition a statement that the plaintiff is not claiming as a mortgagee of the premises. Judgment will be entered in the same way, for possession, arrears of rent, and for 'mesne profits', that is, payment for use and occupation of the premises between the date that judgment is entered and the date possession is taken. The mesne profits will be assessed later, usually by the Master, and form part of the judgment debt: O.13 r4.
3. A claim for unliquidated damages, for example, for personal injuries, or breach of contract. Judgment in this case is given on proof of service as in (1), but is an *interlocutory* judgment. The defendant is adjudged liable to the plaintiff, but the amount of the damages will be assessed later, by the Master, at a hearing at which the defendant may appear: O.37. The judgment therefore gives no right to the plaintiff to levy execution against the defendant's property; it is a judgment as to liability only: O.13 r2.
4. A claim for unlawful retention of goods based upon the tort of conversion, or upon the tort of trespass to goods, or upon unlawful detention of goods contrary to the Torts (Interference with Goods) Act 1977. The plaintiff has the option of entering judgment either for interlocutory judgment for delivery of the goods to

him or their value to be assessed, or for interlocutory judgment for their value to be assessed: O.13 r3.

If the claim does not fall within one of the above classes, it is not possible to enter judgment in default of notice of intention to defend. Instead, the plaintiff must apply by Summons to the Master for judgment: O.19 r7. This is because claims other than money alone normally concern the defendant being ordered to carry out or to desist from some action, and the court screens carefully any such order before making it. Thus, a claim for a mandatory or interlocutory injunction, or for specific performance, or for a declaration, can only be allowed in default on order of the court after hearing evidence or reading affidavits proving the facts giving rise to the claim.

Where judgment is entered in default of Acknowledgement of Service, it may be because the defendant never received the Writ or other originating process; perhaps because it was sent to the wrong address, or because he was abroad either on holiday or at work, or because the process was lost in the post. If the plaintiff knew when effecting service that the process would not be received by the defendant, then any judgment obtained in default will be set aside as a matter of course. The defendant takes out a Summons in action to the Master, and swears an affidavit stating that he had no notice of the proceedings, and requesting that judgment be set aside. This is not an 'appeal' against judgment, for there has been no hearing of the claim on its merits with evidence and argument, and the court has wide powers: O.13 r9. If the plaintiff did not know of the non-receipt of the process, the Master will still in most cases exercise his discretionary power to set judgment aside, though he may order the costs to be borne by plaintiff or defendant, or make no order as to costs.

Where judgment in default is entered after the Acknowledgement has been returned to the court office but states no intention to defend the claim, the Master has the same power to set the judgment aside, and the procedure for application is the same. But the Master will need to have explained to him why a defendant who admittedly received the process and complied with the obligation to return the Acknowledgement did not choose to defend the claim when he had the opportunity. The standard of proof on a defendant is not very high, and reasons such as mistaken view of the facts or the law, or inability to take legal advice, or that there is in fact a defence to the claim, often succeed. The Master does no injustice to the plaintiff by ordering the judgment set aside, for if the plaintiff has a good claim he will succeed at trial. The most important factor is whether the defendant has disclosed a meritorious defence, for which an affidavit should be produced. In a case where setting aside is ordered on these grounds, it is usual for the Master to order that the defendant pay the plaintiff's costs of entering judgment in default and of attending and arguing on the hearing of the application to set aside. On the principles applicable to setting aside judgments, see generally *Evans* v *Bartlam* [1937] AC 473.

The application to set aside judgment in default will most often be made by the defendant in the action, but the court has power to set it aside on application by any person. Third parties will usually only apply where they are themselves affected by the outcome of proceedings. For instance, a landlord has obtained judgment in default against a tenant; if possession is given of the head lease, all sub-leases carved out of it will come to an end. In those circumstances, a sub-tenant may apply, to protect his interest under the sub-lease. Or an insurance company bound to satisfy any judgment given against their insured driver in an action for personal injuries may apply to set aside a judgment in default against the driver, and may even conduct defence of the claim themselves in some cases. There is in addition a power in the court to set aside a judgment in default of its own motion, without application by a party or third party; it is rarely used.

The procedure in the County Court for admitting, defending and/or counterclaiming is dealt with in Chapter 21, section 21.5. There is similar provision for judgment in default which is contained in CCR O.9 r6. The plaintiff can file a request for judgment in a default action if the defendant:

1. fails to deliver a defence or counterclaim or an admission of part of the claim within 14 days of service of the summons; or
2. delivers an admission for the whole of the claim unaccompanied by a counterclaim or a request for time for payment.

In a fixed date action, judgment in default is available (with leave) only in those actions to which automatic directions apply (under CCR O.17 r11).

The procedure for setting aside default judgment is contained in CCR O.37 r4, the same principles applying as in the High Court.

6.3 The defence

Within 14 days of returning the Acknowledgement of Service to the court office indorsed with a statement that he intends to contest the plaintiff's claim, the defendant must usually serve on the plaintiff a formal defence to the claim. The form and content of the defence are considered in detail in Chapter 9; in this chapter the time for service, the claims it may raise, and the effect of failing to serve it in time, will be discussed. It is important to realise that the 14 day period may run not from the date of acknowledging service, but from the date of service by the plaintiff of the particulars of his case in the Statement of Claim. Where the Writ is indorsed specially with a Statement of Claim, time runs from the date of service of the Acknowledgement of Service; when indorsed generally, time runs from the date of service on the defendant of the Statement of Claim: see Chapter 3, section 3.2 and Chapter 5, section 5.10. In the normal case the Writ will be specially indorsed, so that the defendant has 14 days in which to return the Acknowledgement, and a further 14 days in which to serve his defence.

The defence must be served on the plaintiff within the time specified: O.18 r2. If it is not so served, the plaintiff may enter judgment in default of defence in the same way and in the same classes of case prescribed where there is a failure to give notice of intention to defend: see section 6.2; O.19 rr2–7. There is a very similar power to set aside a judgment obtained in default of defence, and the procedure is the same. Where a defendant has however acknowledged service, given notice of intention to defend, and has let the time for service of his defence expire without seeking the agreement of the plaintiff to an extension of time, or applying to the court for an extension, then the Master may take a little more persuading that he has a defence, and that there is good reason for his not having disclosed it when he should, and if judgment is set aside, the defendant must expect to have to pay the plaintiff's costs of entering it and of attending to argue against the application.

6.4 Judgment in default against particular defendants

In the following principal cases, a plaintiff cannot enter judgment in default against a defendant, or the judgment is subject to special restrictions:

1. Where the defendant is a minor or mental patient; no judgment in default of notice of intention to defend. The plaintiff should apply to the court for the appointment of a guardian *ad litem*: O.80 r6 (CCR O.10 r6) and see Chapter 4, section 4.3.
2. Where the defendant is the Crown, the plaintiff must apply to the Master who has a discretionary power to allow judgment to be entered; and see Chapter 4, section 4.9.
3. Where the defendant is deceased, the action is against him or his estate, and no personal representatives have been appointed. The plaintiff should apply to the court for the appointment of an administrator *ad litem*: see Chapter 4, section 4.7.
4. Where the nature of the claim does not fall within one of the classes in which default judgment is allowed: see section 6.2.

6.5 The importance of time limits

Throughout the RSC and the CCR time limits are laid down for the doing of certain acts; the service of proceedings, the service of Statements of Claim, Defences and other pleadings, the discovery of documents and their inspection, the issue of the Summons for Directions and the exchange of expert evidence, the enforcement of judgments and other matters. These will be found in their proper place in the text, but it will be helpful to discuss the importance of complying with them. In general, a failure to comply will not be fatal to the claim or to the defence.

The court has power to extend the time stated in the Rules for the doing of any act, whether the time for doing the act has expired or not, on the application of the party who bears the obligation of compliance; the hearing is before the Master: O.3 r5(1) and (2) (CCR O.13 r5). Unless a party has been guilty of inordinate delay such as to prejudice a fair trial of the action, or has delayed on purpose for some tactical reason, extension is usually granted, though the party applying for it will generally have to pay the other side's costs of the application if it was reasonable to resist it.

The parties may agree between themselves that one should have additional time to serve documents or to file pleadings or to do any other act. This agreement will be enforced by the court, and any application to strike out the claim or defence while the agreed extension is running will be dismissed with costs. In practice, it is usual for agreement to be given; in many personal injury cases a delay of a year or so between service of the Writ and service of the Statement of Claim is not unusual, for negotiations may be continuing for a settlement and the extra cost of drafting pleadings unjustified. Where the claim is for professional negligence in designing a building, for instance, the 14 days period for service of the defence is unreal, for the defendant may first want his expert's comments upon the Statement of Claim before sending the papers to counsel. In the latter example, the court would grant an extension of time almost as a matter of course, so that there is little point in the plaintiff refusing his consent to an extension of time; indeed, if he did so in such a case, the Master may well order him to pay the costs of the defendant's application to the court for extension, for his refusal was unreasonable. Agreements have effect by virtue of O.3 r5(3) (CCR O.13 r5).

It must be remembered that the power to extend time vested in the court cannot be used to alter the substantive law of limitation of some actions, but is confined to time limits prescribed by the rules themselves. The powers to extend the limitation period in personal injury cases have their origin in the Limitation Act, and not the RSC or CCR. See further Chapter 14.

6.6 Counterclaim and set-off

A defendant who is served with proceedings may himself have a claim against the plaintiff. It may be connected with the subject-matter of the plaintiff's claim, as where a plaintiff sues for the price of goods and the defendant wishes to allege that they were faulty. Or it may be totally independent of the plaintiff's claim, as where the plaintiff sues for possession of the defendant's factory premises as landlord, and the defendant has a cause of action against him in respect of a debt. In general, the defendant can raise against the plaintiff in the plaintiff's action any claim which he could bring by starting his own proceedings. Such a claim is termed a *counterclaim*, and procedure for making it is governed by O.15 rr2 and 3 (CCR O.9 and see Chapter 21, section 21.5). The type of claim where the defendant alleges that goods or work done for which the plaintiff claims the price are defective is termed a *set-off*, and is not a truly independent cause of action which the defendant could bring without first being sued by the plaintiff, but it is deemed by the rules to be a counterclaim and may be made in the same circumstances.

Counterclaim and set-off   43

The counterclaim should be made in the defence; this then becomes a 'defence and counterclaim' within the rules of pleading: see Chapter 9. If the claim and counterclaim are of a very different nature and cannot be conveniently tried together, the court may order that the counterclaim be tried separately, and will often do so. The counterclaim may be for an entirely different remedy than claimed by the plaintiff; he may claim damages on the claim, the defendant may seek an injunction on the counterclaim. The rules aim to reduce multiplicity of actions, but not to produce confused trials, so that separate trials on these facts may well be ordered.

The right to counterclaim is subject to the following principal restrictions:

1. It can only be used in an action commenced by Writ.
2. It cannot be used to defend an action brought by the Crown for the recovery of taxes, duties or penalties, or if the counterclaim is against a department of the Crown other than the one bringing the action, or if the Crown sues in the name of the Attorney-General: O.77 r6. In the later two cases, the court may, on application by the defendant, give leave for the counterclaim to be made.
3. Where the counterclaim is a set-off, and may exceed the value of the claim, the excess should be made by counterclaim proper.

In very many respects a counterclaim creates a separate action in which the counterclaiming defendant is 'plaintiff' and the plaintiff against whom the counterclaim is made is 'defendant'. Thus the 'plaintiff' may obtain judgment in default of defence (see sections 6.3 and 6.4), and summary judgment (see Chapter 7), and interim injunctions, payments and other orders. If the plaintiff's claim is settled or discontinued, the counterclaim may survive, particularly if it is not a set-off, and have its own trial and judgment. The question of costs where a counterclaim is made are dealt with in Chapter 17.

The defendant may have a counterclaim against the plaintiff and jointly against some other person. For example, the plaintiff may sue for recovery of a debt, the defendant may have a claim against the plaintiff and against another person for injuries caused to him by the negligence of both. To determine all liabilities in the same proceedings, the defendant is allowed to counterclaim against the plaintiff and to join as a defendant to the counterclaim the other person liable to him. That other person then becomes a party to the action, but only for the purpose of defending the counterclaim. He takes no part in and will not be liable for the costs of the plaintiff's claim against the defendant: O.15 r3. Separate trials may well be ordered.

Where a counterclaim of the type described in the previous paragraph is made, the heading of the action is amended to clarify the position of all the parties (see below):

BETWEEN   A.B.   *Plaintiff*
— and —
C.D.   *Defendant*
(by original action)

AND BETWEEN	C.D.	*Plaintiff*
	and	
	A.B.	*First Defendant*
	and	
	E.F.	*Second Defendant*

(by counterclaim)

6.7 Disputes as to service or jurisdiction

A defendant served with proceedings may consider that the process has been invalidly served upon him, that the rules have not been complied with (see Chapter 5), or that he is entitled to some form of State or diplomatic immunity. He should acknowledge service giving notice of intention to defend (acknowledgement does not amount to an admission that the process was validly served, or that the court has jurisdiction): O.12 r8. Within 14 days of acknowledging service he should take out a Summons before the Master and take his objection and apply to have the whole proceedings set aside or merely the allegedly defective service. The Master may try the objection as to jurisdiction as a *preliminary issue*, for if the defendant succeeds in it there is no point in continuing the action through the many interlocutory stages to a full trial on all issues. A defendant who fails to take out his application within the 14 days takes the risk of being estopped from taking objection later. If, however, the application does not succeed, the defendant may in certain circumstances lodge a further acknowledgement of service within 14 days (or such other period as the court may direct) and in that case paragraph (7) (acceptance of jurisdiction) shall apply as if the defendant had not made the application.

6.8 Security for costs

A defendant does not choose to be sued. He may fear that, if he succeeds in the action, and even though the court makes an order that the plaintiff pay his costs of defending it, the plaintiff will either be unable to pay or will so transfer or conceal his assets that the order for costs is worthless. In certain circumstances he can obtain an order that the plaintiff provide some security for the defendant's costs (usually by depositing with the court a specified sum of money) before proceeding further with the claim. The application for security can be made at any stage after the Writ has been served but is most often made very early in the proceedings.

In general the court has no power to order a plaintiff to give security for a defendant's costs, but in the following cases power exists by virtue of O.23 r1:

1. Where the plaintiff is ordinarily resident outside the jurisdiction that is, he usually lives abroad. The fact that the plaintiff resides within a member State of

the European Economic Community, so that an order to costs against him could be enforced under the Brussels Convention, is a relevant factor, but it is not conclusive against the making of an order for security: *Porzelack KG v Porzelack (UK) Ltd* [1987] 1 All ER 1074 Ch D. Similarly, where some of several plaintiffs reside out of England and Wales, the court is not bound to refuse security for costs merely because other, solvent plaintiffs have their residence within the jurisdiction: *Slazengers Ltd v Seaspeed Ferries* [1987] 3 All ER 967. A plaintiff corporation is 'ordinarily resident' out of the jurisdiction for the purposes of RSC O.23, r1(1)(a), if the central control and management of the company actually abides and is exercised overseas: *Re Little Olympian Each Ways Ltd* [1994] 4 All ER 561.

2. Where the plaintiff is a 'nominal plaintiff' *and* there is reason to believe that he would be unable to meet an order to pay the defendant's costs. A party suing in a representative capacity (see Chapter 4, section 4.12) is not a nominal plaintiff (O.23 r1) nor is the trustee of a bankrupt (*Ramsey v Hartley* [1977] 1 WLR 686); nor the next friend of a person under a disability: *Fellows v Barrett* (1830) 1 Keen 119, and see Chapter 4, section 4.3. The most common example of a nominal plaintiff is one who has assigned to a third party, before commencing proceedings, any damages he may recover.
3. Where the plaintiff's address is not stated or is wrongly stated in the Writ, unless the plaintiff can show that the omission or mistake was innocent.
4. Where the plaintiff has changed his address since service so as to evade the consequences of litigation, for example, where the defendant raises against him a counterclaim greatly exceeding the value of the claim, or the plaintiff has realised that he will lose the action and does not want to pay the costs of it.

In the County Court, only the first of these four grounds is available, under CCR O.13 r8.

In addition, security may be ordered against a plaintiff limited company where there is reason to believe that it will be unable to pay the defendant's costs if it loses: s726 Companies Act 1985. If a company is in liquidation other than a members' voluntary winding-up (in which case the company has been warranted by its shareholders or directors to be solvent) the court will generally presume that it is unable to pay the costs and will require no further evidence of insolvency. It should be noted that the court is not justified in disregarding *unchallenged* evidence by an accountant as to the current ability of the plaintiff company to pay the costs of the action if they are awarded against it: *Kim Barker Ltd v Aegon Insurance Co (UK) Ltd* (1989) The Times 9 October.

There are, apart from the cases stated above, no other circumstances in which a plaintiff can be required to give security except for an appeal, to the Court of Appeal or House of Lords, made by him. However, it should be noted that a defendant who counterclaims other than by pleading a set-off is treated as the plaintiff in the counterclaim, so that an order for security may be made against him in the same cases as against a true plaintiff: see section 6.6.

Even where the defendant can show one of the grounds stated above, no security will be ordered unless the court thinks it appropriate; the Master has a real discretion, but should pay particular regard to the strength of the plaintiff's case, whether the defendant has admitted liability or has made a payment into court (see Chapter 15) or an offer of settlement, and whether the application for security is being used as a means of putting pressure on the plaintiff to discontinue a bona fide claim; and if the basis of the application is (2) above, or s726 Companies Act, and if the plaintiff's feared inability to pay the costs has resulted from the defendant's own acts in, for example, failing to pay the price of goods sold to him, or withholding repayment of a debt, security should not be ordered, for it will prevent the bringing of a just claim: *Sir Lindsay Parkinson* v *Triplan* [1973] QB 609.

The application is made by Summons, but should be preceded by a written request by the defendant to the plaintiff for security. The order may, it seems, be made against one or more plaintiffs rather than against all, even if there is no power to order it against the others: *Pearson* v *Naydler* [1977] 1 WLR 899. An order for security should not be made against a legally-aided plaintiff unless he is ordinarily resident outside the jurisdiction. Where an application is made (whether or not against a legally-aided plaintiff) on ground (1) above, and the plaintiff shows that he has substantial property within the jurisdiction, no order for security will be made unless the defendant can show a real risk that the property will be disposed of or transferred out of the jurisdiction before conclusion of the case (cf Mareva injunctions, Chapter 12).

The court can order security in such amount and in such manner as it thinks fit, but the order is often for two-thirds of the defendant's estimated costs on the 'Standard' basis effective from 28 April 1986 (see Chapter 17, section 17.9). On application the defendant should therefore attach to the affidavit in support of the Summons a draft bill of costs compiled by his solicitors. Security is normally ordered to be in the form of cash paid into the court funds, but less frequently is taken by bond. Further applications for increased security, or for the discharge of an order already made, can be made as the case proceeds. The so-called 'two-thirds rule' is not absolute, and full costs can be ordered: *Procon (GB) Ltd* v *Provincial Building Co Ltd* [1974] 1 WLR 557.

If an order for security is made and the plaintiff fails to comply with it, his action will be stayed, that is, not allowed to proceed further, until he complies. Eventually, if security is not forthcoming, the whole claim may be dismisssed.

6.9 Security on appeal

Where a party appeals to the Court of Appeal, he may be ordered to give security for the respondent's costs of the appeal, whether he was originally plaintiff or defendant, and the cases given in O.23 r1 do not operate to restrict the circumstances in which it may be ordered. Similar rules apply in appeals to the House of Lords.

7

Summary Judgment

7.1   Introduction

7.2   Practice where the action is on a cheque

7.3   Practice in other cases

7.4   Personal injury cases

7.5   Powers of the Master

7.6   Judgment for the plaintiff

7.7   Unconditional leave to defend

7.8   Conditional leave to defend

7.9   Dismissal of summons

7.10 Directions

7.11 Costs

7.12 Appeals

7.13 'There ought for some other reason to be a trial'

7.14 Determination of questions of law or construction: RSC O.14A

7.15 General principles of summary judgment

7.16 Other matters

7.1 Introduction

Every defendant is entitled to give notice of intention to defend and to deny the plaintiff's claim, even if his defence is hopeless. If he does not give notice of his intention to defend, the plaintiff has his remedies under O.13 (CCR O.9 r6): see Chapter 6, section 6.2. In very many cases a defendant will give such notice even though he has no real defence. In commercial cases especially, defendants wish to hold on to money for as long as possible, to delay the day of payment, or simply to try to persuade the plaintiff to give up and to write off the claim against tax. It would be unfair in these and other circumstances if the plaintiff were compelled to wait until a full trial, perhaps several years after the service of proceedings, to obtain the relief he should have been granted at the outset. Although the court's power to grant interlocutory relief in the form of injunction and interim payment go some way towards reducing hardship to plaintiffs with good claims, they are not as valuable as a speedy, final judgment on all issues: see Chapter 13.

To remove the injustice, there is a procedure whereby the plaintiff (or a defendant who is counterclaiming) can obtain summary (that is, quick) judgment on liability and, if the action is for a liquidated amount (or *quantum meruit*), *quantum*. The rules are contained in O.14 and O.86, the latter dealing with summary judgment for specific performance. The procedure is *only* available in an action begun by Writ, and *cannot* be used where proceedings are by Originating Summons, Originating Motion or Petition, or in any of the following cases:

1. Actions for libel, slander, malicious prosecution or false imprisonment: the defendant is entitled to trial by jury.
2. Admiralty actions *in rem*, that is, against ships.

The equivalent procedure in the County Court is contained in CCR O.9 r14: r14(5) states that the provisions of the RSC shall apply to (most) applications for a summary judgment.

7.2 Practice where the action is on a cheque

Summary judgment will only be given when there is no 'triable defence' to the claim. In the great majority of cases this will depend upon the arguments presented before the Master who hears the application, but in one special case a plaintiff is entitled to it almost as of right; when he sues on a cheque given him by the defendant in payment or satisfaction of any debt or demand. In this case, there are very few arguments a defendant can put forward which the Master will consider disclose a valid triable defence. This is because a cheque is regarded as being as good as cash, and to allow a defendant to escape liability to pay upon it would undermine the confidence in the cheque system as a means of 'cash' payment: *Hyland* v *Lamont* [1950] 1 KB 585. Similar rules apply to other promissory notes and bills of exchange, and to letters of credit: *Power Curber* v *Bank of Kuwait* [1981] 1 WLR 1233 and *Bolvinter Oil* v *Chase Manhattan* [1984] 1 All ER 351.

In an action brought upon a bill of exchange such as a cheque, the only cases where the defendant may successfully resist an application for summary judgment appear to be these:

1. where he alleges that it was obtained from him by fraud;

2. where he alleges there has been a total failure of the consideration for which the bill was given; per Lord Denning MR in *Fielding & Platt v Selim Najjar* [1969] 1 WLR 357;
3. where there has been an ascertainable failure of consideration almost but not quite totally; per Lord Wilberforce in *Nova (Jersey) Knit v Kammgarn Spinnerei* [1977] 2 All ER 463;
4. where a misrepresentation is alleged to have induced giving of the bill. In this case it is far from clear whether the misrepresentation must be at least negligent or whether an innocent misrepresentation will suffice: *Clovertogs v Jean Scenes* [1982] Com LR 88.

The defendant in the above cases does not have to prove the fraud, failure of consideration or misrepresentation. He need only persuade the Master that he has some substance to his case, and that it is not an attempt merely to forestall judgment. Even where the Master gives summary judgment on a bill, it is important to remember that the judgment does not prevent the defendant from making a counterclaim or from starting his own separate proceedings against the plaintiff for alleged breaches of contract as to the quality of goods and the like; but he cannot avoid summary judgment merely by setting up that claim as a counterclaim in the plaintiff's action on the bill – the Master would give summary judgment on the bill and give further directions as to the counterclaim.

7.3 Practice in other cases

The plaintiff first serves his Statement of Claim, then takes out a Summons for summary judgment after the defendant has given notice of intention to defend the claim, but usually before the defence is served. If the plaintiff delays issuing his summons under O.14 until after the defence has been served upon him, the court may none the less award him summary judgment, but will take into account his delay as evidence that he perhaps believed there to be a triable issue between the parties: *House of Troy v OMC Group* (1987) The Independent 2 February CA. If the time for service of a defence has expired, the plaintiff could in most cases enter judgment in default of defence (see Chapter 6, section 6.3), but he is better advised to apply for summary judgment, because judgment in default is not a judgment on the merits and can be set aside by the court on such terms as it thinks just (see Chapter 6, section 6.2), whereas summary judgment is a judgment on the merits, usually after evidence and argument, and can only be overturned by an appeal to a High Court judge (see section 7.12). The Summons must be supported by an affidavit sworn by the plaintiff and verifying the facts upon which his claim is based and declaring that in the plaintiff's opinion there is no defence to the claim. Once that is done, the Summons and affidavit must be served on the defendant at least 10 'clear' days (that is, excluding the day of service and the day of hearing) before the 'return day' fixed for hearing: O.14 r2.

The affidavit in effect puts on to the defendant the onus of showing that 'there is a question or issue in dispute which ought to be tried or that there ought for some other reason to be a trial': O.14 r3. The defendant may swear his own affidavit in reply to the plaintiff's and should (though often does not) serve it on the plaintiff at least three days before the return day. Less frequently, the defendant will appear at the hearing before the Master and give evidence orally in rebuttal of the claim. He must show he has an 'arguable defence', one which if true would be a good defence, but the burden upon him is not very great. He must go further than merely denying liability, but need not set out every fact and element of the defence. General principles of what he has to show cannot be given, for all will depend upon the facts of a particular case and the credibility of the affidavits and the strength of counsel's argument. The summary judgment process is however designed only to suppress those defences which have not the slightest prospect of success. Even though the court might be almost convinced that a given defence will fail, leave to defend must be given: *Midland Bank* v *Phillips* (1986) The Times 28 March.

7.4 Personal injury claims

Summary judgment is not forbidden by the rules in personal injury claims, but as a matter of practice is never given where the defendant raises a defence of contributory negligence, as he will do in almost every case. This does not cause very much hardship to the plaintiff, for if he has a good case the court will be likely to award some money on account of damages by way of interim payment: see Chapter 13.

One exception is *Dummer* v *Brown* [1953] 1 QB 710 CA, where summary judgment was given against a driver who had previously pleaded guilty to dangerous driving in respect of the same incident.

7.5 Powers of the Master

The Master has very wide powers on the hearing of a Summons for summary judgment. Apart from giving judgment for the plaintiff or dismissing the application, he may give leave to the defendant to continue his defence, either without restriction (unconditional leave) or upon terms (conditional leave). He may give directions as to the future conduct of the action, as if the Summons were a Summons for Directions issued under O.25, (see Chapter 16, section 16.2) and will deal with the costs of the Summons and hearing.

7.6 Judgment for the plaintiff

This is quite rare, and is given only where the Master is satisfied that there is no 'triable issue' in the case. Where, in an action for damages, the liability of the defendant is clearly established, whether by admissions or by submissions, the court should give judgment for the plaintiff, with costs for damages and interest thereon to be assessed: *O'Connor* v *Amos Bridgman Abbatoirs Ltd* (1990) The Times 13 April. Where the claim is for a debt or liquidated damages, the judgment may be both as to liability and as to the amount adjudged payable, together with interest if claimed. If for unliquidated damages, the judgment is *final* as to liability, but *interlocutory* as to damages, which will be assessed at a later hearing under O.37. Judgment may be for a part of the claim only, or for one of several claims made in the action. The power to give judgment is contained in O.14 r3.

7.7 Unconditional leave to defend

This is the most common order, made under O.14 r4. It *must* be given where a 'triable issue' is raised by the defendant, but may be for a part of the claim only, or in respect of one or more claims in the action. The defendant is allowed to continue his defence as if the hearing for summary judgment had not taken place, and is put under no restrictions in making it other than those that apply to defendants generally; the action proceeds in the normal way.

7.8 Conditional leave to defend

Made under O.14 r4, this is the least common of orders. It is made only when the Master is virtually certain that the defendant has no defence, but is not absolutely certain. For example, a defendant who files an affidavit in reply to the plaintiff's own may fill it with much 'evidence' which the Master finds incredible, but there may be one part of it which does disclose a triable issue. Such a defendant can expect little sympathy from the court, but if there is a triable issue leave should be given. The Master may however properly make it conditional upon the defendant paying into the court fund the total amount claimed by the plaintiff: *Paclantic* v *Moscow Narodny Bank* [1983] 1 WLR 1063. The most common conditions imposed are that the defendant pay into court or give some security for the plaintiff's claim. In assessing the amount payable, the court must consider the means of the defendant, and should not order more than he is reasonably able to pay: *Yorke Motors* v *Edwards* [1982] 1 WLR 444. But regard must be had to the defendant's ability to raise security from friends and others, so that his poverty will not be conclusive against the making of the order.

7.9 Dismissal of summons

Under O.14 r7, the summons can be dismissed if (a) it is not within the scope of O.14, or (b) the plaintiff knew that the defendant would be entitled to unconditional leave to defend. Note that if the summons is dismissed rather than the defendant given unconditional leave to defend:

1. no directions are given (see section 7.10);
2. appeal is without leave if the order is made by a judge;
3. the plaintiff will generally pay costs (see section 7.11).

7.10 Directions

Under O.14 r6, the Master should treat the application for summary judgment as a Summons for Directions, and make orders for, *inter alia*, the place and mode of trial, its estimated length, the time for service of the defence and for the discovery of documents and their inspection, for exchange of expert evidence and the number of expert witnesses: see Chapter 16, section 16.2.

7.11 Costs

Where the application succeeds, the whole costs of the action will normally be awarded to the plaintiff. If unconditional leave to defend is given, the normal order is that whoever wins at trial shall have the costs of the application ('costs in cause'). If giving conditional leave, he will probably make an order that the plaintiff have the costs of the application if he wins at trial, but need not pay the defendant's costs of it if he loses ('plaintiff's costs in cause'). If he dismisses the summons either because the application was brought in a case where the rules forbid it, or where the plaintiff knew on issuing it that the defendant had an arguable defence, the Court of Appeal has urged Masters to order that the plaintiff pay the defendant's costs of the hearing for summary judgment: *Pocock* v *ADC* [1952] 1 TLR 29. The Master may also reserve costs, or make some other order, within his general discretion: see Chapter 17.

7.12 Appeals

Either side may appeal to a judge in chambers against the Master's order on hearing for summary judgment and whether the Summons has been dismissed, judgment given for the plaintiff, or conditional or unconditional leave to defend to the defendant. From the judge an appeal lies to the Court of Appeal in all cases, but where a plaintiff is appealing against an order giving unconditional leave to defend based upon a judge's view of the facts (but not the law), the Court of Appeal will be very reluctant to reverse the judge's order, for it is he who has the real power to judge issues of fact: *Lloyds Bank* v *Ellis* [1983] 1 WLR 569. Where leave was given on the basis of an interpretation of the law, the Court of Appeal is in as good a position as the judge to assess what the law is. The same principle applies where the appeal is brought against a grant of summary judgment or of conditional leave to defend, and the appellate court will form its own view of the law afresh: *Pumfrey Construction* v *Childs* (1985) The Times 12 July.

When appealing against a judge's order, a party may often want to rely upon fresh evidence either that the defence is groundless or that there is a real defence. The rules on admissibility of such evidence are much the same as those that apply to appeal following full hearing at a normal trial; if the evidence was available at the time of the hearing before the judge, but was not used, it cannot be heard by the appeal court unless there is a (very) good explanation for its not being used and it is material and credible: *Langdale* v *Danby* [1982] 1 WLR 1123. The moral of this story must be: use all available evidence at the hearing before the judge, even if as a matter of tactics counsel would prefer to leave some of it aside.

7.13 'There ought for some other reason to be a trial'

In the vast majority of cases the defendant will be able to identify to the Master the general nature of the defence and the broad facts upon which he will rely; this will be to establish a 'triable issue'. Sometimes, however, a defendant will only be able to argue that there is something unusual about the plaintiff's claim which can only be properly investigated on discovery of the documents the plaintiff possesses, or upon interrogating him. Such procedures occur only after a hearng for summary judgment, so that if judgment is given for the plaintiff injustice may be done to the defendant. In such circumstances the court may find that there is some other reason why there ought to be a trial, at least to allow the defendant to defend the action as far as the stage of discovery. For example, where the plaintiff sues for possession of land, and the defendant believes but has as yet no evidence that the claim has been brought and sued after a conspiracy to deprive him of the land: *Miles* v *Bull* [1969] 1 QB 258. Or where the defendant has been unable, before the hearing, to contact a material witness, or to investigate a complicated claim, or if the court thinks that a plaintiff's conduct in bringing the action has been such that a full trial in public is desirable: *Bank fur GA* v *City of London Garages* [1971] 1 WLR 149. In such cases the plaintiff should be put to strict proof of all the aspects of his claim at a full hearing on all available oral and documentary evidence.

An example of where there should usually be a trial is where the issue is one of nervous shock; the law is still evolving and each case should be tried on its own facts: *Rapley* v *P & O European Ferries (Dover) Ltd* (1991) 21 February Court of Appeal transcript 91/0132.

7.14 Determination of questions of law or construction: RSC O.14A

Where the only issue to be determined is one of law or the construction of documents, there is no dispute as to the facts and determination of this issue will determine the whole case. An application may be made by summons, motion, or orally during any interlocutory application to the court. The court may, upon determination of the question, discuss the cause or matter or make such order or judgment as it thinks just.

O.14A r1(3):

'The court shall not determine any question under this Order unless the parties have either –
a) had an opportunity of being heard on the question, or
b) consented to an order or judgment on such determination.'

r1(4):

'The jurisdiction of the Court under this Order may be exercised by a Master.'

The Order is expressed in the widest terms, so that it should operate as an extremely valuable addition to the several modes of obtaining summary adjudication. The underlying policy of this Order is to accelerate the final judicial disposal of an action at the interlocutory stage.

There is no analogous provision in the CCR.

7.15 General principles of summary judgment

The facts of cases vary so much that general guidelines cannot really be given. As an aid, however, some frequently recurring cases will be mentioned where summary judgment will not be available as a matter of practice. Apart from personal injury claims already referred to, summary judgment will not be given where the construction of a contract, deed, will or other document is in issue; or where there is a real dispute as to the facts of a claim; or where the claim involves a difficult point of law. Where the application is in third party proceedings (see Chapter 8), it should not be given if the amount in issue and claimed as indemnity or contribution depends upon evidence which the plaintiff may adduce at the trial of the main action which has not yet taken place: *Heyes* v *Lord Derby* [1989] 1 WLR 777.

7.16 Other matters

Summary judgment is not available against the Crown: s35(2)(c) Crown Proceedings Act 1947 and O.77 r7. If summary judgment is given against a defendant who does not appear at the hearing for it, the judgment may be set aside by the court on such terms as it thinks just: O.14 r11; thus summary judgment in the absence of the defendant is like judgment in default (see Chapter 6, section 6.2). But a defendant who intentionally fails to appear, so as to try to take advantage of this power and so gain further time, cannot expect the court to set the judgment aside. Where the application is for summary judgment for specific performance, it must be made under O.86, which applies to actions begun by Writ in the Chancery Division, and to the less frequent claims of rescission of a contract for the sale of property and the return of money paid over as a deposit on such contracts. Except that judgment for specific performance will not be given at all against a defendant who fails to appear on such an application, the rules of procedure and the powers of the Master are very much the same as those under O.14. summary judgment for the possession of land against squatters is governed by O.113 and dealt with in Chapter 19. Where the claim is for an injunction, which the Master has no power to grant, the Summons must be taken out for hearing by a judge.

Where a defendant has suffered summary judgment, and has satisfied that judgment by paying the entirety of it to the plaintiff, he cannot continue to prosecute any counterclaim raised in that set of proceedings, because the whole action is brought to an end by satisfaction. Instead he must begin fresh proceedings for the cause of action counterclaimed: *CSI* v *Archway* [1980] 2 All ER 215.

Summary judgment may be given on a liquidated claim where there is a small and readily quantifiable unliquidated counterclaim, the court giving judgment for the smallest amount the plaintiff can expect to recover on the assumption that the counterclaim is wholly successful: *Welling Private Hospital* v *Baum* (1988) 10 CL 268.

If one of two or more defendants raises a counterclaim jointly against the plaintiff and against a co-defendant, the provisions of Orders 14 and 16 permit him to apply for summary judgment only against the plaintiff. He cannot obtain summary judgment against the co-defendant if he chooses to proceed by way of counterclaim, since the rules of court relating to summary judgment in third party and contribution proceedings do not apply to his action against the co-defendant: *C E Heath plc* v *Ceram Holding Co* [1989] 1 All ER 203 CA.

An appeal lies from the Master to the Judge in Chambers for both O.14 and O.14A proceedings. An appeal against the decision of the Judge in Chambers in O.14A proceedings will be treated as interlocutory for these purposes. Leave to appeal must be obtained, therefore, from the Court of Appeal.

8
Contribution and Indemnity

8.1 Introduction

8.2 Rights between co-defendants

8.3 Rights where not all potential defendants are joined

8.4 Rights where the plaintiff cannot sue the third party

8.5 Other cases

8.6 Third party proceedings

8.7 Nature of third party proceedings

8.8 Restrictions on third party proceedings

8.9 Joinder of the third party as a defendant

8.1 Introduction

A defendant who is sued may not be the only person liable to the plaintiff in respect of the relief claimed; the plaintiff may have sued others with him, or may have decided not to sue the others even though he could join them as defendants in the action: see Chapter 4, section 4.11. Or the defendant may have rights, against a person whom the plaintiff could not sue directly, to be *indemnified* against the plaintiff's claim or to have that person *contribute* toward any award of damages or other relief awarded by the court. Or the defendant may wish to have that person joined in the action to determine rights related to the subject-matter of the plaintiff's claim and to have the person bound by the court's order. Depending upon whether that other person has been sued as a defendant or is a plaintiff, so that he is already a party to the action, or is not yet involved in it, the procedure will differ.

8.2 Rights between co-defendants

Where a plaintiff sues more than one defendant in the same action, he will probably claim the same relief against each. For example, a pedestrian injured may sue the driver of the car which hit him, and the local authority which was responsible for maintaining the highway; if his injuries arose partly from the negligence of the driver and partly from the failure by the authority to keep the road clear of ice and snow, each will be partly to blame and liable to such proportion as the court adjudges. The court can however order either to pay the *whole* of the damages awarded, and if one pays more than his proper share he will have a right to sue the other for any amount which is really that other's liability; or the defendants may be joint contractors, for example, joint tenants under a lease; if both are sued for breach of the covenants of the lease, the plaintiff can recover the whole of the damages from either, but each will wish to have to pay only an equal share, and recover from his joint contractors any amount he has had to pay over and above his own share.

Where defendants who are sued have these or other rights against their co-defendants, they need not start separate proceedings to claim them. Instead, one defendant can issue against another a *Contribution Notice* under O.16 r8 (CCR O.12), requiring the court to determine, as between the parties to the notice, what their respective liabilities are to the plaintiff. Contribution proceedings brought in this way in effect create an action between co-defendants, to which the plaintiff is not a party. There is however no need to acknowledge service of the notice, and judgment in default is not possible; the court tries the issue of contribution after the trial of the plaintiff's action, though usually before the same judge and at the conclusion of the trial of the plaintiff's claim.

The most common cases of contribution proceedings are these:

1. between joint tortfeasors;
2. between joint contractors;
3. between a debtor and his guarantor;
4. between trustees.

Where the right to contribution arises otherwise than out of a contract between the defendants (where they are liable in tort and have made no arrangement pre-trial to share liability), contribution proceedings are usually begun by *Contribution Letter* rather than notice. This is simply a letter written by one defendant's solicitors to the other, stating that at trial a contribution will be claimed. It is cheaper and simpler than a notice, and does little more than tell the recipient that the sender will ask the court to exercise its power under the Civil Liability (Contribution) Act 1978 to apportion liability between defendants. A defendant who uses a notice when he could have used a letter will find that the costs of preparing and serving the notice will be denied to him if an order for costs is made in his favour in the contribution proceedings. The letter procedure cannot be used where the right to contribution arises out of a contract; there a notice must be served setting out the terms of the contract so that the co-defendant knows what is alleged against him. However, where liability to contribute arises both by contract and otherwise the position is far from clear. When a plaintiff sues in tort against the tortfeasor and against the tortfeasor's employer, the employer is liable vicariously for his employee's wrongdoing, and thus his right to indemnity from the employee arises from tort; but it is also possible to argue that the duty to indemnify the employer arises out of a contract: *Lister* v *Romford Ice* [1957] AC 555. Can the employer make his claim by letter or must he use the more expensive notice? The better view is that a letter is sufficient, for the employee knows the nature of the liability to contribute and need not have it spelt out to him in detail.

Where one defendant serves a notice or letter on the other, it is very common for the other to serve a similar notice or letter in reply, especially where the defendants are joint tortfeasors or joint contractors. Since in the case of most claims for contribution the court has power under the 1978 Act to apportion liability even where no notice has been served and the claim is in tort, the notices are used primarily as a formality and to protect the defendant from allegations that he has taken his co-defendant by surprise in claiming contribution at trial.

Where the main action has come to an end by settlement between plaintiff and defendants, the contribution proceedings begun between defendants survive such settlement, since they create a new 'lis' between those defendants which is unaffected by the settlement: *Harper* v *Gray* [1985] 2 All ER 507.

8.3 Rights where not all potential defendants are joined

In some cases, especially those of personal injury, the plaintiff chooses to sue some only of the persons who might be liable to him. He may be advised that he has a strong case against one, or that another is not worth suing because he has no money or is not insured; or he may not know of the existence or identity of the other. In such cases, it is open to the defendant who is sued to apply to the court to join as co-defendant the persons not sued: O.15 r6 (CCR O.5 r4 and O.15 r1). The court may also, of its own motion, add parties it feels should be joined or would help to resolve the matter.

8.4 Rights where the plaintiff cannot sue the third party

There are very many cases in which, although a plaintiff has no cause of action against a person, he may have a cause of action against one person who in turn has his own cause of action against that person. For instance, a plaintiff cannot sue a defendant's insurers directly, but if the defendant is sued he may have a right by contract with the insurer that the insurer indemnify him against an award of damages made by the court. Or, a plaintiff cannot sue the sub-lessee for a breach of covenant of the lease if the plaintiff is the freeholder; he must sue the head tenant, who in turn may be able to claim indemnity from the sub-lessee for the latter's acts in putting the head tenant in breach of covenant. Or, the plaintiff may be able to sue a contracting party but not the agent who made the contract on the defendant's behalf. If the agent acted ouside the scope of his authority, the defendant may be able to sue him in an independent action to indemnify him against the plaintiff's claim for enforcement of the contract. Or, an employee may sue his employer for providing a dangerous machine which causes him injury. The employer may have a contract with another company who maintain the machine, but whose failure to maintain does not amount to negligence, so that the plaintiff cannot sue them directly. The employer might be able to sue on the contract if it contains a term that the service company will indemnify the employer against awards of damages arising out of the use of the machine, whether or not the employer's liability arises out of the service company's negligence. Or, a plaintiff may sue on a contract for the sale of goods alleging they are defective; he could not sue the manufacturer for the latter gives no warranty to him (cf if the goods cause injury: *Donoghue* v *Stevenson* [1932] AC 562), but if the retailer is sued for breach of his contract with the plaintiff, the retailer might sue the manufacturer for his breach of contract with the retailer.

The essence of all these examples is that in none of them does a plaintiff have any right to sue the third party directly, so the latter could not be joined as a defendant in the action under O.15 (CCR O.12). It is however desirable that the defendant's claim to indemnity be tried in the same proceedings so that separate proceedings are unnecessary and that is possible by use of a Third Party Notice. The procedure is set out below.

8.5 Other cases

It is often convenient, where the action concerns some property or liability in which more than one person has an interest, to have all rights and liabilities in it tried in one set of proceedings rather than in separate actions, even though no question is raised of any rights to contribution or indemnity. Where a defendant requires that a question or issue relating to the same subject-matter as the plaintiff's action be determined as between himself and some other person, he can use the third party procedure to bring that person into the action so that he will be bound by any judgment or order of the court: O.16 r1 (CCR O.12 r1). For example, where the plaintiff claims possession of land against a tenant and the tenant alleges that there are other joint tenants entitled to the land; or where the plaintiff claims ownership of a rare painting, and the defendant in possession alleges that he borrowed it from someone who himself claimed to be the owner. The third party should be a party to the action so that the rights of occupation and ownership can be determined at a single trial rather than at separate trials at increased costs, with increased delay, and the risk of inconsistent findings on the same evidence. The procedure is set out below.

8.6 Third party proceedings

O.16 r1 (CCR O.12 r1): where the defendant:

1. claims a contribution or indemnity;
2. claims substantially the same relief;
3. requires substantially the same question to be determined;

against a third party, a Third Party Notice is issued against the party who is not already a party to the action.

If he issues it before serving his defence to the plaintiff's claim, he can issue it without leave of the court; after serving the defence, he must apply to the Master by Summons for leave to issue: O.16 rr1 and 2. The notice takes the form prescribed in Appendix A of the White Book, and must be served on the third party together with a copy of the Writ and of the plaintiff's Statement of Claim (if one has been served). The third party must acknowledge service of the notice but need not put in a defence, for a Third Party Notice is not a 'pleading': see Chapter 9. The defendant then, within seven days of that acknowledgement, takes out before the Master a Summons for Third Party Directions to decide whether the notice has been issued in proper form and circumstances, and so that the Master gives in respect of the third party proceedings the same sorts of directions as to future conduct of the proceedings (place of trial, discovery, etc) as are given in the action between plaintiff and defendant.

Where a third party is joined in an action, the title of the action is amended thus:

BETWEEN   A.B.   *Plaintiff*
                 — and —
                 C.D.   *Defendant*
                 — and —
                 E.F.   *Third Party*

The procedure in the County Court differs in that leave must be sought (on notice):

1. in a default action to which automatic directions apply (CCR O.17 r11) after pleadings are closed;
2. where automatic directions do not apply and a date has been fixed for the pre-trial review or hearing; and
3. fixed date actions.

There is a prescribed form of notice (Form N15) and a pre-trial review will be held.

8.7 Nature of third party proceedings

In very many respects the third party proceedings are an independent action between defendant and third party, in which the plaintiff takes no part. The defendant may obtain a deemed admission of his claim, or summary judgment (but see *Heyes* v *Lord Derby* (1984) The Times 19 January). The third party can counterclaim against the defendant but not against the plaintiff. If the proceedings between plaintiff and defendant are settled or discontinued before trial, the third party proceedings will usually continue to exist unless they are for contribution or indemnity and the plaintiff's action has failed completely. A third party can claim against other persons not already parties to the action in the same circumstances that a defendant can issue third party proceedings against him. To do this he issues a *Fourth Party Notice*, and the fourth party proceedings take the same form and course as if they were against a third party. This process can be repeated in theory *ad infinitum*; fourth parties can issue a Fifth Party Notice, fifth parties a Sixth Party Notice, and so on. In practice, the only cases where proceedings will go beyond the third party stage are in building disputes or personal injury claims on building sites, where there may be many 'occupiers' of the land or complicated contractual or tortious rights of contribution and indemnity between main contractors, sub-contractors, architects, surveyors and their employees.

When a Third Party Summons for Directions is taken out and heard (see section 8.6) the Master usually orders that the Third Party Notice stand as the defendant's Statement of Claim in the proceedings, and orders the third party to serve a defence to the claim within 14 days. From that time onwards the third party proceedings are from a procedural viewpoint indistinguishable from an action begun by Writ, and the rules apply similarly.

8.8 Restrictions on third party proceedings

A Third Party Notice can almost always be served without leave of the court where the notice is issued before the defence is served. Where the intended third party is the Crown, however, leave to issue the notice is required in all cases (O.77 r10; CCR O.42 r11), and will not be granted unless 'the court is satisfied that the Crown is in possession of all such information as it reasonably requires as to the circumstances in which it is alleged that the liability of the Crown has arisen and as to the departments and officers of the Crown concerned'. This is because the Crown, when defendant in any claim brought against it by a plaintiff directly, can require the plaintiff to supply it with more detailed particulars of the claim than need be given to defendants of other classes: s35(2)(b) Crown Proceedings Act 1947.

Where the third party to domestic proceedings is out of the jurisdiction, the third party claim can still be brought in the domestic jurisdiction. This would be appropriate where it is impossible for a defendant to show that a third party shares responsibility for the plaintiff's damage without all three parties being brought before the same tribunal: *Kinnear* v *Falconfilms NV and Others* [1994] 3 All ER 42.

8.9 Joinder of the third party as a defendant

Where the third party is a person against whom the plaintiff could have issued proceedings directly and joined as a defendant (see section 8.3), either the plaintiff or the defendant who is sued may apply to the court to have the third party joined as a co-defendant, whether or not third party proceedings have already been started. This makes the third party directly liable to the plaintiff, he may raise a counterclaim against the plaintiff, and take part in the trial of the plaintiff's claim. The court has power of its own motion to join him as a defendant even where neither plaintiff nor defendant applies, and in any other case where the court is of opinion that the third party's presence before the court 'is necessary to ensure that all matters in dispute may be effectually determined ... or ... that there may exist a question or issue arising out of or connected with the relief or remedy claimed by the plaintiff which ... it would be just and convenient to determine as between him and' other parties to the action: O.15 r6(2) (CCR O.15 r1). This power is wider than those cases in which third party proceedings are permitted expressly by the rules, but is not often exercised. Special rules apply when the limitation period has expired against the person proposed to be joined: see Chapter 14.

9

Pleadings

9.1 The purpose and types of pleadings

9.2 Time for service

9.3 Trial without pleadings

9.4 Formal contents of pleadings

9.5 Material contents of pleadings

9.6 Special pleading

9.7 Pleading the defence

9.8 Inconsistent defences

9.9 Judgments on admissions

9.10 Further and better particulars

9.11 Reply and Defence to Counterclaim

9.12 Close of pleadings

9.13 Amendment and striking out

9.1 The purpose and types of pleadings

In every action, the defendant must be told what the plaintiff claims, and on what grounds he claims, for otherwise he cannot know what case will be made against him at trial, or even what the claim is about at all. Similarly, the plaintiff should know what defence will be put up to his claim, so that he can choose which evidence he will need and which he need not use; to reduce the costs and length of the trial it must be known on what issues the plaintiff and defendant do not agree. In an action begun by Writ, these ends are achieved by *pleadings*, formal documents served by each party very soon after proceedings have been started.

The most common pleadings in a typical Writ action are:

1. Statement of Claim – served by the plaintiff either with Writ or within 14 days of the defendant giving notice of his intention to defend: see Chapter 5, section 5.10.
2. Defence – served by the defendant within 14 days of him acknowledging service or receiving the Statement of Claim: see Chapter 6, section 6.3.

Or

3. Defence and Counterclaim – served by the defendant in place of a simple Defence, where he counterclaims against the plaintiff: see Chapter 6, section 6.6.
4. Reply – served by the plaintiff within 14 days of receiving the Defence, if he wishes to rebut against the defendant new elements of the claim which were not included in the Statement of Claim and which the defendant has relied upon in the Defence.

Or

5. Reply and Defence to Counterclaim – served by the plaintiff where he wishes to make not merely a Reply but also a defence to the defendant's counterclaim. It takes the place of a simple Reply.

Any of the above types of pleading may be served without leave of the court, but the following types, which have long been in disuse, require leave of the court (usually from the Master) before service. All of them are in the nature of 'replies', but should be unnecessary if the claim and defence have been properly pleaded in full in pleadings already served: Rejoinder, Surrejoinder, Rebutter and Surrebutter: O.18 r4.

The following are *not* pleadings:

1. the Writ itself (though any indorsement upon it is a pleading);
2. an Originating Summons, Originating Motion or Petition;
3. a Third Party Notice (unless and until the Master orders it to stand as the Third Party Statement of Claim: see Chapter 8, section 8.7);
4. *voluntary* Further and Better Particulars of the Statement of Claim, Defence or other pleadings in the action: see section 9.10.

9.2 Time for service

The time laid down by the rules for service of pleadings has been explained at Chapter 5, section 5.10, Chapter 6, section 6.3 and section 9.1. The importance of the time limits, and their extension by agreement or by order of the court appears at Chapter 6, section 6.5.

9.3 Trial without pleadings

In all actions begun by Writ, the rules require service of pleadings within the specified time limits. It is open for either or both parties, however, to apply to the Master by Summons for an order that the whole action, or some issues in it, be tried without pleadings having to be served. This is really only appropriate where there is no substantial dispute of fact, and where the action would have been better begun by Originating Summons: see Chapter 3, section 3.3. This is confirmed by O.18 r21, which allows the Master to make the order unless the action is one for libel, slander, malicious prosecution, false imprisonment or fraud. The application cannot be made before the defendant has acknowledged service, and if made, the order usually requires the parties to prepare a joint statement of agreed facts and of the matters in issue between them. On the hearing of the application, the Master will give directions for the further conduct of the action as if the hearing were a Summons for Directions.

9.4 Formal contents of pleadings

Every pleading of whatever type must contain the following information, by virtue of O.18 r6; the year in which the Writ was issued, the title of the action, the division of the High Court in which the action is proceeding, and any special court of that Division to which it has been assigned (for example, Companies Court or Commercial Court), the description of the pleading (whether it is a Statement of Claim, Defence, etc), and the date on which it was served. Apart from the date of service, which appears at the foot of the pleading, all other formal parts appear before the material contents of it. Pleadings should be divided so far as is convenient into separately numbered paragraphs, each allegation being contained in one paragraph. Dates, sums of money and other figures must be expressed in figures rather than words, the name of the solicitors acting for the party serving must appear on it (usually after the date of service), and if settled by counsel it must bear his signature or (if copied from counsel's original) name.

The equivalent guidelines in the County Court Rules are much less detailed, but based upon the same principles. They are contained in Orders 6 and 20.

9.5 Material contents of pleadings

The style of pleading varies enormously between different counsel, but all pleadings must comply with O.18 r7, and 'contain only, a statement in summary form of the material facts upon which the party relies, but not the evidence by which those facts will be proved, and the statement must be as brief as the nature of the case permits'. The effect of this rule is:

1. cite facts not law;
2. state only the material facts;
3. do not plead evidence;
4. be brief and clear.

Examples of pleadings have their place in manuals on pleading practice, but the rules give the following instruction:

1. Points of law need not be pleaded because everyone is presumed to know the law. Where terms of contracts are alleged to be implied by statute, or defences created by statute, the practice is however to refer to them: O.18 r11.
2. The *effect* of any document or the purport of any oral conversation should be stated briefly, but the actual words written or spoken should not: O.18 r7(2). In practice, a defendant who wishes to rely upon an exemption clause or other term of the contract will be set out the full terms of the material clause.
3. Matters may be pleaded even though they have arisen since proceedings were issued: O.18 r9.
4. The facts should be pleaded in chronological order so far as possible.
5. There is no need to plead any fact or matter the burden of proof whereof lies on the opposing party, unless the opposing party has specifically denied it in his pleading: O.18 r7(3).

9.6 Special pleading

In particular types of case, the rules require that the statement of material facts, the 'particulars' of claim or defence, go further than merely setting out the general nature of the case. In these cases, the prescribed additional matters must be '*specially pleaded*'. The most important of these are the following:

1. The particulars of any misrepresentation, fraud, breach of trust, wilful default or undue influence relied upon.
2. The particulars of any *special damage*, that is quantifiable items of pecuniary loss and expense which the plaintiff has suffered up to the date of service of the pleading (loss and expense between pleading and trial will usually be dealt with by amendment by agreement between the parties).
3. If it is alleged that the opposing party had knowledge of particular facts, the facts relied on to establish that knowledge are often specifically set out though they are not required to be so detailed.
4. Where it is intended to rely upon the criminal conviction of a party as being relevant to an issue in the proceedings, under ss11 or 12 Civil Evidence Act 1968, the date, place and fact of conviction should be pleaded, together with a statement of their relevance: O.18 r7A. This is of great importance in personal injury claims arising out of collisions with vehicles, and in defamation actions where the defence of justification is raised.

5. The facts supporting an innuendo in the law of libel.
6. Facts relied upon to support allegations of illegality of contract which are not raised in an opponent's pleading and which, if not pleaded, might take him by surprise at trial: O.18 r8.
7. A claim for interest whether under a contractual provision for interest or under the courts' statutory power to award it: s35A Supreme Court Act 1981 or under some other statute (in the County Court: under s69 CCA 1984). Where the claim is for a liquidated amount, the claim should include the rate of interest claimed, the period claimed, and a calculation of the claim to the date of service of the pleading, together with a statement of the weekly or daily rate at which interest will accrue after service: *Practice Note (Claims for Interest)* [1983] 1 WLR 377. A failure to plead a claim for such interest, whether by original Statement of Claim or by later amendment in accordance with RSC O.20, prevents the court from making any award of interest for the period preceding judgment: *Ward v Chief Constable of Avon* (1985) The Times 17 July.
8. Facts relied upon to establish any allegation of mind such as mental disorder or disability, malice, or fraudulent intent: O.18 r12.
9. In contract claims, the alleged consideration.
10. Any statutory defence relied upon: see *Nimmo v Alexander Cowan* [1968] AC 107.
11. A claim for provisional damages under s32A Supreme Court Act 1981.
12. Claims for exemplary damages (only in the High Court).

9.7 Pleading the defence

The Statement of Claim often contains many allegations of fact. A defendant may admit any or all of them in his defence, he may not admit them, or he may specifically deny them. The defence must be very carefully phrased, for a defendant who does not specifically deny an allegation, or does not plead that the allegation is 'not admitted' will be deemed to admit the allegation and may later be prevented from withdrawing his deemed admission: O.18 r13. Thus, each and every allegation should be dealt with in a separate sentence, and a defence which merely denies the plaintiff's claim is insufficient: O.18 r12. There are five forms of pleading an answer to any allegation:

1. Admission. Almost all allegations which the plaintiff can prove easily, such as the fact of a collision between vehicles, or of his employment with the defendant, or his address, will be admitted. This saves costs for both sides in proving matters which will not be in dispute. The decision to admit facts depends on the facts of each case, and is always made with the aim of saving costs. Usually an admission is made expressly, but it can be made impliedly by a failure to deny the allegation or 'not to admit it';
2. Non-admission. An express pleading that the defendant 'does not admit' an allegation means that the plaintiff is required to prove the allegation by evidence,

but the defendant will bring no evidence of his own in disproof of it. The most common allegations which are expressed not to be admitted are those of damage and the plaintiff's date of birth.
3. Traverse. This is a denial of the allegation, and must be expressly pleaded. It means that not only does the defendant deny the allegation, but also that he will reserve the right to bring his own evidence to challenge the plaintiff's. In strict pleading theory, a non-admission is a type of traverse. A claim for damages, however, must be specifically traversed in all actions.
4. Confession and avoidance. This is appropriate where the defendant wishes to admit the truth of the allegation but to allege that there are other facts which take away its basis as a cause of action for the plaintiff, for example, where the defendant admits a breach of contract but seeks to rely upon an exclusion clause, or admits negligence but alleges *volenti non fit injuria* or contributory negligence. The facts alleged to negative the cause of action will be pleaded with the denial, for example, the terms of the exclusion clause or the particulars of contributory negligence.
5. Objection in point of law or 'demurrer'. This is an allegation that even if all the allegations in the Statement of Claim are true, they disclose no cause of action. It is not essential that it be made in a pleading, for an application can be made to strike out any such Statement of Claim (see Chapter 10, section 10.8). The most famous example of its use is in *Donoghue* v *Stevenson*, where the defendants did not admit that the ginger beer bottle contained a snail but alleged that, even assuming it did, that could not in law found an action in negligence by the consumer against the manufacturer. In practice, the pleas are very rarely used.

9.8 Inconsistent defences

Civil law permits a defendant to combine traverse, confession and avoidance, and demurrer in answering any allegation; he may thus run more than one defence to the claim at the same time. This is not hypocrisy, for civil trials do not decide whether a defendant has wronged the plaintiff, but rather whether he is *proven* to be liable, which might be quite a different thing. Since the defendant will be allowed to conduct his case at trial only on the basis of what he has pleaded in his defence, it is very common for counsel to protect the defendant's position in this way. Only at trial will it be known how strong the evidence on any issue will be. The classic example of inconsistent defences is that of the schoolboy sued for negligence in breaking the schoolroom window by throwing a brick through it. The defence contained the following allegations:

1. it was not he who threw the brick (traverse);
2. if he did throw it, it was an accident (confession and avoidance);
3. if he did throw it, and it was not an accident, the window was in property outside the jurisdiction of the English courts (demurrer).

The use of inconsistent defences occurs most commonly in personal injury cases, where the defendant denies that he was negligent, alleges that even if he was negligent the negligence caused no damage, and even if it caused damage the plaintiff was guilty of contributory negligence. Judges make no criticism of this practice, for it is well understood that it exists to allow for the evidence at trial being different from what had been expected, a very common occurrence indeed.

9.9 Judgments on admissions

It has been seen that a defendant may specifically admit some or all of the allegations made by the plaintiff, or he may be deemed to admit them because he has failed to traverse them (see section 9.7). It should be noted that the rule that a failure to traverse involves a deemed admission does not apply where the defendant is a person under a disability (minor or mental patient: O.80 r8). Where there are admissions, they may be sufficient to entitle the plaintiff to judgment on the whole or part of his claim. For example, a plaintiff may sue for the price of goods sold and delivered, alleging the unpaid debt to be £100,000. The defendant may admit the contract of sale, admit the delivery of the goods, but allege that the contract price was only £70,000. He therefore (impliedly) admits that he has not paid the £70,000. The plaintiff may thus want to obtain judgment for £70,000 immediately, leaving the balance to be argued about at trial. In such a case, he can apply by Summons to the Master for such judgment as he appears entitled to by reason of admissions or deemed admissions on the face of the defence: O.27 r3. Another example would be where the defendant in a personal injury case admits negligence and causation but does not admit the quantum of damage or the extent of the alleged injuries. In this latter case the judgment will be interlocutory, that is, final as to liability, interlocutory as to damges which will be assessed later, usually at a hearing before the Master (see Chapter 6, section 6.2 and Chapter 7, section 7.6). Admissions made in one action may not be used in other proceedings against the party making them; they are always made with a view to saving costs, and are not generally intended to be made for all purposes: *Thompson-Houston* v *British Insulated* [1924] 1 Ch 203. The application is most often made on the Summons for Directions. It sometimes happens that a defendant has made his admission by mistake. The Master may allow him to withdraw it and refuse judgment to the plaintiff, and usually does so if satisfied that the defendant is not merely seeking to gain time (cf summary judgment, Chapter 7).

9.10 Further and better particulars

Although the rules require that the pleadings disclose sufficient detail of the case which will be raised to prevent the opposing party from being taken by surprise at trial, it is very common for pleadings to state that case in the most general terms, and without much detail. This is done for two reasons. Firstly, to play the case 'close to the chest' and not to reveal to the opposition matters which might give them an advantage in preparing their case. Secondly, the reason stated above, that a party is permitted to argue his case at trial only upon the facts appearing in the pleadings; a party or his witnesses may change their evidence between the start of proceedings and the trial – they may remember extra facts, or forget others – and no counsel wishes to have the differences between the allegations in the pleadings and the evidence at trial pointed out to the judge.

Where the pleading does not contain sufficient particulars to comply with the rules, the opposing party might apply to strike out the pleading for its non-compliance (see Chapter 10, section 10.6). Such an application would almost certainly fail, however, the Master instead ordering the party in default to supply the missing information. The usual course is therefore for the party seeking further particulars to request them from the other side by letter, and should first be done in this way: O.18 r12(6). If the request is complied with, the information given is termed 'further and better particulars' and forms part of the pleading which it amplifies, so that the party is required to present his case at trial on the basis contained in the voluntary particulars.

If the written request is refused, the party seeking particulars will have to take out a Summons for Particulars before the Master: O.18 r12(3). Similarly if, although the request succeeds, he wants the particulars to be supplied by court order and thus form part of the pleading to which they relate. The Master will examine the pleading, consider whether it does indeed need amplification, and order that further and better particulars be given within a stated time (usually 14 or 21 days) of such matters as he thinks necessary. The Master asks himself: do the particulars already given enable the opposing party to know what case he has to meet at trial, so that he can avoid unnecessary expense and being taken by surprise? The answer to that question will vary from one case to another, but particulars will almost always be ordered of matters which should have been, but which have not been, specially pleaded: see section 9.6. It is no answer to the application to say that the party requesting particulars already knows from sources other than the pleadings what the particulars are, for that does not protect him from the case being argued against him at trial on the wide basis of a vaguely pleaded allegation. Where the particulars cannot be given until after the party asked for them has seen documents in the possession of the party asking for them (that is, until after discovery), it is usual for the Master to order that they be given, but need not be given until after those documents have been examined. This applies commonly where a date may be requested, or the names of all parties to a contract, or the precise terms of a contract in the exclusive possession of the party requesting the particulars.

No particulars will be ordered of a mere denial unless the denial is of the 'confession and avoidance' type (see section 9.7), or where the denial does not make clear which of two or more facts is denied. For example, in answer to the allegation 'the plaintiff agreed with the defendant on 30 June 1995' the defendant may plead 'the allegation that the plaintiff agreed with the defendant on 30 June 1995 is denied'. It is not clear from this whether the defendant is denying that there was an agreement, or that it was made on 30 June 1995, or both. Particulars will be ordered to make the issue clear, as in the following form: 'the defendant denies that he agreed with the plaintiff on 30 June 1995 or any other date', if both the fact of agreement and its alleged date are denied.

9.11 Reply and Defence to Counterclaim

If the Defence simply admits or traverses the allegations made in the Statement of Claim, it is not necessary for the plaintiff to serve any further pleadings restating his claim; it is assumed that he continues to allege what is denied by the defendant: O.18 r14. If the Defence contains confession and avoidance, however, it will usually raise new facts not mentioned in the Statement of Claim. For instance, a plaintiff may plead breach of contract. The defendant pleads an exclusion clause. If the plaintiff wishes to rely upon any *facts* showing that the clause was not contained in the contract, or was not intended to cover the breach which occurred, he should raise those in a *Reply* served within 14 days of his receipt of the Defence. If he does not do so, he may be prohibited from alleging those facts at trial: O.18 r1(2).

Where the defendant raises a counterclaim against the plaintiff (see Chapter 6, section 6.6), the defendant becomes a 'plaintiff' in that counterclaim, and the plaintiff becomes a 'defendant'. Therefore, the plaintiff must serve a *Defence to Counterclaim* if he is not to have judgment in default go against him (see Chapter 6, section 6.6). That pleading must comply with all the rules applicable to service of a Defence, and allegations not traversed will be deemed to be admitted. Whether a Reply or a Reply and Defence to Counterclaim, or simply a Defence to Counterclaim, is served, it must contain the same particulars as any other pleading.

9.12 Close of pleadings

The pleadings serve to define the issues in the case. Once they have been exchanged between the parties, they are said to be 'closed', and time limits for other interlocutory stages in the action begin to run, for example, for discovery, inspection, directions. The pleadings are closed either:

1. if the last pleading served was a Defence, 14 days after its service (that is, when the time for serving a Reply has expired);
2. if the last pleading served was a Defence to Counterclaim, or a Reply, 14 days after its service (O.18 r20), unless in either case time has been extended for the

service of any other pleadings, or leave granted for the service of a Rejoinder or subsequent pleading.

In the County Court, pleadings are deemed to be closed 14 days after the delivery of a Defence or 28 days after the delivery of a Defence and Counterclaim.

9.13 Amendment and striking out

Amendment of pleadings, and striking out of pleadings, are dealt with in Chapter 10.

10

Amendment and Striking Out of Pleadings

10.1   Introduction

10.2   Amendment of the Writ

10.3   Amendment of the pleadings

10.4   The practice of amendment

10.5   Amendment in third party proceedings

10.6   Striking out the Writ and pleadings

10.7   Striking out for failure to comply with the Rules

10.8   No cause of action or defence

10.9   Scandalous, frivolous and vexatious pleadings

10.10 Pleadings which may embarrass, prejudice or delay a fair trial

10.11 Pleadings which are an abuse of the process of the court

10.12 Powers on striking out pleadings

10.13 Inherent jurisdiction

10.1 Introduction

Proceedings when issued and served often require amendment. They may have omitted material facts or causes of action by mistake, or have failed to include all necessary parties. Names of parties may be wrongly stated, or the identity of others may not be correct. The particulars may be defective or deficient. After service of pleadings, either side may discover evidence through discovery (see Chapter 11), or through their own efforts in proofing witnesses and obtaining expert reports, which involves adding new allegations to the case already pleaded. Amendment of the Writ and pleadings is the subject of the first part of this chapter; amendment after the expiry of a relevant limitation period is dealt with in Chapter 14.

Pleadings sometimes allege facts which, even if proven, disclose no cause of action or no defence. Although the opposing party may take objection in point of law in his own pleading (see Chapter 9, section 9.7), it is more common to apply to the court to *strike out* the offending claim or defence, so disposing of the action without trial on the merits after a full hearing. There are also powers under the rules for the court to *strike out* a claim on the ground that it has no prospect of success. These and related matters are the subject of the second part of this chapter.

10.2 Amendment of the Writ

Before the Writ has been served, the plaintiff is allowed to make any amendment to its contents that he wishes, though the amendment must be indorsed by the court office out of which it was issued. For the contents of the Writ, see Chapter 3, section 3.2. This unrestricted power does not extend to any Statement of Claim indorsed on the Writ, which can only be amended in accordance with the rules stated above. The most common amendments made before service are the correction of a defendant's address, or of the capacity in which the plaintiff sues or the defendant is sued. Since amendment before service can cause no injustice to a defendant (except where the amendment joins him as a new party after the limitation period against him has expired), no leave is required to effect it: O.20 r1. However, the rule precludes an amendment of the Writ being made without leave after it has been served on one of several parties: *Trafalgar Tours Ltd* v *Henry* (1990) The Times 8 June.

After the Writ has been served, but before the pleadings are closed (see Chapter 9, section 9.12), the Writ may be amended *once* without leave of the court *unless* the amendment has the effect of:

1. adding a new party to the action; or
2. adding a new cause of action; or
3. altering the capacity in which a party sues or is sued.

An amendment which has any of the effects mentioned in (1), (2) and (3) above can only be made with leave of the court; any *second* amendment, even if it does not have these effects, similarly requires leave. It should be noted that there may be several amendments made on the same occasion, but for the purposes of the rules all such amendments are treated as a single one. So that if a plaintiff amends the Writ by correcting a defendant's address and, at the same time, amends a general indorsement so as to delete one of his claims, there is only one 'amendment'.

After the pleadings are closed, any amendment of the Writ requires leave of the court. An amended Writ must be re-served on all defendants, the amendment being made in red ink (if a first amendment): O.20 r1. It must be remembered that if a new party is to be added, leave to amend must always be obtained unless the Writ has not yet been served. New parties cannot be added by amendment of the pleadings alone.

The court has power to allow an amendment to a party's name even after judgment has been given and entered against a defendant, if that amendment is necessary to substitute the defendant's correct name in place of an incorrect name in which he was originally sued: *Singh* v *Atombrook Ltd* [1989] 1 All ER 385 CA.

10.3 Amendment of the pleadings

Amendments to pleadings are of four principal types. The addition or substitution of parties, consequent on amendment of the Writ; the addition or substitution of causes of action; the addition of particulars of claim or defence; and the addition of new classes of relief (for example, an injunction claimed in addition to damages). The amendment of pleadings can sometimes be made without leave.

The pleadings may be amended *once* without leave of the court before the close of pleadings in the same circumstances as amendment of the Writ is so allowed: see section 10.2. The most common amendments are to add further grounds of defence to the claim: O.20 r3. The amendment is made and the amended pleading re-served, after which the other party is allowed to make, without leave, any amendments to his own pleadings made necessary by the re-served pleading.

After the pleadings are closed all amendments require leave. Before trial application will be made to the Master. At trial the application is to the trial judge.

10.4 The practice of amendment

Even where an amendment is made without leave in circumstances where no leave is required, the party against whom it is made can object by himself taking out a Summons to the Master to disallow the amendment. Where leave is required, it is the party making the amendment who must take out the Summons to have it allowed. The onus of making out a case for allowance of the amendment therefore differs according to whether it is one which requires leave, but in practice little distinction is drawn between the two, and they will be considered together.

If the amendment requires leave, but the party or proposed party against whom it is to be made does not object to it, it is only in very rare circumstances that the Master will disallow it. The requirement of leave exists to prevent parties being taken by surprise by late amendments, and to prevent injustice; if the party has agreed he will suffer no prejudice there is no harm in permitting amendment. It is usual however for the Master to order that the party seeking to amend pay any costs of the other party made necessary by the amendment being made during the proceedings rather than at the outset. Such extra costs will be quite small in most cases, and if the amendment is of no substance may be nil.

Where an amendment is proposed, the Master will look carefully at the prejudice caused to the party against whom it is to be made. Where it amounts to merely adding further particulars of negligence or contributory negligence, or is a merely technical amendment, it will usually be allowed. If no prejudice is caused, and it is necessary to do so, an amendment may even be made after the conclusion of evidence and closing speeches of counsel: *Smith* v *Baron* (1991) The Times 1 February. Amendments such as the correction of the name of a party will be permitted if that party already knows that it is him whom the plaintiff intended to sue, even if the correction has the effect of substituting a new party to the action: *Evans* v *Charrington & Co* [1983] 2 WLR 117, where the 'new party' could not claim to be prejudiced by the amendment. If a plaintiff has sued the wrong defendant, and the correct defendant has no knowledge of the proceedings, the amendment will usually be disallowed, and the plaintiff will have to issue a fresh Writ against the correct defendant, although the court might exercise its power under O.15 r6 to substitute the one for the other in the original action (see Chapter 4). Where the amendment consists in the addition of a new cause of action which arises out of the same facts as one already pleaded, amendment will normally be allowed: *Grewal* v *National Hospital* (1982) The Times 15 October and see *Howe* v *David Brown Tractors (Retail) Ltd* [1991] 4 All ER 30.

Cases on amendment are many, and the common thread throughout all is that amendment will be allowed so long as any injustice caused to a party by reason of it can be compensated by an order for costs in his favour. This will depend upon the nature of the amendment and the time at which it is sought to be made. The later it occurs, the greater is the danger that the party will not have preserved evidence needed to counter fresh allegations, or that witnesses who were available at the start of the proceedings, and whose importance was not realised until the amendment is made, have died or moved away: *Clarapede* v *Commercial Union* (1883) 32 WR 262. The court has very wide powers under O.20 r5, but will not exercise them in favour of parties who have omitted material matters on purpose, so as to disable the opposing side from preparing its case fully: see *Cropper* v *Smith* (1884) 26 Ch D 700.

Although leave to amend may be needed in a particular case, it is usual for the parties to attempt to agree that the amendment be allowed and for the actual leave to be given by the trial judge. This saves the costs of a Summons before the Master to do something which both parties wish to be done. In such cases, an agreed amendment is drawn up, and an amended pleading drafted and 'served' on the opposite party, giving him notice of the proposal. Technically, the amendment is invalid until leave is given, but the point is never taken in practice.

Amendments which consist in the addition of new parties or of new causes of action are in strict theory separate actions, and do not form part of the original action: s35 Limitation Act 1980. They are deemed to have been begun on the same date as the original action (s35(1)), and are termed 'new claims' by s35(2). In fact the distinction is of little importance unless the 'new claim' arises out of an amendment made after the limitation period for making the claim has expired, and this is considered in Chapter 14.

10.5 Amendment in third party proceedings

Rights and powers of amendment are broadly similar where what is to be amended is a third party notice or any pleadings ordered to be served upon the third party Summons for Directions (see Chapter 8, sections 8.7 and 8.8). Where the amendment consists in the addition of a 'new claim' within s35 Limitation Act 1980, it is deemed to have been commenced on the date the third party proceedings were commenced: s35(1).

10.6 Striking out the Writ and pleadings

All pleadings must comply with the requirements of O.18 (see Chapter 9). If they do not do so, the court has power to order that they be *struck out*, that is, that the party serving them shall be in the same position as if he had not served them. The power to strike out also applies where, even though the pleading complies with the rules as to form and content, and even if all the facts it alleges are true, it cannot found a cause of action or a defence because the law does not recognise such a claim. There is a further power to strike out an action where it is 'frivolous or vexatious', and to strike out parts only of a pleading, leaving the remainder intact. These now fall for discussion.

10.7 Striking out for failure to comply with the Rules

The court has various powers to strike out a claim or defence where the Rules of the Supreme Court are not complied with. This power applies not only to the Rules for content and service of pleadings, but to all other Rules, such as the obligation to give discovery and inspection, or to comply with any order of the court. Where there is a failure to comply, it is most unusual that any application to strike out the offender's pleading will succeed. The court will in most cases give the party in default an opportunity to comply with the Rules and Orders within a set time, and only after that time has expired will striking out be ordered (see Chapter 14). Especially where a party has given insufficient particulars of his claim, or is only a few days outside the time for service of, for example, lists of documents, an application to strike out for failure to comply is almost certain to fail, and instead the time for serving lists will be extended, or the further particulars will be ordered, by the Master.

The only common case in which a claim will be struck out for failure to comply with time limits in interlocutory proceedings is where there has been 'want of prosecution', that is, the plaintiff has not pursued his action with due speed, and the defendant is prejudiced by the delay. This is dealt with in Chapter 14.

10.8 No cause of action or defence

The court exists to grant remedies where there are recognised rights to those remedies, and a claim will be struck out if, having regard to the substantive law and to the Statement of Claim, the plaintiff's claim *must* fail even though all the alleged facts may be true, or where the facts of a defence, even if all true, can afford no defence in law to the claim. This is solely a question of *law*, and should be contrasted with summary judgment under O.14, which is concerned with the *facts* of a claim where those facts are disputed (see Chapter 7). The power to strike out is contained in O.18 r9, and is exercisable where the pleading 'discloses no reasonable cause of action or defence'. In this context 'reasonable' seems to mean 'even arguable', for a claim or defence which is distinguishable from a previous adverse decision of the House of Lords may be allowed to proceed, on the ground that the law changes constantly, and to strike out every claim or defence which the High Court or the Court of Appeal has in a previous case decided futile would cause the law to stagnate. It is thus only in the clearest cases that the power to strike out will be exercised.

Claims over which the High Court has no jurisdiction will be struck out as a matter of course. A claim which can only be brought in the court of a foreign country, or only before a tribunal established by statute, falls into this class. A claim which is required to be brought in the County Court will always be struck out if the court is of the opinion that the party bringing the action knew or ought to have known the Rules: s40 County Courts Act 1984 as amended by the CLSA 1990. A claim which should have been commenced by arbitration will most often be stayed rather than dismissed at once: s4 Arbitration Act 1950 and O.73.

In other classes of case, the Master, to whom all applications to strike out are made by Summons in the action at first instance, will examine the substantive law to decide whether the rights claimed, or the defence pleaded, are maintainable in law. This depends upon rules of general law, but some recent examples will suffice. A claim by the mother of a baby born after a failed sterilisation, the baby being spastic, will be struck out if it amounts to a claim for damages for allowing the child to be born at all: *Mackay* v *Essex Health Authority* [1982] QB 1166. An action for a declaration of rights under O.15 claiming that the intervention of the Attorney-General to take over and effectively stop a private prosecution is illegal will be struck out on this ground: *Raymond* v *A-G* [1982] QB 839. An action against a witness who gave evidence of a defamatory nature in the course of testifying will be struck out, as the occasion attracts absolute privilege in the law of defamation: *Evans* v *London Hospital* [1981] 1 WLR 184. The list of examples is almost endless, and the reader is referred to the notes on O.18 r19 contained in the White Book.

In deciding whether any reasonable cause of action or defence are disclosed, the Master may look only at the pleadings. He is not permitted to hear any evidence attempting to amplify or explain the pleading. If there are additional facts which render an apparently unmaintainable claim or defence maintainable, the party alleging them should on the application seek to amend the pleading. Similarly, if a claim is made and the defendant knows that there are matters which, if pleaded as they should have been, will ground an application to strike out, he should request further and better particulars and then put these, together with the original pleading, before the Master. For instance, if the plaintiff alleges that 'the defendant on 1 July 1995 uttered words in the sound and hearing of others which implied that the plaintiff was a murderer and a rogue', the defendant could not succeed in an application to strike out the claim. However, if the defendant knows that the words were spoken by him as a High Court judge in sentencing the plaintiff to life imprisonment for murder, they will attract absolute privilege and no claim can be brought against him. He should therefore first request the plaintiff to identify the capacity of the defendant and the occasion on which the words were spoken. If the plaintiff gives the expected particulars, it is apparent from them that the claim must fail, and it will be struck out. If the plaintiff refuses to give particulars, then the court has the power stated at section 10.6 above to strike out his claim for failure to comply with an order of the court.

10.9 Scandalous, frivolous or vexatious pleadings

Such pleadings may be struck out under O.18 r19(1)(b). Pleadings which are scandalous, frivolous or vexatious usually also disclose no reasonable cause of action or defence, and are struck out on that ground. The classes of pleading which fall within the sub-rule seem to concern actions for declarations against government departments and a few other cases where the claim must surely fail: *Pickin* v *BRB* [1974] AC 765 and *Manuel* v *A-G* [1982] 3 WLR 821, the latter case concerning a claim for a declaration that the United Kingdom government had no power to amend the Canadian Constitution, and that an Act of Parliament was *ultra vires*.

10.10 Pleadings which may embarrass, prejudice or delay a fair trial

Under O.18 r19(1)(c), such pleadings may be struck out. The power is normally used to strike out parts of a pleading which raise issues irrelevant to the proceedings and on which much time would have to be spent at trial, or which raise matters on which evidence is not admissible or otherwise fail to comply with the rules of pleading, for example, by pleading evidence rather than material facts, and make allegations of fraud, bad faith or misconduct which are irrelevant to the proceedings in hand. Those parts of a pleading which contained allegations (though true) that a party has been convicted of serious crime would be struck out under this head if the action were for breach of contract in failing to install a proper plumbing system and the convictions were irrelevant to whether the standard of workmanship was adequate.

10.11 Pleadings which are an abuse of the process of the court

The power to strike out these pleadings stems from O.18 r19(1)(d). It is used when the motive for instituting proceedings is not the true vindication of rights, but rather some intention to pressure the defendant or to blackmail him into meeting a demand. The expression 'frivolous or vexatious' includes proceedings which are an abuse of the process: *Ashmore v British Coal Corporation* [1990] 2 WLR 1437, 1443. For an example of its exercise see *Hunter v Chief Constable of West Midlands* [1982] AC 529, which related to a claim by the 'Birmingham Six' that police officers had beaten their confessions out of them and the civil action against those police officers. How the confessions had been obtained had been explored at the criminal trial on a *voir-dire* and so it was held that to allow the civil claim would amount to an abuse of the process.

See also *In re a Company* (1983) The Times 10 May, in which a winding-up petition based upon a debt which only came into existence a few hours before the petition was issued was struck out on the basis that it was not truly presented in order to have the debt paid, but to destroy the company.

A defence may equally be an abuse of process if the court is satisfied that it has been served merely to gain time in the action and without there being any real defence to the claim. This is very similar to the test applied on applications for summary judgment (see Chapter 7), and the plaintiff will usually choose to proceed under O.14 than under this rule.

A plaintiff who issues a Writ but who does not intend to serve a Statement of Claim because he does not yet know what if any causes of action he may have, but who is motivated simply by desire to protect his position under the Limitation Act 1980 (see Chapter 14, section 14.2), is guilty of an abuse of process, and the Writ will be struck out: *Steamship Mutual v Trollope & Colls* (1986) The Times 31 March.

Where the issue had already been tried in another jurisdiction, it may be considered an abuse of process to re-litigate in this jurisdiction: *House of Spring Gardens v Waite* [1990] 2 All ER 990.

10.12 Powers on striking out pleadings

Where pleadings are struck out, the court has power to order that judgment be entered against the party struck out: O.18 r1(3). This it will do if no reasonable cause of action or defence is disclosed, or if the pleading is an abuse of process, unless the party in the former case is given leave to amend the pleading to allege facts which make the claim or defence maintainable (see section 10.8). The effect is that the action is at an end and no fresh proceedings may be started; if they are started, the court will dismiss them as an abuse of process, as an attempt to reopen a claim which is already *res judicata*. The only method of challenging the striking out is thus to appeal from the Master's decision, unless the judgment has been obtained by fraud, or the party can show any of the other grounds to have it set aside (see Chapter 20). Alternatively, the action might be *stayed* (that is, not allowed to proceed further, but not at and end), or *dismissed*, in which latter case it is open to the plaintiff to start fresh proceedings if he wishes.

10.13 Inherent jurisdiction

In addition to the powers under O.18 r19, the court has a very wide jurisdiction of its own, not contained in any rule or order, to strike out a claim or defence. In practice, it is concurrent with powers conferred by the rules to strike out, but is a valuable additional weapon for use when an obviously meritless claim or defence does not fall strictly within the wording of the rules, or when the rules do not expressly cover a particular case: *Valor* v *Application de Gaz* [1977] Eur LR 308, where a pleading which did not give sufficient particulars of alleged breaches of the treaty establishing the EC was struck out.

11

Discovery and Inspection of Documents

11.1 Introduction

11.2 Pre-action inspection

11.3 Pre-action discovery and inspection in personal injury and death cases

11.4 Discovery and inspection against non-parties in personal injury cases

11.5 Discovery and inspection against other non-parties

11.6 Discovery between parties to the action

11.7 Discovery and inspection in actions begun by Writ

11.8 Discovery in other actions

11.9 Failure to make discovery

11.10 Discovery in personal injury actions

11.11 Use of discovered documents

11.12 Interrogatories

11.13 Discovery of expert evidence

11.14 Expert reports in non-personal injury cases

11.15 Expert reports in personal injury and fatal accident cases

11.16 Mutual disclosure of expert evidence

11.17 Medical examination of injured plaintiffs

11.18 Disclosure by agreement of the parties

11.19 Agreement of expert evidence

11.20 Witness statements

11.1 Introduction

Before a claimant starts his action, he may wish to examine documents held by a potential defendant or someone who knows the identity of that defendant; this he can do in only a very few cases. When the action is under way, each side will wish to see all documents in the possession of the other party and relevant to the action; this can almost always be done unless the documents are privileged from production. Sometimes he will want to see documents held by someone not already a party to the action. In all these cases the examination is wanted to see whether there is anything useful to the party's own case or damaging to that of his opponent, in the documents concerned. In limited circumstances, the court can order a party to answer on oath questions concerning matters in issue before the action comes to trial.

Disclosure of the possession of documents is called 'discovery'; allowing a party to see them is 'inspection'. Questions to be answered on oath are 'interrogatories'. Discovery and inspection are sometimes made automatically in an action, sometimes only by order of the court. Interrogatories can only be administered with leave of the court. The CLSA 1990 contains provisions for rules to be made for compulsory pre-trial exchange of witness statements.

11.2 Pre-action inspection

A proposed plaintiff may apply for an order for the inspection of property which may become the subject-matter of proceedings under s33(1) Supreme Court Act 1981. The application is made by originating summons supported by an affidavit describing the property and its relevance to any existing or proposed action. The procedure is contained in O.29 r7A.

The court may order security for costs or impose other terms.

The order for inspection will not be made if it appears to the court that compliance would result in the disclosure of a secret process, discovery or invention not disclosed in the pleadings and that inspection would not have been granted if the application had been made in existing proceedings.

11.3 Pre-action discovery and inspection in personal injury and death cases

Where a claimant is considering whether to start proceedings for personal injuries to himself, or on behalf of the estate of a deceased victim, or under the Fatal Accidents Act 1976, it will in some cases save him time and money in the claim if he can inspect, before issuing proceedings, any documents held by the potential defendant and relevant to the issue of liability. He can then decide whether there is any prospect of success, and can frame his case on what he knows will be the evidence available (in documentary form at least) to himself and the defendant. Very many personal injury cases settle without or soon after the issue of a Writ and s33(2) Supreme Court Act 1981 helps achieve this. By that section, the potential plaintiff may apply by Originating Summons (and not by any other originating process) for an order that the 'defendant' allow him to inspect relevant documents. The conditions in which the court will grant the application are:

1. the applicant must 'appear to the High Court to be likely to be a party' to subsequent proceedings for personal injury or death which 'are likely to be made' in the High Court;
2. the respondent to the Summons must 'appear to the High Court to be likely to be a party' in such proceedings and 'to be likely to have or to have had in his possession, custody or power any documents which are relevant' to an issue or likely issue in the proceedings.

The word 'likely' whenever it appears has been held to mean 'likely, depending upon the outcome of the inspection of the documents', so that the plaintiff need only show that he may well bring an action against the defendant, and is not required to prove that he has, even without inspecting the documents, a good case against the defendant, for to require such proof would defeat the intent of the Act: *Dunning* v *United Liverpool Hospital* [1973] 1 WLR 586. Applications are made under O.24 r7A by Originating Summons supported by an affidavit setting out the grounds for believing both that he and the defendant will be parties to subsequent proceedings, and that the other party has relevant documents.

Discovery under s33(2) has the following principal restrictions:

1. it will not be ordered of documents for which privilege is properly claimed by the defendant; this is a matter for manuals on evidence;
2. the court can restrict disclosure to the plaintiff's legal, medical or other professional advisers, so that the plaintiff does not see them: s33(2)(b).

The power under s33(2) is most useful to obtain hospital records of treatment when a plaintiff is considering an action for medical negligence, or documents concerning the maintenance and accident record of a machine, where the claim is against an employer for breach of statutory duty, or the service records of a motor car, if the claim arises out of a collision with that car and the plaintiff suspects it had a mechanical defect.

The court will take into account, in determining whether it is 'likely' that an action for damages for personal injuries will be brought at some future time, the prospects that the defendant can establish that the limitation period for commencing the relevant action has expired by the time application is made for pre-action discovery under s33(2), though a detailed investigation into those prospects will not normally be carried out at the pre-action stage: *Harris* v *Newcastle Area Health Authority* [1989] 2 All ER 273 CA. See further Chapter 14, sections 14.7 to 14.10.

There is an equivalent power and procedure under the County Courts Act 1984 s52 and CCR O.13 r7.

11.4 Discovery and inspection against non-parties in personal injury cases

When a plaintiff has commenced proceedings against a defendant claiming for personal injury or fatal accident, he generally has a right to see all the documents held by the defendant relevant to the action. He has no right however to see documents held by persons who are not parties, and the only way in which he can inspect them apart from under the power now to be discussed, would be by requiring that person to attend at trial and produce the documents under a subpoena duces tecum. Much time and money might be saved if he can inspect the documents at an earlier stage, and s34(2) Supreme Court Act 1981 so provides. It applies only in personal injury actions as does s33(2) (above), and the following points are worth noting:

1. the application against the non-party is made by ordinary Summons (O.24 r7A), but is served in the same way as a Writ;
2. it can be made by either plaintiff *or* defendant;
3. inspection can be restricted to the party's legal, medical or other advisers: ss34(2);
4. it will not be ordered of documents for which the non-party claims privilege and the claim is upheld.

In addition, the following matters are relevant to applications under both s33(2) and s34(2):

1. they may be made against the Crown: s35(4);
2. the court should not make orders under them if it considers that compliance with the order would be injurious to the public interest: s35(1). This wide and uncertain rule has not been the subject of material case law, and seems to be no more than a statutory confirmation of 'public policy privilege'.

There is also the power under s34(3) Supreme Court Act 1981 to order the inspection, photographing, preservation, custody and detention of property in the possession of a non-party. The County Court equivalent is s53 County Courts Act 1984.

11.5 Discovery and inspection against other non-parties

A potential plaintiff cannot generally obtain discovery against persons who are not already sued in respect of a cause of action other than one for discovery. In other words, a plaintiff cannot bring an action for the sole purpose of obtaining discovery against the defendant; he must have a separate cause of action against him. This is an example of the 'mere witness' rule, that before trial no person who is not a party can be compelled to disclose evidence in his possession even if it is highly material to a party's case. Sections 33 and 34 are statutory exceptions to that rule, and there is another ill-defined exception at common law, developed within the last decade, and the limits of which are uncertain. Where a potential plaintiff knows or believes that his rights have been infringed, but does not know the identity of the wrongdoer, he can it seems bring an action against a person who does know that identity, solely for the purpose of compelling him to disclose it. The limit originally imposed was that the person against whom discovery of the names was sought should have got himself 'so mixed up in the wrongdoing as almost to be a party to it'. This stems from *Norwich Pharmacal* v *Commissioners of Customs & Excise* [1973] 3 WLR 164, where the plaintiffs were holders of a patent in certain drugs. They knew that drugs were being imported which infringed that patent, but did not know who was importing or producing them. The customs authorities kept records of all the drugs imported, for they bore import duty. The House of Lords held that the Customs had 'facilitated' the infringement of patent by allowing the drugs to be imported, and that the plaintiffs were entitled to bring an action to compel the disclosure of the name of the importers.

In the *Norwich Pharmacal* case it was necessary to say that the plaintiffs could have brought an action against the Customs for infringement of patent by participating in the importation knowing the infringement was taking place. It is now clear that the jurisdiction to order discovery of the identity of a wrongdoer against a person who is under no direct liability to the applicant in contract or tort is limited to cases where that person has, unwittingly or otherwise, 'facilitated' the commission of a wrongful act by some third party. It is not enough for the applicant to establish merely that the person has knowledge of the relevant name, even though the applicant could not practically obtain that name from any other source and great injustice might thereby follow to him if no disclosure is ordered. In *Ricci* v *Chow* [1987] 3 All ER 534 the plaintiff sought disclosure, against a person alleged to be involved in the publication of a journal, of the identity of a contributor to that journal who had libelled the plaintiff. The Court of Appeal held that, there being no evidence that the respondent was in any way involved in publication of the journal, no power to order him to disclose the contributor's name could be made, since no 'facilitation' could be proven. The respondent was a 'mere witness', and although he probably knew the name of the true tortfeasor he could not be ordered to reveal it against his will.

Thus far the action has been restricted to the disclosure of the identity of someone whom the plaintiff wishes to sue, and will be prevented from doing so unless the court comes to his aid; it has not been extended to other types of evidence, and the 'mere witness' rule seems to forbid its being so extended. In *British Steel* v *Granada* [1980] 3 WLR 774 it was used to compel disclosure of the name of a person who had 'leaked' confidential information to the television company, but it should be noted that in such a case s10 Contempt of Court Act 1981 provides that the court shall not order that a person responsible for a publication (which includes television and newspaper media) shall disclose the source of information contained in that publication unless disclosure is necessary in the interests of justice or of national security: see *Secretary of State* v *Guardian Newspapers* [1984] 2 WLR 268.

It is fundamental to distinguish discovery against non-parties from that against parties to an action in which discovery of documents or names is merely ancillary to the claim and is used to help prepare the case against that other party; such discovery will normally be ordered, without need to show the *Norwich* conditions, in all cases: *Harrington* v *North London Polytechnic* [1984] 3 All ER 666.

11.6 Discovery between parties to the action

In the usual case, the action will not be about discovery of documents, but rather about some other claim; a breach of contract, a tort, or some other substantive claim. In such cases each party will want to know what evidence the other has. The rules permit however inspection only of *documents* held by other parties, though in rare cases a party may be interrogated on oath (see section 11.12). 'Documents' has been held to include other permanent means of recording information, such as tape recordings and films, and is presumably wide enough to include information stored on computer although it does not take on the form of a document until printed on instruction by the operator. Although it might be thought that a party who realises that he will be obliged to disclose to the other documents which damage his own case would conceal or destroy those documents, this happens surprisingly rarely.

In some actions discovery and inspection are automatic, in others they only occur after court order. In most cases all relevant documents are disclosed, in others only certain classes of document. There may be specific discovery of particular documents. Most of the material rules are contained in O.24 rr1, 2, and 7, O.25 r8 and a few other rules.

11.7 Discovery and inspection in actions begun by Writ

In a Writ action other than for personal injuries, each party must, within 14 days of the close of pleadings (see Chapter 9, section 9.12) serve upon every other party a *List of Documents* stating which documents he has or has had in his possession and which are 'relevant' to any issues in the case: O.24 r2. In practice the 14 day time limit is hardly every complied with, and is usually extended by agreement. The List must be in the form prescribed by O.24 r5, and is divided into Schedule 1, dealing with all documents which the party has at the time of making the List in his 'possession, custody or power'; Part I of the Schedule lists those documents the party is willing to disclose; Part II those for which he claims legal professional privilege or public policy privilege; and Schedule 2 which lists documents which the party did have, but has no longer, in his possession, custody or power, such as the originals of letters sent to other parties, forms reporting accidents sent to the Health and Safety Executive, and other documents he has parted with. Although the Rules of Court provide no express mechanism for amendment of a List of Documents after it has been served, the court has an inherent jurisdiction to allow such amendment, for instance where a party mistakenly fails to claim privilege for relevant material and includes it in Part 1 of Schedule 1 instead of in Part 2: *Re Briamore Manufacturing* [1986] 3 All ER 132 Ch D.

Each document in Part I of Schedule I bears a number, as does each in Schedule 2. Since no party wishes to tell his opponent what privileged documents he has, Part II of Schedule I normally states simply 'instructions to and opinions of counsel, correspondence between the party and his advisers', but does not identify the documents further. The List also states a time and place where the documents in Part I of Schedule I can be inspected by the other parties. This should be not later than seven days after service of the List (again the time limit hardly applies in practice), and is usually at the office of the party's solicitor; if it states an unreasonable time or place, the Master can order it changed: O.24 r11. Facilities must be provided for inspection, such as a tape player or video machine, if the documents require to be 'translated' in such a way.

The rules require that the List contain all documents 'relevant' to the case. The classic definition of this was made in the *Peruvian Guano Case* (1882) 11 QBD 55. A document is relevant:

> '... if it is reasonable to suppose that it contains information which may enable a party either to advance his own case or to damage that of his opponent or which may fairly lead him to a train of inquiry which may have either of these two consequences' Bowen LJ.

It is impossible to state any more general rule as to what is or is not relevant so that it must be included in the List. Everything depends upon the issues in the case, the nature of the claim and defence, and the parties to it. The most recent reported case concerned a plaintiff's claim for personal injuries he alleged he sustained while working for shipwrights, one of the thousands of claims for noise-induced deafness faced by them. B claimed that the only relevant documents were those compiled during the period they employed the plaintiff, and argued that other documents which came into existence before and after that time were irrelevant in that they could neither aid his case nor damage their own. The court ordered discovery of the further documents, on the basis that they might show that B knew, even before the plaintiff started work for them, of the risk of deafness from excessive noise, that is, the documents would have been highly relevant to prove negligence. They should have been included in the List when it was first served: *Drennan v Brooke Marine* (1983) The Times 20 June.

It must be noted that in the following principal cases there is no 'automatic' discovery, and that a List will be served only after specific order of the court or agreement of the parties:

1. where the action is begun otherwise than by Writ;
2. in third party proceedings: O.24 r2;
3. in proceedings by or against the Crown: O.77 r12;
4. where the action arises out of the collision of a vehicle on land (for example, a car crash). In this case the plaintiff makes discovery (but see section 11.10), but the defendant does not do so, automatically: O.24 r2.

11.8 Discovery in other actions

Where the claim falls within any of the classes mentioned in section 11.7, service of Lists will be done only upon order of the court, and a party wishing to see his opponent's documents must apply by Summons and affidavit stating why it should be given: O.24 r3. This was the usual procedure before 1962, and the order will be made if the Master thinks grounds have been made out for the existence of relevant documents. Where the action is of type (4), there is no automatic discovery because there are usually no documents held by a defendant relevant to any issue, but if the plaintiff suspects mechanical defect in the car, and pleads such in his Statement of Claim the Master will often make an order for discovery of the service records of the car and all other documents relating to it. Since this relates to a specific class of documents rather than to general discovery, it is more usual for the application to be made under O.24 r7, which governs discovery of specific documents, but the procedure is the same in either case.

There is no automatic discovery against the Crown because it is realised that many documents it holds may be covered by so-called 'Crown privilege' but on an application to the Master it is usual for discovery to be ordered in the same circumstances as it would be against a private citizen, subject only to the Crown establishing (as may any other party to an action) legal, professional or public policy privilege, or the applicant failing to make out a case either for the existence of the documents or for their relevance to the action.

11.9 Failure to make discovery

A party who is bound to serve a List of Documents and to give inspection but who fails to do so, whether in an 'automatic' case or after an order under O.24 r3, is in breach of the rules, but his pleadings will rarely be struck out (see Chapter 10, section 10.7) unless his failure is intentional or leads to long delay and prejudices a fair trial of the action (see Chapter 14). More usually, the failure consists in a failure to include in the List all relevant documents. If the other party knows of the existence of those others, he will usually apply by Summons for an order for specific discovery to have them included: (O.24 r7), and the Master determines the dispute as to relevancy. If he finds the document(s) relevant, he orders the party to swear an affidavit disclosing whether the document(s) are in his possession. If they are, inspection follows in the normal course of things without further order.

In some cases it will be apparent from the *pleadings*, or from an *affidavit* sworn by a party in proceedings, that that party has some document which may be relevant but which he has not included in his List. To obtain discovery of such documents, the opposing party has a right, enforceable by Master's order which will most often be made, to inspect the documents (O.24 r10), if the opposing party fails to comply with a notice to give their discovery within 11 days of the notice. Where reference is made to a document by a party in his pleadings or affidavits, the court can (though need not) make an order for its discovery even if that document is not in the possession, custody or power of the party who makes reference to it: *Rafidain Bank v Agom Universal Sugar Trading Co Ltd* [1987] 3 All ER 859.

In other cases, documents in the List may themselves refer to other documents which may be relevant and which have not been included. There, the opposing party will most often apply for a *Further and Better List*, seeking discovery of the additional material: O.24 r3. Issues as to the relevancy of the documents are, once again, decided by the Master. This procedure can also be used where, although the undisclosed documents are not known to exist from looking at the List or the documents in it, a party has admitted that he has them. It is not the purpose of discovery to give a party the opportunity to check up whether discovery by the opponent has been properly carried out. If a party does not believe an opponent, he should call for the deponent to appear and be cross-examined: *Berkeley Administration Inc v McClelland* [1990] 2 WLR 1021.

There are cases where a party suspects that his opponent is in possession of relevant documents, but cannot point to any admission, or to anything in the pleadings, affidavits or List, or to the documents in it, to show that such extra documents exist, and the opponent denies their existence. This is very rare indeed, and arises only where a party thinks that his opponent is deliberately concealing material which is known to be relevant, such as a memorandum admitting that the plaintiff has a valid claim, or a vehicle service record which shows that the vehicle was wholly unroadworthy, or some other document damaging to him. If there is such suspicion, the party can apply for an order that the opponent swear an affidavit *Verifying the List of Documents*: O.24 r2(7). If the opponent swears that the List is complete, and that he has no further relevant documents, the court will presume that he is telling the truth and does not wish to incur criminal liability for perjury. Nonetheless, if the party later discovers that the other documents do in fact exist, and that the opponent has them, their discovery will be ordered under O.24 r7.

11.10 Discovery in personal injury actions

Special rules apply to actions for personal injuries. Except where the claim arises out of a collision on land involving a vehicle, both parties must make automatic discovery within 14 days of the close of pleadings, and the procedure and form of Lists, and the remedies where they are defective, are the same as in any other action. The rule governing discovery is however O.25 r8 and not O.24 r2, and if the defendant admits liability there is no discovery except as described below.

In the following personal injury actions, the defendant makes no automatic discovery, but the plaintiff must make discovery of all documents evidencing 'special damages', that is, damage to property in the accident, loss of earnings already suffered, and other items of quantifiable loss and expense sustained as a result of the injuries to the date of discovery. No documents relating to liability, or to general damages, are disclosed:

1. where the claim arises out of a collision on land involving a vehicle; or
2. where the defendant has admitted liability.

Where discovery is automatic under O.24 r2 or O.25 r8, it should take place within 14 days of the close of pleadings, and inspection occur within seven days thereafter but, as explained, the time limits are almost never complied with. The power to order discovery under O.24 rr3 and 7 may be ordered at any stage of the action, and whether or not a party is obliged to give automatic discovery. It may even be ordered before the pleadings have been served, but not if the purpose in seeking it is to find out if there is a cause of action against a defendant. A plaintiff cannot simply start his action with very general allegations, then apply for discovery before pleadings so he can frame his case according to what emerges: *RHM v Bovril* [1982] 1 WLR 661, where the plaintiffs suspected that the defendant had infringed their copyright deliberately, but were unable to give particulars of the deliberate intent. The Court of Appeal dismissed the application for discovery as no more than a 'fishing expedition' designed to discover facts to support the allegations. It was of course open to the plaintiffs to await discovery in the normal way under O.24 r2, and then to seek leave to amend their pleading in the light of discovered documents. The court stated that the power to order discovery before service of pleadings would be exercised only in exceptional cases.

11.11 Use of discovered documents

The purpose of discovery is to enable each side to see the other's documents, and to use such as he chooses, to support a claim *already* pleaded. It is not intended to permit the use of any discovered documents to found a totally new action. In the course of discovery either side may find documents held by the other which relate to different matters, for example, in a claim for breach of contract against him, a defendant may find among the plaintiff's documents some letter he considers defamatory of him and which he did not previously know about; or in an action for one infringement of a patent, the plaintiff may find that the defendant's documents disclose other quite separate breaches of patent. The general rule is that documents disclosed on discovery may be used only for the purposes of fighting the action in which they are disclosed, and not to start a fresh action. Similarly, a party who obtains discovery may not use the documents for any 'improper' purpose, such as disclosing them to non-parties or passing them on to the media, no matter what the public interest may be in bringing scandalous or corrupt dealings to public attention.

There is therefore implied into every High Court action an agreement by the parties that they will use documents disclosed on discovery only for the purposes of the action, and not for any other purpose: *Home Office* v *Harman* [1982] 2 WLR 338. This is termed an implied 'undertaking'. It is open to the court however to grant leave for the use of such documents in another action, and if the documents disclosed reveal a cause of action in fraud or some other strong claim it will often be given. For instance, where a plaintiff brought an action against former employees for breach of fiduciary duty, and on discovery letters were found which implicated other employees in the tort, the court gave leave for such letters to be used in an action begun against those others even though, without discovery in the first action, there would have been no evidence against those others: *Sybron* v *Barclays Bank* (1984) The Times 9 March.

The implied undertaking ceases to bind the party who obtains discovery, however, if the document in question has been read to or by the court, or referred to in open court, unless the court otherwise directs on application of the party giving discovery: O.24 r14A.

Breach of the implied undertaking is a contempt of court, and the use of documents for an improper purpose will be restrained by injunction. This aspect of procedure is thus very similar to the substantive law which restrains the publication and use of confidential information obtained in the course of employment and other activities: see, for example, *Argyll* v *Argyll* [1967] Ch 302.

11.12 Interrogatories

After service of the pleadings, each party may wish to limit the issues in the case further, or to compel his opponent to admit certain easily provable facts, for example, the authenticity of a signature. In general he cannot do so, but the court has a discretion to order that questions be answered by a party on oath before trial if it 'considers it necessary either for fairly disposing of the cause or matter or for saving costs': O.26 r1. When ordered, they must be given within the time specified by the Master (after a hearing on Summons) and are binding on the party giving them; he will not be allowed later to deny their truth. If the answers given are evasive or ambiguous, further answers may be required: O.26 r5. Failure to answer may lead to the defaulter's pleadings being struck out (see Chapter 10, section 10.7) and to punishment for contempt of court.

In practice interrogatories are rarely ordered. The only frequent time they are used is in an action for discovery where the plaintiff seeks the names of persons against whom he has a claim but which he cannot pursue unless the defendant is ordered to disclose the names: see section 11.5. There are alternative methods of attempting to restrict the issues which are usually sufficient, such as requests for further and better particulars (see Chapter 9, section 9.10) and by a Notice to Admit Facts served under O.27 r2, served by one party on the other and requiring him to admit facts which are capable of easy proof (see further Chapter 17).

11.13 Discovery of expert evidence

A plaintiff who alleges he suffered injury, and that the defendant caused it and is liable, bears the burden of proving the extent of the injury. He will be examined by a specialist doctor who prepares a report detailing the seriousness of the injuries. That report is a document which attracts legal professional privilege and the court cannot in any circumstances strike out the plaintiff's claim for his failure to disclose it to the defendant. Rules exist however which provide for the disclosure of the substance of that report (and of any report compiled by the defendant's medical specialist), but the *only* common sanction for failing to comply with these rules is that the party in default will not be allowed to call as a witness at trial the doctor who made the report.

The same principle applies to expert reports of any other kind prepared by any party in the course of or for the purpose of a claim of any kind. The reports of engineers on the safety of buildings or machinery, those of architects on the construction of houses, those of accountants on the future earnings of a party, and those of professional men on the accepted practice of the profession, are common examples. If, and only if, a party intends to call the maker of the report at trial, or to use the report itself, he must seek a direction from the court upon its disclosure to his opponent, subject to agreement between the parties and to the provisions for 'automatic' disclosure under O.25 r8. If he intends to use neither the report nor the maker of the report at trial, he need make no disclosure at all. The rules on pre-trial disclosure apply even where the expert is himself one of the parties, and even though disclosure of his intended testimony would give the opponent the tactical advantage of seeing much of his proof of evidence, since the purpose of the rules is to prevent surprise: *Shell Pensions Trust* v *Pell Frischmann* [1986] 2 All ER 911 QBD. There is an obligation to disclose the substance of an expert's evidence which includes matters which may arise in evidence-in-chief and/or cross-examination. Thus where a defendant obtained an expert's report favourable to his case, but also a covering letter from that expert suggesting possible causes of the accident involving the defendant's own negligence, the defendant was obliged to disclose the covering letter as well as the report: *Kenning* v *Eve Construction* [1989] 1 WLR 1189.

The provisions of the Rules to compel disclosure of such reports, and to limit the number of expert witnesses who may be called by each party, do not permit the Master at an interlocutory stage to rule upon the technical admissibility of such evidence. Such is a matter for the trial judge, whose task it is to determine whether the maker of the report is a suitably qualified person to give 'expert' testimony: *Sullivan* v *West Yorkshire PTE* [1985] 2 All ER 134.

11.14 Expert reports in non-personal injury cases

Where the claim is not for personal injuries, a party who wishes to call at trial the maker of any expert report must apply before trial by Summons to the Master for directions as to whether he should disclose that report to his opponent: O.38 r36. Usually the application will be made on the Summons for Directions, soon after the close of pleadings, but can be made at any time. Until very recently there was a (rather weak) presumption that pre-trial disclosure of expert evidence in cases not involving an element of personal injury or death would not be ordered unless the court thought it 'desirable' so to direct. With effect from October 1987, however, the relevant rule, now O.38 r37, stands amended to reverse that presumption. It is the Master's duty to order that disclosure do take place unless there are 'special reasons' for withholding it, and it will be very rare that such reasons will be found.

On a more general level, note the view of the Court of Appeal that the Rules of the Supreme Court should be amended to enable judges and masters to refuse to allow expert evidence in certain circumstances: *Rawlinson* v *Westbrook and Another* (1995) The Times 25 January; *Liddell* v *Middleton* (1995) The Times 17 July. See Chapter 36, section 36.2 for further details.

11.15 Expert reports in personal injury and fatal accident cases

Where there is expert evidence in such a case which a party wishes to rely upon at trial, the rules provide for 'automatic' disclosure of the substance of that evidence to the other side within ten weeks of the close of pleadings: O.25 r8. Under that rule, however, each party is permitted to call only two medical experts and one expert of another type, for example, an engineer. If a party wishes to do either of the following things, he must apply to the Master by Summons for Directions as to whether expert evidence should be disclosed:

1. If he wishes to call more experts than allowed by r8. This is unusual unless the experts are experts in different fields such as orthopaedic, clinical and neurosurgery, or in mechanical or electrical engineering.
2. If he does not want to disclose the evidence of any expert, even if that expert is one allowed by r8.

In either of the cases above, the Master will order disclosure of the evidence 'unless ... there are special reasons for not doing so'.

In all cases, but particularly those involving permanent injuries, there are commonly several reports by the same or different experts assessing the injuries at stages in time, and giving a prognosis. There will also be reports which are merely commentary upon the reports disclosed by the other side. All fall within O.25 r8 and should be disclosed if a party intends to rely upon them at trial.

11.16 Mutual disclosure of expert evidence

Where each side has prepared an expert report on any issue, and that report must be disclosed whether automatically or under a court order, it is usual that the exchange of reports be 'mutual', that is, that each side send its reports to the other at the same time. This is to prevent one side having the unfair advantage of knowing what the other's expert will say before preparing its own report. The court can however order that exchange be 'sequential', that is, that one side send its report to the other before the other sends its own report. This will only be done where one side cannot properly instruct its expert to investigate allegations until it knows what will be alleged by the other. For instance, in a claim for noise-induced deafness, it is desirable that defendants know the types of noise the plaintiff alleges were harmful, and the places he was exposed to them so that they can tell their own expert where to look and what to look for, rather than being compelled to produce a lengthy and very expensive report covering all possible facts the plaintiff may rely upon: *Kirkup* v *BRB* [1983] 3 All ER 147. Sequential disclosure is appropriate to cases where the plaintiff alleges injuries contracted over a long period, such as deafness, allergies and asbestosis, but will probably not be ordered where the injuries arise from a single incident, such as a car crash or failed surgical operaion, or some other simple 'one-off' event.

11.17 Medical examination of injured plaintiffs

Defendants can only prepare useful medical reports and evidence if they are permitted to examine a plaintiff who claims to have been injured. The defendant has no 'right' to examine the plaintiff, but if the plaintiff refuses unreasonably to be examined by a doctor of the defendant's choosing, the court can stay his claim and order that it proceed no further unless and until he submits to examination: *Edmeades* v *Thames Board Mills* [1969] 2 QB 67. The following additional points should be noted:

1. the plaintiff cannot insist that his own doctor be present at the examination if that would add to the costs of the action: *Hall* v *Avon* [1980] 1 All ER 516;

2. although the plaintiff cannot insist, as a condition of being examined, that the defendant suply him with a copy of any report prepared, the court can impose such a condition: *Megarity* v *Ryan* [1980] 2 All ER 832;
3. if there is a significant risk that examination will cause further injury to the plaintiff, he may refuse to undergo it, and the court will not stay his action: *Prescott* v *Bulldog Tools* [1981] 3 All ER 869.

11.18 Disclosure by agreement of the parties

No order of the court is needed if the parties agree that expert evidence shall or shall not be disclosed, and that the experts concerned shall be called at trial without prior disclosure of their reports: O.38 r36. It is also very common for reports to be exchanged without order, and this has one advantage for the party making disclosure. Expert evidence disclosed by agreement cannot be used by the other side at trial; it sometimes happens that a party making disclosure does not later call the maker of a report to give evidence as a witness, and in such cases the opposing side may want to put the expert's report in evidence because it contains matter favourable to them. Where the evidence is disclosed pursuant to the rules, or by order, such use is allowed: O.38 r42.

11.19 Agreement of expert evidence

After exchange of expert reports, parties make great efforts to try to reach agreement on medical and other expert issues. This is done to save the considerable cost of calling expert witnesses. Sometimes the experts differ only in matters of detail, and parties compromise the detail and agree the substance of the reports, for example, if the plaintiff's doctor states that the injuries will cause him to go off work within five years, and the defendant's doctor estimates ten years, it is common for agreement to be reached on a figure of seven or eight years, since each side has the risk of his expert's opinion being rejected by the judge, and the difference in the value of the claim between five and ten years may be small. Judges encourage agreement of medical evidence wherever possible, and 'agreed reports' should be sent to the court within 14 days of their being agreed, so that the trial judge can read them: *Practice Direction* [1979] 1 WLR 290. In efforts further to define the issues between experts, and to encourage them to come to an agreement which makes it unnecessary for them to be called at trial, the court has power to order a 'without prejudice' meeting before or after reports have been exchanged: O.38 r38.

11.20 Witness statements

Provision has been made since 1989 for the court to order exchange of statements by witnesses as to fact: O.38 r2A. This exchange has been compulsory since 16 November 1992 in cases commenced before as well as after that date. Witnesses whose statements have not been disclosed may not be called to give evidence, nor may a witness statement be added to without leave of the court.

The statements of all non-expert witnesses whom the parties intend to call to give oral evidence must be exchanged within 14 weeks of the close of pleadings in cases governed by automatic directions. In other cases there will be a summons for directions where the direction will be made.

12

Preserving Evidence and Assets

12.1 Introduction

12.2 Anton Piller orders

12.3 Mareva injunctions

12.4 Finding the assets

12.5 The risk of disposal

12.6 Justice and convenience

12.7 Making the application

12.8 Other matters

12.9 Extension of Mareva

12.1 Introduction

In the great majority of actions both sides act with complete honesty. Plaintiffs and defendants do not conceal from each other documents which should be disclosed on discovery, nor do they destroy material evidence, and defendants who are found liable satisfy a judgment if they have the means to do so. There are however occasions when a defendant who knows he is about to be, or is being, sued, will act to defeat the plaintiff's claim by destroying evidence, or will try to deprive the plaintiff of any effective remedy by disposing of his assets or transferring them abroad, out of the plaintiff's reach. To combat such disgraceful conduct, the courts have evolved two very powerful interlocutory weapons, in the form of injunction. These are the *Anton Piller* and the *Mareva* injunctions. These are essentially High Court remedies; although the County Court has limited power to grant *Mareva* injunctions, it has none to make an *Anton Piller* Order: see County Courts Remedies Regulations 1991, SI 1991/1222.

The court has powers under s33 Supreme Court Act 1981 to make orders for the photography and preservation of evidence, but these are exercised mainly where the evidence is likely to deteriorate before trial through no fault of the parties, for example, where a building alleged to have been defectively designed must be demolished at once to prevent danger, or where the court wishes to have the subject-matter of an action independently examined, or to allow one party to have access to the other's premises for the purpose of inspecting the scene of an accident. The powers are not used and are not very useful where a party could destroy the evidence before the order was carried out, (though such destruction would be a contempt of court), and seems likely to do so.

12.2 Anton Piller orders

The acts upon which a plaintiff bases his claim may be, or be very nearly, criminal. There is every reason to suppose that the defendant will try to evade liability by concealing or destroying material evidence and documents. This is especially true where the claim is for infringement of copyright in video tapes, or of industrial processes protected by patent or the law relating to confidential information. Even where the action is not of this type, the court will grant aid to a plaintiff provided he complies with the conditions listed below.

The Anton Piller injunction is an interlocutory injunction now deriving its authority from s37 Supreme Court Act 1981. It allows the plaintiff to enter the defendant's premises and to remove evidence specified in the order (and sometimes orders are very widely worded) against the defendant's will. It has been called 'the civil search warrant' and is an invention, perhaps surprisingly, of Lord Denning. The *Practice Direction (Mareva Injunctions and Anton Piller Orders)* [1994] 4 All ER 52 now governs applications as to the proper manner for execution of orders. The power to issue Anton Piller orders is dealt with under O.29 r3. Anton Piller orders are granted only in the clearest cases, and where the plaintiff's action is almost certain to succeed. They can even be granted *before* the main proceedings have been started, but in such an event the court will require an undertaking from the plaintiff that he will issue and serve his Writ as soon as possible. Because of the need to keep the defendant ignorant of the intention to prevent him defeating the plaintiff's claim, they are always applied for and made *ex parte*. The application must be to a judge, as the Master has no power to grant an injunction of this kind.

To obtain an Anton Piller order, the plaintiff must do the following:

1. Make 'full and frank disclosure'. This means he must tell the court everything about his case, including the facts which may not be in his favour. If the defendant to an Anton Piller injunction contends that the plaintiff failed to make full and frank disclosure in application for the order, the proper forum for argument upon that contention is the full trial and not an interlocutory hearing: *Dormeuil Freres SA* v *Nicolian International Ltd* [1988] 3 All ER 197.
2. Show that he has a 'very strong *prima facie* case'. This entails persuading the court that his action against the defendant is very likely to succeed.

3. Show that any award of damages will be substantial. Anton Piller orders are not made when the value of the claim does not justify invasion of the defendant's rights to property and privacy.
4. Show that the property is likely to be destroyed or concealed if no order is made. This may take the form of showing the defendant's conduct on prior occasions, or his character, or any other reasonable fear that he will act to defeat the plaintiff's action. The plaintiff must adduce 'clear evidence' that the defendant is in possession of the evidence, and a 'real probability' that it will be destroyed or concealed if no order is made: *Jeffrey Rogers Knitwear* v *Vinola Manufacturing* (1984) The Times 5 December. If the defendants are professional people (for example, lawyers) it will be very difficult indeed to prove that the risk of concealment or destruction satisfies this high standard: *Randolph Fields* v *Watts* (1984) The Times 22 November.
5. Show that the English court has (or at least may well have) jurisdiction over the claim made in the main action: *Allertext* v *Advanced Data Communications* [1985] 1 All ER 395.

The injunction if granted is served on the defendant when the plaintiff comes to search for the evidence, and it should specify with precision the nature of the evidence sought. If the plaintiff uses force to enter the premises he is in breach of the injunction, but the defendant cannot raise that issue in the main action, and must bring a separate action for damages for trespass. The order can be drafted to include a right to take the evidence away, but as a condition of this the plaintiff must undertake to pay the defendant damages for any loss the defendant suffers from such removal if the plaintiff subsequently loses his action. The court can if necessary make a rough and ready assessment of the defendant's loss where the plaintiff breaches the undertaking or has obtained his order wrongfully, for instance, where he fails to take reasonable care of property he seizes and it emerges that such property ought never to have been taken away: *Columbia Pictures* v *Robinson* [1986] 3 All ER 338 Ch D.

The plaintiff's solicitor must attend to supervise the execution of an Anton Piller injunction, and, in his role as an officer of the court, explain to the defendant the nature of the order in ordinary language; the consequences of non-compliance, and his rights to obtain its discharge. The solicitor should be one experienced in the area of execution of these injunctions, and should ensure that while in the defendant's property, a list is taken of everything seized by the solicitor, which is then checked by the defendant. In addition, where items are removed, they should be insured if appropriate and third parties should not be informed until after the return date. For a comprehensive list of these duties, see *Universal Thermosensors* v *Hibben* (1992) The Times 12 February and see the *Practice Direction* [1994] 4 All ER 52.

Documents which are validly seized under the terms of an Anton Piller order are, in the judgment of the House of Lords, subject to the same implied undertaking as to the use that will be made of them as are documents revealed in the normal course of *inter partes* discovery under O.24 (see Chapter 11, section 11.11). The seizor may therefore apply them only for the purposes of the action in which he sought and obtained his Anton Piller order, and cannot without leave of the court commence a fresh action based upon further wrongdoing that the seized documents disclose. Since however one of the principal effects of an Anton Piller order is to obtain and preserve evidence of wrongful acts over and above those for which specific complaint is made on application for the order, it will be very common for the court to release the seizor from his undertaking and to permit him to use seized material as the basis for starting fresh proceedings relating to other infringements of his legal rights: *Crest Homes* v *Marks* [1987] 2 All ER 1074.

Where disclosure by the defendant of the evidence sought would put him at risk of criminal prosecution, he can claim the privilege against self-incrimination to refuse to answer questions applicable to other potential criminal defendants, except where the alleged incrimination is as to prosecution under the Copyright Act 1956 or similar statute. This is a matter of privilege and is dealt with in detail in evidence manuals: see s72 Supreme Court Act 1981.

Information obtained on the execution of an Anton Piller order may disclose infringement by a third party. Such information may be used in proceedings against such a third party; its use is not restricted to the proceedings in which it was obtained and the privilege relating to self-incrimination does not apply: see *Twentieth Century Fox* v *Tryare Ltd* [1991] FSR 58.

The defendant to an Anton Piller injunction cannot lawfully refuse to produce documents specified in the order on the sole ground that such production would have a tendency to expose him to proceedings for committal for contempt of court: *Garvin* v *Domus Publishing* (1988) 132 Sol Jo 1091.

A plaintiff to whom an Anton Piller is refused by the judge at first instance can appeal to the Court of Appeal with leave of the latter, but the rehearing will almost always be in open court unless counsel is of opinion that it should be in private.

An Anton Piller order may be made for the first time after judgment has been obtained, if that is necessary to preserve the value of the property ordered restored or otherwise to render the judment effective. The conditions for its issue are those which apply to its grant before judgment: *Distributori* v *Holford* [1985] 3 All ER 750.

12.3 Mareva injunctions

The Anton Piller order aims to prevent a defendant from destroying material evidence before trial. In the mid-1970s the court developed another injunction to curb the evil of defendants who divest themselves of funds before trial so as to make any judgment worthless. Although it is rare for a defendant to act in such a manner, there are cases where the amount of money at stake in the action is so large that the temptation to transfer all one's assets out of the reach of the English courts, or to dissipate them within this jurisdiction, is almost irresistible. There is therefore power in the High Court to grant an interlocutory order restraining a defendant from acting to defeat the value of any future award of debt or damages, by 'freezing' all or some of the property he has or may have in England or Wales or elsewhere in the world, or which may come into the jurisdiction at any time before judgment is given.

This injunction is the 'Mareva' injunction, named after the second case in which it was used. Granted originally under the court's general power to grant injunctions, it now has its basis in s37 Supreme Court Act 1981, which provides so far as is material:

> '1) The High Court may by order ... grant an injunction ... in all cases in which it appears to the court to be just and convenient to do so ...
> 3) The power of the High Court under subsection (1) above to grant an interlocutory injunction restraining a party to any proceedings from removing from the jurisdiction of the High Court, or otherwise dealing with, assets located within that jurisdiction shall be exercisable in cases where that party is, as well as in cases where he is not, domiciled, resident or present within that jurisdiction.'

The injunction can issue to restrain dealings with 'assets' of all kinds, and is not restricted to funds of money. Thus the order can attach to motor cars, works of art, jewellery, and so forth: *CBS* v *Lambert* [1983] Ch 37. It has been used quite regularly to prevent an aircraft leaving the jurisdiction, where that aircraft is the defendant's only substantial asset within it: see *Allen* v *Jambo Holdings* [1980] 1 WLR 1252. It is now also clear that the injunction may prohibit not only a removal of assets out of the jurisdiction, but also any dealing with or disposal of them within it, such as the transfer by a defendant of all his property to his wife, or to a holding or subsidiary company, or his simply spending it on intangibles such as a holiday. In short, the court may prohibit any dealing with the property which might reduce it in value before the plaintiff has the oportunity to execute any judgment he may obtain at trial: see *CBS* v *Lambert* (above).

The application for a Mareva is usually made very early in the proceedings, but can be made at any time after proceedings have been issued (and, it seems, even before their issue in rare cases of urgency), including for the first time after judgment has been given: *Orwell Steel* v *Asphalt* [1984] 1 WLR 1097. The applicant must show a number of things in order to obtain it:

1. That he has a 'good arguable case'. That is, that his claim in the main action is not frivolous, and has some chance of success. He need not prove that he is certain (or even likely) to succeed at trial, for interlocutory applications are not the proper forum for an investigation of the full merits of the claim.
2. That there is a 'real risk' that the defendant will act to defeat the value of an award of debt or damages by dealing with his assets or transferring them so that a judgment in the plaintiff's favour would go unsatisfied.
3. That it is just and convenient to grant the injunction. The Mareva, like all other injunctions, is a discretionary equitable remedy, and the court will look to any conduct by the applicant or defendant, and to all the circumstances of the case, before making an order.

12.4 Finding the assets

A defendant against whom a Mareva injunction is sought is unlikely to be willing to inform the applicant of the existence or whereabouts of his assets, or even to admit that he has any assets within the jurisdiction. The applicant must however prove in the more usual case that there are at least some assets. The following principles seem to have been established:

1. If the applicant can prove that the defendant has an overdrawn bank account within England and Wales, that is sufficient evidence of the defendant's having assets here, for banks do not normally lend money unless secured by some property. The applicant does not need to identify with precision the particular assets which comprise that security: *Third Chandris* v *Unimarine* [1979] QB 645.
2. Where the applicant is also claiming that certain monies or assets held by the defendant have been obtained through breach of fiduciary duty, or by a breach of copyright, or in some other way which gives the applicant some equitable right to trace that property and to have a constructive trust imposed upon it, the court can order the defendant to make disclosure of his bank statements, and to answer interrogatories, in order to identify the location of those assets so that a Mareva can attach to them: *Bankers Trust* v *Shapira* [1980] 1 WLR 1274 and *Bekhor* v *Bilton* [1981] 2 WLR 601.
3. The court *may* have power to order discovery of bank statements, and the administration of interrogatories, even in cases where the applicant's claim does not depend upon equitable rights of tracing, if that is necessary to locate assets which will be subject to the injunction, if the defendant will not reveal them voluntarily. This extension of the ancillary powers of the court to make the Mareva effective is presaged in *Bekhor* v *Bilton* (above) but is thus far in its infancy, evolving a little further in *House of Spring Gardens* v *Waite* (1984) The Times 12 November. If the injunction is to apply to such after-acquired property it must be carefully drawn: *TDK* v *Videochoice* [1985] 3 All ER 345. The power to order cross-examination of the defendant upon his affidavits will however not readily be exercised before the plaintiff has served a full Statement of Claim detailing his allegations, for otherwise the cross-examination could amount to an oppressive 'fishing expedition' by the plaintiff to discover facts later usable to commit the defendant for contempt of court: *Bayer* v *Winter (No 2)* [1986] 2 All ER 43 Ch D.

Even though the court may be unable to discover the location of all or any of the defendant's assets but is satisfied there are some within the jurisdiction, it may grant an injunction to cover all those which are in or which may come into existence within the jurisdiction; the injunction may thus refer simply to 'all or any' assets, and need not specify them. The possible width and effect of such an order is great encouragement to a defendant to tell the court about his assets, so that the injunction may attach only to so many of them as are sufficient to secure the applicant's position with respect to judgment. Thus, if the plaintiff's claim is for £10,000 and the defendant has £100,000 worth of assets within the jurisdiction, the injunction could prevent his dealing with any part of the £100,000 if the court does not know of its whereabouts. If the defendant discloses the location of £10,000 worth of the assets, only that amount will usually be made subject to the 'freezing' order, and he may deal freely with the remaining £90,000.

12.5 The risk of disposal

The court will not grant a Mareva injunction unless the applicant shows that there is a 'real risk' that in its absence the defendant will act to defeat the value of a judgment by transferring his assets or otherwise dealing with them. It is not enough that the defendant is domiciled or resident abroad; something more must evidence the risk: *Third Chandris* (above). That evidence must be 'clear evidence' that the defendant is likely to act to defeat the value of judgment: *CBS* v *Lambert* (above). It seems that the fact that a defendant has transferred his assets out of the jurisdiction in a previous action, in order to avoid judgment in that action, is a relevant factor, as also is evidence that preparations have been made for their removal (for example, by instructions given to a bank to transfer funds abroad), or that the defendant is known to be contemplating their removal or disposal: see generally *Rahman* v *Abu-Taha* [1980] 1 WLR 1268.

The degree of risk, and the evidence in support of it, will vary from one case to another and the High Court has recently restated that the risk *must* be proved to be a real one. A practice had grown up in the late 1970s of granting Mareva injunctions almost automatically and without inquiry into the danger of the judgment going unsatisfied, but the effect of the injunction upon traders (see section 12.6) can be so severe that the injunction is now more strictly controlled: see *Ninemia* v *Trave* [1983] 1 WLR 1420. Where the defendant has allegedly received large sums of money in breach of his fiduciary duty, and lives and works outside the European Union, the risk of his disposing of assets based in the United Kingdom may well be easy to establish: *Guinness plc* v *Saunders* (1987) The Independent 16 April Ch D.

12.6 Justice and convenience

It is now recognised that a Mareva injunction has the effect of 'freezing' the assets and property subject to it, prohibiting any dealings with any of that property unless the court gives permission (on application by the defendant or a third party prejudiced by the order) for a variation of the order. Where the defendant is a trader, and the property 'frozen' is his liquid assets, or those he uses in the course of his business, this can have very far-reaching consequences, and can cause much damage to the defendant's trade. It must be remembered that in most cases, the Mareva injunction is granted long before judgment is given, and the court does not have to be satisfied that the plaintiff *will* win the main action. The interests of both parties (and of third parties who could be affected by the order) must be carefully balanced, and the following principal rules have been evolved. They are guidelines only, and the court can depart from them in appropriate cases where, for instance, the defendant's conduct justifies such a departure:

1. The injunction should not attach itself to any part of the defendant's assets which exceeds the amount the plaintiff is likely to recover in his action by way of debt or damages. Thus, the court must examine the maximum value of the claim, and should make an order restricting dealings with assets only of such amount or value as does not exceed what the plaintiff could possibly recover at trial: *Third Chandris* (above).
2. The value of assets to which the injunction attaches must be taken as their value to the plaintiff and not to the defendant. Thus, an injunction will not be granted to restrain disposal of machinery which has a nominal scrap value (in relation to the amount the plaintiff claims in the action), but which is very valuable to the defendant because it represents a vital part of his business without which he will suffer great loss. The grant of an injunction in such circumstances would amount to 'holding the defendant to ransom' without conferring any real security upon the plaintiff, and the court will not apply such economic pressure: *Rasu Maritima* v *Pertimina* [1977] 3 WLR 518.
3. The injunction will be refused if it would have the effect of interfering substantially with the trade of an innocent third party. For instance, no Mareva will issue to 'freeze' a cargo which is held in the hold of a ship belonging to a third party, because such 'freezing' will deprive the third party of the chance to use his ship to carry other cargo and make further profits: *Galaxia* v *Mineralimportexport* [1982] 1 WLR 539. It is not enough that the plaintiff can offer to indemnify the third party against any such loss of profit, for the third party's loss is, it seems, not merely of money but also of goodwill and of the freedom to trade.
4. The injunction will however not be barred simply because some third party might be affected. If the third party can be adequately compensated by an indemnity from the plaintiff, and will not be prejudiced in his trading activities, the Mareva can issue. Thus, port authorities can be indemnified against loss of income from ships unable to unload cargo, or to move around the port, by reason of the injunction: see *Clipper Maritime* v *Mineralimportexport* [1981] 1 WLR 1262.
5. The injunction should allow for the exercise by innocent third parties of rights of set-off they may have. Thus, where the fund 'frozen' is in the hands of a third party (for example, a bank), the third party should be allowed to claim so much of it as he is entitled to by way of set-off against the defendant, and should not be prohibited from doing so by reason of the entire fund's being 'frozen': *Oceania* v *Mineralimportexport* [1983] 1 WLR 1294.

6. The injunction should not reduce the defendant to a state of poverty by preventing him from using any of his assets without the court's consent. He should be allowed to use such part of it as is necessary for his living expenses, and the injunction should expressly permit this, up to a stated amount: *PCW* v *Dixon* [1983] 2 All ER 158. However, the court will not allow expenditure, or the discharge of debts owed to third parties, out of any of the property to be subject to the Mareva, unless the defendant can show that he has no other funds out of which to make the payments, and that the proposed payments are necessary either for his own use or for the proper conduct of his business. In other words, the balance lies in favour of the plaintiff unless the defendant can show some form of undue 'hardship'.
7. The court has power to impose the injunction upon property which appears to belong beneficially to a non-party, if there is evidence suggesting that it in fact belongs in equity to the defendant, but in such cases the issue of equitable ownership will be ordered tried swiftly to reduce prejudice to that non-party: *SCF* v *Masri* [1985] 2 All ER 747.

Whenever a Mareva injunction is granted, the plaintiff is almost always required to provide an undertaking in damages to the defendant and (where necessary) an indemnity to third parties, in case it should turn out that the injunction was wrongly granted, that is, if the plaintiff loses the main action or recovers less than he claimed, so that the Mareva attached to some or all of the defendant's assets unnecessarily. However, it is open to the court to make the injunction even though the plaintiff could give no worthwhile undertaking, for example, where he is legally aided: *Allen* v *Jambo Holdings* [1980] 1 WLR 1252. Nonetheless, where an undertaking may be of little value, the court may have to be persuaded that the plaintiff has quite a strong case for success in the main action.

12.7 Making the application

Application is by Summons in the Queen's Bench Division, by Motion in the Chancery Division. *The Practice Direction (Mareva Injunctions and Anton Piller Orders)* [1994] 4 All ER 52 governs such applications. The Master has no jurisdiction to grant the injunction and application must be made to the judge. Evidence is normally filed by way of affidavit, and the applicant must take care to comply, as far as possible, with the following requirements:

1. He must make 'full and frank disclosure'. This means he must state all facts known to him, even if they are unfavourable to his case. If an applicant for Mareva fails to make full and frank disclosure in his *ex parte* application, the court will almost always discharge the Mareva with costs against him, but may in its discretion continue the injunction or grant a fresh Mareva if the applicant made his mistake in good faith and remedies it: *Lloyds Bowmaker* v *Britannia*

Arrow Holdings [1988] 3 All ER 178 and *Brink's-Mat* v *Elcombe* [1988] 3 All ER 188. The drastic consequences of non-disclosure were illustrated in *Ali* v *Moneim* [1989] 2 All ER 404 (injunction discharged – without immediate reimposition – even though this meant that the defendant would have an opportunity of making away with his assets; and the defendant allowed to seek damages for non-disclosure without having to wait until after trial).
2. He must give full particulars of his claim, to allow the court to assess both the chances of its success and its likely amount.
3. He must give his grounds for believing that there is a 'real risk' of the assets being disposed of before any judgment against the defendant could be executed: see section 12.5.
4. The applicant should be required, where appropriate, to support his cross-undertaking in damages by a payment into court or by the provision of a bond by an insurance company. Alternatively, a payment by way of such security could be held by the applicant's solicitor pending further order.

12.8 Other matters

The following points should also be noted in relation to Mareva injunctions;

1. The defendant may apply to the court for a variation of the injunction to allow him to make a specific payment or payments from the fund 'frozen' by it. The court will consider whether the variation is reasonably necessary.
2. The injunction does not give the plaintiff any proprietary rights in the property subject to it: it merely provides security for any eventual judgment award of debt or damages.
3. No injunction will be granted unless the main action in which relief is claimed can be properly tried in England. Thus, if the proper forum for trial lies outside England and Wales, no Mareva will issue (*The Siskina* [1977] 3 WLR 803); in cases where it is unclear whether the High Court has such jurisdiction, a Mareva injunction can be granted until the issue of jurisdiction has been determined (usually as a preliminary issue): s24 Civil Jurisdiction and Judgments Act 1982. When s25 of that Act is brought into force, the High Court will have power to grant any injunction even if it is beyond doubt that the English courts have no power at all to try the main action.
4. An injunction cannot attach *in rem* to assets so long as they remain situate outside England and Wales, but the court seems to have power to grant a Mareva in respect of such assets, since Mareva operates only *in personam* against the defendant himself rather than against the property specified in it: see *Babanaft International* v *Bassatne* (1988) The Independent June 30; *Derby & Co* v *Weldon (No 1)* [1990] Ch 48 and *Derby & Co* v *Weldon (No 4)* [1990] Ch 65. The defendant may thus be compelled in appropriate cases to disclose the

whereabouts of assets out of the jurisdiction: *Allied Arab Bank* v *Hajjar* [1987] 3 All ER 739.

Each case must however be taken on its own facts, and there is no presumption that the Mareva injunction will be continued even though the plaintiff shows that he acted in good faith in omitting to make full and frank disclosure. The court must assess the importance of the matters which were not disclosed on the *ex parte* hearing, and the extent to which the plaintiff was to blame for that non-disclosure: *Behbehani* v *Salem* [1989] 2 All ER 143 CA.

5. If the defendant, or any other person who has notice of the injunction, deals with property subject to it in a way forbidden by it, he is guilty of a contempt of court and liable to fine and/or imprisonment (see Chapter 18, section 18.13). Injunctions are therefore carefully worded to inform a defendant and others precisely what they may and may not do with the property.
6. Third parties who are prejudiced by the injunction may apply for its discharge or variation to allow them to be paid from funds subject to it, or to carry on their business (see section 12.6).
7. If a plaintiff has obtained a Mareva over certain of the defendant's assets which are themselves the subject of litigation between the defendant and a third party, the plaintiff cannot intervene in that litigation to protect the value of the assets from being reduced by virtue of any judgment given in that litigation (for example, by an order that they be delivered to the third party), for he has no interest in the assets of any proprietary nature: *Sanders Lead* v *Entores* (1983) The Times 1 December;
8. Although a Mareva granted before judgment is not registrable as a 'pending land action' within the Land Charges Act 1972, according to *Stockler* v *Fourways Estate* [1984] 1 WLR 25, a Mareva granted or continued after judgment probably is so registrable, being given in aid of executing a judgment.
9. While Mareva injunctions and Anton Piller orders are not available in the county court (see section 12.1), they may be obtained in the High Court in relation to county court proceedings upon temporary transfer.

12.9 Extension of Mareva

The width of the power conferred by s37 Supreme Court Act 1981, and its relation to the Mareva and Anton Piller jurisdictions, has allowed the Court of Appeal to grant an order restraining an individual defendant from departing England and Wales pending his revealing the location of assets and evidence to be made subject to one or more of those recognised interlocutory reliefs. Although the duration of such an order will be no greater than is absolutely necessary, it is a powerful weapon in the fight against those intent on defeating the value of the claim and the process of the court: *Bayer* v *Winter* [1986] 1 All ER 733.

There is a growing awareness of the value of this ancillary jurisdiction, and the courts are eagerly invoking it to prevent the controllers of insolvent companies from departing abroad before creditors are able, through the medium of an oral examination by the court, to trace the whereabouts of assets, allegedly transferred in breach of statutory or fiduciary duties: *Re Oriental Credit Bank* [1988] 2 WLR 172.

The jurisdiction is particularly useful where a defendant moves himself and his assets from one country to another in attempts to evade the plaintiff's obtaining a worthwhile judgment: *Arab Monetary Fund* v *Hashim* (1989) The Times 16 January.

13

Interlocutory Injunctions and Interim Payments

13.1 Introduction

13.2 Interlocutory injunctions

13.3 Defamation cases

13.4 Secondary picketing

13.5 Interlocutory injunction in effect whole relief

13.6 Facts and law clear

13.7 Plaintiff or defendant certain to succeed

13.8 The survival of *Cyanamid*

13.9 Undertakings on damages

13.10 Undertakings in lieu of injunctions

13.11 Quia timet injunctions

13.12 Mandatory injunctions

13.13 Procedure

13.14 Interim payments

13.15 Interim payments for debt

13.16 Contributory negligence

13.17 Manner of payment

13.18 Additional matters

13.19 Procedure for interim payment

13.1 Introduction

Between the issue of proceedings and judgment in the action, the plaintiff will want to do all he can to protect his position. Even if all the time limits laid down in the rules are followed, it may be several years before the action is finally disposed of. A plaintiff who claims debt or damages may suffer severe hardship if he has to wait so long before receiving his money. One who claims a final injunction may see his business or property ruined beyond repair before the trial date is reached. It is therefore necessary to see what, if any, 'remedies' are available to a plaintiff pending trial.

The orders to be considered below are interlocutory injunctions and interim payments. In essence, each is a means by which a plaintiff can obtain at least a part of the relief he asks for in his pleadings before the trial, though if he subsequently loses his action he will have to compensate the defendant for being put to the trouble of complying with an injunction or paying money on account.

13.2 Interlocutory injunctions

The court has power by s37 Supreme Court Act 1981 to:

> '... grant an injunction ... in all cases in which it appears to the court to be just and convenient to do so ... either unconditionally or on such terms and conditions as the court thinks just'.

This power when applied to injunctions made pending the trial is exercised according to set principles, though it is always open to the court to depart from those principles if it sees fit. The equivalent power in the County Court is derived from the County Courts Act 1984 s38.

In the early 1970s it was realised that the grant of an injunction before trial often made unnecessary the pursuance of a full injunction at trial. If the plaintiff sought the restriction of publication of a certain television programme, an interlocutory injunction would prevent its being screened, and even if the plaintiff lost the action at trial, that would be so far in the future that the defendant would no longer be interested in showing it. The danger is that interlocutory injunctions are often granted on very little evidence, and always without the full oral hearing and argument that occurs at full trial, and it was thought that mistakes could be made and injustice done by deciding in effect the whole action on an interlocutory hearing.

The House of Lords therefore laid down definite principles to be applied by all courts in granting interlocutory injunctions. As will be seen, it is now accepted that those definite principles are subject to so many exceptions (created by the Court of Appeal and High Court) that they have almost ceased to exist, and the practice of the courts has reverted to the previous law. The leading case is *American Cyanamid v Ethicon* [1975] AC 396, concerning an action for infringement of a patent. The plaintiff asked the court to prevent the defendant producing any more allegedly infringing products until the full trial, and the defendant claimed that if production were not to continue he would be forced out of business and ruined. The House held that the guiding principles were these:

1. The plaintiff must show that there is a 'serious question to be tried' in his action. This seems to mean that the action must not be obviously hopeless; it will not be difficult to prove.
2. He must show that the 'balance of convenience' is in favour of the injunction being granted. The court looks at whether one of the parties cannot be adequately compensated by an award of damages, for instance, if grant will put the defendant out of business, and the plaintiff can be properly compensated by damages, balance of convenience will be against the injunction. If refusal will put the plaintiff out of business, and the defendant can be compensated with damages for loss of profit in the meantime, convenience favours granting the injunction.
3. If both parties or neither party can be adequately compensated by damages, then usually the court will seek to preserve the status quo, for example, if a party is in business, to allow him to continue; if he is erecting a building, to allow it to rise. Difficulties can arise in determining what is the 'status quo' in any particular case. Where, for instance, the defendant's former employer seeks an interlocutory injunction to restrain breaches of a covenant in restraint of trade, it seems that the status quo is judged according to the circumstances as they were at the date before the breaches commenced, and not as they are at the date of the hearing for the injunction, some breaches having by then already occurred and continuing: *Unigate Dairies* v *Bruce* (1988) The Times 2 March.
4. In the last resort, if the status quo is not discernible, or there are factors strongly against preserving it, the court can look to the evidence in the case and see whether one party has a very much stronger case than the other, and grant or refuse the injunction on the 'merits' of that case.

Cyanamid requires the court to disregard the merits of the case, claim and defence, and the relative strength of each, unless no answer is got from balance of convenience. The Court of Appeal did not like this fettering of its discretion, quickly set about exploiting the loophole left by Lord Diplock in his speech that 'other special factors could be considered in individual cases', and found 'individual cases' with amazing regularity. It is now possible to classify cases in which it will be the strength of the evidence presented by each at the interlocutory hearing, and not the balance of convenience, which will determine the grant or refusal of the injunction. The list that follows is not closed, and may well be extended in future cases.

13.3 Defamation cases

In very many cases a plaintiff issues a Writ for libel to stifle unpleasant revelations, but never intends that the action come to trial. This is a 'gagging Writ'. Were the court to apply *Cyanamid*, it would be compelled to grant an injunction against further publications, the balance of convenience being in favour of the grant. It is now clear that no injunction will be granted where the defendant alleges that the alleged defamatory remarks are true (justification), or qualified privilege, unless the plaintiff can show that they were published maliciously, since the right of free speech is not to be lightly stifled (*Bestobell* v *Bigg* [1975] FSR 421 and *Haras* v *Baltic Mercantile* [1982] 1 WLR 959), even though the defendant chooses a 'flamboyant and vulgar method of airing his complaints' such as driving around a housing estate with his house door roped to the front of his Rolls-Royce, a placard attached accusing the plaintiffs of being bad workmen: *Crest Homes* v *Ascott* (1975) The Times 4 February. The public interest in preserving freedom of speech will also be an important factor to be taken into account where the cause of action is conspiracy to injure the plaintiff by publishing allegations against him that he is financially unsound and dishonest: *Femis-Bank (Anguilla) Ltd* v *Lazar* [1991] 2 All ER 865.

13.4 Secondary picketing

Where an employer claims that picketing of his premises is in breach of the law, as secondary picketing, and the pickets claim that their action is not secondary picketing, the court will look to the strength of each claim, in the light of the law, and if the pickets seem unlikely to be able to make out their defence at full trial, an injunction will issue: *Mercury Communications* v *Stanley* (1983) The Times 10 November.

13.5 Interlocutory injunction in effect whole relief

Where the interlocutory order will have the effect of giving the plaintiff substantially the whole of the relief he claims in the action, the court will look at the strength of this case, on evidence and argument, and will refuse the injunction if he seems unlikely to win at trial. This encourages the plaintiff to get on with his claim if he wants a full injunction rather than allowing him to sit back and take things easy in the shade of an interlocutory order: *Cayne* v *Global Resources* [1984] 1 All ER 225, where an injunction to prevent sale of a company's assets on a particular day was refused. This is the same principle applied before *Cyanamid*: see *Woodford* v *Smith* [1970] 1 WLR 806. If the case for the plaintiff is strong then of course the injunction can issue: *Evans* v *BBC* (1974) The Times 26 February, where an injunction was granted to compel the broadcast of a party political message in the days preceding an election and in accordance with a contract: see also *Cambridge Nutrition Ltd* v *BBC* [1990] 3 All ER 523. Similarly, where an employer seeks an interlocutory injunction to restrain breach of a covenant in restraint of trade, and it appears that the time limitation set by the covenant will have expired by the date a full trial of the action can be arranged, the court is very likely to scrutinise the strength of the employer's *prima facie* case for the validity of the covenant, and the fact that the interlocutory order will in substance be decisive of the substantive claim is a very weighty factor in the balance of convenience: *John Michael Design plc* v *Cooke* [1987] 2 All ER 332.

13.6 Facts and law clear

Where all the facts of a dispute are not themselves disputed, and the law on issues is clear, the court can rightly look at the case as if there were a full trial on all evidence, and balance of convenience has no place as it could itself work injustice. This has greatest application to restrictive covenants against competition, where the only issue between the parties is the legality and construction of the covenants: *Office Overload* v *Gunn* [1977] FSR 39 and *Bridge* v *Deacons* (1984) The Times 28 March.

13.7 Plaintiff or defendant certain to succeed

Where from the evidence before the judge it is clear that one side or the other must succeed at full trial, either from admissions of his opponent or from the law applicable, that fact will govern grant or refusal of the injunction: *Re Cable* [1976] 3 All ER 417. It is unreal to compel a judge to disregard the strength of the evidence and to apply the balance of convenience test in such cases.

13.8 The survival of *Cyanamid*

In the light of the serious inroads into the *Cyanamid* rules (on one occasion by the House of Lords itself (*NWL* v *Woods* [1979] 3 All ER 614), the correctness of such decisions as *Fellowes* v *Fisher* [1975] 3 WLR 184 and *Hubbard* v *Pitt* [1975] 2 WLR 254 must now be in doubt. *Hubbard's* case would perhaps be decided the same way today, but on the ground of the strength of the plaintiff's case rather than balance of convenience. *Fellowes'* case also might produce the same result, but on the basis that, although the facts were not in dispute, the law was not clear, so that a defendant should be allowed to continue his business. Until the House of Lords or statute reverse the general principles, all the cases in sections 13.3 to 13.7 must be seen as exceptions, but it is as well to remember that any injunction is a discretionary remedy no matter what are the principles the court must apply in deciding how to exercise its discretion.

13.9 Undertakings on damages

Whenever a plaintiff is granted an interlocutory injunction, he must, unless the court orders otherwise in its discretion, agree that he will indemnify the defendant against any loss the latter might suffer if it later emerges that the injunction should not have been granted, that is, the plaintiff's action fails, or the injunction is discharged because the plaintiff misled the court which granted it. This is an 'undertaking as to damages'. Breach of the undertaking is a contempt of court, and in certain cases the plaintiff may be required to pay into court funds sufficient to meet the undertaking (cf Mareva injunctions, Chapter 12, section 12.6). It is unusual for undertakings to be required from the Crown, though they are often given, and the court can refuse the Crown an injunction if no undertaking is forthcoming: *Hoffman La Roche* v *S of S* [1975] AC 295. When a plaintiff obtains an interlocutory injunction against one or some of several defendants but not against the others, the usual undertaking in damages extends to and can be invoked by all the defendants, not just the defendant against whom the injunction was granted: *Dubai Bank Ltd* v *Galadari (No 2)* (1989) The Times 11 October.

13.10 Undertakings in lieu of injunctions

It is very common for a party against whom an interlocutory injunction is sought to offer to the plaintiff an 'undertaking' in the same terms as the injunction asked for. This saves the time and expense of a court hearing, and the undertaking has much the same force as a court order. Where it is agreed, the undertaking as to damages given by the plaintiff is properly termed a 'cross-undertaking', though that term is much abused to describe a normal undertaking on grant of a formal injunction.

13.11 *Quia timet* injunctions

A plaintiff who fears that his rights are about to be infringed may apply to the court for an injunction to prevent the infringement, even before he has issued his originating process in the action. Such injunctions are termed *quia timet* (what is feared) and are very rare in interlocutory proceedings. It is only granted where the plaintiff has a very strong claim, can show a very real risk that the threatened infringement will occur, that damages will be an inadequate remedy to him if the infringement takes place, and that (where the injunction is to be a mandatory one, requiring the defendant to take some positive step) the cost of complying with the injunction does not place an unreasonable burden on the defendant (unless he has acted in total disregard of the plaintiff's rights). The principles are fully set out in *Redland Brick* v *Morris* [1970] AC 652.

13.12 Mandatory injunctions

Interlocutory injunctions which require the defendant to take some positive step, such as pulling down a building rather than simply stopping to build it, are much less frequently granted than those which merely require him to discontinue an activity. It seems that here again *Cyanamid* does not apply, and that the plaintiff's claim must be very strong if the court is to grant one. Having in mind the extent of the expense and loss caused to a defendant through compliance, a plaintiff should think long and hard before asking for one, since he will undoubtedly be required to give an undertaking in damages: see especially *Shepherd* v *Sandham* [1971] Ch 340. The jurisdiction exists to compel a landlord to restore heating to his tenants pending the trial of an action in which he is allegedly in breach of his covenants to them: *Parker* v *Camden London BC* [1985] 2 All ER 680.

13.13 Procedure

For all interlocutory injunctions the procedure is as follows:

1. Summons or motion in the High Court; or General Form N16A in the County Court.
2. Affidavit setting out the facts of the claim and the grounds for grant of the injunction.
3. The hearing is inter partes unless for some special reason it is *ex parte*, for example, urgency or secrecy is needed as in Anton Piller applications. On *ex parte* applications the court will hear the application even though none of the necessary documents have been filed, and no proceedings yet issued, if counsel undertakes on the plaintiff's behalf to issue and file them as soon as possible.

In the High Court the procedure is contained in O.29 r1; in the County Court, CCR O.13 r6.

13.14 Interim payments

Interlocutory injunctions help plaintiffs who wish to prevent a defendant from doing certain things pending the outcome of the trial, or to compel him to carry out works or some other positive act. They are of no assistance to a plaintiff whose claim is for debt or damages, unless of the Anton Piller or Mareva type (see Chapter 12). The only procedure by which a plaintiff can get money from a defendant before trial (or assessment of damages by the court if liability has been admitted or judgment obtained) is by way of interim payment under O.29 rr9–19, unless the defendant pays voluntarily. These rules also apply to the County Court by virtue of CCR O.13 r12 with some minor variations.

Interim payment means 'a payment *on account* of any debt, damages or other sum (excluding any costs) which a party may be held liable to pay to or for the benefit of another party if a final judgment or order of the court is given or made in favour of that other party': s32(5) Supreme Court Act 1981 (County Courts Act 1984, s50(5) uses virtually the same definition). It is therefore an 'advance payment' and if the party receiving it loses at trial he must repay it, subject to a little-used discretion of the court to direct that it need not be repaid: O.29 r19. It may be made in any claim for damages, including one for 'mesne profits' for the unlawful use of land, though its most frequent application is in personal injury claims. It applies also in cases of claims for debt, for example, the price of goods sold, or money due under a loan or guarantee, and it applies to counterclaims.

No application for an interim payment on account of *damages* will succeed unless the applicant can show the following:

1. that the defendant has admitted liability; or
2. that the plaintiff has obtained judgment against the defendant for damages to be assessed (that is, in default or under O.14); or
3. that, if the action proceeded to trial, the plaintiff would obtain judgment for substantial damages against the defendant, or if there are two or more defendants, against any one of them: O.29 r11(c). The applicant must here prove which of the defendants is almost certain to be liable to him. It is not enough for him to prove that he would succeed against at least one of them – the particular defendant must be identified: *Breeze* v *McKennon* (1985) The Times 23 November.

Where there are two or more defendants to an action, against all of whom damages are claimed, the plaintiff must show that he will succeed against the particular defendant from whom he claims an interim payment. The standard of proof applicable to the interlocutory application is the ordinary civil standard, though it may be difficult to attain: see *Ricci Burns Ltd* v *Toole and Covey* [1988] 1 WLR 993 and *Shanning International Ltd* v *George Wimpey Ltd* [1988] 3 All ER 475.

O.29 r11(c) in (3) above is designed to cover personal injury cases, where summary judgment is hardly ever given because there may be issues of contributory negligence which require a full hearing (see Chapter 7, section 7.4), but it is just that some payment be possible. In addition, if the claim is for personal injuries, the plaintiff has to show one of the following:

1. that the defendant is insured in respect of the claim; or
2. that the defendant is a public authority (who are, even in these difficult times, presumed to be insured or to have the means to pay); or
3. that the defendant is a person whose means and resources are such as to *enable him to make the interim payment* (note that his ability to pay the final judgment is not relevant at this stage): O.29 r11.

13.15 Interim payments for debt

Where the claim is not for damages but for debt (or perhaps *quantum meruit*) the plaintiff has to show either that he has obtained judgment for an account (this is like judgment for damages to be assessed), or that if his claim is for mesne profits for the unlawful use and occupation of land he will recover these profits at trial even if he does not recover possession of the land, or that he would win the action if it went to trial and recover a substantial sum of money: O.29 r12. There is no definition of what is 'substantial' and it is left to the court's discretion.

13.16 Contributory negligence

In deciding to grant interim payments, the court has regard to the likely degree of contributory negligence and to any counterclaim which may be raised. If ordered, the amount is 'not to exceed a reasonable proportion of the damages which in the opinion of the court are likely to be recovered': O.29 r11. Since opinions on the quantum of damages, especially in personal injuries, differ so much between judges and Masters (and members of the Bar) a rule of practice has been evolved whereby a maximum of two-thirds of the expected damages is regarded as 'reasonable'; this is to prevent the Master's opinion, if too high, resulting in the plaintiff having to repay some of the money after judgment because the judge reaches a lower (but equally 'correct') figure. In claims other than for damages, the whole amount may be awarded.

The strength and quantum of a counterclaim are relevant both to determine whether the plaintiff will recover substantial damages at trial and to determine the amount of any interim payment which is in question: *Shanning International Ltd* v *George Wimpey Ltd* [1988] 3 All ER 475.

13.17 Manner of payment

Money ordered to be paid is paid directly to the plaintiff unless the court otherwise directs (and it is rare for it to do so unless it thinks the plaintiff will squander the payment): O.29 r13. But if the plaintiff is a minor or mental patient, payment is into court, where it remains until the court releases it, in whole or by instalments, to the plaintiff's guardian for the plaintiff's benefit. The minimum sum commonly ordered to be paid is £500, whatever the nature of the claim or the identity of the plaintiff.

13.18 Additional matters

The following points should also be noted:

1. The fact that an interim payment has been made must not be disclosed to the trial judge – it might influence him in his judgment of liability and quantum: O.29 r14.
2. After judgment the court takes the payment into account in deciding how much more, if anything, the defendant must pay the plaintiff, or how much of the payment the plaintiff must refund.
3. Further applications can be made as the action progresses, even if past ones have been refused, if good reason is shown.
4. There is apparently power to order repayment of an interim payment at any stage before trial, for example, if the action is discontinued, when, since leave is needed to discontinue, the court adjusts and usually orders repayment: see *Castanho v Brown & Root* [1980] 3 WLR 991.
5. Where an injured plaintiff is the victim of an uninsured driver of a motor vehicle, and seeks to recover his damages ultimately from the Motor Insurers' Bureau under the terms of the Bureau's 1972 agreement with the Secretary of State, the court has no power to make an interim payment against the Bureau, since the claim cannot be brought within the terms of O.29 r11: the Bureau is not the 'defendant' in strict law, and cannot be treated as being the defendant driver's 'insurer': *Powney v Coxage* (1988) The Times 8 March.
6. The court has a discretion to order payment of interest on the interim payment to be repaid.

13.19 Procedure for interim payment

The defendant should first be asked by letter to make a payment. In very many personal injury cases the defendant's insurance company will make a voluntary payment without admission of liability but subject to repayment if the plaintiff loses the case. If the request is denied, the plaintiff takes out a Summons before the Master, and files an affidavit containing the following matters:

1. verifying the facts of the claim;
2. setting out under which head of O.29 r11 the application is made;
3. if the claim is for personal injuries, verifying which of the three classes of defendant (insured, public authority, rich) the defendant falls into;
4. exhibiting (that is, attaching to the affidavit) documents evidencing special damage, for example, loss of earnings, expenses, already incurred;
5. if the claim is for personal injuries, exhibiting any medical reports relied upon, and (sometimes) how much is wanted as interim payment;
6. in a Fatal Accident Act claim, setting out the names and ages of the dependants on whose behalf the action is being brought.

The Summons and affidavit are served on the defendant ten clear days before the hearing. Although the Summons can state how much will be asked for at the hearing, it rarely does so. At the hearing the Master hears argument and reads the affidavit (and any affidavit sworn by the defendant in reply) and makes his order. He may also treat the application as a Summons for Directions even if the parties have not issued one, and give the usual directions for place of trial, exchange of expert evidence, number of expert witnesses, and so forth. If the claim is for personal injuries, and falls within O.25 r8 (see Chapter 11, section 11.10), strictly these directions are not necessary unless either party wants orders different from those given in r8.

Applications for interim payments are commonly joined with a Summons for Directions, or for summary judgment under O.14 or O.113 (CCR O.9 r14; O.24) or for judgment on admissions (see Chapter 7 and Chapter 9, section 9.9). No application may be made until after the Writ has been served and the time for acknowledgment of service has expired (O.29 r10), and no interim payment can be given if the action was started by Originating Summons, Motion or Petition.

14

The Effect of Delay

14.1 Introduction

14.2 Limitation periods

14.3 Contract

14.4 Tort

14.5 Fraud and mistake

14.6 Trespassers and land

14.7 Limitation periods in personal injury actions

14.8 'Significant'

14.9 Identity of the defendant

14.10 Disapplying the limitation period

14.11 Limitation in claims for death

14.12 Claimants under a disability

14.13 Amendment of proceedings after expiry of limitation

14.14 Delay after service of proceedings

14.15 Effect of dismissal

14.16 Dismissal and limitation

14.17 Delay by agreement

14.1 Introduction

Whenever rights are infringed, the substantive law lays down a fixed time within which an action to enforce those rights must be started. If no action is started within that time, the defendant is permitted to plead that the plaintiff's claim to relief is 'statute-barred', but if that defence is not raised the action can properly continue.

The set time is termed the *limitation period*. Except in claims for personal injuries and death, once that time has expired the defendant is entitled to plead a limitation defence as a complete defence to a claim, unless the court exercises powers under s35 Limitation Act 1980 to join him as a defendant in an action which was started, before the limitation period expired, against some other defendant. In personal injury and fatal accident claims, there is a discretion to 'extend' the limitation period. A claim is begun and an action started when proceedings are *issued*.

Even where a plaintiff has started his action within the relevant limitation period, he may be dilatory in pursuing it through the interlocutory stages of service of pleadings, discovery and inspection, setting down for trial, and so forth. The court has power to strike out his action for such delay, but the exercise of that power depends in the main upon the prejudice the delay has caused to the defendant. In such cases, delay by a plaintiff is termed *'want of prosecution'*.

There may be delay by a defendant in the action, in serving pleadings, in giving discovery, and other matters before trial. The plaintiff is obliged to proceed with reasonable diligence once a Writ is issued. Delay thereafter, even if within the discovery period, would be relied upon to support an application to strike out: *Roth v CS Lawrence (P J Cook & Co (A Firm) (3rd Party))* [1991] 1 WLR 399 CA.

14.2 Limitation periods

Where a claim arises in contract, tort or some other field, times are set in which a claim for damages, or an injunction, or some other relief, must be started. It is important to understand that a failure to begin an action within these time limits does not deprive the plaintiff of his rights, but rather provides a defence which a defendant may (and usually will) choose to rely upon. The limits differ according to the nature of the claim. The rules are common to both High Court and County Court.

14.3 Contract

Where the claim is based upon a breach of contract, the plaintiff has six years in which to begin his claim, calculated from the date of the breach, not from the date upon which that breach causes damage. If a solicitor drafts a will in breach of his client's instructions, it is the date that the will is drafted that will be the date the limitation period begins to run, even though no damage is done until the testator dies and it is discovered that incorrect dispositions have been made: *D W Moore & Co Ltd v Ferrier* [1988] 1 All ER 400.

14.4 Tort

A claim founded upon tort (*other* than personal injury) must be started within six years of the occurrence of the damage. The date damage occurs is the date it actually occurs and not the date upon which it could have been discovered or upon which it was discovered, even though the damage could not possibly have been discovered within the six years: *Pirelli* v *Oscar Faber* [1983] 2 WLR 6. Where a plaintiff has an action in both contract and tort, he can choose to sue in whichever cause of action is most favourable to him. If the limitation period has expired for a claim in contract but not for tort, an action in tort will not be statute-barred: *Midland Bank* v *Hett, Stubbs & Kemp* [1979] Ch 384, where the action for negligence was started within six years of the testator's death, which was the date the damage 'occurred' through negligent drafting of the will. See also *Dove* v *Banham Locks* [1983] 3 WLR 1436, *London Congregational* v *Harris* [1985] 1 All ER 335 and *Ketteman* v *Hansel* [1985] 1 All ER 352. Where the plaintiff buys premises on the strength of the defendant's negligent survey of them, time begins to run in tort at the date he becomes bound to buy them, and not at such (later) date upon which the damage manifests itself and the survey is found to be incorrect: *Secretary of State* v *Essex, Goodman Suggitt* [1986] 2 All ER 69 QBD.

The Latent Damage Act 1986 has added ss14A and B to the Limitation Act 1980. They apply to tortious actions in negligence other than personal injury and provide an alternative limitation period of three years from the 'starting date'. This is defined (in s14A(5)) as 'the earliest date on which the plaintiff or any person in whom the cause of action was vested before him first had both the knowledge required for bringing an action for damages in respect of the relevant damage and a right to bring such an action'. In other words, the Latent Damage Act has introduced to general negligence actions a provision similar to that found in personal injury actions (see 14.7 below). However, there is a 'long-stop' limitation period of 15 years under s14B from the date of the alleged breach.

In *Hallam-Eames and Others* v *Merrett and Others* (1995) The Times 25 January, the Court of Appeal considered the question of the knowledge required and held that the plaintiff had to have knowledge of those facts which were causally relevant for the purposes of an allegation of negligence.

14.5 Fraud and mistake

Whenever a claim is based upon a defendant's fraud or a plaintiff's mistake (the latter 'mistake' in contract) the limitation period is six years whatever the nature of the claim, and that time begins at the date the plaintiff discovered the fraud or mistake, or the date when he could with 'reasonable diligence' have discovered it, whichever is the earlier. A plaintiff who buys a painting alleged by the defendant to be by a famous painter is in general entitled to rely upon the plaintiff's representations and need not have it independently valued, so that the six years begin to run only when he is or should be alerted to some cogent facts which put him on notice that the representation is untrue: *Peco* v *Hazlitt Galleries* [1983] 3 All ER 193.

14.6 Trespassers and land

Actions for the possession of land against squatters and others in unlawful possession must be started within 12 years of the first unlawful possession, unless that possession is not continuous. This area of law is termed 'adverse possession' and is subject to special rules, discussion of which falls outside the scope of this book.

14.7 Limitation periods in personal injury actions

Where a plaintiff claims in respect of personal injuries, whether the claim is based upon a breach of contract or a tort, he must begin his claim within a period which in effect creates *two* limitation time limits; or within three years of the injury occurring or within three years of the date of 'knowledge' if this is later. The first period begins at the same time as that of any other tort, at the date the damage 'occurs', even though it was not, and could not possibly have been, discovered within three years thereafter. Thus, a plaintiff injured in a road accident has three years from the date of the accident as his 'first' limitation period, even though in that accident he may suffer brain damage which does not manifest itself for many years, for it is on that date that his cause of action in respect of all damage done accrues to him: s11 Limitation Act 1980.

There is however a 'second' limitation period in personal injury cases, which may apply to extend the time for commencing the action. In the majority of cases this period will begin and end at the same time as the 'first' period, but it may start after that first period has expired, or while it is still running. In addition to the three years from the date the damage occurs and the cause of action accrues, an injured plaintiff has three years from the date of 'knowledge' within which to start his action: s12 Limitation Act 1980. The date of knowledge is the date upon which the plaintiff knew all the following things:

1. that his injury was 'significant'; and
2. that it was *caused* in whole or in part by the act or omission alleged; and
3. the *identity* of the person responsible for the injury; and
4. that he had a cause of action against the person responsible.

These requirements are contained in s14(1) of the 1980 Act, and they are only summarised in this text; the actual wording of the Act is by no means easy to understand, and students should refer to it for a full description of the law. Since an allegation that the plaintiff has brought his action more than three years after he had 'knowledge' is a claim that the action is statute-barred, it is for the defendant to prove that the plaintiff knew all the relevant facts. Where the plaintiff sues his employer and knows, more than three years before issuing his writ, that his injury is attributable to some unsafe system of work, he has 'knowledge' that it is attributable to his employer's acts or omissions even though he does not then know the specific breaches of duty involved. Complete knowledge is thus unnecessary for time to run against him under s14: *Wilkinson v Ancliff* [1986] 3 All ER 427 CA. The issues covered by s14 of the 1980 Act are fully discussed in *Halford v Brookes and Another* [1990] 1 WLR 428.

The scope of s11 Limitation Act 1980 has been defined in *Stubbings v Webb* [1992] 1 WLR 782 to apply *only* to those personal injuries incurred by way of negligence or breach of statutory duty. Hence, deliberate assaults do not attract a three year limitation period but are subject only to a six year period where the tortfeasor is the assailant. This also means, however, that the provisions of s14 and s33 (see section 14.10) do not apply in cases of injuries incurred by deliberate acts of violence.

14.8 'Significant'

A 'significant' injury is defined by the Act as one in respect of which a plaintiff would consider starting proceedings against a defendant who admitted liability and who had the means to pay the damages. Construed literally, *every* injury would be significant within the Act, since what plaintiff would not sue if he were certain of recovering damages? The courts have however limited the definition so that, especially where the injury has been caused by the acts of the plaintiff's employer, it is not significant so long as it is no more than an 'irritating nuisance', such as a buzzing in the ear, or some small discomfort. The justification for this is that good employees are reluctant to sue their employers, and should not be barred from claiming later, when the injury takes on a greater measure of gravity, merely because they have carried on working and have suffered in silence: *McCafferty v Metropolitan Police District Receiver* [1977] 1 WLR 1073.

14.9 Identity of the defendant

A plaintiff injured in a road accident may not discover the identity of the driver who knocked him over until some time after the accident. An employee injured at work may not know who his employer is, especially if he works for a large organisation with many holding and subsidiary companies who sub-contract their workers to associated companies. The requirement that the plaintiff knows who is liable for his injuries has been construed generously in plaintiff's favour, and it seems that the less astute the plaintiff the less the court will expect of him in his understanding of company and employment law, or of the law relating to the liability of occupiers of premises: *Simpson* v *Norwest Holst* [1978] 1 WLR 863 and *Clark* v *Forbes Stuart* [1964] 2 All ER 282.

14.10 Disapplying the limitation period

In personal injury and fatal accident claims *only*, the court has power to order that a plaintiff's action be allowed to proceed even though it was not commenced either within the 'primary' limitation period of three years from the date the injuries occurred or within the three years starting with the date of 'knowledge'. The power is discretionary, and contained in s33 Limitation Act 1980. The House of Lords has however declared that the discretion cannot be exercised when the plaintiff has started an action during the primary period but for some reason that action has been struck out or discontinued, and has then started a second action outside the primary period; in such a case the plaintiff is not 'prejudiced' by the provisions requiring him to begin an action within the period, and the second action will be statute-barred and must fail, there being no discretion to override the limitation period: *Walkley* v *Precision Forgings* [1979] 1 WLR 606 applied in *Deerness* v *Keeble* [1983] 2 Lloyd's Rep 260.

Where the plaintiff has brought no action within the three years of the occurrence of the damage, or within the three years beginning with the date he had 'knowledge' of all the s14 matters, but begins the action only after both those periods have expired, then there is a general discretion to order that the limitation period shall not apply (that is, that the defendant shall not be entitled to plead successfully that the action is statute-barred), and the court may make such an order when it is 'equitable' to do so. These are the widest possible powers which a court can hold, and it seems that an order to 'disapply' the limitation provisions will hardly ever be reversed on appeal: *Thompson* v *Brown* [1981] 2 All ER 296 and *Conry* v *Simpson* [1983] 3 All ER 369.

In applying the discretion, the court must consider *all* the circumstances, but in particular:

1. The length of and reasons for the delay. The court can take into account circumstances arising within the limitation period and can therefore consider prejudice caused to the defendants by a plaintiff's delay in notifying them of the claim: it is not confined to consideration of the period after the expiry of the (possibly extended) limitation period: *Donovan* v *Gwentoys* [1990] 1 All ER 1018. This ruling alters what was previously taken to be the law.
2. The effect of the delay upon the cogency of evidence.
3. To what degree the defendant was responsible for the delay.
4. The plaintiff's conduct, including the extent to which he had access to medical, legal and other advice: s33.

No general rule can be stated as to when the discretion will be exercised in a plaintiff's favour, but in the early years after the passing of the Act it was very freely used, and defendants rarely succeeded in persuading the court that the injustice to them in disapplying the limitation period outweighed the injustice to the plaintiff in maintaining it. Delays in issuing proceedings of six years (*Conry* v *Simpson* above) and even 12 years (*Brooks* v *Coates* [1983] 3 All ER 702) have not deterred the court from allowing the action to continue, especially where the defendant has preserved all the necessary records and documentary evidence, or the plaintiff has sustained very severe injuries. It may be however that there is now developing a more cautious approach to the problem, and that long delay will be a very significant factor in prejudicing a defendant (or his insurance company, which may not have made provision for the claim) after the proper time for beginning the action has passed. See, for example, *Antcliffe* v *Gloucester Health Authority* (1992) The Times 6 May CA where in a medical negligence claim inordinate and inexcusable delay by the plaintiff resulted in prejudice to the defendant in that had action proceeded expeditiously any damages awarded would have been paid by the Medical Defence Union, but if the action was tried now the defendant would have to pay such damages. This prejudice was held to be sufficient to justify dismissing the action.

Where the defendant has proved that the action has been started after the primary limitation period and the period dependent upon the date of knowledge have both expired, the burden lies upon the plaintiff to show why the discretion under s33 should be exercised to allow his claim to proceed. If the issue of limitation is likely to be strongly argued by a defendant, it is common for the court to order that it be tried as a preliminary issue, that is, that there be first a trial on all the evidence relating to limitation and, if the plaintiff succeeds on that issue, a trial on liability and quantum will follow later. This course saves time and money for court and parties alike.

14.11 Limitation in claims for death

An injured claimant may die before starting proceedings, and his cause of action generally survives death, under the Law Reform (Miscellaneous Provisions) Act 1934. Or his death may give rise to claims by his dependants under the Fatal Accidents Act 1976. The relevant time limits for these actions are as follows:

1. the deceased's own claim must not be statute-barred, that is, he must have died before the primary period or that dependent upon 'knowledge' have expired; and
2. the action by the estate or dependents must be started within three years of the death or within three years of the date of 'knowledge' of the personal representative of the deceased (the requirements of 'knowledge' are the same as those for a plaintiff who is still alive): s11(4) and (5) Limitation Act 1980.

The court has similar powers to disapply the limitation period in claims for death as for claims by living plaintiffs for their own injuries, and the conditions for exercising that power are identical (see section 14.10).

14.12 Claimants under a disability

Where a plaintiff is a minor or mental patient, the relevant period of three or six years limitation does not start to run at all, whatever the nature of his claim, unless and until the disability ceases but, once it has ceased, nothing will stop it. Thus a plaintiff injured at the age of five years has until the day of his 21st birthday in which to begin his action, but of course his date of 'knowledge' may be later so that the time is further extended. A plaintiff who has a cause of action in tort for, say, a nuisance to his land, but who at the time the cause of action accrues is a mental patient, has six years in which to bring his action, calculated from the date he recovers his mental health; but if during that six years he once more lapses into insanity, the time continues to run and is not suspended until he is once more sane. These provisions stem from s28 of the 1980 Act.

It should be remembered that an unborn child can have a cause of action in respect of things done to him before he is born, so that the limitation period for such acts must be at least 21 years from the date of birth: Congenital Disability (Civil Liability) Act 1976.

14.13 Amendment of proceedings after expiry of limitation

The powers and practice of the court in renewing for service a Writ which has expired without being served have been discussed already (see Chapter 5, section 5.2) and it has been noted that the court will very rarely, if ever, renew if the relevant limitation period has expired. It now falls to consider to what extent a plaintiff may amend his Writ and pleadings after the limitation period has expired against the defendant to the action or some other person the plaintiff now wishes to add as a party. The general rule is that no such amendment will be allowed.

If a plaintiff wishes to amend his Statement of Claim so as to allege a further cause of action which arises out of the same or substantially the same facts as those already in issue in a claim already started, the court may allow him to do so: s35 Limitation Act 1980. The theory is that it causes no injustice to a defendant to have a further cause of action argued against him if he has already been made aware of the facts upon which it will be based. For example, a plaintiff injured in an accident at work may sue for common law negligence. Later, after the limitation period has expired, he may want to add allegations of breach of the Occupiers' Liability Act 1957, or of the Factories Act 1961, arising out of the same accident and almost the same facts. The court has power to allow the amendment. The relevant date for the expiry of the limitation period is the date at which the amendment is actually made: *Welsh Development Agency* v *Redpath Dorman Long Ltd* [1994] 1 WLR 1409.

The plaintiff may have named the wrong defendant in the Writ by mistake, so that the correct defendant is not a party to the action. If the limitation period has expired, a claim against the correct party may fall. The court has power to allow the name to be corrected so as to name the proper defendant provided that defendant was not, in effect, misled by the mistake: O.20 r5 (CCR O.15 r1). For example, an action may be begun against a company not the true occupier of premises, but the true occupier may be all along aware of the error and not in any way prejudiced by it, knowing all along that it was him whom the plaintiff really intended to sue; the court may allow the amendment: *Evans* v *Charrington* [1983] 2 WLR 117.

The capacity in which the plaintiff sues or in which the defendant is sued may be amended if the amendment alleges a capacity he held at the date the proceedings were issued: O.20 r5(4). Thus, if it is necessary to allege that the plaintiff was the personal representative of a deceased, or the defendant trustee of a trust fund, the amendment will be allowed to add the proper capacity even though the limitation period has expired and the amendment amounts to a change of party (in strict theory). Once again, the amendment is little more than a formality and can cause no real prejudice to the party against whom it is made.

Greater difficulties arise where the plaintiff (or defendant) wishes to add a party to the action, and cannot use the provision to 'correct' a mistaken nomination, after the limitation period has expired. Since any joinder of that additional party will have effect as if he had been a party from the start of the proceedings, it deprives him of his defence of limitation. Accordingly, a new party may only be added to an action after the period of limitation has expired *against him* if it is 'necessary' to do so or if the court uses its powers under the Limitation Act. It is necessary only if:

1. either the new party is to be substituted for a party whose name was given in the original claim in mistake for his (see *Evans* v *Charrington* above); or
2. the claim made by or against the existing parties cannot be maintained unless the new party is joined (this aims principally at cases where not all joint contractors have been joined in the original Writ, for all must be joined if the action by them is to succeed).

It must be remembered that the powers of the court to allow amendment before limitation has expired are very much wider (see Chapter 10 above), and that even after expiry amendments which do not amount to the allegation of a completely new cause of action or to the addition of a new party are permissible with leave. Amendments which do have either of these two latter effects are termed 'new claims' by s35. However, the substitution of a National Health Service Trust for the original plaintiff, a regional health authority, was held by the Court of Appeal not to amount to a 'new claim' within s35. The court considered that the words 'the addition or substitution of a new party' in s35(2)(b) did not apply to claims which did not involve a new cause of action: *Yorkshire Regional Health Authority* v

Fairclough Building Ltd (1995) The Times 16 November. See Chapter 36, section 36.3, for further details.

It should also be remembered that where an amendment is allowed, whether before or after expiry of limitation, the party making it may be ordered to pay the costs incurred by the other side in meeting the amended claim at a late stage; it should have been made before the Writ was served.

The rules as to amendment after expiry of limitation periods apply equally to defendants making counterclaims, and to both sides in third party proceedings, as they apply to plaintiffs: s35(8). One further point merits mention: where a proposed amendment by a defendant amounts to his blaming some person not already a party, after the period for the plaintiff beginning an action against that other person has expired. It sometimes happens that a defendant does not know at once that a third person is really to blame for the plaintiff's damage, but only discovers so at a late date when, for example, his expert reports have been delivered and those reports criticise a third person. It may by then be too late for the plaintiff to sue the third person, because the limitation period against him has expired. Provided that the defendant has not delayed on purpose so as to deprive the plaintiff of his claim against that person, the court can allow the amendment: *Turner* v *Ford Motors* [1965] 2 All ER 583. Since this case was decided before the provisions as to 'knowledge', and the court's discretion to override time limits in personal injury and death claims, were introduced, it may be that such amendments will be more freely allowed in personal injury actions, since the amendment may be the first the plaintiff knows of the identity of the person blamed (so that his claim would not be statute-barred), or the revelation may suffice to allow the court to exercise its s33 discretion to allow a *prima facie* barred claim to proceed against that person.

14.14 Delay after service of proceedings

The effect of delay before issue of proceedings has been considered under the heading of Limitation. The effect of delay between issue and service of the Writ, and the practice of renewal, have also been outlined (see the first part of this Chapter). Even if a plaintiff has successfully started his action, and has served his Writ in time, and has surmounted any objection taken by the defendant that the action is statute-barred, he may delay so much in bringing the action to trial that the defendant is seriously prejudiced; evidence deteriorates, witnesses forget material facts, the anxiety of being sued, all these and other factors hinder a fair trial and put the defendant under increasing pressure. Less commonly the delay consists in deliberate refusals by the plaintiff to comply with direct orders of the court as to the discovery of documents, and the power of the court to strike out a claim for such refusal has already been mentioned (see Chapter 10, section 10.7). More usually the delay is caused by the plaintiff's wish to be sure that he has all available evidence, or to assess how serious is an injury, or simply because, having started the action, he loses enthusiasm to persue it, or lacks money to continue, or is advised that the claim is not a strong one. Whatever the reason, the action may 'go to sleep' for a considerable time. The court places no duty upon a defendant to do the plaintiff's job for him in reminding the plaintiff that the action exists.

Where the defendant considers that the delay has been more than is justifiable, he may take out a Summons before the Master applying for the plaintiff's action to be dismissed for 'want of prosecution'. The court considers all the circumstances, but will only make the order in one of two situations:

1. if the plaintiff has delayed intentionally and the delay is such as to amount almost to a contempt of the court's orders; or
2. though not intentional, the delay has been inordinate and inexcusable and is such as to create a substantial risk of prejudice to a fair trial of the action, or as to cause serious prejudice to the defendant. Whether any given delay is 'inordinate' is in every case a question of fact, but a general definition appears in *Tabata* v *Hetherington* (1983) The Times 15 December: 'a delay materially longer than the time regarded by the profession and the courts as an acceptable period'.

These principles emerge from the decision of the House of Lords in *Birkett* v *James* [1978] AC 297. They are of general application to both High Court and County Court, and the following things will be considered when the ground of application is 'inordinate and inexcusable' delay:

1. Has the defendant admitted liability? If so, the action will be dismissed only if the defendant is prejudiced in arguing the issue of damages: *Gloria* v *Solokoff* [1969] 1 All ER 204.
2. Has the delay been caused or contributed to by the defendant's delay in discovering documents or providing evidence, or in otherwise complying with the rules? If so, the action will not be struck out, for the defendant cannot rely upon his own misconduct.
3. Is there an excuse for the delay? It is no excuse to say that the papers were with counsel, and counsel was too busy to deal with them, for other counsel should be instructed: *Thorpe* v *Alexander* [1975] 1 WLR 1459. It may be an excuse that the plaintiff is imprisoned abroad and cannot give instructions to his legal advisers: *Akhtar* v *Harbottle* (1982) The Times 4 August. Where the reason for delay was that the plaintiff wished to wait until the defendant was more solvent, the action was dismissed, even though the decision was a reasonable one to make in commercial terms: *Claremount* v *GCT* (1983) The Times 17 June.
4. Has the limitation period expired? If it has not, it will only be in the most exceptional circumstances that a claim will be struck out, and probably only if the delay has been intentional and akin to a contempt of court, for on dismissal the plaintiff is entitled to start a fresh action: *Tolley* v *Morris* [1979] 1 WLR 205. If it has expired, so that if the claim were struck out no further action could be maintained, the court will take into account delay before the issue of proceedings

as well as after their issue, in deciding whether there is an excuse. The greater the delay since the cause of action accrued (and limitation began to run) the less excusable it will be: *Biss* v *Lambeth* [1978] 1 WLR 382.

5. What prejudice is caused to the defendant? Even if the delay is very long, and is inexcusable, the claim will not be dismissed unless the defendant can show some prejudice other than mere delay: *Halls* v *O'Dell* (1991) The Times 5 November. It is not enough for the defendant to show that memories have grown fainter during the delay: *Rowe* v *Glenister and Others* (1995) The Times 7 August; see Chapter 36, section 36.3, for further details. If the evidence has been preserved, and there is no significant risk that it will be less cogent, and especially if the defendant is also insured (so that the spectre of litigation hanging over him causes him no real concern) there will be no order for dismissal: *Abouchalache* v *Hilton Hotels* (1982) The Times 15 November (a claim arising out of an explosion at the hotel in the early 1970s in which the plaintiffs were injured). In contrast, in *Hayes* v *Bowman* [1989] 1 WLR 456 the Court of Appeal held that delay in presenting a claim for personal injuries tended to increase the damages the defendant would eventually have to pay to the plaintiff, and that this might be so prejudicial to the defendant that the plaintiff's action should be struck out on account of inordinate and inexcusable delay prejudicing the defendant; however, on the actual facts of that case this step was not justified.

The House of Lords hoped, through the principles of *Birkett* v *James*, to encourage plaintiffs to proceed with their actions promptly, and thereby to reduce the delays which plague High Court litigation in particular. That hope has not been fulfilled, but the House has declined to alter the principles and now wishes the legislature to impose a stricter timetable on interlocutory proceedings: *Department of Transport* v *Chris Smaller (Transport) Ltd* [1989] 1 All ER 897 HL.

Counterclaims can also be dismissed for want of prosecution. The court has an inherent jurisdiction to control litigation, and further it is clear that a counterclaim is equivalent to a separate action: *Owen (trading as Max Owen Associates)* v *Pugh; Beamish and Another* v *Owen (trading as Max Owen Associates)* [1995] 3 All ER 345. For further details, see Chapter 36, section 36.3.

14.15 Effect of dismissal

Where an action is dismissed for want of prosecution, whether because of delay by the plaintiff in complying with orders of the court (intentional and contumelious delay) or because of inordinate and inexcusable delay causing a risk of prejudice to the defendant through the chances of a fair trial being reduced or the threat of litigation hanging over him for an unnecessary time, the plaintiff may start a fresh action provided the limitation period has not expired, for a dismissal of action does not amount to a judgment on the merits. However, where the action has been dismissed on the first ground, the court has a discretion to strike out the second action unless the plaintiff gives some good explanation of his failure to comply with the rules in the first action: *Janov* v *Morris* [1981] 1 WLR 606 explained in *Bailey* v *Bailey* [1983] 3 All ER 495. Where the plaintiff offers no explanation for his failure to comply with the court's peremptory order to serve a Statement of Claim, as a result of which a first action was struck out, a second action will be similarly dismissed even though begun within the limitation period: *Palmer* v *Birks* [1985] NLJ 1256.

In the absence of special circumstances the court would not exercise its inherent jurisdiction to dismiss for want of prosecution unless it caused the defendant a real risk of prejudice: *Costellow* v *Somerset County Council* (1992) The Times 25 November. Prejudice may be economic as well as to the conduct of the trial: *Gascoigne* v *Haringey Health Authority* (1992) The Times 21 January.

14.16 Dismissal and limitation

It has been noted that dismissal will hardly ever be ordered where a relevant period of limitation is still running. Where that period has expired, however, dismissal will be an absolute bar to any further (successful) action by the plaintiff by way of a fresh Writ, for the defendant can rely upon his plea that the second action is statute-barred. Some confusion, however, has arisen as to whether, in a claim for personal injuries or death, the plaintiff can avoid having the first action struck out by persuading the court to exercise its powers under s33 and to declare that, even if it would have struck out the action for want of prosecution, it will not do so because it would allow any second action to continue and disapply the limitation period, that is, that since a new action would be permitted, there is no point in striking out the first one. Although not clear, the law seems to be as follows:

1. the court should disregard its powers under s33 when deciding to strike out for want of prosecution;
2. if, but for the power to disapply the limitation time limits, the court would strike out the claim, it should strike it out;
3. if the plaintiff wishes to argue the limitation issue, he must start a fresh action, after the first one has been dismissed, and argue in that action for an exercise of the s33 discretionary power.

These principles are stated as obiter dictum in *Firman* v *Ellis* [1978] 2 All ER 851, by the Court of Appeal. The problem is however this: if the plaintiff has started an action within the limitation period, and has had it struck out for want of prossecution after the period has expired, the court has *no power* to allow the second action to proceed, and *cannot* exercise its s33 discretion. This is because the House of Lords in *Walkley* v *Precision Forgings* [1979] 1 All ER 102 held that s33 does not apply where an action has been brought within the limitation period but has been struck out, and the plaintiff brings a second action outside the period. In simple terms, the effect of *Firman* and *Walkley* is that a plaintiff whose action is struck out has absolutely no remedy against the defendant if the limitation period has passed. The only substitute for him is to sue his solicitors for negligence in allowing his first action to fail, and this will give him a remedy for as much, if not more, damages than he would have recovered from the defendant he can no longer sue. But that alternative is useful only so long as the solicitor is fully insured (a fact which seems to have caused the House of Lords some peace of mind in *Deerness* v *Keeble* [1983] 2 Lloyd's Rep 260). If the solicitor is not insured, and has not the means to pay, or if the plaintiff has acted without solicitors, he is left with no remedy against anyone at all.

So long as this injustice reigns, there is perhaps a way in which the courts can circumvent it. They could find as a matter of discretion that the first action should not be struck out for want of prosecution (deciding the case really on the basis that striking out will leave the plaintiff without a remedy, but not referring to that factor in the judgment), and such finding could be challenged only if it is so unreasonable that no court could have made it. This requires a robust judge who is prepared to fill the gap in the law until (hopefully) Parliament fills it with amending legislation.

14.17 Delay by agreement

It is always open to the parties to agree that periods of limitation shall not apply to an action, or that the plaintiff may have extra time in which to prosecute his claim after he has begun it. If such an agreement is still extant, a limitation defence will fail, and the claim will not be struck out for want of prosecution. The agreement may be implied from the defendant's conduct, but it has been held that a voluntary interim payment does not without more amount to it, nor does a continuation of correspondence between the parties' solicitors after the limitation period has expired: *Deerness* v *Keeble* (above).

15

Payment into Court

15.1 Introduction

15.2 Procedure

15.3 Acceptance of the payment

15.4 Other matters

15.5 Acceptance with leave of the court

15.6 Disclosure of the payment in

15.7 Miscellaneous points

15.1 Introduction

The provisions by which a defendant can be ordered to pay money into court as a condition of being given leave to defend the action have been discussed in Chapter 7. The payment of interim sums before trial and on account of debt and damages are dealt with in Chapter 13. The subject of this chapter is the time, conditions and procedure by which a defendant can pay into court voluntarily and before judgment in the action a sum of money which the plaintiff may accept in full and final settlement of his claim or of part of it. The governing rules are contained in O.22 (CCR O.11).

A defendant from whom debt or damages are claimed will attempt to settle the claim for less than the plaintiff wants. Probably before proceedings have been issued there will be negotiations between the parties, and the defendant may offer a lesser sum to 'get rid of the claim' and avoid the time, trouble and expense of litigation, even if he thinks he has a good chance of winning at trial. Once proceedings have been served, he may offer more, and the bargaining will continue until trial (something over 50 per cent of all personal injury claims are settled at the doors of the court just before trial, if they have proceeded so far). The advantage of paying into court is that the plaintiff has a difficult decision to make; should he be tempted into accepting the payment in and abandon his claim for the full amount he thinks he might recover, or reject the payment and risk recovering not only less than it at trial but also having to pay his own costs and those of the defendant from the date the payment was made?

15.2 Procedure

The defendant can make a payment in at any time, even before the Writ has been served (O.22 r1) (CCR O.11 r1), though of course not after judgment in the action, but the most common time it is made is a few weeks or months before trial. The payment may be of any amount, but the defendant usually calculates it so as to be sufficient to tempt the plaintiff into acceptance but not so much that, on the available evidence, it exceeds what the defendant thinks the court will award at trial. As a rule of thumb, in personal injury claims a payment in of about 75 per cent of the estimated damages is made, taking account of the chance that the plaintiff may lose altogether or have his award cut for contributory negligence (these are some of the 'hazards of litigation' always considered when making the calculation).

Payment is made into the Bank of England, Law Courts Branch, and the money is credited to the defendant's name and invested, at the present time in the court's short-term account earning about 6 per cent interest: O.22 r13. In the County Court, the equivalent provisions are contained in the Court Funds Rules 1987. The defendant then serves on the plaintiff a Notice of Payment into Court which states the following:

1. the date of the payment;
2. the amount;
3. whether in making the payment the defendant has taken account of any counterclaim he is making, and failure to do this may cause the court to disregard the payment in when making orders for costs at the conclusion of the trial: *Humber Asphalt* v *Squire W Swift Ltd* (1987) The Independent 6 April CA.
4. if the plaintiff claims in respect of more than one cause of action, in respect of which cause or causes the payment is made;
5. what proportion of the payment is in respect of interest, and what capital (if this is not stated, the payment is deemed to include all interest due to the date of it);
6. a notice stating the terms on which the payment may be accepted by the plaintiff; O.22 r1.

Within three days of receiving the Notice, the plaintiff must send a written acknowledgment, of the receipt of the Notice, to the defendant: O.22 r1(2). He may also apply for the Notice to be amended so as to specify, where the plaintiff claims in respect of more than one cause of action, and the Notice does not already do so, how much of the payment in relates to which of the causes of action. This is only done where it would be very difficult for the plaintiff to tell how much is in respect of each, and it is essential that he know the 'split': O.22 r1(4). In *The Talamba* [1965] P 433, several tugs had assisted the defendant's ship into port, but the defendant refused to pay them their charges. The plaintiff, the tugs' owner, sued for the charges, and the defendant paid into court a single sum, not specifying how much was apportioned to each tug. The plaintiff did not therefore know how much should be paid to each, if he accepted the sum. The court ordered the defendant to state the proportion of the sum allocated to the cause of action of each tug.

In the following principal cases, where a single payment in is made in respect of two or more causes of action alleged by the plaintiff, the court will not order the defendant to specify how much is apportioned to each:

1. claims by a personal representative under the LRMPA 1934 for the estate of the deceased which are coupled with a claim by the personal representative on behalf of the dependents under the Fatal Accidents Act 1976: O.22 r1(6).
2. where the causes of action are substantially the same, for example claims for damages for personal injury alleging common law negligence and breach of statutory duty, both based upon the same facts.

The rules governing the County Court are essentially the same, one minor difference being that service of the notice is by the Court.

15.3 Acceptance of the payment

A payment in is not an admission of liability or of the quantum of a plaintiff's claim. It is an offer to settle the claim once-and-for-all for the amount paid in (plus any interim payment already made and taken into account). The plaintiff has 21 days from receiving the Notice of Payment In during which he can give notice of acceptance and acquire a right to take the money out of court in satisfaction of his claim: O.22 4.3 (CCR O.11 r4). If he lets the 21 days expire before trying to accept it, the money remains in court and will only become his if the court gives leave. The defendant may however increase the amount of the payment in at any time, and if he does he must serve a Notice of Increase in similar form to the Notice of Payment In. On receiving the Notice of Increase, the plaintiff has a fresh period of 21 days in which to accept the whole of the payment including the amount of the increase without the court's leave.

Where a plaintiff accepts within the 21 days, he can generally withdraw the money paid in (though not apparently the interest it has earned) without leave of the court, and can make up his bill of costs to the date of the payment, have it taxed (see Chapter 17) four days after taking the money out, and sign judgment for those taxed costs two days later: O.62 r10. The action is stayed and proceeds no further, but there is no judgment on liability or quantum; the action is settled without admission or liability on either.

Although the most normal payments in are made long before trial, a payment may be made or increased after the trial has begun. In these circumstances, the following different rules apply:

1. the plaintiff has only two days, and not 21, in which he may accept the payment and withdraw it without leave of the judge: O.22 r3;
2. if the judge begins his judgment before the two days are past, it is the moment before the judgment begins that is the last moment for acceptance without leave;
3. where a payment is accepted without leave at trial, the plaintiff cannot tax and sign judgment for his costs; they are in the discretion of the judge: O.22 r4(3).
4. in the County Court, a payment in should not be accepted less than three days before the hearing (CCR O.11 r3). Where payment is made after the trial has begun, the plaintiff may accept within 14 days but before judgment is delivered.

15.4 Other matters

In addition, the following points should be noted:

1. If a payment in is made or increased less than 21 days before the trial begins, the plaintiff has only until the start of the trial in which to accept without leave. However, a payment in made less than 21 days before trial commences is effective to provide the defendant with protection in costs, and has to be taken into account when awarding costs, the contrary statement in the White Book 22/1/9 is erroneous: *King* v *Weston-Howell* (1989) The Times 28 March (CA).
2. Where the time for acceptance has expired, the court will usually give leave for acceptance of the payment in, if the defendant makes no objection to the application for leave.
3. Once a payment in has been made, it is only in rare cases that the defendant will be allowed to reclaim it and draw it out (and in any event leave is required to do so) before all questions of liability and quantum have been decided, or the claim has been struck out or discontinued. If the defendant shows some good reason why he should be given leave, such as new evidence which indicates that there is a more substantial defence, or that the plaintiff's claim is a fraud, then leave might be granted: the fact that after paying in the defendant has become bankrupt or has gone into liquidation is not a sufficient reason for allowing withdrawal, since the effect of payment in is to render the plaintiff a secured creditor in the bankruptcy in respect of the payment: *Sherratt* v *John Bromley* [1985] 1 All ER 216.
4. A payment may be made in foreign currency if the claim is expressed in that currency, and will be held in a special account: *Practice Direction (Foreign Currency)* [1976] 1 WLR 83.
5. Where a defendant states in his Notice of Payment In that he has taken account of a counterclaim made by him, and the plaintiff accepts the payment, the counterclaim is stayed as well as the plaintiff's claim, and is in effect settled in the same way.
6. Where two or more defendants are sued jointly or in the alternative (that is, are

alleged liable in respect of the same cause of action), and not all of them make a payment in, acceptance without leave is possible only if the plaintiff discontinues the action against all defendants so sued: O.22 r4(1) (CCR O.11 r4).
7. If the plaintiff claims damages and some other relief (for example, injunction), acceptance of a payment in appears to have the effect of staying the claim for that other relief and thus the whole of the plaintiff's claim in respect of the cause of action is stayed: *Hargreaves* v *Limeside* (1982) The Times 3 July.
8. When a payment into court is paid out to the plaintiff following a judgment at trial (rather than in pursuance of a settlement before trial) interest accruing to the payment into court before the date of judgment will most often be paid out to the party who lodged the capital payment. Interest accruing after the date of judgment will usually be apportioned between the parties according to the destination of the capital payment under the trial court's order: *Practice Direction* [1988] 3 All ER 896.
9. If the defendant pays money into court in satisfaction of only one of two or more causes of action and the plaintiff then abandons the other causes, the plaintiff is entitled by O.65 to all his costs of the entire action, including the abandoned claims: *Hudson* v *Elmbridge Borough Council* [1991] 1 WLR 880.

15.5 Acceptance with leave of the court

In the following cases, a payment in can only be accepted and withdrawn by the plaintiff with leave of the court:

1. Where the period for acceptance without leave has expired.
2. Where the plaintiff is a minor or mental patient. The court must be satisfied that the payment in represents a fair basis for settlement of the claim, taking into account the strength of the plaintiff's case, and any risk of findings of contributory negligence. The court will generally accept the opinion of counsel for the plaintiff that the payment in is such a fair way of dealing with the claim, but the application for leave will be heard by the judge rather than the Master: O.80 r12. The same procedure exists in the County Court (CCR O.10 r11).
3. Where the claim is under the Fatal Accidents Act 1976 on behalf of more than one person. The requirement of leave allows the court to apportion the money among the dependants in proportion to their dependencies.
4. Where the payment was made by some, or one, but not by all persons sued jointly or in the alternative, and the plaintiff does not discontinue his action against those who have not paid in, or if one of those other defendants objects to the payment being accepted (note that this rule does not apply where money is paid into court on behalf of all the defendants sued; the term 'sued jointly' here does not mean the same thing as 'joint liability', but only that other defendants have been joined together in action).

5. Where the money was paid into court under a court order other than as a condition of being given leave to defend on a hearing for summary judgment (see Chapter 7).
6. Where the claim is for debt and there is a defence of 'tender before action', that is, the defendant alleges that before the proceedings were started he offered to pay the plaintiff the whole sum the plaintiff claims in the action. Tender before action is only appropriate to liquidated claims.

15.6 Disclosure of the payment in

A judge may be influenced if he knows that a defendant has made a payment in, especially a substantial one, while maintaining a denial of liability at trial. The fact of the payment in must therefore not be pleaded, and must not be mentioned to the trial judge (unless there is the defence of tender before action) until after he has given judgment on all issues of liability and quantum: O.22 r7 (CCR O.11 r7). It is not however contrary to the rules to mention the fact of the payment to the Master in interlocutory hearings, since he makes no decision on final liability, thus the fact of the payment may be mentioned on an application for an interim payment (see Chapter 13, section 13.18): *Fryer v London Transport* (1982) The Times 4 December. Further, the fact and date (but not the amount) of a payment in may be mentioned to the court where the question of liability has already been decided but that of quantum remains to be tried (that is, where there has been a 'split' trial), and the court is hearing argument solely upon the question of the *costs* of proving the liability: O.22 r7(2).

Complications can arise, however, when the plaintiff wishes to accept the payment in after the trial has started and needs leave to do so. The Court of Appeal laid down the following principles in *Gaskins v British Aluminium* [1976] QB 524:

1. the application for leave should not be made unless the defendant consents to it (if he does consent, it is almost certain that the judge will grant leave, so that no damage is done to the defendant's case because the action will come to an end without judgment);
2. if the judge refuses leave, he has a discretion to continue hearing the action and need not order a new trial in front of a different judge;
3. if the fact of a payment in is mentioned by accident (for example, by a witness, or by counsel), the judge should continue to hear the case so as to prevent the plaintiff having the advantage of a new trial, but he retains his discretion to stop the trial.

15.7 Miscellaneous points

The effect upon orders for costs where there has been a payment in are considered in Chapter 17. A plaintiff who is in the position of a defendant in a counterclaim may make a payment in in the same circumstances as any other proper defendant. A third party may pay in in respect of the defendant's claim against him, but not in respect of the plaintiff's claim against the defendant.

16

Arrangement for and Conduct of a High Court Trial

16.1 Introduction

16.2 Summons for Directions

16.3 Additional directions

16.4 Arranging for trial

16.5 Adjournment before trial

16.6 Exchange of evidence and other pre-trial matters

16.7 Trial

16.8 Submissions of no case to answer

16.9 Defendant's case

16.10 Judgment

16.11 Form of judgments and orders

16.12 Interest

16.13 Family Division Practice Direction

16.1 Introduction

The trial of almost every High Court action which proceeds as far as trial takes place in London. Puisne judges do go 'on circuit' to the principal provincial towns and cities, but spend most of their time in the law courts in The Strand. Before trial there is, as has been seen, a large number of interlocutory applications which may be made. One of these which has been mentioned but not so far discussed is the Summons for Directions; it is dealt with in the first section of this chapter.

When all interlocutory stages are complete, the parties may have a long time to wait until trial, as they advance slowly along a queue of cases ahead of them.

The conduct of the trial, when it arrives, is the subject of the second section of this chapter. The *Practice Direction (Civil Litigation: Case Management)* [1995] 1 WLR 262 provides additional steps to be taken in order to streamline the preparation and conduct of trials and to save costs. The most important of these are as follows:

1. Judges should assume tighter control over the preparation for and conduct of hearings and should penalise lawyers who do not conduct cases economically.
2. Accordingly, the court would exercise its discretion to limit:
   a) discovery;
   b) the length of oral submissions;
   c) the time allowed for examination and cross-examination of witnesses;
   d) the issues on which it wished to be addressed;
   e) reading aloud from documents and authorities.
3. Unless otherwise ordered, every witness statement should stand as the evidence-in-chief of the witness comcerned.
4. Detailed provisions are given as to the preparation of documentation, estimates of time, provision of skeleton arguments and opening speeches. A 'pre-trial checklist' is provided.

This *Practice Direction* foreshadowed the reforms recommended by Lord Woolf's committee of inquiry into the civil justice system. The interim Woolf report, published in 1995, suggested the 'uncontrolled nature of the litigation process' was the cause of the current malaise. The focus of Lord Woolf's proposals concentrated on two areas: the pre-trial stage and the trial itself. Pre-trial, Lord Woolf recommended greater judicial involvement in case management. The court will assume greater control through a number of initiatives to include: changes in the allocation of cases between the High Court and county court; cases categorised as fast track or multi-track with differing procedural rules and greater judicial control at the 'discovery' stage. At the trial stage, Lord Woolf suggested: revising the permitted content of pleadings to allow not only a statement of the facts relied upon but also the identity of witnesses and documents to be tendered at the trial and to refer to issues of evidence; the instigation of a case management conference and reforming the role of witness statements and expert evidence.

The common theme of Lord Woolf's report, the *Practice Direction (Civil Litigation: Case Management)* and the Family Division *Practice Direction* (see section 16.13) is that the parties are under a duty to the court to cooperate, actively seek to reduce the issues of disagreement between them and to reduce the present extravagances often associated with the discovery stage and the instruction of expert witnesses.

Whilst the changes proposed and implemented during 1995 have received a large measure of support from practitioners and the judiciary, the hard part has yet to come. Long-established working and procedural practices will have to be put aside in favour of the new streamlined approach. There also needs to be a radical change in the culture of litigation from the profligacy of the present system to the realism of the 'post-Woolf era'. Inevitably the issue of reform will again be the dominant theme for civil litigators during 1996 and for some considerable time to come.

16.2 Summons for Directions

Within one month of the close of pleadings (see Chapter 9, section 9.12) the plaintiff must take out and serve upon the defendant a Summons before the Master asking for directions for the further conduct of the action: O.25 r1. The 'return date' for hearing must not be less than 14 days after service. If the plaintiff fails to take out the Summons within the time stated, the defendant may do so: O.25 r1(4). Despite the apparently strict time limit, it is very common for some very considerable delay to occur before a Summons for Directions is issued, and the parties expressly or impliedly agree that the time be extended.

A Summons for Directions is unnecessary in the following principal cases:

1. where the action is begun otherwise than by Writ;
2. where directions have already been given on the hearing of some other interlocutory application, for example, O.14 application (see Chapter 7), hearings for interim payments (see Chapter 13), or for trial without pleadings (see Chapter 9, section 9.3), or for trial of a preliminary issue before discovery;
3. in actions for the infringement of patent, or which have been transferred for trial by an official referee (such as complicated building disputes);
4. in actions for personal injuries except where the action alleges medical negligence or is an Admiralty action: O.25 r8. In the cases to which r8 applies, the directions are 'automatic', but if either party wishes to have different orders than those given by the rule he must apply by Summons for a variation of the directions.

The Summons is in standard form listing a large variety of directions the Master can be asked to make. The plaintiff deletes those he does not want and states any further additional directions he requires. The function of the Summons is to deal, so far as is possible, with all interlocutory matters at a single hearing. A defendant can serve a Notice in reply to the Summons specifying any additional or alternative directions for which he will ask the Master, and that Notice should be served not less than seven days before the return date: O.25 r7.

Either party can ask for a large number of directions at the hearing, and there are some which the Master will give even if not specifically requested to do so. The most common requested directions are:

1. Place of trial. Usually this will be in London (if the Crown is a party, it can insist on trial in London: O.77 r13), though for convenience it may be ordered at

a court in the provinces, for example, where there are to be many witnesses all of whom live in the north of England.
2. Mode of trial. Except where the action involves allegations of libel, slander, fraud, malicious prosecution or false imprisonment, the order will be for 'trial by judge alone' rather than by judge and jury. The action then goes into the Non Jury List and, if expected to last no more than half a day, into the Short Cause List.
3. Listing category. The Master makes an assessment of the importance and difficulty of the case and lists it A (great substance or difficulty or great public importance), B (of some difficulty), or C (other cases). Category C is the most common ordered.
4. Expert evidence. The Master gives directions as to the discovery of the substance of expert witnesses the parties intend to rely upon at trial, and for which directions are needed under O.37 r36 (see Chapter 11, section 11.13).
5. Setting down. All actions must be put into the queue of those awaiting trial. The Master will order that the plaintiff 'set the action down for trial' within a specified time.

16.3 Additional directions

In addition to the above, the Master will rule upon any applications of the following types:

1. Security for costs (see Chapter 6, section 6.8).
2. Amendment of Writ and/or pleadings (see Chapter 10).
3. Further and better particulars of pleadings (see Chapter 9, section 9.10).
4. Interrogatories (see Chapter 11, section 11.12).
5. Discovery of documents (see Chapter 11, sections 11.7 and 11.8).
6. Consolidation of actions. Where there are two or more actions proceeding separately, but concerning the same subject-matter or incident, it may be convenient that all be heard together or that the same directions apply to each. Consolidation does not mean that all the actions become a single action; they remain separate, but have joint trial. If actions are consolidated, all plaintiffs must be represented by a single firm of solicitors. Consolidated actions may later be 'deconsolidated': O.4.
7. Stay of proceedings. Where the defendant alleges a binding arbitration agreement, the Master may stay the High Court action and in effect compel the arbitration. Similarly, if the defendant alleges acceptance of a payment in, or a settlement of the action.
8. Striking out. The defendant may use the Summons for Directions to apply to strike out the plaintiff's pleadings and claim (see Chapter 10, sections 10.7 and 10.8) or to dismiss for want of prosecution (Chapter 14, section 14.14 *et seq*).

9. Transfer to the County Court. There is a wide jurisdiction to transfer cases, especially those where there is no substantial difficulty of fact or law involved in the claim: see further Chapter 21.

16.4 Arranging for trial

Following the Summons for Directions, the plaintiff sets the action down for trial, and informs the defendant that he has done so: O.34 r8. If, before trial, either party becomes aware of matters which may lengthen the trial beyond the estimate made at the Summons for Directions, he should inform the court. If the action is set down for trial outside London, the plaintiff must file with the Registrar a 'certificate of readiness' stating the up to date position in respect of compliance with directions, issues remaining in dispute between the parties, and other matters laid down in *Practice Direction (Trial out of London)* [1988] 1 WLR 1322.

The parties then wait until their case is reached in the relevant List of actions. Sometimes a fixed date is given well in advance, but more commonly the parties' solicitors must watch the 'Warned List' published daily by the High Court in the Daily Cause List, and which contains the names of cases expected to come to trial shortly. It is very common for parties to have only a few hours notice of the date of trial, the name of the judge, and the number of the court where the action will be heard. Since many cases settle at the doors of the court, it is not unusual for four or five cases to be listed in the same court at the same time; three may settle, one may be tried in that court, and the other transferred at a few minutes' notice to a different court and a different judge, all of whose listed cases have settled. This somewhat chaotic procedure aims to make the most efficient use of judges' time, but if the number of cases which settle is lower than expected, some cases may be 'put over' to the following day, with much loss of time by counsel, solicitors and witnesses in waiting around outside court in the increasingly forlorn hope that their case may be 'reached' and begun before the close of the judicial day.

16.5 Adjournment before trial

Cases which have been allotted a fixed date, or have appeared in the Warned List, may be adjourned with consent of the court. Sometimes a party is not ready for trial, or has material evidence unavailable. If the other party consents to the adjournment it will usually be allowed, and the case will be 'stood out of the List' until a future day or perhaps 'sine die', until the parties are ready. Where the case is a fixture, or the application for adjournment is opposed, the court must be satisfied by the applicant that there is some good reason for it, and that it is just to adjourn.

16.6 Exchange of evidence and other pre-trial matters

Before trial each party will have to prepare its evidence and serve any necessary notices, such as those under the Civil Evidence Acts, interview its witnesses, consult with counsel, serve schedules of alleged special damage up to date, and collect documentary evidence into bundles to be put before the judge. Evidence may be agreed, to dispense with the need to call witnesses. The defendant may increase his payment into court (or make a first payment in) in an attempt to settle the case and to protect his position as to costs at trial. At the doors of the court the case may settle on agreed terms. Preparation is probably the most important stage of any action, and the stage at which counsel plays the greatest part before the trial begins in advising on liability, quantum and evidence.

A new *Practice Direction* specifies the procedure for citing from Hansard as an aid to statutory interpretation: *Practice Direction (Reference to Extracts from Hansard)* (1995) The Independent 11 January. The extract and summary of the argument in support of the party's submission must be served on the court and the other parties at least five working days before the hearing. This *Practice Direction* applies where a party in the circumstances permitted by *Pepper* v *Hart* [1993] AC 593 seeks to refer to parliamentary proceedings reported in Hansard only, and to the Supreme Court, including the Crown Court, county court and to both final and interlocutory hearings.

16.7 Trial

If the action has proceeded through the court doors without settlement, the trial begins. The plaintiff usually begins with an opening speech from counsel, unless from admissions made or the rules of evidence it is the defendant who bears the burden of establishing fact and issues. If there are several plaintiffs, they present their cases usually in the order in which their names appear on the originating process. This is not mandatory, however, and the trial judge has discretion with regard to the order of speeches and whether or not there are to be any opening speeches. The speech outlines the facts of the case and the relief sought. The plaintiff's witnesses then give their evidence (usually the plaintiff is the first witness), are cross-examined and re-examined, and documents are tendered in evidence and given exhibit numbers (for example, 'P1' is the first document put in the plaintiff's case). Procedure at trial is quite flexible, so that the judge may permit the evidence to be given in such order as he thinks convenient, often allowing a defendant's witness to be heard in the middle of the plaintiff's case if there is some urgent reason why that witness should not be detained at court longer than necessary (this is particularly common where the witness is a doctor who has other patients to attend to).

If neither party appears at trial, the judge may order the case struck out of the

List (very rare). If only one party appears, the trial may continue, judgment being given for a defendant on the plaintiff's claim, for the plaintiff on the defendant's counterclaim, and so forth. Like any other judgment given in a party's absence, it may be set aside on such terms as the court thinks just, without need to appeal; but if the party has deliberately absented himself from trial, for example, because he was refused an adjournment and wished to delay trial, the court will not exercise its discretion to set aside: *Re Barraclough* [1965] 3 WLR 1023.

Building on the Court of Appeal's well-established policy towards written and oral submissions, Sir Thomas Bingham MR has given a *Practice Direction* [1995] 1 WLR 1096. Its most important provisions are as follows:

1. If a case is reported in the Official Law Reports published by the Incorporated Council of Law Reporting for England and Wales, that report should be cited. These are the most authoritative reports; they contain a summary of argument; and are most readily available.
2. If the case is not yet reported in the Official Law Reports, but is reported in the Weekly Law Reports or the All England Law Reports, that report should be cited.
3. If a case is not reported in any of these series, a report in any authoritative specialist series may be cited. Photostats of the leading authorities or the relevant parts should be annexed to written submissions.
4. Counsel are reminded that lists of authorities, including textbooks, should be delivered to the Head Usher's office not later than 5.30pm on the working day before the day when the hearing of the application or appeal is due to be commence: see *The Supreme Court Practice* 1995, vol 1, p926.

16.8 Submissions of no case to answer

At the close of the plaintiff's case, the defendant may submit that the plaintiff's claim is bound to fail, either because, even if all the plaintiff's evidence is accepted, no cause of action is disclosed (for example, because in an action for negligence there is no evidence of damage), or because the plaintiff's witnesses have been so discredited in cross examination that they cannot be believed. The judge should not make a ruling unless the defendant agrees to call no evidence whatever the result of the judge's decision on the submission; the defendant is 'put to his election'. Thus if the submission fails the defendant cannot call any evidence of his own, and any appeal from a judgment against him is restricted to matters of law and fact arising from the plaintiff's case alone: *Alexander v Rayson* [1936] 1 KB 169.

Because a submission of no case will prevent the defendant setting up any evidence in his own case, it is extremely rare. If the case has been properly prepared by the plaintiff's counsel, and he has correctly advised on evidence, there should be no scope for its succeeding unless the witnesses are wholly incredible. And a defendant's counsel will be very reluctant to restrict his conduct of the case to a simple attack upon the plaintiff's evidence; he will almost always want the judge to hear his own witnesses.

16.9 Defendant's case

If no submission of no case is made, the defendant is allowed to call his evidence. He need call no witnesses, in which case (even though he may have put documents in evidence) the plaintiff makes his closing speech at once and the defendant's counsel has the 'last word' before the judge: O.35 r7. If witnesses are called for the defence, they are examined, cross examined and re-examined, documents are put in evidence and numbered (for example, 'D1', 'D2') and defence counsel makes his closing speech, raising any points of law he wishes. This is followed by the plaintiff's counsel's closing speech which, if it raises points of law not canvassed by the defendant's counsel in his speech, is itself followed by the defendant's counsel's speech in reply on those fresh points of law: O.35 r7(2).

16.10 Judgment

Once all the evidence and speeches have been given, the case is closed, though the judge does have power to allow further evidence to be given, or to call witnesses of his own, or to recall witnesses to clarify points he is not clear about, subject to counsel having further rights to speak on matters raised by the fresh evidence. The judge then gives judgment, either immediately or at a later time (a 'reserved judgment'), and the parties make submissions on costs. In personal injury cases, judgment is usually given at once, or after a short adjournment, unless the case has complexities of law. The judge may assess damages at once or refer the assessment to the Master, or adjourn the case for argument on damages at a later date: see generally O.37.

If the trial has been before judge and jury, the judge sums up the evidence to the jury, directs them upon the law, and they retire to consider it. On returning to court the verdict is given and the jury assess the damages themselves, but the judge decides what orders should be made for costs.

The procedure to be followed where the Court of Appeal makes available its reserved judgment is given in *Practice Direction (Court of Appeal Handed Down Judgments)* [1995] 1 WLR 1055. The most important points are as follows:

1. Copies of the written judgment are made available to the parties' legal advisers on the afternoon before judgment is due to be pronounced on condition that the contents are not communicated to the parties until one hour before the listed time for pronouncement.

2. Where a party's legal adviser has special ground for a relaxation of the usual condition restricting disclosure to the party itself, a request for the relaxation of the condition should be made through the clerk of the presiding Lord Justice.
3. A copy of the written judgment will be made available to any party who is not legally represented. It must be treated as confidential until judgment is given.
4. When the court hands down its written judgment, it will pronounce judgment in open court. Copies will be given to recognised law reporters and media representatives. Members of the public can read copy in court but not remove it.

As well as prescribing the procedural guidelines to be followed for 'handed down' judgments the Master of the Rolls emphasised the restrictions on disclosing and reporting the judgments.

16.11 Form of judgments and orders

In the Queen's Bench Division, the court itself draws up the judgment which is then 'entered' in the court records. If the judgment contains clerical errors the court has an inherent power and a power under the rules (O.20 r11) to correct the defect; but the judge cannot have second thoughts and after giving judgment alter his award, for he has by then terminated his jurisdiction to hear the case and is *functus officio*. A very different procedure exists in the Chancery Division, and is discussed in Chapter 19.

16.12 Interest

From the date of judgment until the date an award of debt or damages is paid, the judgment carries 'automatic' interest under the Judgments Act 1838, at a rate which varies from time to time and is set by statutory instrument. The rate is usually around the Bank of England's minimum lending rate, but lags a little behind changes in that rate. The interest runs from the date judgment is entered (that is, all necessary court records have been compiled and formal notice of judgment issued) or from the date damages are assessed by the Master under O.37, whichever is the later: O.42 r1. The current rate of interest upon judgment debts is 8 per cent per annum simple.

The award of interest for periods before trial is governed by s35A of the Supreme Court Act 1981. The court has power to award interest at such rate and for such period as it thinks just, but interest should be specifically pleaded for in the Statement of Claim and, wherever possible, there quantified if the claim is for a liquidated demand and the rate claimed does not exceed that currently payable on judgment debts: *Practice Note (Claims for Interest)* [1983] 1 WLR 377. The following points should be noted:

1. If interest is payable by reason of some contract between the parties, no award of interest under s35A will be made, though the contractual provision for interest will be upheld in most cases; there is no award of 'interest upon interest'.
2. In claims for damages for personal injuries or death, there is a statutory presumption that interest will be awarded under s35A if the award is of more than £200; the current rates approved by case law are:
    a) upon special damages, half the court's short term investment rate during the relevant period from the date of accident to the date of trial (*Jefford* v *Gee* [1970] 2 QB 130), though there may be special factors which require a higher or lower rate or a different period of calculation: *Dexter* v *Courtaulds* [1984] 1 All ER 70;
    b) upon general damages for pain, suffering and loss of amenity, at 2 per cent per annum from the date of the service of the Writ until the date of trial;
    c) upon future loss of earnings, loss of earning capacity, cost of future care and other post-trial loss, no interest at all.
3. Where a plaintiff alleges that he has been compelled to borrow money in order to mitigate his loss pending trial and recovery of damages, and the judge finds that such borrowing is a recoverable item of loss, the interest so incurred forms part of the *damages* and no award is made under s35A. For example, see *Tate & Lyle* v *GLC* [1983] 1 WLR 65 per Forbes J.
4. Interest awarded under s35A is simple and not compound interest.
5. In claims for payment of a dishonoured bill of exchange (for example, a cheque) the plaintiff is entitled to recover, in addition to the amount of the bill, damages from the date of dishonour until the date the bill is paid, and there is no prescribed rate of interest. The plaintiff may claim any reasonable rate justified by commercial practice, but if there is a dispute as to the amount the judge will resolve it: s57 Bills of Exchange Act 1882. In general, a claim for the full short-term investment rate will usually be regarded as reasonable.

16.13 Family Division *Practice Direction*

The President of the Family Division has issued a *Practice Direction* [1995] 1 FLR 456 applicable to all family proceedings in the High Court and in all care centres, family hearing centres and divorce county courts. The most important provisions are as follows:

1. The importance of reducing the cost and delay of civil litigation makes it necessary for the court to assert greater control over the preparation and conduct of hearings. Failure by practitioners to conduct cases economically will be visited by appropriate orders for costs, including wasted costs.
2. The court will accordingly exercise its discretion to limit:
    a) discovery;

b) the length of the opening and closing submissions;
c) the time allowed for the examination and cross-examination of witnesses;
d) the issues on which it wishes to be addressed;
e) reading allowed from documents and authorities.
3. Unless otherwise ordered, every witness statement or affidavit shall stand as evidence-in-chief of the witness concerned.
4. It is the duty owed to the court both by the parties and by their legal advisers to give a full and frank disclosure in ancillary relief application and also in all matters in respect of children. The parties and their legal advisers must also use their best endeavours:
    a) to confine the issues and the evidence called to what is reasonably considered to be essential for the proper presentation of their case;
    b) to reduce or eliminate issues for expert evidence;
    c) to agree which are the main issues in advance of the hearing.
5. Unless the nature of the hearing makes it unnecessary and in the absence of specific directions, bundles should be agreed and prepared for use by the court, the papers shall be in A4 format where possible and suitably secured.
6. The opening speech shall be succinct. At its conclusion, other parties may be invited briefly to amplify their skeleton arguments. In a heavy case the court may, in conjunction with final speeches, require written submissions, including the findings of fact for which each party contends.

17

Costs

17.1　Introduction

17.2　General principles

17.3　Judicial discretion

17.4　Successful plaintiffs

17.5　Successful defendants

17.6　Trustees

17.7　Legally-aided parties

17.8　Wasted costs

17.9　Bases of taxation

17.10　Costs on appeal

17.11　Appeals from costs orders

17.12　Interlocutory orders for costs

17.1 Introduction

At the several stages of an action, both parties will incur costs in lawyers' fees and witness expenses and the like. At the stage of taking advice before issue of a Writ, upon issuing it and serving it, upon applying for interlocutory relief, upon making and serving lists of documents and giving discovery, in preparing for trial and appearing at it, lawyers will charge and expect to be paid. When the proceedings, or some part of them, are concluded, the court will consider what orders should be made with respect to those costs, and whether one side should pay the other's costs as well as his own, or whether each side should bear its own costs, and whether any part of any item of costs or any stage of the proceedings should have its own order. Even if an order is made, the amount of costs may be reduced, so that the party in whose favour the order is granted does not recover from the other all the costs he has to pay his own lawyer. Finally, the position of legally-aided parties must be examined.

Costs in the County Court are dealt with in Chapter 21, section 21.14.

17.2 General principles

The rules as to costs are contained in O.62, which qualify the power conferred by s51 Supreme Court Act 1981. Section 51 (as amended):

> 'Subject to the provisions of this or any other enactment and to rules of court, the costs of and incidental to all proceedings in the civil division of the Court of Appeal, the High Court and any county court shall be in the discretion of the court ... [which] shall have full power to determine by whom and to what extent the costs are to be paid ...'

The court is therefore given a discretion in the matter of costs, but it is a discretion which must be judicially exercised on proper materials and for proper reasons. There is no unfettered discretion to award or refuse an order for costs.

In the great majority of cases, an order for costs will be made in favour of the party who succeeds in the action, and the order will cover all stages of the proceedings. This is confirmed by O.62 r3(3), which provides:

> 'If the Court in the exercise of its discretion sees fit to make any order as to the costs of any proceedings, the Court shall order the costs to follow the event, except where it appears to the Court that in the circumstances of the case some other order should be made as to the whole or any part of the costs.'

This is the general rule that 'costs follow the event', that is, quite simply, that the winner receives his costs of the action, and the loser pays both his own costs and those of the winner. It is the most usual order where neither party is in receipt of legal aid.

Even where a party loses the main action, the court is directed to make in his favour an order for so much of the costs as are referable to particular issues or matters in the proceedings. In each of the following cases, there is a 'presumption' that the court will make an order for costs, even in favour of the losing party, by O.62 r6(5)–(7):

1. The costs incurred by a party against whom an amendment was made to the Writ or pleadings without leave of the court. The costs of taking advice and of drafting any counter amendments required by the amendment should be awarded against the party making it, even if he succeeds at trial on the main issues (see Chapter 10, section 10.1 *et seq*).
2. The costs incurred by a party who resists an application by the other to extend the time for doing any act, for example, serving lists of documents, giving discovery, disclosing expert evidence. Such costs should be paid by the party who made the application; they will usually consist in the briefing of counsel or the instruction of a solicitor to attend the hearing for extension of time.

3. The costs of proving facts specified in a Notice to Admit Facts served under O.27 r2. Such a Notice is appropriate where one party is easily able to prove a fact which the other disputes, for example, that he was employed by that party, or that a collision occurred between vehicles, or that a particular date fell on a Tuesday in a particular year. The cost of proving these facts will be borne by the party against whom they are proved, if the court takes the view that they should have been admitted by that party because of the ease of proof. The basis of the rule is that a party should have to pay for the luxury of putting the other to proof of every single item of his claim or defence, so far as concerns items which are so easily proved that they really ought not to have been disputed.
4. Section 4(6) CLSA states:

> 'In any proceedings ... the court may disallow or (as the case may be) order the legal or other representative concerned to meet the whole of any wasted costs or such part of them as may be determined in accordance with rules of court.'

Section 4(7) defines 'wasted costs' as 'any costs incurred by a party:

> a) as a result of any improper, unreasonable or negligent act or omission on the part of any legal or other representative or any employee of such a representative; or
> b) which, in the light of any such act or omission occurring after they were incurred, the court considers it unreasonable to expect that party to pay.'

For each of the classes above, the costs will be paid by the 'guilty' party unless the court otherwise directs. Thus, if there was a good reason to dispute a fact contained in a Notice to Admit, or to challenge the authenticity of a document, it can be expected that the court will apply the more normal rule that costs follow the event.

There is a very important presumption in awards of costs that a party who fails to recover at trial more than the amount of money paid into court under O.22 (see Chapter 15 above) shall pay the costs of the other party (usually the defendant) from the date the payment in was made. The Rules of Court direct only that such a payment in should be 'taken into account' (O.62 r9 (b)), but the courts have laid down principles of discretion. This means that if the plaintiff fails to 'beat the payment in', he can expect to have to pay the costs which the defendant incurred after the payment in was made (that is, after the date the court thinks the plaintiff should have taken the amount paid in and brought the action to an end). This can lead to quite complicated calculations, where there have been several payments in, or the court awards large sums in interest on the debt or damages awarded. The rules are these:

1. There are some cases in which a defendant cannot as a matter of practicality pay money into court and is unable to protect his position as to costs by making a payment in. For instance, a claim by the plaintiff to an injunction, or to a declaration, cannot be the subject of payment in. If the defendant in such cases wishes to invoke the presumption that a claimant should pay the costs of his opponent after rejecting an offer of settlement equalling or exceeding the benefit

conferred by the court at trial, he can make a written offer expressed to be 'without prejudice save as to costs': O.22 r14. If the plaintiff turns down the terms of the offer and obtains at trial some equally or less favourable judgment, the court is likely to award costs as if there had been a rejected payment into court.
2. The court asks itself whether, if the amount of damages awarded at trial had been awarded at the date of the payment in, together with the interest upon it to that date at the rate interest was awarded at trial, the payment in was more or less than that award would have been, that is, if the trial had been held at the date of the payment in, would the plaintiff have recovered in *total*, including interest, more than the payment in?

This calculation is useful only where the payment in was in respect of both damages and *interest*, as it now normally is. The following example may assist:

Date of accident	1 June 1992	
Date of payment in	1 June 1993	£5,000 (including interest)
Date of trial	1 June 1996	£4,500 + £1,000 interest

It appears that the plaintiff has beaten the payment in, having recovered £5,500 as against a payment in of £5,000. However, what must be examined is: if the plaintiff had been awarded damages of £4,500 on 1 June 1992, would the interest added to that figure if it had been awarded on that date have brought the total award above £5,000? Since the award of interest at trial has been at £250 per year from the date of the accident to the date of trial (ignoring the fact that interest may not start to run until proceedings are actually issued: see Chapter 16, section 16.12), if the action had come to trial in June 1992 the plaintiff would have recovered £4,500 plus one year's interest, that is, £250, a total of £4,750. He has therefore *not* beaten the payment in, if the payment in included any interest to the date of it.

Where there are different rates of interest over different periods and in respect of different items of damage the calculation can become very complicated indeed, added to which is the well-known fact that awards of damages for personal injury rise to keep pace with inflation; working out whether a payment in has been beaten can therefore involve speculation as to what level of general damages the court would have awarded at the date of it, the interest levels then payable, and what the total award would then have been. In practice, it is very rare for the court to make such a detailed assessment, and the fact that the plaintiff has recovered more at trial, including interest, than was paid in, is usually taken as sufficient unless the defendant strenuously objects.

Where there has been more than one payment in, the court looks to which of the payments in should have been accepted. Thus, if the defendant paid in £1,000, and later increased it to £6,000, and the plaintiff recovers £5,000 at trial, it will be the date of the increase which is material, not the date of the first payment. Similarly, if he pays in £1,000, then increases it to £4,000, then increases it again to £6,000, the defendant's liability to costs usually stops at the date of the increase to £4,000 if the plaintiff recovers no more than that sum at trial; the fact that the defendant thought he might get more damages is irrelevant.

If a plaintiff beats the payment in, he normally gets his costs of the whole action, under the usual principle that costs follow the event. If he fails to beat it, the court is presumed to be obliged to order that the defendant pay the plaintiff's costs down to the date the payment in was made, and that the plaintiff pay the defendant's costs for any period thereafter. Although these presumptions are merely guidelines, it is very unusual for the court to depart from them and to exercise its discretion to apportion the costs in some other manner: *Hultquist* v *Universal Pattern* [1960] 2 All ER 266.

A defendant who, instead of paying money into court under O.22, makes an offer of settlement by letter in correspondence 'without prejudice' may sometimes obtain an order for costs in his favour as if he had paid in, if the plaintiff at trial recovers less than the amount offered, but there is no presumption that the trial judge will make such an order, and use of the letter procedure is thus of less protection to the defendant than a proper deposit of money with the court under O.22: *Cutts* v *Head* [1984] 2 WLR 349 and *Corby* v *Holst* [1985] 1 All ER 321.

17.3 Judicial discretion

The award of costs is in most cases a matter entirely for the discretion of the trial judge, and the Court of Appeal will interfere with his order only if he has failed to exercise any discretion at all, or has exercised it upon wrong principles or in the absence of any evidence which gave him grounds for departing from any of the normal, accepted principles discussed above. Throughout the examples which follow, the practice is stated of what the court will normally do, but it must be remembered throughout that the facts of an individual case may call for a departure from the normal rules; so long as there is good reason for that departure, the costs order alone will not be challengeable. A notable extension of judicial discretion in the matter of costs is provided by s51(8) Supreme Court Act 1981 which states

> 'Where:
> a) a person has commenced proceedings in the High Court; but
> b) these proceedings should, in the opinion of the court, have been commenced in a county court in accordance with any provisions made under s1 of the CLSA or by or under any other enactment,
> the person responsible for determining the amount which is to be awarded to that person by way of costs shall have regard to those circumstances.'

17.4 Successful plaintiffs

The general rule is that a successful plaintiff will obtain an award of costs in his favour to cover the whole proceedings. It is no ground for depriving him of his costs that his witnessses exaggerated their evidence, or that the action was brought without prior warning to the defendant. But if he has presented a false case or false evidence then, notwithstanding that he may win the action, he can be deprived of his right to seek costs from his opponent. Also, where the plaintiff carries on the action not for his own benefit, but rather for the benefit of some non-party, so that the non-party may obtain a ruling on some interesting point of law, the court can justifiably deprive him of costs (but need not do so), for his intention in prosecuting the case was not to establish his own legal rights: *Hobbs* v *Marlow* [1977] 2 WLR 777. Similarly, if the defendant has, before the action was brought, offered the plaintiff the whole relief to which the court holds him entitled (this is different from a payment into court, and normally concerns claims to injunctions).

In the following special cases, statute prescribes that a successful plaintiff shall not necessarily obtain an order for costs against the loser:

1. Slander of Women Act 1891: the amount of costs shall not exceed the amount of damages awarded unless the trial judge certifies that there were 'reasonable' grounds for bringing the action. This provision aims to discourage actions in which the allegation of unchastity causes little if any actual damage to the plaintiff and apparently succeeds in its aim.
2. Where plaintiffs in an action for breach of contract recover only nominal damages and do not establish anything which is the least value to them, they are not to be regarded as successful plaintiffs, and the court will normally award the defendants the costs of the action.

The cases thus far considered have turned upon whether the court can order that the plaintiff who succeeds should not recover from the defendant any part or some part of his own costs. It is also within the court's power to order that a successful plaintiff pay a part or even the whole of a defendant's costs, in addition to being deprived of his own. One example of this is the failure to beat a payment into court, already discussed, but it will be unusual that a successful plaintiff will in any other cases have to pay any part of his unsuccessful opponent's costs. The only common cases in which this will happen are those where the plaintiff has misconducted himself, for instance by proceeding by some method which was unnecessarily expensive, or has presented some false evidence which the opponent has incurred costs in rebutting, or where the item of costs falls within one of the cases in O.62 r3 (see section 17.2). And see *Kierson* v *Thompson* [1913] 1 KB 587.

In addition to these cases, the rules as to payment into court described at section 17.2 must be noted, as must the special rule applicable to parties who are legally-aided, outlined at section 17.7.

17.5 Successful defendants

A defendant who succeeds in the action can expect an award of costs in his favour, under the normal principle that they follow the event. It is no ground for depriving him of costs that he won on a technicality, or that his defence was devoid of merit. However, he may be deprived of costs where he presents a false case, or where he fails to make discovery of an expert report in time for the trial but is allowed to call the expert witness. Similarly, a defendant who acts with the deliberate intention of increasing his opponent's costs, and without any intention to aid his own case, may be deprived of his costs, as may one who 'misconducts' himself in some other way quite improper for the due conduct of litigation: *Andrew* v *Grove* [1902] 1 KB 620. However, a defendant who is not wholly successful can be properly deprived of his costs, particularly those referable to the issues or matters upon which he was not successful. Thus, if the plaintiff claims a mandatory injunction to compel the demolition of a building, and the court instead awards a prohibitory injunction to prevent its being built any higher, the defendant has not wholly succeeded, may well not recover his whole costs of defending the action, and may be deprived of all his costs.

The court cannot however make an order that the defendant be not only deprived of his own costs, but also pay the *whole* of the plaintiff's costs of the action, if the defendant succeeds on every issue, unless there is something very unusual about the case and very reprehensible about the defendant's conduct. The most that can usually be done is to order that the successful defendant pay a part of the plaintiff's costs: *Foster* v *Great Western Railway* (1882) 8 QBD 515.

Where there are two or more defendants, it sometimes happens that the plaintiff succeeds against some but not against all of them. For example, where he joined two defendants, one as principal, the other as agent, in an action on a contract, not being certain which of them was liable, and suing them in the alternative: see Chapter 4, section 4.11. Or he may sue the drivers of two cars which crashed into him, and the court find that the accident was entirely the fault of one. If the trial judge wishes to make an order for costs in favour of the defendant who has been held not liable, he has two choices:

1. He can order that the *plaintiff* pay the successful defendant's costs, and that the unsuccessful defendant then reimburse the plaintiff in respect of what he has had to pay. This is known as a *Bullock* order.
2. He can order that the *unsuccessful defendant* pay the successful defendant his cost direct. This is a *Sanderson* order.

The orders take their names from *Sanderson* v *Blyth Theatre* [1903] 2 KB 533 and *Bullock* v *London General Omnibus* [1907)] 1 KB 264. The choice of which to make lies in the judge's discretion, but the following principles apply:

1. A Sanderson order is appropriate where the plaintiff may be insolvent, for it gives the successful defendant a better chance of recovering his costs; but not where the defendants were not sued in the alternative, nor where the causes of action against each defendant were different.
2. A Bullock order is appropriate where the unsuccessful defendant may be insolvent or where the plaintiff has been injured and claims against the drivers of

two or more vehicles, suing them reasonably in one action. But if each defendant has tried to put all the blame upon the other, the court might well think a *Sanderson* order more justifiable.

Whether the court makes a Sanderson or Bullock order is nonetheless a matter of discretion, and there is no settled inflexible rule: *Goldsworthy* v *Brickell* [1987] 1 All ER 853 CA. Thus, the House of Lords has ruled that where the trial judge considers that the hardship to a successful plaintiff will be unduly greater through the Bullock order than through the Sanderson formula, perhaps because an unsuccessful defendant is insolvent, he is entitled in his discretion to choose the latter form of order if to do so will spread more equitably the burden of unrecoverable costs among the successful parties: *Bankamerica Finance Ltd* v *Nock* [1988] 1 All ER 81.

17.6 Trustees

Where trustees of a trust fund conduct litigation on behalf of that fund, then whatever the result of the litigation, the court should order that the trustees recover their costs from the trust fund unless they have acted unreasonably or for their own benefit rather than the benefit of the trust: O.62 r6. The court may in addition make an order for costs in favour of the trustees against any other party to the litigation, but this will be rarely done where the litigation is 'friendly', for example, an application for directions upon the construction of the trust document. Trustees who act in good faith thus recover very nearly all their costs of the action, win or lose, in most cases. The same rule applies to actions by personal representatives of a deceased litigating on behalf of his estate, and to mortgagees litigating to protect mortgages property.

17.7 Legally-aided parties

The nature of legal aid is that the person to whom it is granted has a limited liability to contribute to the costs of the action should he lose it, to the extent of the 'contribution' assessed after inquiry into his means; the legal aid fund in effect insures him against his own costs. However, there are severe restrictions upon what can be recovered *from* a legally-aided party by the other party to litigation. The general rule is that if the court would otherwise make an order for costs in favour of the non-legally-aided party (that is, usually, because he has won the case), no order will be made either against that party or against the Legal Aid Board.

The court does have power to order a legally-aided party to pay costs, just as if he were not legally aided, but in very many cases no such order is made or, if made, is for a small amount, by reason of s17(1) Legal Aid Act 1988, which provides:

'The liability of a legally assisted party under an order for costs made against him with respect to any proceedings shall not exceed the amount (if any) which is a reasonable one for him to pay having regard to all the circumstances, including the financial resources of all the parties and their conduct in connection with the dispute.'

The effect of s17 is that the court may consider making an order against the legally-aided party personally, but must inquire into his means as they appear to the court to be, on the evidence available at the time of judgment. If the legally-aided party is a defendant, and has a 'nil' contribution, his apparent means are nil, and thus no order will usually be made against him. The s17 restriction therefore means that there are only two main cases in which an order for costs will be made against a legally-aided party:

1. Where he has recovered something by way of debt or damages. The court can order that some proportion of that award be set off against the costs of the other party. This is relevant where the legally-aided party is the plaintiff and fails to beat a payment into court: see section 17.2 and *Anderson* v *Hill* [1965] 1 WLR 745.
2. Where the legally-aided party is the plaintiff, recovers damages, and loses an appeal against the quantum of those damages. The court can order the defendant's costs of the appeal paid out of the damages awarded: *Bloomfield* v *BTC* [1960] 2 QB 86.

It can be seen that the power to order costs paid personally is of little use in most cases, and that a party in whose favour the court would otherwise award costs may be substantially out-of-pocket through having to fight with his own money an opponent supported throughout by the Legal Aid Board. All is not lost, however, for the court has power to make an order for costs against the Board itself, rather than (or in addition to) an order against the party supported by it. The power arises from s18(2) of the 1988 Act. The conditions for making such an order are as follows:

1. the court would, but for the fact of legal aid, have awarded costs against the legally-aided party (that is, the only bar to an order for costs against that party personally is the futility of an order); and
2. the proceedings were not begun by the party who is seeking the order (for example, the party applying for the order against the Board was a defendant in the action whether to claim or counterclaim, and did not choose to be sued); and
3. the court has considered what order, if any, to make against the legally-aided party personally under s17 (that is, such an order is either not called for because that party is too poor, or the amount of the order is insufficient to protect the other party's costs position); and
4. the court is satisfied that the non-legally-aided party (the 'unassisted' party) will suffer severe financial hardship unless an order is made against the Board; and
5. it is just and equitable to make the order, in all the circumstances of the case.

Conditions (1) to (3) call for no further explanation. The requirement of 'severe financial hardship' was liberally interpreted by the former Master of the Rolls, who recognised that High Court litigation is expensive, and a party who cannot recover his own costs because the other party is legally-aided and too poor to pay them personally almost always suffers severe financial hardship. In *Hanning* v *Maitland* [1970] 1 QB 580 Lord Denning MR advised that almost any litigant can prove 'severe financial hardship', with the exception of 'insurance companies, commercial concerns who are in a considerable way of business, and wealthy folk who can meet the costs without feeling it'. Thus, even quite well-off litigants have been the beneficiaries of a s18 order, including a Chief Constable against whom proceedings were brought by a legally-aided Plaintiff claiming legal representation at a disciplinary hearing; an order was made in his favour for the costs of an appeal to the Court of Appeal: *Maynard* v *Osmond* [1979] 1 WLR 31.

In determining the existence of 'severe financial hardship', the court is usually obliged to leave out of account the capital and income of the applicant's spouse, and should determine the question solely upon the basis of the applicant's own means, except to the extent that the spouse has substantial resources of his or her own and could, without reliance upon the applicant, maintain himself or herself and thereby relieve the applicant of the need to provide day-to-day support: *Adams* v *Riley* [1988] 1 All ER 88.

Thus, even traders and limited companies can suffer severe financial hardship. It must be noted that where a case is taken on appeal to the Court of Appeal, such hardship is presumed in very nearly every case, for the costs of an appeal are great, and judicial notice is taken of that expense: *General Accident* v *Foster* [1973] 1 QB 50. It is thus more common for a s18 order to be made in respect of the costs of a successful unassisted appellant or respondent, but the conditions for the order are otherwise the same, that is, the unassisted party must not have begun the proceedings at first instance (though he may be the appellant in the appeal), the court must consider making an order against the assisted party, and be ready to have made one but for the fact that his means were insufficient, and it must be just and equitable to make the order.

The requirement that it be 'just and equitable' to make the order confers on the court a very wide discretion to make or refuse an order against the Board under s18. If the unassisted party has in no way misconducted himself, he can expect it to be just and equitable to make an order in his favour (provided all the other conditions of s18 are satisfied), but the court might deprive him of an order if he has been guilty of any misconduct in the litigation.

17.8 Wasted costs

Under s51(6) Supreme Court Act 1981 (as substituted by the Courts and Legal Services Act 1990) the court has the power to order the legal or other representatives concerned to meet all or part of any wasted costs. Similarly, the court can disallow costs on the same basis. These provisions apply to the Court of Appeal, High Court and county court. 'Wasted costs' are defined in s51(7) as (a) any costs incurred by a party as a result of any improper, unreasonable or negligent act or omission on the part of the representative, or (b) costs which, in the light of any such act or omission occurring after the costs were incurred, the court considers it is unreasonable to expect that party to pay.

In *Ridehalgh* v *Horsefield* [1994] 3 All ER 848, the Court of Appeal considered the making of wasted costs orders and held that the court should only make such an order if it was satisfied that the conduct characterised as 'improper, unreasonable or negligent' directly caused the wasted costs complained of. The Court of Appeal further held that an advocate would not be held to have acted improperly, unreasonably or negligently simply because he acted for a party who pursued a claim or defence which was doomed to fail, so long as the proceedings were not an abuse of the court.

17.9 Bases of taxation

Whenever a court awards costs to or against a party, it is very rare indeed that the beneficiary of the order recovers every penny he has incurred in costs, or that the party liable to pay them to the other must reimburse him for every penny so spent. Orders for costs thus concern only one question: to what extent is the party in whose favour they are made to be indemnified against the legal and other expenses he has incurred in the case? An order for costs has no effect whatever upon the amount a party has to pay his own lawyer, but affects only the amount he may receive from the other party to help him pay his own lawyer's bills. The court has a limited choice of bases upon which to award costs, each of which will provide a different degree of reimbursement.

With effect from 28 April 1986, the bases of taxation of costs are as follows. 'Taxation' means assessment of items of costs and allowance, in respect of each, of a certain sum:

1. 'Standard': the beneficiary of such an order recovers a reasonable amount in respect of all costs reasonably incurred, but will be very unlikely to receive full reimbursement.
2. 'Indemnity': the holder of the order recovers all costs except insofar as they are of an unreasonable amount or have been unreasonably incurred.

In almost all cases the standard basis will be ordered (and it applies automatically if the judgment is silent as to the basis awarded). Indemnity taxation will probably be confined to cases where the conduct of the losing party has been very reprehensible, for example, a flagrant breach of copyright: *EMI* v *Ian Cameron Wallace* [1983] Ch 59. The standard basis of taxation has absorbed the older bases of 'party and party', 'common fund' and 'trustee', and in litigation between trustees and beneficiaries the standard basis should be ordered in the absence of special circumstances rendering indemnity taxation appropriate: *Bowen-Jones* v *Bowen-Jones* [1986] 3 All ER 163 Ch D.

Whichever basis is given, the costs must then be 'taxed' by the court unless the parties agree their amount. Taxation takes place by delivery to the court of a bill of costs prepared by the party benefiting from the costs order. The court officer, the Taxing Master, then works through each item of costs in the bill and decides whether he will allow any amount, and if so how much, in respect of it. According to the terms of O.62, he may disallow items which he thinks unreasonably incurred. The Taxing Master may request the parties to attend to argue allowance of any particular items, and will give his decision which may be challenged at a hearing before him and further on appeal to a judge in chambers, the costs of such challenge being treated in effect as a separate action and normally 'following the event'.

Interest accrues upon the taxed costs of an action from the date the order for costs is made rather than from the date taxation of those costs is completed: *Hunt* v *R M Douglas (Roofing) Ltd* [1988] 3 All ER 823.

17.10 Costs on appeal

The costs of bringing or defending an appeal normally follow the event. A successful appellant may be deprived of his own costs where he only partly succeeds, or wastes court time, or succeeds on a point not raised in the notice of appeal but only argued at the appeal after the Court of Appeal gives leave for it. A successful respondent may be deprived of his costs where his defence is discreditable, or he raises a new point on appeal not taken at first instance, or argues a point on which the Court of Appeal is bound by clear authority of the House of Lords, among other cases. The Court of Appeal has much the same discretion as to costs as does a first instance judge, and can vary any order made at first instance, though it will rarely do so (cf where the appeal is as to costs only: see section 17.11).

17.11 Appeals from costs orders

Where a party to the action appeals against any judgment or order made at first instance, the Court of Appeal has power to vary the order for costs made below if the appeal is in substance upon grounds other than or additional to the costs order alone, and even if the appeal on those other grounds fails. However, there is a general prohibition upon appeals against orders for costs alone, not coupled with a true appeal against some other party of the judgment: s18 Supreme Court Act 1981 provides:

> '(1) No appeal shall lie to the Court of Appeal –
> ... (f) without the leave of the court in question... from any order of the High Court relating only to costs which are by law left to the discretion of the court.'

The effect of this section is as follows:

1. Leave of the *trial judge* is necessary; the Court of Appeal cannot give it if he refuses leave.
2. NO leave is required if the appeal is in substance in respect of matters additional to costs.
3. NO leave is required if the ground of appeal against the costs order is that the trial judge exercised his discretion *wrongly*, that is, upon wrong principles, or by taking into account irrelevant matters or leaving out of account relevant ones, or if there were no materials upon which he could reasonably depart from the normal principle that costs follow the event.
4. Where the Court of Appeal has jurisdiction to hear the appeal as to costs whether because the trial judge gave leave for it or the appeal is on the basis of other matters, or of wrong exercise or non-exercise of discretion, the Court of Appeal may substitute its own order for costs: *Alltrans Express* v *CVA Holdings* [1984] 1 WLR 394.

17.12 Interlocutory orders for costs

In dealing with the costs of an interlocutory application, the Master or judge will very often make a specific order as to who is to pay those costs. In rare cases he may order the costs of such an application taxed and paid immediately, without regard to the outcome of the trial to be held at some future date. This type of order, made only where the court considers that the application ought never to have been made or defended, entitles the party in whose benefit it is made to tax and claim his costs forthwith, and will usually take one of the following forms:

1. 'Costs to be paid forthwith'.
2. 'Application dismissed with costs'.
3. 'Costs to be paid'.
4. 'Plaintiff's (or defendant's) costs'.

The more usual order is that costs be not paid until all questions of liability and quantum have been decided, but that the trial judge be bound by the Master's opinion upon the interlocutory hearing, quite independently of any order for costs the judge might make in respect of the trial itself. Interlocutory costs orders take various forms and are in the discretion of the court:

1. 'Costs reserved': the party in whose favour an order is made shall be entitled to his costs of the application, but must apply for them to the trial judge.
2. 'Costs in any event': the benefiting party shall be entitled to his costs of the interlocutory application whatever the outcome of the full trial, but must

ordinarily await conclusion of the case before being able to tax and claim his costs.
3. 'Costs in the cause': the party in whose favour an order for costs is made at the conclusion of the case shall be entitled to his costs of the interlocutory application (and will thus ordinarily follow the event).
4. 'Plaintiff's (*or* defendant's) costs in the cause': the benefiting party shall only be entitled to his costs of the interlocutory proceedings if judgment is given in his favour at the conclusion of the case. Thus the named party will get his costs of the application if he wins, but will not have to pay his opponent's costs of that application if he loses, at the full trial.
5. 'Costs thrown away': where proceedings or any part of them have been ineffective or set aside, the party in whose favour this order is made shall be entitled to his costs of those proceedings or of part.
6. 'Costs of the day': the benefiting party recoups his wasted expenses of a particular attendance at court, usually because of an adjournment made necessary by his opponent's actions.
7. 'No order as to costs': each party bears his own costs of the application or proceeding.

18

Enforcement of Judgments

18.1 Introduction

18.2 Fieri Facias

18.3 Garnishee proceedings

18.4 Charging orders

18.5 Appointment of a receiver

18.6 Bankruptcy and liquidation

18.7 Liquidation of limited companies

18.8 Enforcement in the County Court

18.9 Attachment of earnings

18.10 Writ of Delivery

18.11 Writ of Sequestration

18.12 Writ of Possession

18.13 Committal for contempt of court

18.14 Foreign judgments

18.15 The importance of insurance

18.1 Introduction

The time, trouble and expense of bringing an action and obtaining a judgment will have been in vain if there is no effective means of enforcing that judgment. Consideration of the means of a defendant to pay an award of damages, or of the court's liability to compel him to comply with an injunction, should be made before any proceedings are issued. The means by which the plaintiff can protect his position pending trial have already been discussed under the topic of Mareva injunctions: see Chapter 12. It now falls to discuss the means of enforcing a High Court judgment for debt, damages or some other remedy.

In aid of the means about to be discussed, the court has power to continue a Mareva injunction granted before trial, and has a further power to grant such an injunction for the first time after judgment, if there is reason to fear that the defendant will dispose of his assets to defeat that judgment: *Orwell Steel* v *Asphalt & Tarmac* [1984] 1 WLR 1097. Additionally, there is it seems an inherent jurisdiction to order a debtor to supply full particulars of the nature, value and location of all his assets within the United Kingdom, and to require those particulars verified by affidavit from the debtor or his duly authorised agent: *Maclaine Watson & Co Ltd* v *International Tin Council (No 2)* [1987] 3 All ER 886.

18.2 Fieri Facias

Where the judgment is for money, whether debt or damages, the plaintiff can issue a Writ of Fieri Facias (commonly termed 'FiFa') out of the Central Office addressed to the Sheriff of the county in which goods and chattels belonging to the defendant are situated, commanding the Sheriff to seize sufficient of that property to satisfy the judgment, any costs awarded with it, and the Sheriff's costs of carrying out the seizure. This is the most common way of 'levying execution', and the Writ can be issued without leave of the court unless more than six years have elapsed since judgment was entered: O.47. If the plaintiff does not know what property the defendant has, or where it is, he may apply first for an examination on oath of the defendant (now termed the 'judgment debtor') before a court officer: O.48. The judgment debtor must answer, or risk being committed for contempt of court, and must answer truthfully, or be guilty of perjury.

In executing the Writ, the Sheriff may not break open the outside doors of residential premises (though he may enter forcibly premises which are used for a predominantly commercial purpose), but can break open interior doors once he has entered peaceably. He may take away with him any goods belonging to the debtor, including any money, banknotes, bills of exchange or other securities, and other moveable property, but he may not seize any of the following:

1. wearing apparel of the judgment debtor and his family, or tools of the debtor's trade, insofar as the aggregate of such does not exceed £100 in the case of apparel and £150 in the case of tools;
2. property which the debtor holds on trust for some third person;
3. property held on hire-purchase (since it belongs to the finance company until the hirer pays the final instalment).

The Sheriff is empowered to sell goods seized and to remit the sums realised on sale, having deducted his costs. If the judgment is for less than £600, the debtor is not liable for the costs of execution, since it will usually have carried no order for costs in favour of the plaintiff (see ss19 and 20 County Courts Act 1984). If the sale does not realise the amount of the debt (and sales by Sheriffs usually bring in less than the full value of the goods, since the sale is a 'forced sale' and there is not time properly to advertise or to haggle over price), further execution may be necessary.

Special forms of Writ are used where the debtor is a member of the church and church property is to be seized; these are *Writs de bonis ecclesiasticis* under O.47 r5, and are executed by the bishop's officers rather than the Sheriff. The ordinary form of Writ of FiFa is contained in Appendix A to the White Book Form 53. It should be noted also that no execution may be levied against the Crown for the enforcement of any judgment: s25(4) Crown Proceedings Act 1947.

FiFa has several disadvantages. Firstly, there may be nothing worth seizing at the debtor's premises, in which case the Sheriff returns the Writ *nulla bona*. Secondly, even though goods are seized apparently sufficient to pay the debt, the amount realised on sale may be only a fraction of their true worth. Thirdly, once the seizure has occurred, some third person may appear who claims the property as his own. It is then dangerous for the Sheriff to sell them, for he risks not only a civil action for conversion but also some criminal liability for theft. In the latter event the Sheriff should take out an *Interpleader* Summons, requiring the court to decide which of the debtor and the claimant is the true owner: O.17. This then proceeds like any other High Court action, and may take a considerable time. The position of a third person who acquires the goods between the date the Writ is delivered to the Sheriff, and the date execution is levied, is regulated by s137 Supreme Court Act 1981; if he has acquired title in good faith and for valuable consideration and without notice of the Writ, he has a good title which the plaintiff cannot disturb.

18.3 Garnishee proceedings

The debtor may have owed to him debts from third persons, such as banks at which he has an account in credit. The existence of such debts will usually come to light during an examination under O.48. The debt may be of other types such as a trading debt, or accounts with a building society, or the National Savings Bank, or the Post Office, or a local authority. Provided the amount owed to the judgment debtor is at least £50, application may be made to compel payment of the debt to the plaintiff rather than to the judgment debtor: s40 Supreme Court Act 1981.

The plaintiff applies *ex parte* to the Master by an affidavit which identifies the judgment debtor, his address, and the amount of the judgment unpaid. It names the person who owes money to the judgment debtor (the proposed 'garnishee') and states that to the best of the plaintiff's knowledge and belief the money is owing to the debtor. At the hearing the Master will usually make a *garnishee order nisi*, an order in effect forbidding the garnishee to pay his debt to the judgment debtor, and commanding him to attend before the Master to show some reason why the order should not be made *absolute*. The order nisi has effect from the time the garnishee is given notice of it, and he must be served with it; a copy is served on the judgment debtor. No less than 15 days later, all attend before the Master (though if there is no dispute that the money is owed to the debtor, it is rare for either him or the garnishee to appear at the resumed hearing). The Master will make the order absolute if no reason is shown that it should not be, and from that time the garnishee becomes in practice a judgment debtor of the plaintiff, who may execute the order as if it were an ordinary judgment. See generally O.49.

Garnishee orders may be made against the Post Office and the National Savings Bank, even though they are departments of the Crown: s40 Supreme Court Act 1981. No order can be made which will have the effect of reducing below £1 the amount standing to the judgment debtor's credit in a building society: O.49 r1(4).

18.4 Charging orders

FiFa is of little use if the judgment debtor has no sufficient moveable property, and garnishee proceedings are futile if he has insufficient debts owed to him by others. It may be however that the debtor has an interest in land, either legal or equitable, which the plaintiff could take as security for the debt and, perhaps, sell later to realise the award and judgment. If so, application for a charging order over that interest may be appropriate. The rules are found in the Charging Orders Act 1979 and O.50. The order can also be made over stocks and shares registered in the debtor's name and over his interest in the property of a partnership.

The High Court may only make a charging order to enforce one of its own judgments if the amount of the judgment exceeds £5,000; in other cases, the County Court has jurisdiction to make the order, and the judgment should be transferred to it (see Chapter 21). All cases for the payment of a sum of money exceeding £5,000 which it is sought to enforce against goods are to be enforced by the High Court. The plaintiff applies *ex parte* to the Master, by an affidavit setting out the amount of the judgment unpaid, the address and description of the land or other interest to be charged, and the belief that the debtor has the alleged interest in it. The Master will make a charging order nisi, which in effect imposes a charge on the property; a time is fixed for a second hearing, for further consideration of the order, and notice of hearing, together with a copy of the order nisi, must be served on the judgment debtor at least seven days before that hearing: O.50 r2. At the hearing as resumed, the court must exercise a real discretion before making the order absolute, but the burden of showing that it should not be rests upon the debtor. All the circumstances must be considered, including the position of other creditors of the judgment debtor, and any scheme proposed for a composition with creditors: *Roberts Petroleum v Kenny* [1982] 1 WLR 301.

A charging order can be obtained over an interest in land, even where the judgment debtor holds only a beneficial interest in it. However, the order is incapable of being registered under the Land Charges Act 1972 (and cannot therefore confer priority over subsequent purchasers of interests in the property) if the debtor holds merely a beneficial interest in the proceeds of sale of the land, concurrent with other persons whose interests in those proceeds are not subject to the charge, by operation of the statutory trust for sale: *Parry v Phoenix Assurance plc* [1988] 3 All ER 60. In *Howell v Montey* (1990) The Independent 28 March the Court of Appeal considered the question of priorities as between a plaintiff who had obtained a charging order and a purchaser of the charged property, and discharged a charging order where 'the balance of equities came down decisively on the side of the purchasers', exercising the very wide powers to discharge such an order conferred by s3(5) Charging Orders Act 1979.

The charging order gives security for the judgment debt, but it does not provide either a quick or easy means for the recovery in ready cash of the amount of that debt. If the plaintiff wishes to realise his security, he must apply in the Chancery Division for an order for sale: O.50 r9A and O.88. The application is made by Originating Summons. If the property charged is a residence and the judgment debtor's matrimonial home in which his wife has an interest, the court will weigh carefully the competing interests of plaintiff and family, and may well refuse to order sale: *First National Security v Hegarty* [1983] 1 WLR 865. If the order is made over a share in partnership property, it is common for the order to contain a provision that the other partners have the opportunity of purchasing the judgment debtor's share, payment being made to the plaintiff, and if they do not do so the plaintiff's remedy is to appoint a receiver to manage the affairs of the partnership and realise the amount of the debt. If the order is over stocks and shares in a company, the court may make a 'stop order' to prevent the transfer of them pending discharge of the charging order.

18.5 Appointment of a receiver

There are some cases in which the remedies already discussed will not be available. For example, if the judgment debtor will, but has not yet, become entitled to receive money from a third person (that is, future debts, which cannot be the subject of a garnishee order, for they do not yet exist). Equity developed the remedy of appointment of a receiver, who in effect received the money when it became payable, and prevented it coming into the hands of the judgment debtor. The equitable power does not however extend to cases where there is a means of execution at common law; it is a substitute rather than a complement to the powers of FiFa and garnishee, despite the apparently unqualified words of s37(1) Supreme Court Act 1981, which allow the appointment whenever the court thinks it just and convenient. The procedure is governed by O.51. The principles upon which an equitable receiver will be appointed are fully set out in the judgment of Millett J in *Maclaine Watson & Co Ltd v International Tin Council* [1987] 3 All ER 787.

There is one exception to the rule that a receiver cannot be appointed where an alternative method of execution is available; in relation to legal estates and interests in land, whether or not a charging order has been made over them: s37(4) Supreme Court Act 1981. The court here has parallel powers to appoint a receiver in addition to making a charging order, or instead of the order, and in aid of enforcement of the order by sale. The court must consider the cost of the appointment (receivers' charges may exceed the amount of a judgment debt if the debt is small or the receivership is lengthy), and the amount of the debt: O.30 r2 *et seq*.

By statute, a receiver may be appointed to manage the affairs of a partnership where the judgment debtor is a partner in the firm, where a charging order is made over the partner's interest. The receiver collects debts already due to the firm, and receives future payments, which would form the judgment debtor's share of the profits: s23 Partnership Act 1890.

18.6 Bankruptcy and liquidation

If all else fails, the plaintiff might consider threatening the recalcitrant judgment debtor with bankruptcy (if he is an individual) or compulsory liquidation (if a limited company). These remedies are a last resort, since if carried through, the judgment creditor plaintiff is in the same position as other unsecured creditors, ranking behind secured creditors (usually banks and other moneylenders) and preferential creditors (the Inland Revenue, former employees, local authorities) who may pick the debtor's bones clean, leaving little or nothing to be divided equally between the unsecured creditors.

It is thus generally true that if a judgment debtor does not pay up under the immediate threat of bankruptcy or liquidation, there will be little point in proceeding to make him bankrupt or to wind up the company. It is always better to attempt one of the other methods of execution first, for if it succeeds then, notwithstanding that the judgment debtor is very shortly afterwards made bankrupt or wound up on the application of some other person, provided the plaintiff has 'completed' his execution before that occurs, the assets or money he recovers will not be available for distribution to any other creditors of the judgment debtor. Completion usually takes place when the goods seized have been sold, or the garnishee order made absolute, or the charging order made absolute. Where it is known that a judgment debtor is or may be insolvent, there is often an unseemly race by his creditors to obtain judgment against him and to complete execution of judgment before an order for bankruptcy or winding-up is made.

The procedure for bringing a judgment debtor to the brink of ruin, and for helping him over the brink, differs according to whether he is an individual or a limited company. If the debtor is an individual, the procedure is governed by the Insolvency Act 1986 and by the Insolvency Rules 1986:

1. The creditor serves on the debtor a notice in prescribed from requiring him to pay the debt within 21 days. The debt must equal or exceed £750.
2. If the debtor fails to comply with the statutory demand (IA 1986 s268) or it is a judgment debt and execution has not been satisfied (IA 1986 s268) or the debtor has failed to comply with a voluntary arrangement, then:
3. The creditor files a bankruptcy petition asking the court for a receiving order.
4. The court hears the petition and, if it thinks it just, makes the order. From that date, all assets and affairs of the debtor are taken from him and vest in his trustee in bankruptcy, who collects all debts due to him, and distributes his estate to creditors in order of priority. The official receiver will normally take first possession of the bankrupt's estate until a trustee is appointed. No court proceedings may commence or continue against the bankrupt without leave of the court, and the order of priority of application of the assets is governed by s328 of IA 1986: claims to income tax, value added tax, national insurance contributions by central government have a 'preferential' status, as do those by former employees for unpaid wages and accrued holiday pay, and transactions effected by the bankrupt in attempts to transfer his assets to disguised nominees shortly before the bankruptcy may be set aside.

The procedure on petitions, and the powers of the court are very involved, and difficult questions arise of priority, preference and payment. The reader is referred to *Williams & Muir Hunter on Bankruptcy* for full details. The County Court has a very wide jurisdiction in bankruptcy, and it is usually preferable to begin proceedings there.

18.7 Liquidation of limited companies

If the debtor is a limited company, the procedure is as follows:

1. The creditor serves on the debtor a statutory demand for payment of the debt; Insolvency Act 1986.
2. If the debt is not paid within three weeks of the receipt of the demand, the company is deemed to be unable to pay its debts.
3. The creditor presents a petition for the compulsory winding-up of the company, complying with the Insolvency Rules 1986.
4. The court hears the petition and, if it thinks it just and equitable to order winding-up, makes the order: s125. A liquidator is appointed to collect all assets and to pay creditors in order of priority. The procedure for meetings of creditors, collection and distribution of assets, supervision of proceedings and replacement of liquidators are governed by Part IV Insolvency Act 1986, and are further defined by Insolvency Rules 1986.

Problems of priority, preference and payment arise equally in liquidation as in bankruptcy. The standard practitioner's text is *Palmer's Company Law* . It should be noted that, whether the debtor is an individual or a company, the notice or statutory demand can only be properly served where the amount of the judgment debt outstanding is £750 or more.

18.8 Enforcement in the County Court

The holder of a judgment of the High Court can usually gain access to two additional means of enforcement of his judgment, attachment of earnings and payment by instalments. To do this he must apply for the judgment to be transferred to the County Court for the district in which the judgment debtor resides or carries on business. This is effected by issuing in the County Court a request for a *Judgment Summons* or *Application for Attachment of Earnings* (CCR O.25 r11), setting out the details of the judgment and verifying the amount due. The court compels the attendance of the debtor and inquires into his means and income: CCR O.28 rr1–10.

A judgment or order of the County Court for under £2,000 must be enforced (if enforcement is sought by execution against goods) in the County Court. If the sum is £5,000 or over it must be enforced in the High Court (SI 1991 No 724).

18.9 Attachment of earnings

If the court orders attachment of earnings, it orders the debtor's employer to pay to the County Court (which then remits the money to the creditor) such part of the earnings of the debtor as it thinks fit, but makes two assessments:

1. the 'normal reduction rate': this is the rate at which the court thinks it reasonable for the debtor's earnings to be applied in meeting his liability to pay the judgment; and
2. the 'protected earnings rate': this is the rate below which, having regard to the debtor's resources and needs, the court thinks it reasonable that the earnings actually paid to him should not be reduced: s6 Attachment of Earnings Act 1971.

Both rates are calculated taking into account the debtor's liability to income tax and other deductions, the amount of the debt, and the period during which it will be repaid. Although the debtor should not be left to receive less in any one period than the amount prescribed as 'subsistence level' by the social security legislation, it is not illegal to fix the protected earnings rate at below that level: *Billington* v *Billington* [1974] Fam 24. The combination of the two rates is thus that the employer is to deduct and to pay over to the court the figure specified as the normal deduction rate unless in the relevant period (weekly or monthly) that would reduce the amount of earnings left over for payment to the employee debtor below the protected earnings rate, in which case he should deduct only so much as does not reduce that amount below the protected rate.

An order for attachment of earnings may be made against a servant of the Crown, and the head of the department in which the servant works is treated as his 'employer' for the purposes of the Act: s22. There may be more than one order in force against a debtor at the same time. The order can be discharged or varied if the debtor loses or changes his employment. If on the application for an order it appears to the court that the debtor has other debts, the County Court may instead make an *administration order*, appointing an administrator to collect in assets and pay all creditors: County Courts Act 1984 Part VI and CCR O.39.

18.10 Writ of Delivery

A judgment for the delivery of goods or chattels which does not give the judgment debtor the option of paying damages may be enforced by the issue without leave of the court of a Writ of Delivery under O.45 r4. The Sheriff is commanded to seize the goods and deliver them to the plaintiff. If the judgment has been for delivery of the goods *or* payment of their value, the debtor having the option in which way he satisfies the judgment, the plaintiff has two courses:

1. issue of a Writ of Delivery *without leave* which orders the Sheriff to seize the goods in question or, if this cannot be done conveniently, to levy execution as in FiFa upon sufficient other property to realise the damages already assessed payable (the damages musst be assessed before the Writ is issued); or
2. issue a Writ of Delivery *with leave* which directs the Sheriff to seize the goods, but itself gives no power to levy other execution (though it may be combined with a separate Writ of FiFa).

18.11 Writ of Sequestration

This is an order of the High Court to four commissioners appointed by the court, the 'sequestrators', to seize the property of the defendant and to keep it, and all it earns, until the defendant complies with an order of the court. It is a form of punishment for contempt of court, used recently to enforce compliance by trade unions with prohibitory injunctions. It is available whatever the nature of the judgment, be it for money, goods, or the doing or abstaining from doing of any act (for example, picketing, making a nuisance), but is subject to the following principal restrictions, under O.45 r7:

1. it can issue only with leave of the court;
2. the judgment sought to be enforced must have borne on its face a time limit within which it was to be complied with;
3. that time must have expired without compliance;
4. the judgment served on the defendant must have had indorsed on it a 'penal

notice' warning the defendant that unless he complied within the stated time he would be liable to process of execution (the need for service can be waived by the court if the defendant has had notice in some other way of the terms of the judgment and the possible consequences of non-compliance);
5. none of the property seized can be sold without leave of the court.

Application for the Writ is by motion to the judge, supported by an affidavit setting out the terms of the judgment, the defendant's failure to comply, and the goods to be seized, served personally on the defendant.

In the County Court, there is also jurisdiction to order sequestration, the principles of practice in the High Court being adopted (CCA 1984 s76).

18.12 Writ of Possession

A judgment for the possession of land may be enforced by a Writ of Possession commanding the Sheriff to enter upon the land, evict those adjudged in unlawful possession, and give possession to the plaintiff: O.45 r3.

It can be combined with a Writ of FiFa if the judgment is also for damages or for mesne profits (that is, payments for the use and occupation of land during a period of unlawful occupation). The Writ can only be issued with leave of the court unless:

1. the judgment is in an action on a mortgage; or
2. the judgment has followed an application under O.113 (see Chapter 19).

Application is by affidavit showing that all persons in possession of the land have been given notice that they may apply for relief against having to give up possession, and that there is no obstacle in law to the recovery of possession, such as statutory protection under the Rent Acts.

18.13 Committal for contempt of court

Where the judgment consists of an injunction ordering the defendant to do or to refrain from doing any act other than to pay money, the court may commit him to prison for contempt of court if he refuses to obey the order. Failure to pay money (other than under a maintenance order or fine by a criminal court) is not punishable by imprisonment: s11 Administration of Justice Act 1970. The following restrictions are imposed by O.52 and by the Contempt of Court Act 1981:

1. a time limit must have been specified for the doing or refraining from doing of the act in question;
2. the defendant must have been served personally with a copy of the judgment or order within the time specified for compliance with it;

3. the copy must have borne a 'penal notice';
4. the time for compliance must have expired without compliance;
5. the application for committal can only be made by a judge on motion in open court;
6. it must be supported by an affidavit setting out the grounds of the application;
7. the court cannot commit the contemnor for a period exceeding two years: s14 of the 1981 Act.

It seems that the mere fact of non-compliance with the court judgment or order is sufficient to be contempt of court, and that there need be no *mens rea* on the contemnor's part, though an unintentional contempt, or one made even after attempts to comply with the order, may be excusable: *Heaton's Transport v TGWU* [1973] AC 15. The less blameworthy the defendant, the less the court is likely to order imprisonment.

18.14 Foreign judgments

The High Court has powers to allow enforcement in England and Wales of judgments obtained in foreign courts. The procedure is laid down in O.71, and consists briefly in the judgment being 'registered' at the High Court, and leave being obtained to use one of the methods described above to obtain money or compliance with the judgment or order. Various conventions govern which countries' judgments are capable of enforcement here, and the law in this field has been substantially amended by the full provisions of the Civil Jurisdiction and Judgments Act 1982.

18.15 The importance of insurance

The great majority of judgment debtors satisfy judgments for the payment of money if they are able to do so. The process of execution is inconvenient and embarrassing for them. This is especially true where the defendant is insured in respect of the liability found against him. It is almost unheard of for an insurance company to fail to pay promptly an award of damages against their insured. If they do fail to pay, the plaintiff usually only has rights against them directly if he first makes the insured bankrupt, under the Third Parties (Rights Against Insurers) Act 1930, unless the judgment arises out of a motor accident when rights of direct action are provided by ss151–152 Road Traffic Act 1988. The latter rights depend upon the insurance company having been given notice of the issue of proceedings within seven days of their issue. If the driver was uninsured, or if the insurance company successfully avoid liability by avoiding the policy of insurance, there may be rights against the Motor Insurers Bureau for the injured plaintiff. These topics are fully discussed in *McGillivray & Parkington's Law of Insurance*.

19

Miscellaneous Proceedings

19.1 Introduction

19.2 Withdrawal and discontinuance

19.3 Interpleader proceedings

19.4 Proceedings in the Chancery Division

19.5 Summary possession of land

19.6 Judicial review

19.7 References to the European Court of Justice

19.8 Confiscation orders under the Drug Trafficking Offences Act 1986

19.1 Introduction

This chapter discusses proceedings which cannot easily be related to any considered elsewhere. They are grouped together simply because it is convenient to describe them here, but there is no common link between them. The subjects are withdrawal and discontinuance of action, inter-pleader proceedings, proceedings in the Chancery Division, actions for the summary possession of land, and applications for judicial review.

19.2 Withdrawal and discontinuance

There are three main circumstances when a plaintiff will want to stop his action against a defendant before it reaches trial:

1. where he decides he has a weak case and does not want to risk further costs by continuing;
2. where the action has been settled, whether by acceptance of a payment in (see Chapter 15) or some other agreement on terms;
3. where he thinks he may recover greater damages, or have a better chance of success, in a foreign court.

If the action has been commenced by Writ, the plaintiff may discontinue it without leave of the court at any time before the defence is served or within 14 days of the service of the defence: O.21 r2(1). Notice must be served upon the defendant, and the plaintiff will be liable for the costs already incurred by the defendant: O.62 r10. Unless the defendant agrees to discontinuance, the leave of the court is required to discontinue at any later stage of the action, and the court may impose a condition, when granting leave, that no further proceedings be brought in respect of the claim: O.21 r3. Leave is also required where, even though the notice is served before the defence, or before the 14 days after service of the defence have expired, the plaintiff has received an interim payment under O.29 r11 (see Chapter 13, section 13.14), so that the court can consider ordering repayment of it to the defendant as a condition of giving leave.

Where the action has been commenced by Originating Summons, the plaintiff may discontinue the action without leave at any time before the expiry of 14 days after service upon him of the defendant's affidavit evidence filed pursuant to O.28 r1, by notice in the prescribed form: O.21 r2(3A). Leave is required in the same cases as is required in actions commenced by Writ. It seems that leave is always required to discontinue proceedings begun by Originating Motion or Petition, and third party proceedings.

Instead of discontinuing the entire action, the plaintiff may wish to remove a part of it, for instance a cause of action under statute, leaving the remainder of the action intact. The conditions for doing this (which is termed 'withdrawal') are the same as those for discontinuance. A defendant may withdraw or discontinue any counterclaim he makes in the same cases as the plaintiff may do so to his claim, and upon the same terms as to leave and costs.

Unless the court imposes a condition that no further action be brought, the plaintiff may commence a fresh action to revive the claim, limitation periods permitting.

19.3 Interpleader proceedings

A person in possession of property may find himself 'caught in the middle' between two others each of whom claims the property as his own. There is danger in yielding to the claim of either, because it may turn out that the other was the true owner, and the true owner may then sue for damages for conversion. The position of the Sheriff levying execution has already been mentioned (see Chapter 18, section 18.2). The problem can arise in other ways. Property left with the innocent holder for repair may be claimed by the person who passed it to him, or by a finance company, or by someone who claims it was stolen from him. It is equally dangerous for the holder to refuse both claims, because he will be liable to whomever is the true owner, for wrongful interference with goods.

The holder of the goods may wait to be sued for their return, and the court will then determine the question of title to them. That may not occur for some time, and the holder (termed the 'stakeholder') is permitted to start an action of his own, requesting the court to tell him to whom he should deliver the property; this is the interpleader Summons. The action is begun by Originating Summons under O.17 r1, served on all those who, to the stakeholder's knowledge, claim an interest in the property. The stakeholder must not himself claim any interest in it other than for, for example, the costs of repair or of storage. The Summons is heard by the Master, who usually orders that there be a trial between the claimants, and that the property be lodged with the court pending its outcome, permitting the stakeholder to deduct his costs if the property is money. The stakeholder thus in effect 'drops out of the picture' and is relieved of any liability to the true owner.

If the holder has already been sued by one of the claimants, he takes out an Ordinary Summons in the action instead of an Originating Summons, but the powers of and procedure before the Master are broadly the same; the Master will usually order that the claimant who has not sued be joined in the action as defendant in addition to or substitution for the stakeholder, and that the question of title be tried between them: O.17 r5.

The Master may try the issue of title himself if the parties consent to that course, or one of them asks for it, or if the question is solely one of law: O.17 r5. However, the Master should direct a full trial before the judge if the property is of a substantial value or if difficult questions of law may arise: *Fredericks* v *Wilkins* [1971] 1 WLR 1197.

The interpleader brought by the Sheriff who is faced with rival claims to goods taken in execution is different in form from that of the stakeholder, but the procedure is similar: *Practice Direction (Interpleader Proceedings)* [1982] 1 WLR 2. An appeal from the Master's decision on any interpleader lies to the judge in chambers rather than to the Court of Appeal, since interpleader is in essence an interlocutory proceeding.

19.4 Proceedings in the Chancery Division

The specialised nature of actions brought in Chancery has from time immemorial set its procedure (and that of its predecessors) apart from the Queen's Bench Division. Although there is gradual change to bring the two closer together, significant differences remain. Most relate to the detailed nature of pleading and judgment. In general, actions take longer to come to trial and, even after trial, it may be a considerable time before the parties agree on a form of judgment to embody the judge's decision.

Actions begun by *Writ* in Chancery follow much the same course as those so begun in Queen's Bench, but with the following variations:

1. the pleadings are longer and far more detailed, setting out all facts and matters in support of a claim for the exercise of a discretion;

2. the Master has all the powers of a judge in chambers (including the power to grant injunctions on interlocutory applications), except those relating to certain applications for inheritance claims, administration actions and the approval of compromises: O.32 r14;
3. applications for judgment in default are made by motion to the judge in open court, rather than to the Master;
4. applications for interlocutory relief, for example, injunction, are usually made by motion to the judge on two clear days' notice to the defendant, or *ex parte* in cases of urgency, or on 'short' notice to the other side;
5. trials take place almost always in London;
6. applications for summary judgment are rare, and if specific performance is claimed are made under O.86, which allows the Summons to be issued as soon as the action is started (in the Queen's Bench it can be issued only after service of the Statement of Claim).

Actions begun by *Originating Summons* in Chancery are begun, and the Summons served, as in a Writ action. At the first hearing before the Master, he gives directions as to the future conduct of the action, but there is no formal pleading by way of defence. Instead, the usual order is that each party file evidence by affidavit within a stated time (since the Summons procedure is applicable only where the facts are unlikely to be disputed), but the Master has additional powers to give the same directions as if the action had been begun by Writ (O.28 r4), and can order that the action be treated for all further purposes as if it had been so begun (O.28 r8). The Summons is then usually adjourned for hearing by the judge, either in open court or in chambers at his choice, and it is unusual for there to be any other interlocutory stages.

Whatever the nature of the case, and the mode by which the claim was begun, the judge gives judgment after trial but, unlike the procedure in Queen's Bench, it is for the parties and not for the court to embody his judgment in a form which is entered on the court records. Much time may therefore be spent by junior counsel after the conclusion of the case in drafting a very carefully-worded document called the 'minutes of order' which both sides agree contains no less and no more than the judge decided; the judge may be consulted on points of difficulty which arise in the drafting, and eventually he signs the minute and this is entered. In long and acrimonious disputes, it often takes longer to reach agreement on the meaning of the judge's judgment, and the precise words in which it should be expressed, than it took to bring the case to trial.

For about three hundred years a power existed by which the Master hearng an application in a Chancery action could, either of his own motion or on the application of one of the parties, decline to determine the issues raised before him and 'adjourn' the application into court before the judge for 'further consideration' – this was then a continuation before the judge of the hearing before the Master, and not technically an appeal. This power was removed in 1982, so that now any party aggrieved by a Chancery Master's order on any interlocutory matter must appeal formally to the judge within five days of the making of the order; the procedure is identical to that in the Queen's Bench Division: O.58 r1 and O.32 r14.

19.5 Summary possession of land

The length of time taken by proceedings by Writ renders this method unsuitable for the recovery of land from squatters and trespassers.

A rapid procedure is provided by O.113 for the recovery of possession. Its terms and conditions are as follows:

1. The persons in possession must be there without the licence and consent of the person entitled to possession: O.113 r1.
2. The proceedings must be commenced by Originating Summons: O.113 r2.
3. The Summons need describe the unlawful occupiers only as 'persons unknown' if their names cannot be discovered. The plaintiff must swear an affidavit that he does not know the name of any person occupying the land who is not named in the Summons.
4. The Summons must be served on every defendant named in it either by personal service or by leaving a copy at the premises, or in such other manner as the court directs: O.13 r4(1).
5. It must also be served on unnamed defendants, and upon the premises themselves, by affixing a copy of the Summons to the main door or other conspicuous part of the premises: O.113 r4(2).
6. No final order for possession may be made less than five clear days after service of the Summons, except in cases of urgency: O.113 r6(1).
7. The order may only be made by a judge.
8. Persons who are in occupation of the premises but who are not named in the Summons and who wish to be heard on its trial may apply to be joined as named defendants in the action: O.113 r5.
9. The order for possession may relate to parts of the premises not in the occupation of the squatters at the date of the issue of the Summons and/or the hearing date, if there is reason to fear that the squatters will move into those other parts: *University of Essex v Djemal* [1980] 1 WLR 1301.
10. The order can be enforced without leave of the court at any time within three months of its being made, by Writ of Possession (see Chapter 18, section 18.12).

19.6 Judicial review

Students of constitutional and administrative law will be familiar with the High Court's role in controlling the activities of inferior decision-making tribunals, and with the prerogative Writs of certiorari, mandamus and prohibition. Judicial review under O.53 is the procedure by which these remedies are obtained (the Writs themselves have now been abolished). It applies only to those tribunals exercising a judicial or quasi-judicial function and established by statute, for example, the magistrates' court, local authorities, licensing justices, but not to tribunals exercising some jurisdiction only by virtue of a contract. Thus an employee who is dismissed after a hearing before his employer's internal disciplinary tribunal cannot bring judicial review of that tribunal's decision: *R v BBC, ex parte Lavelle* [1983] 1 WLR 23. Similarly, it does not lie to review the decision of a tribunal responsible for enforcing the terms of licences granted to trainers of greyhounds, the tribunal being established under the rules of the national association and exercising jurisdiction only over the association's members: *Law v National Greyhound Club* [1983] 3 All ER 300. Nor is it generally available where the plaintiff applicant has some alternative remedy, for example by way of a Writ action for a declaration, though there is presently a conflict of judicial opinion on this principle: *ex parte Goldstraw* [1983] 3 All ER 257 and *ex parte Cowan* [1983] 3 All ER 58.

It seems that the court is reluctant to grant judicial review if the applicant for it is already pursuing or could readily pursue effective alternative remedies: *R v Civil Service Appeal Board, ex parte Bruce* [1988] 3 All ER 686.

Judicial review must be applied for; it can only be heard fully on leave given by the court. The requirement of leave helps filter out unmeritorious applications. Application for leave is made *ex parte* in the prescribed form, supported by an affidavit, in the Queen's Bench Division. The applicant must show that he has a *prima facie* or arguable case, and that his application is not trivial, but the court does not go into the merits of the application and confines itself to deciding whether an arguable case is disclosed: *R v Inland Revenue, ex parte National Federation of Self-Employed* [1981] 2 WLR 722.

The application must normally be brought within three months of the making of the decision complained of, though the court has power to extend the time, but where the court considers that there has been undue delay it may refuse leave: s31(6) Supreme Court Act 1981 and O.53 r4. If the court grants leave, the plaintiff may then issue and serve an Originating Summons or, more commonly, an Originating Motion to the Divisional Court of the Queen's Bench with at least eight clear days between service and hearing: O.53 r3. A grant of leave to bring judicial review operates as a stay of the proceedings to be reviewed, and of any enforcement of them, until the application is determined or the court orders otherwise: O.53 r1(5). The court has an almost unfettered discretion to extend the time for applying for judicial review. For instance, if the delay in application has been caused by the need to obtain legal aid it will often be excused: *Ex parte Jackson* [1985] 3 All ER 769.

19.7 References to the European Court of Justice

As the amount of directly applicable European Union legislation increases, the courts may more often require the authoritative determination of the European Court of Justice upon the interpretation of that law. The procedure for such references is contained in O.114, and the circumstances in which they should be made by courts of first instance are conveniently summarised in *An Bord Baine* v *Milk Marketing Co-operative* (1984) The Times 26 May by Neill J:

1. A reference should be made only if the court considers that a decision on the question of European Community law is 'necessary' to the decision in the case before it.
2. 'Necessary' means 'reasonably necessary' and not 'unavoidable', but imports something stronger than merely 'desirable or convenient'.
3. The court has a discretion to refuse to grant a reference, and to decide at what stage of the proceedings a reference should be ordered, if at all.
4. In general, no reference should be made until all the relevant facts have been found upon which it can be made, and should not therefore be ordered at an interlocutory stage.

19.8 Confiscation orders under the Drug Trafficking Offences Act 1986

Order 115, introduced pursuant to the Drug Trafficking Offences Act 1986, allows a court to confiscate the assets of a person convicted of any 'drug trafficking' offence.

20

Appeals

20.1 Introduction

20.2 Appeal from Master's orders

20.3 Appeals from orders of High Court Judges

20.4 Appeals direct to the House of Lords

20.5 Procedure on appeal to the Court of Appeal

20.6 Hearing of the appeal

20.7 Fresh evidence

20.8 Judgment

20.9 Appeal to the House of Lords

20.10 Other matters

20.1 Introduction

A party not satisfied with the decision of a Master or judge may wish to re-argue the decision, or a part of it, at a higher level. The tribunal to which he can appeal, the procedure to be followed, the time limits applicable, and the powers of that higher court, vary considerably according to the nature of the decision. In some cases there is no right of appeal, but only a right to apply for leave to appeal; in others, there can be no appeal at all. Rights of appeal in and from the County Court are dealt with at Chapter 21, section 21.15.

20.2 Appeal from Master's orders

Either party may appeal from the decision of a Master of the Queen's Bench or Chancery Divisions to a High Court judge in chambers, without leave of the court, in any *interlocutory* matter: O.58 r1. The appeal takes the form of a complete rehearing before the judge. The definition of 'interlocutory' has never been clearly set. The following are the most common interlocutory orders;

1. amendment of Writ and pleadings;
2. interim payments;
3. discovery of documents;
4. orders made on the Summons for Directions;
5. garnishee orders;
6. striking out of pleadings under O.18 r19, or for want of prosecution;
7. extension of time for service of pleadings, lists, etc.

Procedure on appeal is by Notice of Appeal issued within five days of the making of the decision complained of and served within five days of issue and not less than two clear days before the hearing of the appeal.

The appeal is, in the Queen's Bench Division, then entered in a 'general list' unless the hearing of it seems likely to last for more than 30 minutes, in which case it joins the 'chambers appeals list'. Whichever list contains it, the parties must then lodge with the court at least 48 hours in advance of the hearing a full bundle of documents, including the notice of appeal, the pleadings, copies of all affidavits and exhibits to affidavits on which reliance will be placed, and the order appealed against: *Practice Note (Chambers Proceedings)* [1989] 1 All ER 1120 QBD.

By contrast, an appeal from any decision of a Master which is a *final* order lies to the Court of Appeal and not to the judge in chambers, no leave being necessary: O.58 r2. The general distinction between interlocutory and final orders is that the latter finally dispose of the rights of the parties: *Haron Zaid* v *Central Securities* [1982] 3 WLR 134. The following are the principal types of final order:

1. an order for summary judgment under O.14;
2. assessment of damages by the Master under O.37.

The CLSA now provides that Rules of Court may be made prescribing certain classes of case for which an appeal may lie to the Court of Appeal only with the leave of the Court of Appeal or other court or tribunal.

Where the Master's order is final in the sense described, the procedure for appealing to the Court of Appeal is the same as that applicable to appeals from a judge: see section 20.3.

20.3 Appeals from orders of High Court Judges

Except where statute otherwise provides, there is an appeal from the order or judgment of any High Court judge, to the Court of Appeal. Where the appeal is on an *interlocutory* matter (and the same problems of definition apply here as they do to appeals from Masters), leave is required from the judge or from the Court of Appeal unless the appeal is of the following types:

1. concerning the liberty of the subject;
2. against the grant or refusal of an injunction;
3. concerning the custody of or against a refusal of access to a minor;
4. in other cases prescribed by s18(1)(h) of the SCA 1981.

Applications for leave should first be made to the judge himself, but if refused should be renewed before the Court of Appeal itself by much the same procedure as a full appeal. The appeal is heard usually by two Lords Justices.

Appeal lies from the judgment or order of a High Court judge of the *final* type, and without leave of the court, except in the following principal cases, contained in s18(1)(a)–(g) Supreme Court Act 1981:

1. An order granting an extension of time for giving notice of appeal. No appeal is possible.
2. Where the parties have agreed not to appeal and the agreement has been recited in the judgment or order. O.25 r5. No appeal is possible.
3. Where the judgment was by consent of the parties. Leave must be obtained from the trial judge.
4. As to costs only (see Chapter 17, section 17.11).
5. From any judgment in a criminal cause or matter by the High Court. No appeal is possible.
6. From any decision which statute declares to be final.

In the Chancery Division, orders made by the judge in chambers cannot normally be appealed to the Court of Appeal unless either the judge or the Court of Appeal gives leave: O.58 r6. Application should first be made by motion to the judge in open court to set aside or discharge his order.

20.4 Appeals direct to the House of Lords

In exceptional circumstances it is possible for an appeal to side-step the Court of Appeal and to go direct to the House of Lords, under ss12 and 13 Administration of Justice Act 1969. This is the so-called 'leap frog' appeal and is used only where the Court of Appeal would be bound to decide the case by reason of some binding House of Lords or Court of Appeal authority, and the appellant wishes to have that authority over-ruled by the House. It can only be made where all parties consent, the trial judge certifies that the case involves a point of law of public importance concerning either the construction of a statute or statutory instrument or (more usually) a matter upon which the Court of Appeal is bound by a previous House of Lords ruling, or one its own, and the House of Lords itself gives leave for the bringing of the appeal. Its use is very rare in civil cases. It was first used in *American Cyanamid* v *Upjohn* [1970] 1 WLR 1507, and later in *O'Brien* v *Robinson* [1973] 2 WLR 393.

20.5 Procedure on appeal to the Court of Appeal

Applications for leave to appeal, where necessary, are heard by a single Lord Justice, and from his decision there is no further appeal: s54(6) Supreme Court Act 1981. Whether leave is or is not required, the appellant must file a Notice of Appeal within four weeks of the judgment complained of being signed, entered or perfected though there is power to extend the time on application to the Registrar of Civil Appeals: see for example *Hollis* v *Jenkins* (1984) The Times 31 January. The usual procedure on an application to appeal out of time involves the court in an examination of the merits of the appeal, to assess whether, if leave were granted, the appeal has any prospect of success. Where however the reasons for a failure to observe the time limit are cogent, and the prejudice to the potential respondents small, the merits will be left for consideration on the hearing of the appeal itself, and not investigated at the stage of determining leave: *Palata Investments* v *Burt & Sinfield* [1985] 3 All ER 517, where the respondents had been notified immediately after trial that an appeal was likely, but Notice of Appeal was served three days late because the appellant's solicitors had not received the most recent edition of *The Supreme Court of Practice* and were not aware that the time for appealing had been reduced since 1982.

The Notice of Appeal must state the ground of appeal and the precise nature of the relief sought on appeal: O.59 r3. No ground can be raised at the hearing of the appeal that is not contained in the Notice, though there is power to allow amendment of the Notice on application to the Registrar: O.59 r7. Again, amendment will rarely be allowed unless the appellant can show some good reason why it was not made before the Notice was lodged. The Court of Appeal has power to amend the Notice at the hearing of the appeal itself, but very rarely does so.

Within 21 days of the service of the Notice of Appeal, the opposing side (the 'respondent') may file a Respondent's Notice, which is in effect a cross-appeal by him seeking also a variation or revocation of the trial judge's order: O.59 r6. This should be as specific as the Notice of Appeal in describing the grounds of cross-appeal and the relief sought. The Respondent's Notice is only a true cross-appeal if it relates to parts of the judgment not challenged by the appellant in the Notice of Appeal, and is then more properly termed a Notice of Appeal, subject to the same time limits as to service, and content.

Within seven days after service of the Notice of Appeal, the appellant must apply to 'set down' the appeal in one of the 15 or so different lists covering such areas as chancery, admiralty, patent, employment, revenue and general Queen's Bench appeals. There are separate lists for interlocutory and final appeals: O.59 r5. On setting down the Notice of Appeal is filed, together with a copy of the judgment or order appealed against. The respondent must be informed of the application to set down within two days of its being made. The seven-day time limit will be strictly enforced, and extensions rarely granted by the Registrar.

The parties then wait until the case appears in the 'list of forthcoming appeals', which may be some time after it is set down. Within 14 days of such appearance, the appellant must lodge with the court three bundles of documents for use by the appeal judges and consisting of the Notice of Appeal, any Respondent's Notice, the judgment or order appealed against, the pleadings in the action, and transcripts of the evidence and judgment below, suitably screened to prevent the Court of Appeal detecting that there had been a payment into court before or during trial: O.59 r9 and 12A. The appellant should also give an estimate of the length of the appeal, having consulted with the respondent. Because there was much delay in filing these documents in the procedure before 1982 (that required filing only seven days before the hearing of the appeal), the Master of the Rolls has made it known that the time limit will be very strictly applied: *Practice Note (Civil Appeals)* [1982] 1 WLR 1312. Modifications to the appeal procedure, intended to expedite hearings still further, came into force in October 1987. See *Practice Note (Court of Appeal: Appeals: Timetable)* [1987] 3 All ER 434.

Once the bundles of documents have been filed, the Registrar has the power to call the parties before him to take directions as to the future conduct of the appeal: O.59 r9(3). It will not be in every case that this is done, but the power exists to prevent waste of time at the appeal by reason of missing documentation, or absence of relevant authorities. A skeleton argument must be delivered to the Court of Appeal in advance of the appeal's being heard except in cases of exceptional urgency: *Practice Note (Skeleton Argument)* [1989] 1 All ER 891 CA. Skeleton arguments must be exchanged between the parties and filed with the court not less than four weeks before the date on which the appeal is scheduled to be heard. A full list of authorities must be contained in that skeleton so that the members of the court can 'preread', and the main points of argument must be clearly set out. A chronology of factual events must also be included.

Once the appeal is entered in the 'list of forthcoming appeals', it may be listed by the Registrar for hearing at any time after the expiry of 14 days from its entry into that list. The Civil Appeals Office then liaises with counsel's clerks and supplies information on the likely progress of the appeal towards being listed for a full hearing. The 'Warned List', which made inefficient use of time and resources in planning for the date of a hearing, was abolished in October 1987.

Certain cases require expedited hearings. Examples would include appeals against committal orders, cases in which children are likely to suffer, possession orders. In *Unilever plc* v *Chefaro Proprietaries Ltd* [1994] NLJ 1660, the Court of Appeal issued guidelines as to the features of a case that would suggest an expedited hearing was appropriate. These are: a party losing its livelihood, business or home or suffering irreparable loss or extraordinary hardship; the appeal becoming futile; delay in the resolution of numerous cases pending the appeal; widespread divergences of practice continuing pending the appeal; serious detriment to good public administration or to the interest of members of the public not concerned in the instant appeal.

20.6 Hearing of the appeal

An appeal to the Court of Appeal is by way of rehearing: O.59 r3. It is however exceptionally rare for the court to hear oral evidence, and it usually confines itself to the transcript of the evidence and judgment, requiring counsel for the appellant to point to some part in it where the trial judge made errors in his findings of fact, or his interpretation or application of the law. In general, no argument may be raised before the court that was not raised at first instance; but the court can consider changes in the facts or the law which have occurred since the judgment, for example, the death of an injured plaintiff, or a decision of the House of Lords; see *Curwen* v *James* [1963] 1 WLR 748.

The court will be very slow to overturn any finding of fact by the judge which was dependent upon which of the witnesses he believed, unless he 'has abused the manifest advantage of seeing and hearing the witnesses give their evidence' (*Evans* v *Bartlam* [1937] AC 473), but they are not so chary of interfering with his inferences from those 'primary' facts. Questions of law are argued afresh, and there is no presumption that the trial judge was correct.

The Court of Appeal will hardly ever reverse the decision of a trial judge on a matter which was within his discretion, unless he has decided in a way which the court considers will cause injustice to be done on appeal. Thus the following judgments are, among others, almost never successfully appealed:

1. To disapply the time limits under s33 Limitation Act 1980: see Chapter 14, section 14.10 and *Conry* v *Simpson* [1983] 3 All ER 369.
2. Apportioning blame between two or more joint tortfeasors: *British Frame* v *McGregor* [1943] AC 197.
3. Granting or refusing an interlocutory or final injunction, or other equitable remedy: *Hadmor* v *Hamilton* [1982] 2 WLR 322. However, the Court of Appeal will interfere with the exercise by a judge of his discretion not to grant an interlocutory injunction, where he appears to have ignored an outstandingly relevant factor, such as the public interest, in deciding the balance of convenience: *Associated British Ports* v *TGWU* (1989) The Times 9 June.
4. Ordering or refusing security for costs: *Fawcett* v *Johnson's* [1939] 3 All ER 377.

If the court does decide that it must interfere with a judge's findings, it may make its own, and may make any order that the trial judge could have made, or substitute its own view of the exercise of a discretionary power: *Yorke Motors* v *Edwards* [1982] 1 WLR 444 and O.59 r11. There is a rarely-used power to order a new trial, used in practice only where the original trial was before judge and jury, or when the court considers that fresh evidence adduced before it justifies a complete rehearing on oral evidence.

20.7 Fresh evidence

The court may hear fresh evidence not used at first instance, but will only do so in the following circumstances:

1. the evidence could not with reasonable diligence have been discovered before the trial at first instance, or there is a very good reason why, if it was available below, it was not used; and
2. it is credible; the court first looks at the evidence or the proofs of witnesses proposed to be called and sees whether the fresh evidence fits in with that already given; and
3. it would, if it had been used below, very probably have produced a different verdict or judgment: *Ladd* v *Marshall* [1954] 3 All ER 745.

Where fresh evidence is received, the court usually orders a new trial. Reasons for its reception when it could have been used below have included misleading action by an opposing party: *Skrzypkowski* v *Silvan* [1963] 1 WLR 525. Before ordering a new trial, the court must consider the hardship caused to the other party from having the matter reopened. In general, the longer the delay before the appeal, and the less blameworthy is the respondent, the less willing the court will be to go against the principle that judgments should be seen to be final, and the matters in dispute disposed of forever: *Sincroflash* v *Trusthouse Forte* (1983) The Times 7 January. In particular species of appeal, for instance those arising upon points of law from the Revenue Commissioners, an even more restrictive rule is applied, and the court will almost never receive fresh evidence unless the respondent has knowingly misled the court at first instance: *Brady* v *Group Lotus plc* [1987] 2 All ER 674.

20.8 Judgment

In the drive for the saving of time by the Court of Appeal, judgments which are reserved are now often printed and 'handed down' without being read orally in open court, thus eroding the practice of nine centuries. It is also becoming increasingly common for the court to decide the appeal after hearing only the appellant's argument, if it is bound to fail, rather than to call upon the respondent to present his case. This may be efficient but doubts are expressed as to the long-term effects upon the image of justice.

20.9 Appeal to the House of Lords

An appeal lies to the House of Lords, in most cases, from the Court of Appeal, and in exceptional cases from the High Court directly (see section 20.4). The appeal may be on points of fact as well as law, though the latter are the most common. Appeal is only by leave of the Court of Appeal or of the Appeals Committee of the House. Applications for leave to the House itself are brought by way of petition. If leave is granted, there is an enormous amount of preparatory work by both sides, including special printings of judgments and orders, detailed disclosure of the arguments which will be presented, complete lists of authorities relied upon, and the deposit with the House of security for the costs of the appeal, by the appellant, of £4,000. The procedure is contained in Standing Orders of the House to be found in Part 7 of Volume 2 to the White Book.

20.10 Other matters

Appeals to the Court of Appeal (Criminal Division) and to the Divisional Court of Queen's Bench are dealt with in the section on criminal procedure. Costs on appeal are explained in Chapter 17.

Where a jury in a civil trial has made an award of damages (for example, in a false imprisonment or libel case) the Court of Appeal will be enabled through Rules of Court to be made under the CLSA to substitute a sum as appears proper to the court (as an option to ordering a new trial).

21

County Court Procedure

21.1 Introduction

21.2 Transfer of proceedings

21.3 Transfer to the High Court

21.4 Commencing proceedings

21.5 Issue and service of proceedings

21.6 Parties

21.7 Pre-trial review and automatic directions

21.8 Summary judgment

21.9 Pleadings

21.10 Interlocutory proceedings

21.11 Trial

21.12 Enforcement of judgments

21.13 Small claims procedure

21.14 Costs

21.15 Appeals

21.16 Nonsuit

21.1 Introduction

The procedure of the County Court is similar to that of the High Court. Where no special procedure is laid down by the County Courts Act 1984 or the County Court Rules 1981 then the Rules of the Supreme Court apply (CCA 1984 s76).

Throughout this textbook, the emphasis has been upon the High Court with parallel Orders in the County Court being referred to where appropriate and differences are highlighted. In this chapter, these differences are examined in greater detail. In particular, section 21.13 looks at the Small Claims procedure, which is unique to the County Court and of increasing importance.

21.2 Transfer of proceedings

At any stage of proceedings begun in the High Court the High Court may, either of its own motion or upon application by the parties or one of them, transfer those proceedings to such county court as it thinks convenient: s40 County Courts Act 1984. The power applies however only insofar as the only reason why the action was not commenced in the County Court was because the sum claimed or the value of the subject-matter of the action was above the County Court limit. In other words, the action must be of a type which could be commenced in the County Court, disregarding the financial limits upon its jurisdiction. The following types of action cannot be transferred:

1. matrimonial causes and those relating to the custody of children;
2. actions in which the Crown is a party, unless the Crown consents to the transfer.

Section 40 CCA 1984 as amended provides that the High Court shall transfer any proceedings that are required to be in a County Court or, if it is of the opinion that the party bringing the action knew or ought to have known that it was to be started in the County Court, strike out the proceedings. An order for transfer or striking out under this provision may be made on an application by either party or of the court's own motion.

The High Court may also transfer any proceedings on the application of any party or of its own motion (for example, where the amount is large but the issues are simple).

If there is a counterclaim proceeding with the claim, both will be transferred. The parties then lodge with the District Judge of the County Court to which transfer has been ordered (depending on the convenience of the parties and the work-load of the county courts) copies of the Writ and other documents. The action then proceeds as if it were a County Court action for all purposes, including rights of appeal, but the County Court judge is empowered to award any relief in the action which could have been given if the action had remained in the High Court: s40(10).

The documents which should be lodged with the Central Office or District Registry, and with the County Court to which the action is to be transferred, are specified in procedural directions of the High Court: *Practice Direction* [1988] 2 All ER 64 and [1988] 3 All ER 95.

Application for transfer may be made at any time, but is usually made on the Summons for Directions (see Chapter 16, section 16.2). An action which has been transferred to the County Court may be transferred back to the High Court under the powers discussed below.

The backlog of cases awaiting a trial in the Chancery Division of the High Court has led to the recent adoption of a procedure whereby transfer to a County Court (usually the Mayor's and City of London Court) under s40 of the 1984 Act will be considered as of course by the Master on hearing of the Summons for Directions, and a transfer ordered if the matter appears relatively straightforward: *Practice Direction (Chancery: Transfer of Business)* [1988] 3 All ER 96. In particular, applications for the sale of property held on trust for sale, for new tenancies of commercial premises, for the appointment and replacement of trustees, and for the resolution of disputes over boundaries to land and rights of way across it, will probably make their way to a County Court trial unless there is some important question of law or fact raised in them.

The transfer from High Court to County Court of civil actions which would normally be tried by jury, such as malicious prosecution, false imprisonment and assault, is to become more frequent. The High Court judge charged with responsibility for maintaining the list of jury actions is thus to be given the task of reviewing these actions once they are set down for trial, to determine whether they are suitable for transfer to a County Court jury trial: *Practice Note (County Court: Transfer of Jury Cases)* [1989] 2 All ER 128 QBD.

21.3 Transfer to the High Court

An action begun in the County Court may be transferred to the High Court of its own motion, under s41 of the 1984 Act, or by order of the County Court of its own motion or on application of the parties or one of them, under s42. These provisions mirror those of s40 as amended. See generally RSC O.78 and CCR O.16 r10.

Proceedings may also be transferred from one County Court to another for reasons of convenience or fair conduct of the action (for example, if the judge of the County Court where the proceedings should properly be begun is a party to or otherwise interested in the action) (O.16 r1), or where the action has been begun in the wrong court by mistake: O.16 r2.

21.4 Commencing proceedings

County Court proceedings are of two main types: *actions* or *matters*. However, the vast majority of proceedings are actions. Actions are divided into default and fixed date actions (CCR O.3 r2). A default action is used to recover money, both liquidated and unliquidated sums. A fixed date action is used where the claim or any part of it is for some relief other than money; for example, possession of land or equitable remedies.

To issue proceedings in an action, the intending plaintiff completes a request form or a form of summons. This gives the names and addresses of the parties, a brief description of the claim and the relief being sought. If brief particulars of claim are not indorsed on the form then a fully pleaded Particulars of Claim must be enclosed with the request or summons. Where the action is for personal injuries, the plaintiff must also enclose a medical report and a statement of special damages. Lastly, notification of Legal Aid must also be enclosed if appropriate.

Default actions can be commenced anywhere (CCR O.4 r2(1)(c)), but under CCR O.9 r2(8) will be automatically transferred to the defendant's home court on the filing of a defence. Fixed date actions may be commenced: (a) in the court for the district in which the defendant or one of the defendants resides or carries on business; or (b) in the court for the district in which the cause of action wholly or in part arose (CCR O.4 r2(a),(b)). Where proceedings are for the recovery of land, they may only be commenced in the court for the district in which the land or any part of it is situated (CCR O.4 r3).

Matters are defined in s147 County Courts Act 1984 as 'every proceeding in a county court which may be commenced as prescribed otherwise than by plaint'. Statutes, statutory instruments or the CCR will provide for the minority of proceedings that are matters and they will be commenced by originating application or petition. For example, CCR O.43 r2 states that proceedings under the Landlord and Tenant Acts 1927, 1954, 1985 and 1987 shall be commenced by originating application.

21.5 Issue and service of proceedings

When the court receives the request or summons and other documents from the intending plaintiff, it issues the summons by sealing it with the court seal. A return day is fixed for those fixed date actions not subject to automatic directions under CCR O.17 r11. The plaintiff is sent a plaint note which notifies him of the issue of the summons.

The court serves the summons on the defendant (in contrast with the High Court) along with the Particulars of Claim (if any) and forms for admission, defence and counterclaim. However, the plaintiff can elect to serve a summons personally (CCR O.7 r10). Also, under CCR O.7 r10A, the plaintiff's solicitor can serve the summons by first-class post in personal injuries cases.

The defendant has a number of choices upon receiving the summons (CCR O.9 rr2–4):

1. if it is a money claim, admit it and pay the money directly to the plaintiff;
2. admit the money claim but seek time to pay by delivering the form of admission together with a statement of his means and a request for time;
3. dispute liability for all or part of the claim by returning a defence and, if appropriate, a counterclaim within 14 days of service. The defence (and any counterclaim) can either be fully pleaded or on the forms sent to the defendant.

Note that the time limits for the service of the defence may be varied by agreement between the parties: *Heer* v *Tutton and Another* (1995) The Times 5 June; see Chapter 36, section 36.4, for further details.

21.6 Parties

The rules as to joinder of parties are much the same as in the High Court, but by contrast a minor may sue in his own name, without the intervention of a next friend, for wages, and may be sued without the need for a guardian *ad litem* in any claim for a liquidated sum in any case where the court so directs: O.10 r8 and s47 of the 1984 Act.

21.7 Pre-trial review and automatic directions

In all fixed date and default actions, there are now automatic directions. There are, however, a number of exceptions to this rule, for example, there are no automatic directions in actions for delivery of goods; actions for trial by jury; small claims arbitration; actions for recovery of land: CCR O.17 r11. Where there is a pre-trial review instead it is broadly similar in function and form to the Summons for Directions in the High Court.

The automatic directions provide a timetable which begins with close of pleadings. This is deemed to occur 14 days after service of the Defence or 28 days after service of a Counterclaim. The Timetable is as follows:

Subject	Action	Time
Discovery and inspection	serve list of documents, indicating where and when inspection can occur	28 days (after close of pleadings) with a further seven days for inspection
Witness statements	exchange of statements (including experts) that will be adduced at trial	ten weeks
Photographs and plans	agree before trial	any time
Fix trial date (Plaintiff only)	request court to fix date; estimate length of case and number of witnesses	six months
Documents (Defendant only)	inform Plaintiff of documents wish to use at trial	not later than 14 days before trial
Documents (Plaintiff)	send court documents both parties will use	not later than seven days before trial

In personal injury claims, where the injury arises out of a road traffic accident, only documents relating to quantum need be discovered. In addition, each party will be limited to two medical experts and one other expert unless the parties agree otherwise.

The timetable is flexible to the extent the parties may agree a longer period for each step. However, if a trial date has not been requested within 15 months, the case will be automatically struck out. The court does have jurisdiction under O.13 r4 to extend time retrospectively for the making of a request and thereby reinstate the action. However, the plaintiff must show that he has conducted his case overall with reasonable diligence and that his failure is excusable before the court will consider whether to reinstate: *Rastin* v *British Steel* [1994] 1 WLR 732. A failure to deliver witness statements on time must be explained on affidavit by the party seeking the exercise of the court's discretion to allow oral evidence from those late witnesses: *Taylor* v *Remploy* [1995] 3 CL 434. See Chapter 36, section 36.4, for further details.

21.8 Summary judgment

Powers to give summary judgment for the plaintiff at the pre-trial review are contained in O.9 r14. The procedure and conditions for granting it are very similar to those of the High Court, and there is power to give conditional and unconditional leave to defend. The application can be made however only if the following terms are met:

1. the action is a default action;
2. the amount claimed is £1,000 or more (whether liquidated or unliquidated) (in other words summary judgment is not available where an action is referred to arbitration under O.19 r3);
3. the defendant has filed a document purporting to be a defence (in the High Court O.14 is usually applied for before the defence is served);
4. the plaintiff files an affidavit verifying the claim and averring that he believes there is no defence to the claim;
5. notice of the application, together with a copy of the affidavit, have been served on the defendant at least seven days before the hearing (in the High Court the period is ten clear days).

21.9 Pleadings

The principles governing the drafting of pleadings are the same as those in the High Court, save that the plaintiff's statement of his claim is termed Particulars of Claim (O.6 and O.9), though the pleadings are generally far less detailed. There are similar powers to order further and better particulars, to strike out pleadings, and to dismiss for want of prosecution and give judgment in default of pleadings: O.6 r7, O.13 r5, O.13 r2 and O.9 r6. Unlike proceedings in the High Court, pleadings are sent to the court rather than to the opposing party; the court sends them on to the other side.

21.10 Interlocutory proceedings

There are usually fewer interlocutory hearings and applications in the County Court, but the powers to give relief are similar with respect to discovery of documents, interrogatories and interpleader. The following however are to be noted:

1. there is no power to order interim payments on account of debt or damages unless the sum claimed or amount involved is substantial: O.13 r12;
2. leave is required to issue third party proceedings in all fixed date actions and in default actions where a day has been fixed for trial or pre-trial review: O.12 r1;
3. the court has a limited power to grant Mareva injunctions, but no power to make an Anton Piller order (see County Court Remedies Regulations 1991, SI 1991/1222).

21.11 Trial

The mode of trial is very similar to that in the High Court except in relation to small claims (see section 21.13). The defence however may not make a closing speech without leave of the court if it made an opening speech. The trial may be before the judge or, with the parties' consent, before the District Judge: O.21 r5.

21.12 Enforcement of judgments

Judgments for money in the County Court must be paid within 14 days of the judgment, unless the court orders otherwise, but the court can order payment by instalments having regard to the defendant's means to pay: s71 of the 1984 Act and O.22 r10. The methods of enforcement are much the same as those in the High Court, but have different names:

1. Warrant of Execution under O.26 r1 – like FiFa, but executed by the County Court Bailiff rather than the Sheriff;
2. Warrant for Possession under O.25 r17 – like Writ of Possession, for recovery of land.

There are powers to commit for contempt, to garnishee debts, to make charging orders, and to appoint receivers. The powers of enforcement are contained in O.26, O.27, O.28, O.29, O.30, O.31, O.32 and O.33.

21.13 Small claims procedure

Where the plaintiff begins a default action for £3,000 or less, and the defendant files a defence, the case is automatically referred to informal arbitration by the District Judge: O.19 r3 (the only exception to this procedure is claims for the possession of land or personal injury claims exceeding £1,000). The use of arbitration is intended to encourage the bringing of small claims by litigants unable to afford the costly services of lawyers. The case is heard by the District Judge in private, and the normal rules of procedure and evidence do not usually apply; the District Judge may adopt such procedure as he considers fair and convenient: O.19 r7. However, the District Judge has no right to exclude from the hearing any duly qualified solicitor or barrister properly instructed by a party, or to disallow cross-examination of witnesses: *Chilton* v *Saga Holidays* [1986] 1 All ER 841 CA.

One very great advantage of the procedure is that there is an almost absolute 'no costs' rule (O.19 r4); win or lose, neither party has to pay the other's costs or is able to recover his own. This discourages the use of lawyers, especially by defendants, and the plaintiff acting in person can conduct his case in the sure knowledge that if he loses he need not pay for the solicitors instructed by the defendant. The exceptions to the rule are as follows:

1. a plaintiff who succeeds can claim his costs of commencing the action and of enforcing the District Judge's award;
2. if either party has acted 'unreasonably', he may be ordered to pay the costs of the other: O.19 r4.

The increase to £3,000 in the small claims limit came into effect from 8 January 1996, and the change is part of the first phase of the implementation of the recommendations of the Woolf report.

A claim for £3,000 or less may involve difficult questions of fact or law, and provision is made for rescinding the automatic reference to arbitration and taking the case into the same procedure as a normal default action in the County Court, with pre-trial review and full trial and orders as to costs. The power to rescind is given by O.19 r3, and is exercisable by the District Judge after considering the defence, either on the application of a party or of his own motion. He must be satisfied:

1. that a difficult question of law or exceptionally difficult question of fact is involved; or
2. that a charge of fraud is in issue; or
3. that the parties agree to rescind the reference; or
4. that it would be unreasonable, having regard to the subject-matter of the claim, the circumstances of the parties, or the interest of other persons likely to be affected by the award, to proceed to arbitration; for example, if the claim is a personal injury case between motorists, and one party will be funded throughout the case by his insurers but the other will not, there is inequality, for the unfunded plaintiff cannot recover the costs he must personally incur to defend the action properly: *Pepper* v *Healey* (1982) The Times 9 March.

Order 19 r3 was considered by the Court of Appeal in *Afzal and Others* v *Ford Motor Co Ltd* [1994] 4 All ER 720. This concerned 22 minor personal injury actions brought against employers, in 16 of which successful applications had been made to rescind the reference on the basis that the nature of the claims – industrial personal injuries – made them unsuitable for arbitration given the importance of statutory duty, medical evidence and discovery. In three of the cases, the automatic reference had been avoided by inflating the damages beyond £1,000, which was the small claims limit at the time. The Court of Appeal held that the question of law had to be difficult and the question of fact exceptionally complex to justify rescission and there was nothing inherently different about industrial accident cases to justify approaching them differently. Further, the intentional overstatement of the amount involved to avoid a procedure was a clear misuse of power.

There is also provision (in O.19 r9) for voluntary reference to arbitration on application by a party, either within the pleading or on notice under O.13 r1.

The mechanism for setting aside an award made where proceedings are referred to arbitration is contained in O.10 r8. There are only two grounds: misconduct by the arbitrator or an error of law. The application to set aside must be made within 14 days on notice and will be heard by a Circuit Judge or District Judge.

21.14 Costs

The award of costs other than in proceedings referred to arbitration is governed by the same principles as in the High Court. The winner usually recovers his costs, the loser usually pays, but the position may be changed by payments into court, conduct of the parties, or the other principles which allow unusual orders to be made (see Chapter 17). The difference is that costs in the County Court are calculated on three 'scales', relating to the amount claimed or recovered in the action; if the plaintiff succeeds the appropriate scale is that relating to the amount actually recovered. If he loses, it is the amount he unsuccessfully claimed which governs his costs liability. The court can order that a different scale apply, but only does so in practice where the claim was very complicated. The scales are:

Lower scale	£25.01 to £100
Scale 1	£100.01 to £3,000
Scale 2	more than £3,000

There is a scale of 'fixed costs' where the amount of costs is stated on the Summons, and taxation of costs is done by the court by reference to scales laid down in the Green Book. The allowance of items of costs for services of counsel are quite restricted, and in general the aim of the costs scales is to discourage parties from retaining expensive lawyers in what is meant to be a court for quick resolution of simple disputes. The basis of taxation of costs is almost without exception 'party-and-party', the meanest of the possible bases. There is no power in the County Court for the judge to order a fixed sum in his order of costs.

The rules concerning payment into court differ slightly in that the plaintiff cannot accept without leave of the court less than three days before the start of the trial (CCR O.11), but the principle that a plaintiff who accepts is entitled to his costs insofar as they relate to the period before payment in is broadly similar: *Seacroft Hotel* v *Goble* [1984] 1 WLR 939.

21.15 Appeals

An interlocutory decision of a District Judge can be appealed as of right to a Circuit Judge (CCR O.13 r1). The appeal is made on notice within five days of the order being made and is usually heard in chambers.

Appeal of a final decision by a District Judge also lies to the Circuit Judge (CCR O.37 r6). Notice must be filed within 14 days, stating grounds of appeal. If these are established, the Circuit Judge can vary or set aside all or part of the decision, remit the case for a rehearing or order a new trial before a judge.

Appeal of a decision by a Circuit Judge lies to the Court of Appeal (CCA 1984 s77), notice of appeal being served within four weeks. The general provisions concerning whether leave is required are contained in RSC O.59 r1B and rules specific to the County Court are contained in the County Courts Appeals Order 1991. This latter states that leave will be required:

1. in an action in tort or contract where the value of the appeal does not exceed £5,000;
2. where proceedings come within the court's equitable jurisdictions and the capital value of the estate, fund or assets does not exceed £15,000;
3. where the value of the appeal is not quantifiable;
4. where the determination sought to be appealed from was made by a judge acting in his appellate capacity.

If leave is required, it is first sought from the Circuit Judge, failing which leave must be obtained from the Court of Appeal.

21.16 Nonsuit

One further procedure, unique to the County Court and long ago abandoned by the High Court, deserves mention: the nonsuit. This is a power to order at trial, instead of judgment for the defendant, that the plaintiff has failed to prove his claim but shall not be prevented from bringing a fresh action on the same facts and for the same relief. Its grant is regulated by O.21 r2 and is subject to the following principles:

1. At any time up to the time the facts are found, if the plaintiff elects to be nonsuited he is entitled to claim nonsuit as of right and the court cannot refuse. Thus at any time before judgment, in effect, the plaintiff can insist that he be allowed to start from the beginning again by bringing a fresh action.
2. If, after all the evidence has been given, but before the facts are found, the plaintiff refuses to be nonsuited, the court has a discretion to nonsuit even against his wishes.
3. Once the facts are found, the court has a complete discretion whether to nonsuit or to give judgement for the defendant, if the plaintiff has failed to prove his case.

The right to claim, and the discretion to grant, nonsuit, have been retained in the County Court to assist the plaintiff who acts in person without legal representation, and who does not understand the technicalities of procedure and evidence. He may fail to bring evidence of a vital fact, for example, damage in a claim for common law negligence, or have pleaded his case on an incorrect basis. Although the nonsuit is not restricted to plaintiffs acting in person, its use is most common by them on the suggestion of the judge, who does not wish to cause the plaintiff injustice by giving judgment for the defendant when, if the plaintiff were properly advised, his claim has a prospect of success.

Appendix:

Rules of the Supreme Court

The following is a summary of the Rules of the Supreme Court. The general nature of the subject-matter of each is given, together with a list of the most important and frequently used Rules of each Order. In the column headed 'CCR' is the County Court Order (if any) most closely similar to that of the High Court.

RSC Order	CCR	Subject-matter	RSC Rules
1	1	Interpretation of the RSC	
2	1	Effect of Non-Compliance with RSC	1
3	1	Definition of Time and Time Limits	2, 5
4	13	Assignment, Transfer, Consolidation	
5	3	Mode of Commencing Proceedings	2, 3, 4
6		Writ: General provisions as to Form	8
7		Originating Summons: as to Form	
8		Originating Motions: as to Form	
9		Petitions: Motions: as to Form	
10	7	Service of Writ, OS etc	1, 4
11	8	Service of Writ, etc, outside jurisdiction	1
12		Acknowledgement of Service	1, 7
13	9	Failure to Give Notice of Intent to Defend	1, 2, 7, 9
14	9	Summary Judgment	1, 2, 3, 4, 11
15	5	Joinder of Parties and Causes of Action	1, 2, 3, 4, 6, 6A, 7, 16
16	12	Third Party Proceedings	1, 3, 5, 8, 9, 10
17	33	Interpleader	
18	6	Pleadings: Form and Content	1, 2, 3, 6, 7, 7A, 12, 19
19	9	Default of pleadings	1, 2, 3, 8
20	15	Amendment	1, 3, 5, 10
21	18	Withdrawal and Discontinuance	1, 2, 3
22	11	Payment into Court	1, 3, 4, 7
23	13	Security for Costs	1
24	14	Discovery and Inspection	1, 2, 3, 7, 7A, 10, 16
25	17	Summons for Directions	1, 8
26	14	Interrogatories	1, 8
27	9	Admissions	2

Appendix: Rules of the Supreme Court 205

Order	CCR	Subject-matter	Rules
28		Originating Summons Procedure	1A
29		Interlocutory Orders	1, 10, 11, 17
30		Receivers	
31	22	Sale of Land by Court Order	
32		Proceedings in Chambers	
33		Mode of Trial	
34		Setting Down for Trial	
35	21	Proceedings at Trial	
36	21	Trial by Master or Referee	
37	21	Assessment of Damages by Master or Referee	
38	20	Evidence	1, 2, 2A, 4, 21–30, 35–39
39	20	Depositions and Court Examiners	1
40		Court Expert	
41	20	Affidavits	
42	22	Judgments and Orders: Form and Content	
43	23	Accounts and Inquiries	
44		Judgments and Orders: Chancery Division	
45	25	Enforcement of Judgments and Orders: General 1	
46	26	Writ of Execution	
47		Fieri Facias	
48	28	Examination of Judgment Debtor	
49	30	Garnishee Proceedings	1
50	31	Charging Orders	1
51	32	Receivers	
52	29	Committal for Contempt of Court	
53		Judicial Review	1, 3, 4
54		Habeas Corpus	
55		Case Stated: Appeals to the High Court	
56		Case State: Appeals to the High Court	
57		Divisional Court Procedure	
58	37	Appeal from Master's Decisions	1, 7
59		Court of Appeal	3, 4, 11
60		Restrictive Practices Court	
61		Appeals from Tribunals by Case Stated	
62	38	Costs	2, 3, 5, 12, 28–31
63	50	Administration and Sittings of High Court	
64		Administration and Sittings of High Court	

Order	CCR	Subject-matter	Rules
65	7	Service of Documents	1, 2, 3, 4
66		Specification of Type of Paper	
67		Change of Solicitor	
68		Official Shorthand Note	
69		Foreign Proceedings	
70		Evidence for Foreign Courts	
71		Reciprocal Enforcement of Judgments	
72		Commercial Actions	
73		Arbitration	
74		Merchant Shipping Act Proceedings	
75	40	Admiralty Proceedings	
76	41	Contentious Probate Proceedings	
77	42	Crown Proceedings	3–4, 6–9, 12, 16
78	16	Transfer from County Court	
79		Criminal Proceedings (rr1–7 REVOKED)	
80	10	Persons under a Disability	2, 8, 10, 11
81	5	Partnership Proceedings	9
82		Defamation Proceedings	5
83	49	Consumer Credit Act Proceedings	
84		REVOKED	
85		Administration Actions	
86		Specific Performance	1, 4
87		Debenture Holders Actions	
88		Mortgage Actions	
89	47	Proceedings between Husband and Wife	2
90		REVOKED	
91		Revenue Proceedings in Chancery	
92		Lodgement of Funds in Chancery	
93		Applications under various Acts: Chancery	
94		Applications under various Acts: QBD	
95		Bills of Sale Act Proceedings	
96		Mines (Working Facilities) Act Proceedings	
97	43	Landlord and Tenant Act Proceedings	
98		Local Government Act Proceedings	
99	48	Inheritance (Provision) Act Proceedings	
100		Trade Marks Acts Proceedings	
101		Pensions Appeal Tribunal Act Proceedings	

Order	CCR	Subject-matter	Rules
102		Companies Act 1985 Proceedings	2, 3, 5
103		REVOKED	
104		Patent Act Proceedings	
105		REVOKED	
106		Solicitors Act Proceedings	
107		County Courts Act 1959	2
108		Charities Act Proceedings	
109		AJA 1960 Proceedings	
110		Environmental Control Proceedings	
111		Social Security Act Proceedings	
112		Blood Tests in Paternity Actions	
113	24	Summary Possession of Land	1, 3, 4, 6
114	19	References to European Court	
115		Confiscation orders under the Drug Trafficking Offences Act 1986	

PART II
CRIMINAL PROCEDURE

22

Introduction

The rules of civil procedure are concerned mainly with what happens *outside* the courtroom; the issue of process, service, discovery, and other interlocutory matters. By contrast, the principal rules of criminal procedure concern events *inside* court. There are interlocutory stages in any prosecution, but it is with the conduct of the trial itself that this book is occupied, together with the other occasions upon which an accused person may come before the court preliminary to his full trial.

Just as the civil courts have two main types, so in the criminal law there are two courts which try offenders; the magistrates' court, which has a local jurisdiction, and the Crown Court, where trials take place with judge and jury. It is important to have in mind that some 97 per cent of all criminal trials take place in the magistrates' court, and that only some 3 per cent are tried before a jury. The newly-called barrister can expect to appear in his or her early career in the 'lower' of the two courts; briefs to the Crown Court will be rare and very simple. A thorough knowledge of the workings of summary trial before lay magistrates is thus essential. Particularly in criminal cases, points of procedural law may arise in the course of a trial – it is undignified and embarrassing if counsel cannot quickly find the answer to them, or asks for an adjournment in order to consult his textbooks or, worse still, misleads the court by giving a wrong answer.

The standard works on procedure are lengthy and expensive, but should be consulted for detailed study of the law. For the Crown Court, the recognised authority is *Archbold Criminal Pleading and Practice*; for the magistrates, there is a massive work which contains much obscure substantive law and in which students may have difficulty in finding specific references – this is *Stone's Justices Manual*, published annually in three volumes. *Blackstone's Criminal Procedure* is a very good alternative to *Archbold* and is possibly more appropriate for the newly practising barrister. Much of the law is derived from statute, with judicial precedent grafted upon it. The use of the law reports will also be required. Although not strictly within the terms of reference, mention will be made of proposals for changing the law, where these seem particularly relevant and likely to be implemented within the next few years.

Throughout what follows, the following abbreviations are used in reference to statutes:

CLA   Criminal Law Act
CJA   Criminal Justice Act
CAA   Criminal Appeal Act

CJPOA	Criminal Justice and Public Order Act 1994
JA	Juries Act
JPA	Justices of the Peace Act
LAA	Legal Aid Act
MCA	Magistrates' Courts Act
PCC	Powers of Criminal Courts Act
SCA	Supreme Court Act
PACE	Police and Criminal Evidence Act 1984

Other statutes and rules are referred to by name in their appropriate places.

23

Arrest and Prosecution

23.1 Introduction

23.2 Arrest with warrant

23.3 Arrest without warrant

23.4 Procedure on arrest

23.5 Detention and police bail

23.6 Decision to prosecute

23.7 Director of Public Prosecutions

23.8 Attorney-General

23.9 Government departments

23.10 Private individuals

23.11 Caution

23.12 Time limits

23.13 Motoring offences

23.1 Introduction

Many, but by no means the majority, of criminal prosecutions begin with the arrest of a suspect. The arrest may be with or without a justices' warrant. Following arrest the suspect will be questioned and the decision taken whether to charge him. He may be remanded in custody or given bail by the arresting authority, or by the court. If the arrest has been unlawful or the period of detention excessive and unjustified, the suspect may have remedies for false imprisonment.

23.2 Arrest with warrant

A warrant for arrest is a formal document issued by a justice of the peace, a magistrate, ordering the police force for a named area to take the person named in the warrant into custody and to bring him before the court to answer a charge made against him. It is used mainly only where there is no power to arrest the suspect without warrant (see section 23.3) and there is reason to believe that the suspect will abscond and fail to appear at court if the more normal procedure of Summons is used. A Summons is a formal document addressed to the suspect requiring him to appear at court. Warrants can be issued only by a justice of the peace, and only if the following conditions are satisfied:

1. the charge in respect of which the warrant is sought has been put into writing and the truth of its contents sworn to on oath (usually by the police officer applying for the warrant); and
2. the accused is either a juvenile or the offence is punishable with imprisonment or accused's address is not readily establishable: s1 MCA 1980.

The warrant remains in force until revoked by the court or executed by arrest of the person named in it. Provided the police act in good faith, they will be protected against an action for false imprisonment by an arrested person if it turns out that the warrant was wrongly issued. Usually the arrest will be effected at the accused's home, and reasonable force may be used to enter any premises where the accused is. The warrant 'runs throughout England and Wales', so that the accused can be arrested on it even though he is outside the area for which the court which issued the warrant has jurisdiction.

Once arrested on warrant, the custody and questioning of the suspect follow the same course as on arrest without warrant. The warrant itself may however direct the police to release the suspect on bail, with a condition that he 'answer for bail' by appearing before the court on a stated date. The warrant is then said to be 'backed for bail'. The suspect must be shown the warrant if he asks to see it, though the police need not have it in their possession at the time of executing it; where a warrant is known to have been issued, the accused may be found by chance by an officer who does not possess it – the arrest can be made and the accused shown the warrant on his arrival at the police station where it is kept: see s33 PACE 1984.

23.3 Arrest without warrant

There is a very wide range of suspected offences for which the police or private citizens, or various government departments, may arrest a suspect without having to obtain a warrant. Most of these are of a serious nature, or are most commonly committed in circumstances where, if there were no power to make an immediate arrest, the offender would disappear or cause further harm. The principal offences for which power of arrest without warrant is given to the police are as follows:

1. drunken driving or unfitness to drive through drink or drugs;
2. breach of the peace committed in the officer's presence;
3. possession of controlled drugs;
4. any offence which is punishable on first conviction with a maximum of at least five years' imprisonment.

The offences in (4) above are termed 'arrestable offences', and include all the most serious offences, for example, murder, robbery, rape, theft, burglary, actual or grievous bodily harm, blackmail and criminal damage. It is not the sentence which the particular offender may receive which determines whether the offence is arrestable, but the maximum prescribed by statute for an adult. Thus a shoplifter who steals items of low value will probably be sentenced to no more than a fine, but since the maximum sentence for theft is seven years he may be arrested without warrant even though there is no chance that he will receive so severe a penalty. Similarly, the hooligan who breaks a small pane of glass will as likely as not receive only a non-custodial penalty, but since there is a maximum sentence of ten years for criminal damage, he may be arrested without warrant. Arrestable offences are governed by s24 PACE 1984.

The power to arrest for arrestable offences is given to private citizens as well as to the police, but the conditions for its exercise are different for each. A police officer (whether on or off duty, and whether or not in uniform) may arrest any person whom he reasonably suspects to be in the act of committing the offence, for example, the burglar with his jemmy forcing open a window, any person whom he reasonably suspects to be *about to commit* an arrestable offence, and any person he reasonably suspects of committing an arrestable offence which he reasonably suspects has been committed or which has in fact been committed. The private citizen however has far more limited powers of arrest. He can arrest only where the offence is in the act of being committed or where it has actually been committed (not merely suspected of having been committed), and may arrest the person he reasonably suspects of committing it. The dangers of a citizen arresting are illustrated by *Walters* v *W H Smith* [1914] 1 KB 595. W was the manager of a bookstall. He took books home with him. His employers suspected him of stealing the books and arrested him. At his trial the court accepted that he had taken the books only for safekeeping, and had no intent to keep them; therefore no theft had been committed. And since there was no theft, there could be no arrestable offence which had been actually committed and which could found a power of citizen's arrest. W's action for damages for false imprisonment succeeded. He could have been lawfully arrested by a police officer, but not by the employers. In a more recent case (*White* v *WP Brown* [1983] CLY 972) a 72-year-old woman was awarded approximately £1,000 for false imprisonment and trespass to her handbag after being stopped by a shop security guard and detained for two hours.

It should be noted that private citizens have other powers of arrest not restricted to 'arrestable offences' within s24 PACE 1984. Apart from the power to arrest for a breach of the peace committed in the citizen's presence, all are conferred by statute and are subject to the conditions the statute prescribes. For example, there is a power of arrest without warrant for reasonably suspected offences of making off without payment under s3 Theft Act 1968 if the offence is in the act of being committed. The offence carries a maximum penalty of two years and is thus not 'arrestable' within PACE 1984. Where an arrest is effected by a citizen, whether under PACE 1984 or some other statute, the person arrested must be handed over to a police officer or brought before a magistrates' court as soon as is reasonably possible, though it seems that a moderate amount of questioning is permitted before the police are called, if its purpose is to decide whether or not to press charges: see *John Lewis* v *Tims* [1952] AC 676.

Section 25 PACE empowers a police officer to arrest a person for any 'non-arrestable' offence, provided one of the general arrest conditions is satisfied, for example, that the offender may cause harm to himself or others.

23.4 Procedure on arrest

An arrest is usually made by taking hold of the suspect and placing him under some physical restraint. The use of handcuffs is discouraged unless there is some reason to believe the suspect will try to escape or could do further injury or damage to himself or others. Unless the offender makes it difficult to tell him by running away he must be told the nature of the offence for which the arrest is made, though reasonable attempts to explain the fact of the reasons for arrest will suffice, for example, if, unknown to the arresting officer, the suspect is deaf or speaks no English: *Christie* v *Leachinsky* [1947] AC 573 and *Wheatley* v *Lodge* [1971] 1 WLR 29. This requirement is created by s28 PACE 1984.

Anyone making an arrest may use reasonable force to effect it: s3(1) CLA 1967. What is reasonable depends upon the circumstances. Use of excessive force may render the arrest unlawful and expose the arresting officer or citizen to civil claims for assault or criminal charges for assault or bodily harm. A police officer may, but a private citizen may not, enter premises (if need be by force) where he with reasonable cause believes an offender to be, for the purposes of making an arrest with warrant: s17 PACE 1984. He may also carry out a search of those premises in order to locate the offender and the evidence of the offence.

23.5 Detention and police bail

Once arrested, a suspect should not generally be kept in police detention for a period exceeding 24 hours without being charged, calculated from the moment he is brought to a police station in the area in which he has been arrested or (if arrested in one area and conveyed to another) arrives at the police station of the area where he is to be fully interrogated: s41 PACE 1984. Where a person has been arrested for a serious arrestable offence (murder, rape etc), he may be detained without charge up to a maximum of 36 hours, on the authority of an officer of the rank of at least superintendent, to enable sufficient evidence to be gathered. For such offences, further detention without charge may occur up to a maximum of 96 hours from arrival at the police station as outlined above, with the authority of 'warrants of further detention' issued by a magistrate under s43 of the Act and intended to assist the investigation of serious crime in similar manner. It should be noted that under the Prevention of Terrorism (Temporary Provisions) Act 1989, suspects detained without charge on suspicion of terrorist offences may be so detained for up to 48 hours in the first instance, a period which can be extended by a maximum of five days by order of the Home Secretary.

Special rules apply to the detention or release of juveniles. The juvenile's parent or guardian must be informed if practicable, and the juvenile may be detained upon the additional ground that such detention is reasonably thought necessary in his own interests: s38(1)(b).

Regular reviews should be made during the period of detention to assess whether the conditions which originally justified its continuance remain. The first review is after six hours, then nine hourly: s40.

Very many arrested persons are not kept long in custody after their arrest. After conveyance to the police station they are either released without charge, the police being satisfied that no point will be served in bringing proceedings, or are released on bail to appear in court at a later date. Bail is the release from custody of a person subject to a duty upon him to surrender to the court on a stated date, and it may be subject to further conditions. Where bail is granted by the police following an arrest but before appearance before the magistrates' court, the following must be noted:

1. The grant of 'police bail' is governed by ss37, 38 and 47 of the PACE 1984 and is deemed to occur under the provisions of the Bail Act 1976 (see Chapter 35). Section 47 has amended s43 MCA 1980.
2. As soon as the suspect arrives at a police station under arrest, the police officer responsible for reviewing his case (termed the 'custody officer') shall determine whether there is sufficent evidence to bring a charge. If no such evidence exists, the suspect should be released, either on bail or without bail unless the custody officer has reasonable grounds for believing that his continued detention without charge is necessary to secure or preserve evidence relating to an offence for which he is under arrest or to obtain such evidence by questioning him: s37(1) and (2).
3. If there is sufficient evidence to justify the making of a charge, the suspect must either be charged or released with or without bail (unless he is not at the time in a fit state to be charged or released, in which case he may be kept in police detention pending his recovery): s37(9).

4. If the suspect is charged, he should be released on bail unless his name and address cannot be ascertained or that which he has given is reasonably believed to be false, or his continued detention is reasonably believed necessary for his own protection or to prevent his causing injury to other persons or loss of or damage to property, or there are reasonable grounds for believing that the suspect will fail to answer bail or interfere with the administration of justice or the investigation of a particular offence: s38(1).
5. A suspect who, being charged, is not released with or without bail must be brought before a magistrates' court 'as soon as is practicable and in any event not later than the first sitting after he is charged with the offence': s46(2). Special provisions apply for the arrangement of sittings outside normal court hours and for detention during public holidays.
6. If bail is granted, the suspect is released on condition that he surrender himself at a stated time either at a police station or a magistrates' court. Additionally, the suspect can be required to furnish 'sureties' for his good behaviour during the period of bail, and to guarantee his observation of it, from persons considered by the police to be suitable guarantors of his conduct. Such persons enter into 'recognisances' which they become liable to forfeit if the terms of the bail are breached.
7. None of the foregoing statutory provisions applies if the suspect was arrested by a warrant which *itself* ordered the release of the suspect or his appearance before a particular magistrates' court. In such circumstances, the terms of the warrant take priority over those of the Act. If the warrant directs the police to release the suspect on bail (it is then said to be 'backed for bail'), he must be so released unless there is some other reason for his continued detention (for example, the suspected commission of other offences which themselves justify that detention). If the warrant directs that the suspect be brought forthwith before a court he must so appear and will not be entitled to the presumption of early release created by ss37 and 38: see generally s117 MCA 1980.

23.6 Decision to prosecute

Whether or not a suspect has been arrested, a decision must be made upon the commencement of a prosecution. Since 1986 the decision whether or not to commence or continue a prosecution has been taken out of the hands of the regional police forces and largely conferred upon a new department of government, the Crown Prosecution Department established by the Prosecution of Offences Act 1985. If the police make a charge following arrest, the officers of the department may resolve to take the matter no further, and no summons will issue. Alternatively, proceedings may be brought against a person whom the police consider should not be prosecuted. Much bureaucracy attends the new service in an attempt to achieve nationwide consistency of prosecution policy, and the service is severely understaffed, hampered by the relatively low salaries it offers its lawyer members. There is also a fear that in some areas the department may submit to police pressure in its decision-making, undermining its role as an independent and impartial body.

23.7 Director of Public Prosecutions

Under s2 Prosecution of Offences Act 1985 the Director of Public Prosecutions, one of the Law Officers of the Crown, has power to institute proceedings. In the following principal cases, *no* prosecution may be begun without his express consent:

1. homosexual offences where one of the parties is under 21;
2. incest;
3. offences of theft or criminal damage committed by one spouse against another.

In the following principal cases the Director must be informed by the police that prosecution is being considered, and may himself take over the case:

1. perjury;
2. criminal libel;
3. complaints against the police;
4. robbery with use of firearms;
5. serious drugs offences;
6. serious offences against the immigration laws.

Cases may also be referred to the Director if the police consider they are of special difficulty, for example, murder of a child, for his advice on appropriate charges and to give him the chance to adopt the prosecution and conduct it through his own office. Except where his consent is expressly required for the commencement or continuance of proceedings, the Director has no power to stop a prosecution taking place; but he may exercise his power to take over the case and to prevent it continuing by 'offering no evidence', which secures the accused's acquittal and prevents a re-trial.

23.8 Attorney-General

The Attorney-General is the senior Law Officer of the Crown, appointed by the government. He loses office when the government falls. It is he who supervises the work of the DPP, but he has extensive powers of his own. In the followng principal cases his consent is necessary before proceedings can be begun:

1. major charges of corruption of public officials;
2. offences against the Official Secrets Act 1989;

3. public order offences involving membership of proscribed organisations such as the Irish Republican Army, and the wearing of uniforms of such organisations, and offences of inciting racial hatred.

In addition, the Attorney-General has an unlimited power in exercise of the Royal prerogative to stop any prosecution whatsoever once it has begun. This is done by entry of a *Nolle Prosequi*, an order commanding the court to discontinue hearing the case, and preventing any further steps being taken in it. The decision to enter a *Nolle Prosequi* cannot be reviewed by the courts: *Gouriet* v *Union of Post Office Workers* [1978] AC 435. The *Nolle Prosequi* can be entered only where the trial is proceeding on indictment, that is, before judge and jury in the Crown Court. Where the trial is in the magistrates' court, the Attorney-General can intervene and take over the proceedings and achieve the effect of a NP by offering no evidence. Once again, his decision to do this, and that of the DPP where he takes over a case (see section 23.7), are not subject to the control of the courts, and are unfettered powers to prevent proceedings: *Raymond* v *Attorney-General* [1982] QB 839. Although most often used only to stop private prosecutions which are frivolous or against the public interest (see section 23.10), the power is not restricted to such cases.

For the purposes of statutes which require the Attorney-General's consent to be given before proceedings are 'instituted', it seems that so long as the consent is obtained before committal proceedings start (or perhaps before the trial begins, if the offence is to be tried summarily) a resultant conviction will stand even though the consent was not granted before the accused was formally charged by the police: *R* v *Elliott* (1984) The Times 13 December.

23.9 Government departments

The majority of prosecutions not brought by the police are begun by government agencies responsible for enforcing the law broken. The Factories Inspectorate prosecutes for breaches of the Health and Safety at Work Act 1974 and the Factories Act 1961; the Inland Revenue prosecutes for offences of avoidance of taxes, the Office of Fair Trading for false descriptions of goods, the Department of Social Security for fraudulent claims to benefits, and so forth. Most prosecutions are brought on the advice of individual inspectors or the department's legal advisers, and the decision to prosecute is very similar to that exercised by the police. The Attorney-General and the DPP have similar powers to intervene in, take over and bring to an end the proceedings so begun. The Prosecution of Offences Act 1985 (see section 23.6) has preserved the prosecuting functions of these bodies.

23.10 Private individuals

In one sense all prosecutions which are not brought solely in the name of the Crown or of one of its Law Officers are 'private' prosecutions. They are brought in the name of a citizen who may happen to be also a police officer or an official of a government department. The term 'private prosecution' is used however in practice to describe a prosecution brought other than by the police, the Crown or some governmental or official body or one of its employees. Except in the very few cases where the consent of the Attorney-General or the DPP is needed (see sections 23.7 and 23.8), any person may institute proceedings for any offence, even though he may not be the victim of it and have no connection either with the offence or the offender. The most common type of private prosecution is by major retail shops against shoplifters; it is often cheaper for all concerned to have the store bring the case from start to finish, and much police time is saved. Other examples would be where the police have decided not to prosecute, but a private citizen is so aggrieved by their decision that he feels the offender should be punished, and brings his own prosecution. Since the cost of the prosecution may not be recoverable, especially if it fails, such cases are rare. The victim of an offence can usually obtain a better, cheaper and more easily proved remedy against the wrongdoer in the civil courts.

Although the right to bring private prosecutions in the sense described has been retained, the Attorney-General exercises a supervisory jurisdiction by the power to enter a *Nolle Prosequi* in a trial on indictment, or to take over a magistrates' court summary trial and to offer no evidence (see section 23.8). Oppressive prosecutions, or those where the public interest is not served by prosecuting, can therefore be stopped. Although the right to bring a private prosecution has not been formally abolished by the Prosecution of Offences Act 1985 (see section 23.6), it is rarely exercised due to the substantial risk that the full costs of such prosecution may well not be recoverable even if it succeeds.

23.11 Caution

One further way of dealing with a suspected offence must be mentioned. Instead of prosecuting, the police may release the suspect without charge or comment. Although this does not prevent any prosecution being brought in respect of the offence, in practice it is the end of the matter. There is an additional power to record some warning against the offender, but not to proceed to charge and trial. This is the formal caution. It is most commonly employed in motoring offences of a minor nature, for example, speeding, 'jumping' red traffic lights, having defective indicators or tyres, failing to wear seat belts, but appears to be increasingly frequent for progressively serious offences including those of violence. Since little point is served by prosecuting each and every infringement of these technical laws, it may well suffice to remind the offender of his misconduct. This is done by letter, but is not a 'conviction', so that in theory a prosecution could follow; it never does, however.

23.12 Time limits

The commencement of civil claims is governed by periods of limitation fixed by statute; a failure to begin the action within the time provides a defence to the defendant. These matters were discussed in Part I, Chapter 14. In criminal cases a failure to bring proceedings within a relevant time limit renders a subsequent trial null and void. There is no limitation period at common law for the bringing of proceedings, and the statutory periods differ according to the nature of the offence.

Where the offence in question is 'indictable' or 'triable either way' (see Chapter 29, sections 29.2, 29.3 and 29.4), that is, could be tried by judge and jury in the Crown Court, proceedings may be commenced at any time after the commission of the offence unless otherwise provided for by statute: see s18 CLA 1977. The most important of these limits are:

1. Homosexual offences – proceedings must be begun not more than 12 months after the commission of the offence: s7 Sexual Offences Act 1967.
2. Unlawful sexual intercourse with a girl under the age of 16 but of age 13 or over – 12 months from the commission of the offence or of an attempt to commit it: s37 Sexual Offences Act 1956.
3. False trade descriptions – three years from the date of commission of the offence or one year from the date of its first discovery by the person who brings proceedings, whichever is the earlier: s19 Trade Descriptions Act 1968;
4. Corrupt election practices – 12 months from the date of commission of the offence: Representation of the People Act 1983.

Where the offence is triable summarily only, that is, before magistrates, proceedings must be commenced within six months of the date of the commission of the offence, unless statute otherwise directs: s127 MCA 1980. The most important of the exceptions to this general rule are:

1. False statements to obtain social security benefits – three months from the date on which evidence sufficient to justify prosecution comes to the knowledge of the Secretary of State or 12 months from the date of the commission of the offence, whichever is later: s11 Child Benefit Act 1975 and s12 Family Income Supplements Act 1970.
2. Section 6 of the Road Traffic Offenders Act 1988 provides for an extended time limit for certain road traffic offences. Proceedings may be commenced within six months of the date on which sufficient evidence came to the prosecutor's knowledge, but no more than three years after the offence.

For the purposes of any relevant time limit, proceedings are 'commenced' on the following dates:

1. In the case of offences to be tried on indictment, when the indictment is preferred (if there are no committal proceedings) or the information laid (see Chapter 24, section 24.3). It may also be that the application for a warrant for the arrest of the accused is a sufficient act of commencement, though this is almost certain to be after the information has been laid and sworn to on oath: *R v West* [1898] 1 QB 174.
2. In the case of offences to be tried summarily only, the date upon which the information is laid. In each case, the day of commission of the offence is excluded from the calculation, but the day on which the proceedings are commenced is included: *Radcliffe* v *Bartholomew* [1892] 1 QB 161.

The foregoing time limits relate to the time after the date of the alleged offence within which a prosecution must be commenced. For the separate question of the time within which certain stages of the prosecution process must be reached *after* the prosecution has been commenced: see Chapter 27, section 27.3.

23.13 Motoring offences

In relation to certain motoring offences, there is a further restriction on prosecution (ss1 and 2 Road Traffic Offenders Act 1988). The accused shall not be convicted unless either:

1. he was warned at the time the offence was committed that he would be considered for prosecution for the offence or some other offence committed on the same occasion; or
2. within 14 days of the commission of the offence he has been served with a Summons (that is, proceedings have been begun); or
3. within 14 days of the commission of the offence he was served with a 'notice of intended prosecution' detailing the offence and informing him that proceedings might follow. The notice is deemed to have been duly served if proved to have been posted, unless the accused proves the contrary; or
4. the offence consisted of or was followed by an accident due to the vehicle's presence on the road. These include reckless driving, careless driving, reckless and careless cycling, failing to comply with traffic directions, leaving vehicles in dangerous positions, speeding on specially restricted roads, and exceeding general speed limits on any highway.

24

Prosecuting a Summary Offence

24.1 Introduction

24.2 Summary offences

24.3 Commencing proceedings

24.4 Issue of the Summons

24.5 Form of the information in the Summons

24.6 Course of the trial

24.7 Pleading guilty by post

24.8 Adjournment

24.9 Proceeding in the absence of the parties

24.10 Acceptance and change of plea

24.11 The magistrates' clerk

24.12 Conflicts of interest

24.13 Composition of the court

24.14 Powers of sentencing for summary offences

24.15 Variation of findings and sentences

24.16 Defects in information and variance with evidence

24.1 Introduction

There are two modes of English criminal trial: by magistrates ('summary' trial) and before judge and jury (trial 'on indictment'). There are three classes of offence: those triable only summarily, those triable only on indictment, and those which could be tried by either mode. The latter are termed 'offences triable either way'. The classification is explained in greater detail in Chapter 29. This chapter is concerned with prosecution and trial of offences which may only be tried summarily; the procedure for commencing proceedings, the mode of trial, and the basic powers of sentencing. Appeals from summary trial are dealt with in Chapter 33.

24.2 Summary offences

To determine whether an offence is a summary offence, and can therefore be tried only in the magistrates' court, it is necessary to refer to the statute creating the offence. If no penalty is provided for by the statute on conviction on indictment, the offence is summary only.

The majority of minor road traffic offences are summary, for example, failing to comply with traffic signals, speeding, careless driving, having defective tyres or lights. As a general rule, any offence for which there is no power of imprisonment will be summary, but the following exceptions to that rule should be noted:

1. assaulting a police officer in the execution of his duty, contrary to s51 Police Act 1964. This carries a maximum penalty of six months' imprisonment but is only a summary offence;
2. making false statements to obtain driving licences, etc, contrary to the Road Traffic Act 1988. There is a maximum penalty of four months' imprisonment, but the offence is a summary one.

To the above list of exceptions there are others, and the appropriate statute should be consulted. Although most offences under the Theft Act 1968 are indictable, the offences under s12 (taking conveyances) are now triable only summarily when they appear as the sole charge against an accused: s37 Criminal Justice Act 1988. In like manner, common assault is now triable only summarily in most cases: s39 CJA 1988.

24.3 Commencing proceedings

It having been determined that an offence may be prosecuted summarily only, and the decision to prosecute having been taken, the process of prosecution begins. The time limits for prosecuting summary offences have already been discussed (see Chapter 23, sections 23.12 and 23.13). The appropriate court must be chosen. In general, a magistrates' court has jurisdiction to try summary offences only if the offence is committed, commenced or completed within the county for which the court sits, or within 500 yards of the boundary of that county: ss2 and 3 MCA 1980. The county may extend beyond its coastline and include territorial waters If an offence is begun in one county and completed in another, the courts for each have a concurrent jurisdiction. There is power to try in one county a summary offence committed entirely within another if either:

1. the accused is already on trial for an offence of any kind in the county which does not have jurisdiction prima facie to try the other offence – he may be tried for all summary offences wherever committed: s2(6) MCA 1980 s2(6). All charges may thus be dealt with at once, and it is not necessary that all arise out of the same incident; or
2. the accused is being tried in one county, and it is 'necessary or expedient' that some other person be tried with him: s2(2). Where there has been a series of offences committed in different counties by different persons, it may be better that all offences and offenders be tried in the same place.

It must be noted that a magistrates' court has jurisdiction to try *any* offence triable either way, and to hold committal proceedings for any offence triable only on indictment, regardless of whether the offence was committed within the county or not. There are several courts in each county, the county being divided into 'petty sessional divisions', all of which have concurrent jurisdiction with each other, and the choice of court depends largely upon the prosecutor; usually, the petty sessional division selected will be the one closest to the place of commission of the offence.

24.4 Issue of the Summons

The prosecution of a summary offence may start with an arrest, but is more likely to begin with the laying of an information, a complaint of an offence made by the intending prosecutor to the court. It need not be in writing, but most often will be so, complying with r100 MCR 1981, and identifying the accused and the particulars of the alleged offence. The court inquires into the case and decides whether the offence is known to law, the prosecution begun within any relevant time limit, and whether the court has jurisdiction. Although there is a discretion to refuse to accept the information and to decline to act upon it, this is only used where the intended prosecution appears frivolous or very unlikely to succeed on the evidence adduced at this early stage.

Satisfied that the information is proper, the court through its clerk issues a *Summons*, addressed to the defendant and detailing the particulars of the offences alleged, and ordering the defendant to appear at court on a named date to face trial in respect of them. It must be served on the defendant, and although personal service is permitted, the more usual practice is to serve by post to his usual or last-known address: r99 MCR 1981.

24.5 Form of the information in the Summons

A Summons may contain more than one information and more than one charge. In motoring offences particularly, the same incident may give rise to several charges, for example, speeding, failing to have a current MOT certificate, failing to produce a certificate of insurance, failing to comply with traffic signals. All these will usually be charged in the Summons, but will appear in separate informations in it. There are however important rules as to the form of the information and the trial of a defendant on a Summons which contains more than one information:

1. An information which charges more than one offence is 'bad for duplicity' (see further Chapter 26, section 26.5). It is often difficult to decide whether a single information does so charge, or whether a Summons which is divided into separate paragraphs, not each of which is headed 'information', contains several different informations or a single information alleging separate offences: *Shah* v *Swallow* [1984] 2 All ER 528 HL.
2. An information which is bad for duplicity cannot be validly tried unless and until the prosecution elects which of the offences charged in it will be proceeded with (and only one may be chosen) and which abandoned.
3. Where a Summons contains more than one information, the court cannot try more than one information at the same time unless either the Summons charges an offence and an attempt to commit that offence in the alternative (s4 Criminal Attempts Act 1981) or the accused consents to that joint trial or the court considers it is 'in the interests of justice' to have joint trial: *Chief Constable of Norfolk* v *Clayton* [1983] 2 WLR 555.
4. Where more than one Summons has been served against the same defendant, the court may try the Summonses together only if he consents expressly or impliedly, or if it is 'in the interests of justice'.
5. Two or more defendants may be charged in the same information. This alone does not make the information bad for duplicity, nor does each defendant have any right to be tried separately from the others, if the allegation is that they committed the offence jointly.
6. If two or more defendants are charged in separate informations in the same Summons, they may not be tried together unless each consents expressly or impliedly to a joint trial or the court considers a joint trial 'in the interests of justice'.
7. Where two Summonses have been served, one *against* a defendant alleging one offence, the other *by* that defendant alleging an offence committed by the prosecutor of the first offence, the court may not try the Summonses together: *Ex parte Gibbons* [1983] 3 All ER 523. This may arise where a policeman prosecutes for an assault upon him, and the defendant issues a Summons (a 'cross-summons') alleging the policeman assaulted *him* on the occasion in question. Because of the difficulties of procedure, for example, who has the right to begin calling evidence, who has a right to a closing speech, there must be separate trials of each even though the trials will concern the same incident and the same evidence, and may reach inconsistent verdicts.

24.6 Course of the trial

On the named hearing date the prosecution and defence appear for trial in most cases. Each may be represented by solicitor and/or counsel, or may represent himself. There is a right of an accused to have with him in court a friend who, while not legally qualified, sits with him and whispers advice as to the questions he should ask and speeches he should make: *MacKenzie* v *MacKenzie* [1970] 3 All ER 1034. After moves and judgments to the contrary, the right to a 'MacKenzie friend' has been maintained. The prosecution makes an opening speech, usually a very brief one, and calls its witnesses and puts in its documentary evidence. The defence are then entitled to make a submission of 'no case to answer' if the prosecution evidence fails to make out one or more of the elements of the offence. If this is successful, the defendant is acquitted, if not, the defence then presents its case, calling witnesses and adducing documentary evidence as necessary. The defence may make a closing speech (or, sometimes, an opening one). If points of law are raised in the defence speech, the prosecution has a right of reply upon them. The magistrates then deliver their decision; they may announce it at once or after a brief retirement from the courtroom. It is necessary to discuss in detail the provision for pleading guilty by post, the powers of the court to adjourn the hearing, the powers to proceed in the absence of the prosecution or the defendant, and the provisions for accepting pleas of guilty.

24.7 Pleading guilty by post

Trials are expensive, for the prosecution as much as for the court and the defendant. If the defendant is to plead guilty, there is often little point in his coming to court to hear what sentence will be given, if that sentence is a low one and unlikely to involve imprisonment. In certain limited cases the accused can notify the court of his intention to plead guilty, and the court may try and sentence him in his absence. One of these cases is plea of guilty by post, and the following points should be noted:

1. It can be used in the prosecution of any summary offence where the maximum penalty does not exceed three months' imprisonment. This covers almost all summary offences.
2. The accused is sent a prescribed form together with the Summons. He may state on that form the fact that he intends to plead guilty, and he may set out any matters he wishes the court to consider in mitigation of sentence.
3. The notice of intention to plead guilty may be withdrawn at any time up to the trial, preferably in writing, and if this is done the court is not told of the intention so withdrawn.
4. If the statement of mitigating facts seems to disclose a real defence to the charge, the court may refuse to accept the tendered plea of guilty and adjourn the case for a full hearing.

5. If, having entered a plea of guilty by post, the accused is found guilty on acceptance of the plea, the court may sentence him in his absence unless they are considering imprisoning him or (if the offence carries power to disqualify from driving) disqualifying him: ss12 and 13 MCA 1980.

The plea of guilty by post procedure is most commonly used in motoring offences, and an accused so charged must send his licence to the court together with the notice of intention to plead guilty. It must be remembered that it is not the notice which constitutes the conviction, but the finding of the court when the offence is tried and the notice accepted as a formal plea of guilty. Where the mitigating circumstances are unusual, it is often better for the accused to present them to the court in person rather than to rely upon a written account of them; magistrates are more impressed with oral evidence than with written assertions of a defendant they had no opportunity of hearing or seeing. The procedure is not available in the youth court. Although postal pleas have greatly reduced the workload of magistrates' courts, a great deal of court time remains taken up in dealing with them. A new system of Fixed Penalty Notices is in force for minor road traffic offences which renders a court hearing of any kind wholly unnecessary if the offender pays a predetermined sum to the police on receipt of a notice affording the opportunity to pay. Only if liability is contested will a trial be arrranged. Detailed consideration of this scheme falls outside the syllabus, but it is expected to remove some 500,000 cases annually from the lower courts through replacement of a judicial process by an administrative one.

24.8 Adjournment

At any stage of a trial in their court, magistrates may adjourn the hearing to another day: ss5 and 10 MCA 1980. If the adjournment is after conviction and before sentence, it may be for not more than four weeks unless the defendant is remanded in custody to prison, in which case the adjournment period must not exceed three weeks. Adjournment after conviction must not be confused with the power to defer sentence under s1 Powers of Criminal Courts Act 1973 (see Chapter 30, section 30.3). Adjournments before conviction are most common where at the request of the prosecution or defence on the ground that one or other is not ready to proceed, or where one or other fails to appear on the due date (see section 24.9). Following conviction, the commonest reason for adjournment is to allow preparation of reports upon the offender, or to secure his attendance for sentence if he has been convicted in his absence.

24.9 Proceeding in the absence of the parties

The power to hear a case and convict a defendant where he has pleaded guilty by post have been discussed at section 24.7. In other summary trials, the court has the following principal powers to try the case where either prosecution or defence fail to appear:

1. if the prosecution fail to appear, the magistrates may dismiss the case, which has the effect of an acquittal preventing a retrial for the offence; or
2. if the prosecution does not appear, adjourn the case to another day; or
3. if the prosecution fail to appear, proceed with the case; this is only useful if all the prosecution evidence was given at an earlier hearing which was itself adjourned: s15 MCA 1980;
4. acquit the defendant: *R v Sutton Justices, ex parte DPP* (1992) The Times 6 February.

Where the defendant does not appear the court has slightly different powers. In general, the accused need not be present at trial, and the court can proceed to try him in his absence once proof has been adduced that the Summons informing him of the hearing date was either served personally on him or was posted without being returned marked 'gone away' or 'address unknown' or the like: s11 MCA 1980. Where the offence is a summary offence only, the accused *must* be present if the trial is to continue if:

1. he has been bailed to appear at court. The court will then most usually issue a 'bench warrant' for his arrest and adjourn the hearing until he is found; or
2. having convicted the accused in his absence, the magistrates are considering sending him to prison or disqualifying him from driving. The case should be adjourned and the accused notified of the magistrates' intention: s11(4). If the conviction has followed a plea of guilty by post, no warrant for his arrest may be issued, but if the conviction follows a simple failure to appear, a warrant may issue to secure his presence. If, having received notice of the magistrates' intention to disqualify him from driving, the accused does not appear to make representations, he may be disqualified in his absence. No sentence of imprisonment may be passed on anyone following conviction of a summary offence unless he is present before the court: s11(3) MCA 1980;
3. if, having begun to hear a case in the absence of the accused, the magistrates consider that the matter is so serious that it would be undesirable to continue without the accused being present, they should adjourn the case and issue a warrant for arrest: s13 MCA 1980.

For the purposes of the above rules, a party is deemed to be present at court if he is represented there by counsel or solicitor, even though he may not himself be personally present in court: s122 MCA 1980. The only exception to this rule is that a person bailed to appear at court is not 'present' unless he appears personally in answer to the bail. Despite the power to proceed in an accused's absence, magistrates commonly adjourn a case where he does not appear, unless there is evidence to suggest that he has deliberately absented himself. The power to proceed in summary cases must be contrasted and must not be confused with the position where the offence is indictable only or is triable either way (see Chapter 29, sections 29.2 and 29.3). Where both prosecution and defence fail to appear, the court may deal with the matter in the same way as if the prosecution had failed to appear but the accused were present: s16 MCA 1980.

24.10 Acceptance and change of plea

A defendant who is present or deemed to be present may plead not guilty to the charge, and may change his plea to guilty at any stage of the case. A defendant who is absent or deemed to be absent, and whose case the magistrates proceed to try summarily under s11 of the 1980 Act, will have a plea of not guilty entered on his behalf. Problems arise however where a defendant wishes to plead guilty but later desires to change his plea to not guilty, and where the magistrates refuse to accept a guilty plea tendered by him.

Magistrates have a general discretion to refuse to accept a plea of guilty offered by a defendant, although they will hardly ever exercise it if the accused is legally represented and has taken advice upon the elements of the offence and the consequences of the plea.

A plea when tendered may be 'equivocal', that is, although the defendant may say he wishes to plead guilty he adds something which gives notice to the magistrates that he has a real defence to the charge. For example, he may say on a charge of theft 'I took the goods, so I am guilty, but I did not mean to keep them'. In such cases the court should ask him questions and explain to him the nature of the charge and the elements of the offence, and ensure that his intended plea is a voluntary one made with full knowledge of the law. A failure to make this explanation will render the plea involuntary and an appeal lies to the Crown Court to reverse the magistrates' decision and to order a retrial: *Foster Haulage* v *Roberts* [1978] 2 All ER 751. The magistrates must comply with an order of the Crown Court to retry the accused after his conviction has been quashed on appeal because the original plea should have been treated as equivocal: *R* v *Plymouth Justices, ex parte Hart* [1986] 2 All ER 452 DC.

Although unequivocal when entered, the defendant's plea of guilty may become equivocal in the light of information emerging during proceedings before sentence; it may be only when asked whether he wishes to say something in mitigation of sentence that he says 'I did not intend to keep the goods'. In these circumstances the magistrates must consider rejecting his guilty plea and permitting him to change it to not guilty. They have a discretion to allow or to refuse the change, and so long as they do not exercise it manifestly unreasonably, it will be only in very rare cases that their decision will be struck down on appeal: *Ex parte Rowland* [1983] 3 All ER 689 where the court was held entitled to conclude that the defendant's motive for seeking to alter her plea was a desire to avoid a custodial sentence the magistrates had made it clear they were minded to impose.

Where however it must be clear to the court that the defendant or his advisers made a genuine mistake in entering an initially unequivocal plea of guilty, the magistrates will be virtually compelled to allow the plea to be withdrawn and replaced by one of not guilty: *Ex parte Sawyers* [1988] Crim LR 754 QBD.

24.11 The magistrates' clerk

The clerk to the magistrates sits in court throughout the hearing of the case, taking notes of the evidence and dealing with such matters as putting the charge to the defendant, recording the verdict, advising the accused of his right to speak and to give evidence and call witnesses. He is also the adviser to the magistrates on points of law; they may consult him for his opinion on the law and will usually accept that opinion though not bound to do so. The clerk must not however take any part in suggesting to or conferring with the magistrates on issues of fact, that is, who is telling the truth, and whether the defence case is credible; his task is confined to advice on the law. If there is a real risk that the clerk has taken part in discussions on the facts, the conviction may be quashed, for justice has not been seen to be done. So, the clerk who retires with the magistrates to their private room for consideration of their decision acts improperly if there is no reason for him to be there, even if there is no evidence that he has in fact assumed a judicial instead of an advisory role. A recent decision confirms that the clerk should only retire with the magistrates when it is plainly necessary: *R v Birmingham Magistrates' Court, ex parte Ahmed* [1995] Crim LR 503. See Chapter 36, section 36.5, for further details and see generally *Practice Direction* [1981] 1 WLR 1163.

24.12 Conflicts of interest

It is a fundamental rule of law that there should be no suspicion that anyone with the task of judging cases has been swayed in his decision by reason of a personal connection with the outcome of the case, such as his acquaintance with a party or his witnesses, or a shareholding in any company which appears as a party or which will be affected by the result of the trial, or some other less direct interest in the case. If a magistrate's financial interests could be affected by any case, he should not sit to judge it and, if he does so, it is almost certain that his decision will be quashed even if there is not the slightest evidence that his interest in fact clouded his impartiality. Thus a magistrate should not hear an application for a gaming licence by a club of which he is a member, or sit to hear a prosecution of a company of which he is a director or shareholder.

If the magistrate's connection with the case is of a type other than one which could affect his financial interest, for example, his acquaintance with parties or witnesses, or his membership of the governing body of the social services department of which the accused is an employee, it is always advisable that he withdraw from the case to avoid totally the suspicion of bias. He may however continue to hear it, but would do well to declare his interest to the parties and offer to withdraw if one of them wishes him to do so. If he hears the case without declaring his interest, the decision will often be quashed on appeal, but only if the appellant can show that there was some 'real likelihood of bias' arising from the interest. Such likelihood will depend upon the facts of each case, but the closer the magistrate's connection with parties or witnesses, the greater it will be: *Ex parte Pennington* [1975] 1 QB 459. Thus, if a magistrate has in the course of a summary trial inadvertently gained sight of a list of the defendant's previous convictions while the issue of guilt is being tried then, even though the court is sure that it did not in fact affect the verdict (because he did not communicate that information to his two colleagues, who both found the defendant guilty), the conviction will be quashed because a reasonable bystander might think that justice was not being done: *Ex parte Robinson* (1985) The Times 11 October. It will however rarely be a valid ground of complaint that a magistrate knew or might have known, when deciding the question of guilt, of other *charges* outstanding against the accused (as opposed to other convictions already recorded against him), where he derived or could have derived that knowledge from a perusal of the published list of cases to be heard in the court on the same day: *R v Weston-super-Mare Justices, ex parte Shaw* [1987] 1 All ER 255.

Where one of the parties to summary proceedings is a local authority, and any of the magistrates listed to hear the case is a member of that authority, as a councillor or member of one of its committees or boards, statute prescribes that that magistrate shall not hear the case: Justices of the Peace Act 1979 s64. Although not yet the subject of any reported cases, it seems that a breach of the statute will lead to a decision being quashed automatically on appeal, even if there is no proof of real likelihood of bias.

24.13 Composition of the court

In connection with the withdrawal of magistrates from cases in which they have or might have an interest, it should be mentioned that a magistrates' court consists normally of either three lay magistrates (unpaid, not legally qualified part-time judges) or a single stipendiary magistrate (salaried, qualified, full-time judge). The number of magistrates sitting to hear a case may vary from two to seven, and a stipendiary may sit with lay magistrates. Where one of a bench of three withdraws through some interest in the case, the court often gives the parties the opportunity of seeking an adjournment of the hearing to allow a new bench of three to be assembled; if the case continues with two only, there is the risk that they will be divided in their decision (there is no casting vote given to the chairman) so that the case would have to be reheard at further cost to parties in time and money.

24.14 Powers of sentencing for summary offences

If magistrates find the case proved, and convict the accused, they will proceed to sentence him. The prosecution produces evidence of the defendant's previous convictions and of his circumstances (the 'antecedent evidence') including his age, address, marital status, earnings, employment and character and other things known about him which may be relevant to sentence. The defendant is then allowed to state facts which he wishes to draw to the court's attention in reduction of sentence ('mitigation'), and the magistrates consider all these matters. They acquaint themselves with the range of sentences open to them, and will often announce their decision at once. The range of sentences available, and the combinations which can be given, are discussed in greater detail in Chapter 30, but it will suffice here to say that statute will lay down a maximum term of imprisonment or fine, and that other types of dealing with the convict will usually be open to the court. If the offence is more than merely technical, and involves some element of dishonesty or violence, it is common for the court to adjourn before sentence to allow social inquiry or probation reports to be prepared.

24.15 Variation of findings and sentences

A magistrates' court having tried an accused for a summary offence and having sentenced him for that offence has quite wide powers to amend its decision retrospectively. The powers of amendment are most often used where the magistrates have doubts about their decision to convict or about the severity of the sentence. The power arises from s142 MCA 1980 (as amended by Criminal Appeal Act 1995), and can be used to correct clerical errors in the form of findings and sentences, as well as to amend them in substance.

This power may be exercised regardless of the plea made by the defendant. Following the Criminal Appeal Act 1995, the court may vary, rescind or replace a sentence where it appears to be 'in the interests of justice to do so': s26 CAA 1995. A magistrates' court may also rehear a trial before a different bench (again, whether the defendant pleaded guilty or not), where it would be in the interests of justice.

24.16 Defects in information and variance with evidence

It has been seen that an information which charges more than one offence is bad for duplicity and a resulting conviction liable to be quashed (see section 24.5). If the defect in the information is of this type, it cannot be cured unless the prosecution amends it as has been described. In the case of other formal defects in the information, or the Summons, s123 MCA 1980 provides that 'no objection shall be allowed ... for any defect in it in substance or form', but this apparently general prohibition is subject to the following principal exceptions:

1. it cannot prevent object being taken to a Summons or information which alleges an offence unknown to law, or which does not state the statute (if any) which creates the offence;
2. it does not allow the court to convict of the offence charged if the facts emerging in evidence disclose not that offence but some other which has not been charged.

Section 123 also provides that 'no objection shall be allowed to any variance between' the Summons or information 'and the evidence adduced on behalf of the prosecutors', so that a defendant cannot generally complain that the evidence alleges a different date for commission of the offence than that stated in the Summons, or that the subject-matter of the offence differs in evidence from the Summons. The section is intended to prevent technical objections to matters of detail which cannot really prejudice a defendant, and continues 'if it appears to the court that any variance between a Summons and the evidence adduced by the prosecutor is such that the defendant has been misled by the variance, the court shall, on the application of the defendant, adjourn the hearing'.

Variance between charge and evidence is quite common, and whether the defendant has been misled depends upon the facts of each case. Where a defendant has prepared his alibi for the date charged, and the evidence alleges a different date, the magistrates should usually adjourn to allow fresh alibi evidence to be prepared: *Wright* v *Nicholson* [1970] 1 WLR 142. If there is a variance then, even if not satisfied that the defendant has been misled, the court will usually require the prosecution to amend the charge to substitute the new correct facts.

Although s123 gives the court a wide power to convict even if there is a formal defect, it is very common for the defect to be cured by amendment of the Summons or information at the start of or during the course of the trial, and such amendments are permissible with the court's leave at any time before sentence. Nonetheless, if the amendment in substance charges a different offence, or otherwise could cause prejudice to the accused in presenting his defence to the charge, an adjournment should be allowed at his request (*Garfield* v *Maddocks* [1974] QB 7) and, if the variance has misled him, the request for adjournment *must* be granted.

Magistrates have no power to convict the accused of an offence which is not specifically charged in the Summons: s6 Criminal Law Act 1967 does not apply to a magistrates' court. Thus, on a charge of committing an offence, the court cannot return a verdict of guilty of an attempt to commit it, unless and until the information is amended to charge an attempt (and the amendment can be made at any time before sentence, so that it will usually be applied for by the prosecution when the magistrates have made it known that they are minded to dismiss the charge of the full offence but to find the case proved if an attempt is charged). Similarly, no conviction of failing to comply with a traffic signal could be returned on a charge of dangerous driving, the facts of which allege the accused drove through a red traffic light; the information must first be amended, and the court consider the prejudice caused to the defendant by the amendment when deciding whether to adjourn the case.

25

Committal Proceedings

25.1 Introduction

25.2 Committal with consideration of the evidence

25.3 Submission of no case to answer

25.4 Procedural points

25.5 Committal without consideration of the evidence

25.6 Ancillary orders

25.7 Place of trial

25.8 Witness orders

25.9 Bail

25.10 Alibi warning

25.11 Legal aid

25.12 Costs of the committal proceedings

25.13 Publicity at committal proceedings

25.14 Additional evidence

25.15 Voluntary bill of indictment

25.16 Committal of summary offences

25.17 Transfer for trial

25.1 Introduction

The course of proceedings in a magistrates' court where the offence charged is summary only has been examined in Chapter 24. It now falls to discuss the second role which the magistrates play in the criminal process; as examiners of the evidence adduced by the prosecution on a charge which may or must be tried in the Crown

Court before judge and jury, but which will not come to that trial unless a magistrates' court thinks that there is a 'case for the defendant to answer'.

This chapter therefore concerns the function of magistrates' courts in scrutinising evidence of an offence presented to it by the prosecution, in those cases where the offence is triable only on indictment or, if triable either way, is to be tried on indictment. The purpose of the preliminary proceedings before the magistrates is to filter out cases which are bound to fail if prosecuted further, and to make certain orders ancillary to sending the case on to trial: 'committing for trial to the Crown Court'. The course of committal proceedings applies equally to those offences which only the Crown Court has power to try, and to those in which the mode of trial is at the defendant's option and he has elected for jury trial.

However, committal proceedings will be abolished and replaced with transfer for trial procedures when s44 Criminal Justice and Public Order Act 1994 comes into force. The target date for commencement is August 1995. These are dealt with in section 25.17.

25.2 Committal with consideration of the evidence

It is the duty of the prosecution to persuade the magistrates that there is sufficient evidence upon which a jury in the Crown Court could convict the accused. The general rule is that all the evidence upon which they intend to rely shall be put before the magistrates at committal proceedings. The traditional means of doing so was for the prosecutor to outline the nature of the case, and to call all his potential witnesses to give evidence on oath before the justices. That evidence was then taken down in longhand and the resulting record signed by the witness; it then became his 'deposition' and formed the basis of the Crown case. The witnesses would be examined by the Crown, cross-examined by the defendant or his legal adviser, and re-examined by the Crown. This long and tedious process is known as 'committal with consideration of the evidence' or 'old-style committal' under s6(1) MCA 1980, and is now rare. Nonetheless, it must be examined in some detail.

The defendant can insist upon an old-style committal. He is usually advised to do so only when there seems to be a prospect of so discrediting the prosecution witnesses in cross-examination that the magistrates are persuaded that the charge must fail. Additionally, there is always the chance that in cross-examination a witness will make a statement which can be used against him later if his evidence at the jury trial is inconsistent with the evidence he gave at committal. In general, however, the cross-examination will elicit few, if any, useful pieces of evidence in the accused's favour, and the time and expense of the procedure is not justified. Cases where the defence alleges mistaken identity are considered below at section 25.4.

It is important to understand that at the stage of committal the magistrates are concerned only with the strength of the prosecution evidence. The defence cannot under any circumstances be compelled to produce any of its own evidence, though it may do so in rare cases where it thinks that allowing the court to hear those witnesses will show the prosecution witnesses in such a bad light that the case will be thrown out and will not be ordered committed for trial. The procedure is, therefore, in the vast majority of cases, one-sided, for no defence evidence is put before the court; instead, the defence keeps the nature of its evidence 'up its sleeve' until trial (with the exception of alibi evidence and any evidence to be used to make out a plea of truth as defence to charge of criminal libel).

After all the prosecution evidence has been led, the magistrates consider whether there is a *'prima facie* case to answer'. They must ask themselves: 'on the evidence we have heard, taken at its highest and most credible, could a reasonable jury properly directed on the law and the facts reasonably convict the defendant of the offence charged?' If the answer is in the affirmative, the prosecution have discharged the fairly low burden of showing a *prima facie* case. If the answer is in the negative, the magistrates must refuse to commit for trial and will dismiss the proceedings. The test of *prima facie* case has been laid down in many cases, and there is no consistent form to the question the court must address to itself: s6(1) states simply that 'if a magistrates' court is of opinion ... that there is sufficient evidence to put the accused on trial by jury ... the court shall commit him for trial'.

25.3 Submission of no case to answer

It can be seen that the prosecution has a relatively easy task in persuading the court that the case should go to trial. It is always open to the accused, however, to submit that there should be no committal. This is done by making a submission of no case to answer at the close of the prosecution evidence. If the defence has called evidence of its own a second submission of no case may be made at the close of the whole of the evidence. It is likely to succeed only where either of the two following conditions is met:

1. the Crown evidence has been so discredited in cross-examination, or by evidence called by the defence, that no reasonable jury properly directed could reasonably convict upon it; or
2. there has been no evidence led by the prosecution, or contained in the defence case, of an essential element of the offence charged, for example, of the fact that goods were stolen, or of the death of a person with whose homicide the accused is charged. It should be remembered that evidence of the fact that goods were stolen can be inferred from the circumstances in which the accused received them, and that the absence of a body does not prevent a man being convicted of homicide; it will thus be very rare that there is no evidence from which a jury could *infer* an element of an offence, unless the prosecution have omitted by mistake to call the necessary witnesses, or have commenced the prosecution realising that it must fail.

Since in deciding whether to commit for trial, or whether to uphold a submission of no case to answer, the magistrates are entitled to consider the whole of the evidence they have heard, it is often wiser for the defence to call none of its own evidence; it may be the defence's own witnesses who provide the evidence sufficient to justify committal for trial!

25.4 Procedural points

In addition to the broad picture drawn above of the course of s6(1) committal proceedings, the following should be noted:

1. The accused should be present at all stages of the proceedings: s4 MCA 1980. This means physically present in court himself. Exceptionally the proceedings may be heard in his absence if his disorderly conduct makes it impracticable to continue the proceedings with him present in the court, or if he is legally represented at court and has consented to the proceedings continuing in his absence, but is unable himself to attend due to illness: s4(3) and (4).
2. Once each witness has given evidence, the presiding magistrate and the witness himself sign the written record of that evidence made contemporaneously by the clerk – this becomes the deposition.
3. If a submission of no case to answer is made at the close of the prosecution evidence, and fails, the charge is written down and read to the accused; it is at this stage that he decides whether to call any evidence of his own, or to make any statement to the court, in an attempt to persuade them not to commit for trial. There may, therefore, be two submissions of no case: the first at the close of the prosecution evidence, the second after any defence evidence has been produced.
4. A committal may be partly upon written statements tendered under s102 MCA 1980 and partly upon depositions of witnesses who give oral evidence before the justices. It is an old-style committal nonetheless (see section 25.5). This course will often be appropriate if any of the witnesses upon whose testimony the prosecution will rely at trial is under the age of 14 and the offence includes an assault or a sexual element: see s33 Criminal Justice Act 1988.
5. Where the defence case will be mistaken identity, committal proceedings under s6(1) will usually be appropriate unless the parties indicate that they do not wish the identifying witnesses to be called but will instead accept their s102 statements. It had been thought prior to 1979 that cases which depended largely upon identification of the accused should always proceed with consideration of the evidence of the witnesses to identification, even if both sides did not want it, but that caused much wasted court time.
6. The court can direct an old-style committal even if no application is made for one by either prosecution or defence; it rarely does so.

7. Section 53 Criminal Justice Act 1991 provides for committal proceedings to be by-passed in certain sexual violence and cruelty cases involving a child witness (see section 25.17).

25.5 Committal without consideration of the evidence

Committal under s6(1) is now uncommon. Since the prosecution need only show a *prima facie* case to answer, and will have little difficulty in doing so in most cases, there is little point to having a laborious 'pre-trial trial' to decide an issue which both sides know will result in a committal for trial. The most frequent power now therefore used is to commit for trial without consideration of the evidence, under s6(2) MCA 1980. There are no witnesses present, no defence evidence is called, and the committal takes only a few minutes. The procedure can only be used if the following conditions are all satisfied:

1. all the prosecution evidence (apart from real evidence) is in the form of statements made by witnesses and signed by them in the format prescribed by s102 MCA 1980: this really requires only that the statement contain a declaration that the maker makes it from his own knowledge and to the best of his belief, and is aware that if it is false he risks prosecution – it need not be a sworn statement; and
2. the defendant or, if more than one, all defendants, are 'legally represented': s6(2)(a). It is not necessary that the accused or his legal representative be physically present in court, and suffices if he has a solicitor acting for him in the case: s61 CJA 1982; and
3. the s102 statements have been served on the accused before the proceedings commence. Sometimes the 'before' means a few moments before the hearing starts; and
4. the defendant or, if more than one, all the defendants give consent to the procedure being used.

If all conditions are met, the procedure is as follows:.

1. The charge is written down and read to the accused. He is asked whether he wishes to submit that there is no case to answer, or to call evidence of his own, or to make any objection to the contents of the s102 statements. If the accused wishes to do any of these things, the court must adjourn the case for hearing as an old-style committal.
2. The s102 statements are handed to the clerk by the prosecution. Most often the prosecution are represented by the police officer attached to the court, since the procedure hardly calls for the expertise of a qualified lawyer.
3. The magistrates commit for trial without reading any of the statements, and make the ancillary orders detailed below (see section 25.6).

25.6 Ancillary orders

Incidental to the proceedings, and whether under s6(1) or s6(2) MCA 1980, the magistrates will have to make certain orders once the decision to commit for trial has been made. These are the place of trial, the orders to compel attendance of witnesses, the grant of bail, the alibi warning, legal aid, and the costs of the committal proceedings. They will be considered in turn.

25.7 Place of trial

Committal will usually be to the Crown Court for the district in which the proceedings were held. The court considers whether any different court should try the case, perhaps because of the difficulty in finding an impartial jury in the locality. The defence is allowed to make representations as to the appropriate place of trial. Exceptionally, a case heard on committal outside London may be committed to the Central Criminal Court if it is of great public importance. Place of trial is governed by s7 MCA 1980, which requires the court to have regard to the convenience of all parties and their witnesses, and to the delay which might occur before trial, and by the Lord Chief Justice's Directions (*Stone's Justices Manual*), which lay down duties upon the justices to consider the seriousness of the charge, whether the offence is rarely charged, and the importance and identity of the defendant.

The magistrates' choice of trial court can be varied by the Crown Court on application by the prosecution or any defendant, or of its own motion. In theory, the place of trial can be varied an infinite number of times by the Crown Court, shifting the case from court to court perhaps in attempts to obtain a speedy trial.

25.8 Witness orders

In respect of every witness who gives evidence at committal proceedings, or whose written statement is tendered under s102 at a committal without consideration of his evidence, the magistrates must decide whether to order that he attend the trial in the Crown Court. There are two types of witness order:

1. *Full* – the witness is 'fully bound' to attend the trial, and must do so on notice to him of the date of the trial. If he fails to appear, a warrant may issue for his arrest, and he may be fined and/or imprisoned for his non-appearance, by the Crown Court.
2. *Conditional* – the witness is 'conditionally bound' to attend to give evidence at trial only if he receives a notice requiring him to do so.

It is for the accused to choose whether he wishes witnesses fully or conditionally bound. In general, all will be fully bound, and only those witnesses whose evidence is purely formal and will not be challenged by the defence will be the subject of a conditional order; their statements will be read at trial as evidence of the truth of what they contain, if they comply with s9 CJA 1967 and the defendant consents to them being so used. It should be remembered that it is only the prosecution witnesses who are the subject of witness orders made in the committal proceedings; no orders are made in respect of any defence witnesses.

25.9 Bail

On committing to the Crown Court, the magistrates must remand the accused to come up for trial. He may be remanded in custody or on bail: s6(3) MCA 1980. The subject of bail is more fully discussed in Chapter 35.

25.10 Alibi warning

The defence cannot be compelled to disclose at committal proceedings the nature of their case. Even if the committal is without consideration of the evidence, that is not automatically taken to be an acceptance by the defendant that he admits presence at the scene of the alleged offence, and will not later allege mistaken identity and bring witnesses to testify to his presence elsewhere. Unless a defendant has been given at committal a warning that he must disclose any alibi upon which he seeks to rely at the trial, there is no restriction on the adduction of such evidence, and the prosecution will be put to serious difficulty in investigatng the truth of his claim.

The magistrates must therefore consider whether to give an alibi warning. This consists in telling the defendant that he must notify the prosecution, within seven days of the conclusion of the committal proceedings, of the names and addresses of any alibi witnesses he proposes to call in the Crown Court; the accused is warned that a failure to give notice may result in the trial judge rejecting the evidence as inadmissible. The warning is given under s11 CJA 1967.

The magistrates may decide not to give the alibi warning if, having regard to the nature of the offence charged, it appears unnecessary: rr6 and 7 MCR 1981. Usually the defence is asked whether it considers the warning appropriate. If they are in any doubt as to its necessity, the warning will be given; it can do no harm if the defence raises no alibi, and protects the prosecution if the defence seeks to raise it.

25.11 Legal aid

The accused may already have been granted legal aid for the proceedings at the time of his first appearance in court, perhaps after an arrest or at a remand prior to committal. If so, the court will be asked to continue it to trial in the Crown Court.

If the accused has not obtained legal aid already, the court may be asked to grant it. If the court refuses to extend legal aid or to grant it, the accused may apply to the Crown Court for it: s28 Legal Aid Act 1974. The subject of legal aid is dealt with in Chapter 34.

25.12 Costs of the committal proceedings

The magistrates may order the costs of the committal proceedings paid out of central funds, that is, out of money set aside by the government for the payment of legal costs. The order may be made in favour of the prosecution if the proceedings are successful, and even if the eventual trial at the Crown Court ends with the acquittal of the accused ('costs in any event'), or in favour of the defence if the case is dismissed and no order is made for committal. In addition, the court may order that the prosecution pay the defence costs if the case is dismisssed without committal, but only if the charge was not made 'in good faith' by the prosecution. It is important for a party who seeks an order for costs to apply for it at the close of the committal proceedings. See generally *Stone's Justices Manual* vol 1.

25.13 Publicity at committal proceedings

The nature of most committals, whether with or without consideration of the evidence, is that only the prosecution evidence is disclosed; the defence case does not emerge until trial. To allow publication of the entirety of the prosecution evidence, unbalanced by the defendant's, may prejudice a fair trial – if potential jury members have read the lurid and one-sided reports of the committal, they may assume that 'there is no smoke without fire' and form their view of the accused's guilt far in advance. To prevent this possibility of prejudice, there are severe constraints upon what is permitted to be published of the proceedings at committal.

By s8 MCA 1980, a full report of the proceedings, including details of the evidence given, may be published or broadcast (by newspaper or television or wireless) only in two main circumstances:

1. if the committal proceedings result in the magistrates *refusing* to commit the accused for trial; or
2. if the proceedings result in a committal for trial, after the trial has ended.

In all other cases, the only report which may be published or broadcast is one which confines itself to some or all of the following matters:

1. the identity of the court, the justices, parties and witnesses;
2. the offences charged, or a summary of them;
3. the charges upon which the accused has been committed and thoseupon which he was not committed;

4. the identity of counsel and solicitors for the parties;
5. any decision on the grant of bail and legal aid for the accused.

If a report breaches s8 the offending publisher (newspaper editor, proprietor or publisher, or broadcasting body) is liable to a fine on summary conviction. Proceedings for the offence cannot however be instituted without the consent of the Attorney-General (see section 23.8). The restrictions imposed by s8 extend to any court hearings prior to committal, for example, remands and applications for bail. It will be noted that a private report of the proceedings not intended for publication to 'the public' falls outside s8; thus the person who describes in detail to his neighbour the evidence adduced at committal commits no offence. Section 8 aims at preventing prejudice to a fair trial by the general dissemination of information into the eyes and ears of those who may later form the jury at the accused's trial.

Since the purpose of s8 is to protect the interests of accused persons, they may waive that protection and allow publication of a full and very detailed report of the proceedings, including the evidence taken before the justices: s8(2) MCA 1980. If the proceedings concern only one accused, the magistrates must comply with any application made by him to 'have reporting restrictions lifted'. If two or more accused are involved in the committal, and not all make the application, the magistrates may only lift the restrictions if they are satisfied that it is in the interests of justice to do so: s8(2A). Thus, there is a presumption that, in cases where two or more accused are appearing together for committal, the restrictions will not be lifted if at least one of them objects to that course.

Applications to remove reporting restrictions are rare. The only common occasion of their use is where the accused considers that a full report of the proceedings might lead to the discovery of evidence useful to him. For instance, witnesses who can support his intended defence of alibi. Those reading the report may remember some vital piece of information, or have relevant evidence to give. The detailed report of proceedings is however a double-edged sword; it may lead to the discovery of evidence more useful to the prosecution than to the defence. The dangers are well illustrated by the case of *Vaquier* in 1924. V was charged with poisoning a public house landlady by arsenic. He was arrested, but the police could trace no arsenic to his possession. Prior to his committal, and solely for the purposes of personal vanity, V gave interviews to the newspapers and allowed them to publish his photograph. A chemist recognised the photograph as that of a customer who had bought a large quantity of arsenic, and contacted the police; it was his evidence that sent V to the gallows. Had V kept silent, and allowed the proceedings to take their normal, low-key course, he might well have been acquitted.

As an incident of publicity, it should be noted that committal proceedings almost always take place in public, so that anyone may attend and hear the full evidence if they wish: s4 MCA 1980. The justices may however conduct them in camera if they consider that the ends of justice would not be served by their sitting in open court, or when statute so directs or permits: s4(2). The hearing may be partly in open court and partly in camera. 'The ends of justice' include taking a deposition from a witness too ill to attend at court. Examples of statutory powers include s37 Children and Young Persons Act 1933 (child giving evidence at committal) and s8 Official Secrets Act 1920 (public to be excluded from hearing evidence, on the application of the prosecution, that publicity would be prejudicial to the national safety).

25.14 Additional evidence

In almost all cases, the prosecution leads at committal all the evidence on which it will or may rely at trial; it may indeed lead some which it does not later employ. It is a fundamental rule that the defence should be told of and shown all the intended trial evidence, but it seems that this need not, as a matter of law, be done at committal stage. Provided the prosecution leads sufficient evidence to make out a *prima facie* case, it can keep other evidence back, serving it only after committal, in the form of a 'Notice of Additional Evidence', a collection of further statements made under s102 MCA or s8 CJA 1967 (see section 25.5): *Ex parte Massarro* [1973] 1 QB 433. This is a bad practice, for it deprives the accused of his right to cross-examine, at an old-style committal, those witnesses whose evidence is disclosed in the Notice. Nonetheless, now that very few committals are made under the old style, it is unlikely to cause serious injustice.

The Notice of Additional Evidence can also be used to inform the defence of evidence discovered or taken since the committal proceedings were heard, and which the prosecution intends to use at trial. If the Notice is served at or very close to the trial, the defence may well successfully claim an adjournment to consider their position and prepare evidence in rebuttal to meet the fresh allegations.

25.15 Voluntary bill of indictment

Before an accused can stand trial in the Crown Court, there must be some preliminary proceeding at which the evidence is considered and upon the basis of which the formal charge against him can be reduced into an *indictment*. In very nearly every case that preliminary consideration will be by magistrates at committal proceedings. There is in addition a rarely-used power to send the accused for trial without his having been committed by the justices. This is the *voluntary bill of indictment*. It is ordered 'preferred' by a High Court judge, and has the effect of committal for trial. The statutory authority for it lies in s2 Administration of Justice (Miscellaneous Provisions) Act 1933. Although in theory available as an alternative to committal proceedings in every case, it is used in only three common cases:

1. Where committal proceedings have failed because the magistrates have refused to commit an accused for trial. A refusal to commit is not an 'acquittal'.

2. Where, after one accused has been committed for trial, another is arrested and charged whom the prosecution wish tried jointly with the one already committed. A voluntary bill may issue against both, joining them in one indictment for trial, and without committal proceedings in respect of the second accused.
3. Where, after quashing a conviction on the ground of fresh evidence, or because the trial was a nullity, the Court of Appeal (Criminal Division) orders a retrial of the accused. There is no need for fresh committal proceedings since the accused already knows the evidence which will be adduced against him at the new trial.
4. Where, after a reference to and preliminary inquiry by the Serious Fraud Office, it is decided that sufficient evidence has been adduced to justify the trial by jury of an accused charged with an offence of serious fraud: see generally the Criminal Justice Act 1987.

The disadvantage of the powers described in (1) and (2) above is that in none of them does the accused have any right to have the witnesses who will be called against him at trial cross-examined at an old-style committal, or to submit that there is no case to answer. Where the application is made by the prosecution under (1) or (2) above, the judge receives an affidavit from the Crown setting out the reason for the application, enclosing a copy of the proposed indictment, and including the depositions of intended witnesses or their s102 statements. The judge almost always considers the application in private without argument from either prosecution or defence.

25.16 Committal of summary offences

Section 40 CJA 1988 provides magistrates with a power to commit summary offences to be tried with the either-way offences. If the defendant is then convicted of the either-way matter(s), the Crown Court decides on the defendant's guilt in relation to the summary matters. If, however, the defendant is acquired of the either-way offences, the summary matters may then be tried at a magistrates' court.

Section 40 CJA 1988 enables the drafter of an indictment to include counts for certain summary offences, where the accused has been committed for an indictable offence, the summary offence arises out of the same facts or evidence or is part of the same series and the facts or evidence relating to the summary offence are disclosed on the committal papers. This section applies to common assault: s12(1) Theft Act 1968; driving while disqualified; criminal damage (under £2,000 worth).

25.17 Transfer for trial

By s44 Criminal Justice and Public Order Act 1994 it was intended that transfer for trial would streamline committal proceedings between magistrates' and Crown

Courts. The new guidelines would have meant that the most serious cases would be transferred automatically from the magistrates' court to the Crown Courts. As a result, committals under s6(1) MCA 1980, which account for 7 per cent of all committals, were to be abolished.

In April 1996, Michael Howard, the Home Secretary, announced that plans to introduce transfer for trial had been dropped. It remains the government's intention, contained in the Criminal Procedure and Investigations Bill, that committals under s6(1) will be abolished. Witnesses will be required to attend and evidence taken at the 'committal stage', only when the defence makes an application to dismiss the charges.

The test for 'dismissal' is likely to be similar to the present test under s6(1) MCA 1980, ie 'is there sufficient evidence to put the accused on trial by jury?'

A procedure similar to transfer for trial will continue in two existing circumstances: serious fraud and child witness cases. Under s4 Criminal Justice Act 1987, the prosecuting authority is entitled to give notice in 'a case of fraud of such seriousness and complexity that it is appropriate that the management of the case should without delay be taken over by the Crown Court'. The accused may apply to a Crown Court judge for the charges in the notice to be dismissed. Similarly, under s53 Criminal Justice Act 1991, where there is a sexual offence involving a child or an assault upon a child, and a child who is the victim or who has witnessed the offence will be called as a witness, then notice may be served. Again there is a procedure for challenging the charges in the notice in front of a Crown Court judge.

26

The Bill of Indictment

26.1 Introduction

26.2 Form of indictment

26.3 Time for and procedure on drafting

26.4 The rule against duplicity

26.5 Duplicity in the Particulars of Offence

26.6 Reasons for the duplicity rule

26.7 Joinder of accused in the same count

26.8 Joinder of counts in an indictment

26.9 Joinder of defendants in one indictment

26.10 Combination of defendants and counts

26.11 Severance: separate trials of defendants and counts

26.12 Amendment of the indictment

26.13 Comparison with Summons in summary trial

26.1 Introduction

When an accused is to be tried before judge and jury in the Crown Court, the court must have before it the concise details of the offences charged and the alleged offenders. This is the function of the Bill of Indictment, the formal document setting out the names of the accused, the names of the offences with which each is charged, and brief details of the facts of each offence. In a very broad sense it is equivalent to the general endorsement on a Writ of Summons in civil proceedings.

26.2 Form of indictment

Every indictment must comply with the provisions of the Indictments Act 1915 and the Indictment Rules 1971. It is drawn up, often by counsel, and signed by an officer of the Crown Court where the accused will be tried. In certain circumstances it may charge more than one accused and more than one offence, and if it does so a separate trial of accused or charges may be ordered. It may be amended in the course of the trial.

26.3 Time for and procedure on drafting

Unless the accused has been committed for trial by means of a voluntary bill approved by a High Court judge, the indictment is drafted following the conclusion of the committal proceedings. Usually it will contain the same charges as those upon which the justices made their order for committal, but it is not bound to do so, and may charge any offence which is disclosed by the s102 statements or the depositions tendered or taken at committal, even if the justices have refused to commit on that other charge: s2 AJ(MP)A 1933. There must however have been a successful committal on at least one charge known to law, else the power to draft an indictment does not arise at all. The indictment may be drafted by the clerk of the Crown Court to which the accused was committed, but is often drafted by counsel instructed by the prosecution if there is any complexity in the case. The bill must be 'preferred', that is, drafted by the court itself or sent to the court by counsel who drafts it, within 28 days of the accused being committed for trial (r5 Indictment Rules 1971), but this rule is directory rather than mandatory, and a bill preferred 'out of time' will be nonetheless valid: *R v Sheerin* (1976) 64 Cr App R 68 at 70. However, an indictment which is not signed by the proper officer of the Crown Court is invalid, and a trial which is based upon it is a complete nullity. A retrial may thus be ordered: *R v Morais* [1988] 3 All ER 161.

Every indictment contains certain formal parts identifying the court, the number of the case, the identity of the prosecutor (almost always the Crown), and a number of 'counts', the list of charges. Sometimes there is only one count. Each count contains two parts:

1. The *Statement of Offence* – this is just the name of the offence charged, together with any statute which creates it. For example 'Theft, contrary to s1 Theft Act 1968', or 'Murder', or 'Taking a conveyance, contrary to s12 Theft Act 1968'. This part of the count does not name the accused or give any details of the facts of the offence.
2. The *Particulars of Offence* – this names the accused charged with the offence, and gives brief details of the facts. By r3 of the 1971 Rules it must contain 'such particulars as may be necessary for giving reasonable information as to the nature of the charge'. Normally very few specific details are given, and the count alleges

merely the names of the accused, the date of the offence (or the dates between which it has been committed, if no specific date is known), the subject-matter of the charge and the victim of it (if any). There is no set formula for Particulars, and the reader is referred to the *GP I Textbook* and to *Archbold*, where precedents for the more commonly charged offences are listed. Despite the requirement to give charged particulars sufficient to allow the accused to know the case put against him: see *R* v *Teong Sun Chuah and Teong Tatt Chuah* [1991] Crim LR 463. This was a case where there had been a failure to set out particulars of the false representations relied upon in counts that charged offences of obtaining mortgage advances by deception. The Court of Appeal held that it was plain what the particulars were in the case against the appellants and no injustice had, therefore, resulted from the failure to spell out those particulars in advance.

26.4 The rule against duplicity

Few aspects of criminal procedure give so much difficulty as the requirements of r4 of the 1971 Rules that 'where more than one offence is charged in an indictment, the statement and particulars of each offence shall be set out in a separate paragraph called a count'. This means that each count may charge one, and only one, offence. A count which charges more than one offence is 'bad for duplicity' and liable to be quashed. This matter was considered in outline in relation to informations in summary offences at Chapter 24, section 24.5, and the following discussion should be taken as equally relevant to the contents of individual charges in an information.

It will sometimes be clear that a count charges more than one offence. For example, a count alleging 'Theft, contrary to s1 Theft Act 1968 and Taking a Conveyance, contrary to s12 of the said Act', quite obviously infringes the rule that only one offence may be charged in any one count. The problems arise however when, although the count alleges only one 'offence', the statute creating the offence, or the particulars given of the offence, disclose that more than one is being charged. It is best to approach the problem thus:

1. looking at the Statement of Offence, is more than one offence charged; if not, then
2. looking at the Particulars of Offence, do the particulars show one offence, or separate offences committed at different times or places?

It is only in respect of statutory offences that problems arise with duplicity in the Statement of Offence, and only where the statute lists several modes of committing an offence under it. The question is: does the statute create different ways of committing the *same* offence, or ways of committing different offences? For example, s22 Theft Act 1968 makes it an offence to receive stolen goods, or to assist in their retention, removal, disposal or realisation by or for the benefit of another. Which of the following alternatives is correct:

1. That there is one offence of 'handling', but that offence can be committed either by receipt or by assisting in retention or by removal or by disposal or by realisation.
2. That there is an offence of receiving and a separate offence of assisting in retention, removal, disposal or realisation.
3. That there is an offence of receiving, a separate offence of assisting in retention, a separate offence of assisting in removal, etc?

It has been held that (1) is the correct answer: s22 creates only one offence. Therefore a count which alleges 'Receiving Stolen Goods or Assisting in their Retention, Removal, Disposal or Realisation by or for the benefit of another' does not contravene the rule against duplicity. As a matter of practice, two counts are usually charged, one alleging 'receiving', the other alleging 'assisting' but there is no rule that this must be done: *R v Deakin* [1972] 1 WLR 1618.

By contrast, an example will suffice to show that the words of one section of a statute can create separate offences which must be separately charged. Section 2 Road Traffic Act 1927 (now replaced by the differently worded ss2 and 3 Road Traffic Act 1988, and other provisions) provided that 'any person who drives a motor vehicle on a road recklessly or at a speed or in a manner dangerous to the public ... shall be guilty of an offence'. It was held that the Act created separate offences of:

1. driving recklessly; and
2. at a speed or in a manner dangerous to the public.

Therefore a count which alleged 'Driving ... recklessly or at a speed or in a manner dangerous to the public' was bad for duplicity, for it charged two offences. It should have read *either* 'Driving recklessly' *or* 'Driving at a speed or in a manner dangerous to the public': *R v Wilmot* (1933) 24 Cr App R 63.

It is extremely difficult to state with precision when a statute will be interpreted so as to create one rather than two or more offences in each section. The following principal cases have been decided:

1. Section 22 Theft Act 1968 creates only one offence.
2. Section 5 Public Order Act 1936 'using threatening or abusive or insulting words or behaviour' creates only one offence: *Vernon v Paddon* [1973] QB 663.
3. Section 4 Road Traffic Act 1988 driving whilst 'unfit to drive through drink or drugs' creates only one offence, of driving whilst unfit: *Thompson v Knights* [1947] KB 336.
4. Section 9 Theft Act 1968 creates separate offences of burglary under s9(1)(a) and (b), so that the count must specify which of the subsections is charged, or be bad for duplicity.

If a statute's section creates separate offences, each of those must be charged in a separate count or, if only one count is charged, it must specify which of the offences created by the section is intended to be charged. Rule 7 of the 1971 Rules provides that 'where an offence created by or under an enactment states the offence to be the doing or the omission to do any one of different acts in the alternative ... the acts or other matters stated in the alternative may be stated in the alternative in the indictment'. This however begs the question, for the matters can only be stated in the alternative if the statute creates only one offence. Rule 7 therefore gives no guidance as to when a statute does or does not create more than one offence per section; it cannot cure a count that is bad for duplicity.

26.5 Duplicity in the Particulars of Offence

The discussion in section 26.4 has concerned duplicity in the Statement of Offence. Even if that is not bad for duplicity, the Particulars may show that more than one offence is charged. This almost always centres upon a series of acts done over a shorter or longer period of time, and whether they form part of one offence or are separate offences in their own right. Duplicity in the Particulars is totally distinct from duplicity in the Statement of Offence. The question is: what is the accused alleged to have done – a series of acts which are one offence, or a series of acts each of which is a separate offence and should be charged in a separate count? The answer is a question of fact in each case (duplicity in the Statement of Offence is a question of law).

The classic example of the problem is the shoplifter who enters a store and moves from shelf to shelf, or from department to department, taking items as he goes. Does he commit one offence of theft of all the articles taken, or a separate offence of theft in respect of each article? If the latter, a separate count for each item must be charged, and a single count for theft of more than one item is bad for duplicity. The answer lies in the notion of a 'system' or close connection between the takings. Are they in the same shop, on the same day, and follow one after another without significant interruption in time? If so, they may all be charged in a single count, for there is only one offence of theft, though different articles are taken; the position is seen as being identical with that where the accused takes all the items at the same time: *R* v *Wilson* (1979) 69 Cr App R 83. If there is some break in the chain of takings, such as the accused going for lunch between two of them, or moving to a different store, or leaving the store and then returning later having formed some new and previously absent intent to steal another item, the takings do not truly form part of the same 'system' of activities, and are properly charged in separate counts: *R* v *Ballysingh* (1953) 37 Cr App R 28 and *Heaton* v *Costello* (1984) The Times 10 May.

Similar problems arise where employees take money from their employer's till on several occasions over a period of time. Are there several offences, each taking being charged in a separate count, or one offence of taking committed at different times? This is a difficult case.

It seems that, if the prosecution does not know the specific dates of each taking, a count charging all as one offence will survive, but that if the individual dates are known each should be separately charged unless they form part of a closely connected and systematic course of crime: *Cain* [1983] Crim LR 802. There is often no correct answer; see also *R v Balls* (1871) 1 CCR 328. In *Jemmison v Priddle* [1972] 1 QB 489 the accused was charged in one 'count' of an information with shooting two deer with two consecutive shots from his rifle, both killings following almost immediately the one after the other. The Divisional Court held the charge properly made in a single count, since there was only one offence of killing even though two victims of it. Had the killings been more separated in time or place, for example, if the accused had moved to a different part of the wood after the first killing, or had done the killings more than a few minutes apart, there would have been two offences which would have had to have been separately charged.

If however the statute under which a charge is drawn provides specifically that a separate offence is committed by the possession, destruction or other dealing with a particular item, a single count which alleges that the accused possessed, destroyed or dealt with several such items will be bad for duplicity. In *R v Ward* [1988] Crim LR 57 the defendant was charged with possession of many illicit copies of several different motion pictures, contrary to s21 Copyright Act 1956. The Court of Appeal held that, on a proper construction of the statute, a separate offence was committed in respect of each of the motion pictures, since each was entitled to its own distinct copyright protection. Thus the count fell foul of the duplicity prohibition.

26.6 Reasons for the duplicity rule

The rule against duplicity has grown up to combat two different problems, each related to the prejudice an accused faces in being charged on a duple count:

1. That if a count charges more than one offence, the accused does not known which of the offences charged he is required to defend, if not both. This is the basic rationale of the rule in respect of the Statement of Offence. If the account alleges 'burglary contrary to s9 Theft Act 1968', how does the accused know which type of buglary (s9(1)(a) or (b)) is alleged? The answer surely is that he can tell easily from the Particulars of Offence, and that the rule serves no purpose.
2. More seriously, that if a verdict of guilty is returned on a duple count, the court does not know of which offence the accused has been convicted, or whether he had been convicted of both. For example, a count alleging theft of a video recorder worth £500, and a video cassette worth £5. If the jury say simply 'Guilty', has D been convicted of theft of goods totalling £505 in value, or £500, or only £5? It is necessary to know, for the value of the goods stolen will materially affect his sentence. Provision exists for taking a 'special verdict' from

the jury specifying which of the offences they found proved, but it is rarely used. However, since most offences are tried by magistrates, who will give their findings specifically, the rule is to all intents redundant in summary proceedings. Difficulty in knowing which offence has been proved also affects the accused's ability to plead 'autrefois acquit' or 'autrefois convict' at a subsequent trial founded on the same facts. But such occasions are very rare (see Chapter 27). On the issue of ignorance of which offence has been proved: see *R v Cain* [1983] Crim LR 802.

26.7 Joinder of accused in the same count

If an accused is alleged to have committed an offence jointly with some other person, or if that other is charged with being a secondary offender, such as an aider or abettor, both may be charged in the same count, and the count will not be bad for duplicity if it later emerges that, although each committed the offence, they did not act jointly; the jury may convict each as if he had been charged in a separate count. Similarly, where more than one accused is charged in a single count, the jury may convict one or more and acquit the others or other of the offence charged: *DPP v Merriman* [1973] AC 584. It must be remembered that, even where two or more are so charged, the count must still, apart from the special power to return verdicts of guilty described above, satisfy the duplicity rule.

26.8 Joinder of counts in an indictment

The indictment may contain more than one count against the accused (if he is the only defendant named in the indictment) if the counts sought to be joined 'are founded on the same facts, or form or are a part of a series of offences of the same or a similar character': r9 Indictment Rules 1971. The rule creates two distinct powers, which must be considered separately. For offences to be 'founded on the same facts', they must be related to each other and, generally, arise out of the same incident. Thus a hotel fire which leads to several deaths allows counts for arson and for each of the deaths to be charged in the same indictment, for there is a single 'transaction': *R v Mansfield* [1977] 1 WLR 1102. Similarly, where there is a course of criminal conduct one piece of which is closely related to another as a matter of causation, the whole course is founded on the same facts and may be charged by several counts in the same indictment: *R v Barrell* (1979) 69 Cr App R 250. The prosecution may join in a single indictment against the same accused a number of mutually exclusive counts which are 'founded on the same facts', even though the accused could lawfully be convicted on only one of them at the conclusion of the trial: *R v Bellman* [1989] 1 All ER 32.

Where the alleged offences cannot be viewed as founded on the same facts, or as a causally connected list of offences, then they may only be joined in the same indictment if they 'form part of a series of offences of the same or a similar character'. This has been interpreted to mean that there must be some 'nexus' both in fact and in law between them: *Ludlow* v *MPC* [1971] AC 29. An offence of burglary of a public house and one of theft of money from a public house in the same area about two weeks later have a nexus of fact (public houses, locality, offences of dishonesty) and law (offences of dishonesty, both arising under the Theft Act 1968), and may therefore be joined in the indictment in separate counts: *Ludlow's* case. A charge of handling, burglary and a further charge of handling, committed on different days and at different places and in respect of different property may have a sufficient nexus of fact (locality) and law (all are offences under the Theft Act) to permit joinder, even though there is no other similarity between them: *R* v *McGlinchey* [1983] Crim LR 808.

From authorities since *Ludlow* it seems that the nexus required is very slight indeed, and that provided the offences are of roughly similar types committed in roughly the same locality, that will suffice to permit joinder under r9. In *R* v *Baird* (1993) The Times 12 January, for example, offences committed nine years apart were held to have been properly joined. The test of whether a sufficient nexus existed depended largely on whether evidence in one count would be admissible in the other. Nonetheless, there will still be cases where joinder would be wrong, for example, a charge of theft and a charge of indecent assault allegedly committed on different days, or even on the same day but at different places. If the offences were connected, for example, theft from the victim of the assault, they would be 'founded on the same facts' and therefore joinder permissible under the first branch of r9, but apart from that it is difficult to conceive of them having any nexus in law and fact.

Where a trial proceeds upon an indictment which fails to comply with r9 1971 Rules, the judge having wrongly refused to quash a count or counts which ought never to have been included, it seems that the resultant conviction of the accused is void, the entire proceedings being a nullity and the accused never in danger of valid conviction upon the defective indictment: *R* v *Newland* [1988] 2 WLR 382. The court can however issue a Writ of *Venire de Novo* (see further Chapter 33, section 33.15) and the accused can be retried on an indictment containing only the counts which should properly have been joined together. The trial judge has power to permit the original defective indictment to be replaced by a fresh indictment containing only those counts from that original which can properly be joined under r9, notwithstanding that the fresh indictment is preferred out of time. Proceedings on the original defective indictment can then be stayed, the trial continuing on the fresh bill: *R* v *Follett* [1989] 1 All ER 995 CA.

26.9 Joinder of defendants in one indictment

The position of joinder of defendants in the same count has already been discussed at section 26.7. Where the prosecution seek to join in one indictment counts against individual defendants (that is, not all the accused are charged in all the counts), the counts which do not charge a defendant or defendants who appear in other counts may be joined with the other counts which charge all others if there is some common connection between all the accused and all the offences which makes it desirable that all be charged in the same indictment and therefore tried together. For example, where all have committed separate offences on the same occasion, a joint trial seems appropriate to decide who is to blame the most. A fight in which all accused participated would fall into this category. Even though no two or more accused could be charged in the same count, it is in the interests of justice that all be tried together.

Similarly, where two accused, both employees of the same club, assault on the same night different customers who have not paid their bills, a joint trial is convenient, so that both will be joined in the same indictment, but in separate counts: *R v Assim* [1966] 2 QB 881.

26.10 Combination of defendants and counts

It should be noted that all the principles thus far discussed may work together in one indictment. There may be one count which charges A and B jointly with an offence, one which charges A with an offence founded on the same facts as the joint charge, one which charges B with a totally different offence which forms part of a series of offences of the same or a similar character to the joint charge, and a further count which charges C with an offence connected with the joint charge but with which he could not be charged jointly with A and B. The possible permutations are almost endless, and the best approach is to take first each count separately; is it bad for duplicity, are the defendants properly joined in it? Then take the second count and consider whether it is properly joined with the first or some other count; repeat the process for each count in the indictment.

26.11 Severance: separate trials of defendants and counts

The rules as to joinder of defendants and counts in the same indictment are difficult even for experienced judges to apply. The effect upon a jury of having to consider all the evidence they have heard, and to use some of it on only some of the counts but not on others, or against some of the accused but not against all, can seriously prejudice the chances of a fair trial. The practice has therefore evolved that the indictment should not be 'overloaded' with too many counts or too many accused, even if that course is in theory permitted by the joinder rules. This is a contraceptive measure. The prosecution should select the real offences in the case and not add everything of which the accused may possibly be guilty on the facts alleged – the likelihood of concurrent sentences for offences committed on the same occasion makes joinder of more than the most serious futile: *R v Stanton* [1983] Crim LR 190, and confuses the jury, leading to a risk of injustice.

If the prosecution have not heeded the advice of the Court of Appeal, or have joined counts or defendants in one indictment, the defendant(s) may apply to the trial judge that some counts be tried separately from others, or that some defendants be tried separately from others. This is known as 'severing' the indictment, in the sense that two or more trials take place on the basis of a single indictment. Where only one defendant is named in the indictment, but there are several counts properly joined against him, the court may order that one or more of the counts be tried separately from the others 'when it is of opinion that he would be prejudiced or embarrassed in his defence' if they are tried together or if 'for any other reason it would be desirable' to order separate trials: s5(3) Indictments Act 1915. From this wide discretion given the trial judge case law seems to have established the following principles:

1. If all the evidence on each of the counts is admissible on all counts (as 'similar fact' or for some other reason) it is unlikely that an application for severance will succeed, for it serves no purpose.
2. If the evidence on each count would be inadmissible on other counts, so that the jury would have to split the evidence into 'compartments' and take each count separately from the others, that is not conclusive in favour of severance: the judge can warn the jury with a suitable direction to keep the evidence on each count separate: *Ludlow v MPC* (above) and *McGlinchey* (above).
3. The judge is under no duty to order separate trials unless there is some special feature that would make it difficult to direct the jury to keep the evidence separate on each charge, or would cause serious and inevitable prejudice to the accused, for example, a large number of sexual offences of a similar type: *DPP v Boardman* [1975] AC 421. Even though the evidence on each count would be admissible on all the others, it may be appropriate to order separate trials of sexual offences.
4. The Court of Appeal is very reluctant to interfere with a trial judge's refusal to order separate trials, unless he has acted manifestly unreasonably or upon a wrong view of the law: *R v Wells* [1989] Crim LR 67 CA.
5. The only types of case where applications for separate trials now succeed with any regularity are those of indictments alleging a large number of sexual offences in which the 'similar fact' test is not satisfied or the number of counts exceeds three or four (*R v Brooks* (1991) 92 Cr App R 36), but if the case is not one of 'similar facts', the Court of Appeal will be reluctant to interfere with a judge's decision: *R v Dixon* (1991) 92 Cr App R 43. The expense of separate trials cannot easily be justified: *Mansfield* (above).

The preceding discussion has concerned the separate trials of counts against the same defendant. It now falls to discuss separate trials of defendants charged in the same count, or in different counts in the same indictment. The judge has a discretion to order separate trials, on similar grounds of embarrassment, prejudice and delay, and the following principles can be deduced:

1. Separate trials may be appropriate if an essential part of one accused's defence is an attack upon his co-accused (so that to make it the accused risks the loss of his shield under s1(f)(iii) Criminal Evidence Act 1898). However, the mere fact that each accused will blame the other is not conclusive in favour of separate trials, for the public has an interest in finding the truth: *R v Hoggins* [1967] 1 WLR 1233.
2. Where defendants are joined in a single count, it will be very rare that the interests of justice require a separate trial: *R v Moghal* (1977) 65 Cr App R 56.
3. The fact that evidence may be admissible against one defendant but not against another is one factor to consider, but is not conclusive in favour of separate trials, for the judge can give the jury a suitable direction to disregard that evidence so far as it is inadmissible against one of the accused (though this of course depends upon the facts of each case): *R v Lake* (1977) 64 Cr App R 72 and *R v Maloney* [1985] Crim LR 49.
4. Separate trial may well be ordered where a joint trial would be so long and complex as to cause injustice to the defendants or one or more of them. This is particularly relevant where there is no joint charge but numerous defendants, or numerous counts which do not each charge all the defendants. In this type of case it is probably true to say that the counts and defendants should never have been joined together in the first place: *R v Thorne* (1978) 66 Cr App R 6.
5. The Court of Appeal is equally reluctant to interfere with the trial judge's exercise of his discretion unless it is clearly wrong: *R v Maloney* [1985] Crim LR 49.

The question of severance is really a matter of fact in each case. Some judges are more willing to grant it than others. It does no harm to apply for it, but clients must be advised that, according to the known disposition of the trial judge, the application has little prospect of success and an even smaller prospect of founding an appeal against conviction if the client is convicted on the unsevered indictment. It should be remembered however that before asking for severance it should be considered whether the counts desired severed have been properly joined at all – improper joinder will almost automatically lead to the improperly joined counts being quashed, and may be a good ground of appeal if the judge refuses severance and conviction follows on the unsevered counts.

26.12 Amendment of the indictment

The court may give leave for the indictment to be amended at any stage up to the beginning of the summing-up: s5(1) Indictments Act 1915, 'unless, having regard to the merits of the case, the required amendment cannot be made without injustice' to the accused. Once again, what appears to be a wide discretion has been made subject to restrictive rules, of which the following are the principal ones:

1. The indictment must be 'defective'. This includes being bad for duplicity, or for joining counts or defendants improperly but extends also to an indictment which does not charge all the offences which could have been charged on the basis of the committal evidence, that is, a charge which could have been, but was not, charged when the indictment was preferred (see section 26.3): *R v Radley* (1973) 58 Cr App R 394. The additional counts must however be founded upon the same facts as one or more of the counts which formed part of the indictment as originally drafted, or be or form part of a series of offences of the same or a similar character with one or more such original count. Section 5(1) 1915 Act and s2(2) Administration of Justice (Miscellaneous Provisions) Act 1933 do not permit a breach of r9 Indictment Rules 1971 (see section 26.8) which exclusively governs the joinder of several counts against a single defendant: *R v Lombardi* [1989] 1 All ER 992 CA.
2. Amendments are more frequently allowed before the accused is arraigned and pleads to the indictment than after (for arraignment see Chapter 27, section 27.4), for they cause no injustice (though the accused may well be entitled to an adjournment to consider his position, if the trial has already started or is fixed for a date in the near future).
3. An amendment to add further charges after arraignment, but before the jury is empanelled, is permissible if it causes no injustice to the accused. For instance, a formal amendment to correct a name, or a new count based upon the same facts as those charged: *R v Johal & Ram* [1973] 1 QB 475.
4. Amendments after empanelling of the jury will very rarely be allowed. See *R v Gregory* [1972] 1 WLR 991 and *R v Bonner* [1974] Crim LR 479. In the latter case an amendment was allowed immediately before the summing-up, but the Court of Appeal considered that in such circumstances the defence must be granted an adjournment if they ask for one, and given the chance of calling further evidence to combat the amended charge.

Where an indictment is bad for duplicity, defence counsel is best advised to make no application for amendment at trial; it is the prosecution's task to ensure that the indictment is correctly drafted. The defence can reserve their challenge to the duple count(s) until after conviction, and have reasonable prospects of success if the conviction has been by jury and it is unclear which of the two or more offences charged in the count have been found proved by the jury. The defendant thus gets 'two bites at the cherry'; there is the chance that the jury will not convict at all on the duple count, and the chance that, if they do, the conviction will be quashed on appeal. It is no part of defending counsel's duty to point out to the prosecution or to the court ways in which his client's conviction can be made more certain and unappealable.

If an indictment has been improperly preferred, or is so defective that it cannot be cured by minor amendments, the judge will often quash it totally on the application of prosecution or defence. For example, an indictment which charges an offence unknown to law, or which, even if all the allegations of fact are true cannot sustain a conviction, will be quashed as of right: this is a matter of law for the judge: *R v Yates* (1872) 12 Cox CC 233. Duple counts should be quashed rather than amended.

The indictment may be quashed in whole or in part. If quashed in whole, a new indictment may be preferred, for the quashing does not amount to an acquittal; the new indictment must be preferred by a High Court judge. If an indictment has been improperly preferred, for example, signed by the wrong official of the court, and no application is made at trial to quash it, no objection can betaken to the technical flaw if the accused is convicted: s2(3) AJ (MP) A 1933. Cf s123 MCA 1980 (Chapter 24, section 24.16).

26.13 Comparison with Summons in summary trial

In very many respects the form and purpose of the indictment is the same as that of the Summons upon which an accused stands summary trial in the magistrates court (see Chapter 24, section 24.5). The following principal differences should however be noted:

1. The 'count' in the indictment is the 'information' in the Summons.
2. A defendant can be tried on more than one count against his will; he may be tried on more than one information only with his consent, unless the second information charges an attempt to commit the first or it is in the interests of justice to have joint trial.
3. Counts in an indictment of committing an offence impliedly include a charge of attempting to commit the offence. In a Summons, an attempt must be separately charged.
4. Defendants can be tried together on indictment without their consent; in summary trial this can only happen if they agree to joint trial, unless they are charged jointly in one information or the court considers joint trial in the interests of justice.
5. An indictment is almost always drafted after a preliminary hearing by the justices in open court. A Summons never is, but is issued simply upon the laying of an information.

27

Arraignment and Plea

27.1   Introduction

27.2   Place of trial and composition of court

27.3   Time for trial

27.4   Arraignment

27.5   Standing mute

27.6   Answers less than proper pleas

27.7   Equivocal plea

27.8   Not guilty plea

27.9   Guilty plea

27.10 Plea bargaining

27.11 Other pleas on arraignment

27.12 Presence of the accused

27.1 Introduction

When committal proceedings have concluded with the committal of the accused for trial in the Crown Court, the indictment is drafted and preferred as described in the preceding chapter. It is this which forms the basis of the trial. The defence knows the substance of every item of the prosecution evidence but (with the exception of alibi) it is unlikely that the prosecution will know the nature of the defence case. This chapter describes the procedure at arraignment and on the taking of the plea, and of ensuring the accused's attendance at trial.

27.2 Place of trial and composition of court

The trial will usually be at the location of the Crown Court to which the justices committed the accused. That location can however be altered either by the court of its own motion or upon application by prosecution or defence (see Chapter 25, section 25.7). It should be remembered that there is only one 'Crown Court', but that it sits at different places around the country: its jurisdiction is therefore unlimited, and any trial on indictment can be held in any place the Crown Court sits, regardless of where the offence was committed (provided the English courts have power to try it).

Mode of trial is by judge and jury. The jury are the 'judges' of the facts of the case, the judge instructs them on the law and decides points of evidence and procedure as they arise. The composition of the jury will be examined later at Chapter 28, section 28.3. The judge may be one of the four following types:

1. High Court judge – puisne judge, almost always of the Queen's Bench or Family Division.
2. Circuit judge – 500 or so full-time judges attached to particular courts or districts.
3. Recorder – part-time judge, usually a practising barrister, who sits as a judge for about four weeks per year.
4. Assistant recorder – part-time judge, usually a practising barrister, who will later become a recorder after some time as a 'deputy' judge.

The type of judge appointed to preside over the trial depends largely upon the seriousness of the offence.

The Lord Chief Justice has issued a *Direction* amending directions previously given on the classification and allocation of the business of the Crown Court: *Practice Direction on Classification and Allocation of Crown Court Business* (1995) The Independent 31 May. Its most important provisions are as follows:

For the purposes of trial in the Crown Court, offences were to be classified as follows:

1. Class 1 offences – any offence for which a person might be sentenced to death; misprision of treason and treason felony; murder; genocide; any offence under s1 Official Secrets Act 1911; incitement, attempt, or conspiracy to commit any of the foregoing.
2. Class 2 offences – manslaughter; infanticide; child destruction; abortion; rape; sexual intercourse with a girl under 13; incest with a girl under 13; sedition; an offence under s1 Geneva Convention 1957; mutiny; piracy; incitement, attempt or conspiracy to commit any of the foregoing.
3. Class 3 offences – all offences triable only on indictment other than those in classes 1, 2 and 4.
4. Class 4 offences – wounding or causing grievous bodily harm with intent; robbery or assault with intent to rob; incitement or attempt to commit any of the foregoing; conspiracy at common law, or conspiracy to commit any offence other than those included in classes 1 and 2; all offences triable either way.

The different classes of offences were to be allocated as follows:

1. Class 1 offences to be tried by a High Court judge. A case of murder, or incitement, attempt or conspiracy to commit murder might be released by or on the authority of the presiding judge, for trial by a circuit judge approved by the Lord Chief Justice.
2. Class 2 offences to be tried by a High Court judge unless a particular case was released for trial by a circuit judge.
3. Class 3 offences might be tried by a High Court judge or in accordance with general or particular directions by a presiding judge, by a circuit judge or recorder.
4. Class 4 offences might be tried by a High Court judge, circuit judge a recorder or assistant recorder. A class 4 case should not be listed for trial by a High Court judge except with his or the presiding judge's consent.

27.3 Time for trial

A trial on indictment cannot begin less than two weeks after the date the accused was committed for trial by the justices; nor should it begin more than eight weeks after committal: s4 Courts Act 1971. These requirements are directory rather than mandatory, so that a failure to comply with them does not make the trial void. In view of the delay which inevitably occurs in preferring the indictment, instructing prosecution counsel, and finding suitable dates for the hearing ('listing for trial'), it is very unusual for a trial to begin within eight weeks of committal. Instead, the accused can expect to wait several months to have his trial. In the Scottish criminal system, a failure to begin the trial within 110 days of committal is often an absolute bar to proceedings, and the accused must be discharged. An approximation to this system, but more complicated, was enacted in s22 Prosecution of Offences Act 1985, this is being introduced in a piecemeal way in different parts of England and Wales; the details are too complicated to this text.

Supreme Court of Judicature Practice Direction (Crown Court: Plea and Directions Hearings)

The Lord Chief Justice has issued a *Practice Direction* ((1995) The Times 31 July) which established plea directions and hearings (PDHs) in the Crown Court and would apply to all cases, other than serious fraud, in Crown Court centres which had notified the magistrates' court that PDHs had been introduced. The PDH scheme builds upon recommendation 92 of the pre-trial issues working group and the reports of a pilot study at three Crown Court centres in 1992 and 1993. The rationale underlying the changes is that it seeks to encourage the early preparation of cases and to reduce the waste of time and expense incurred by trials 'cracking'. The initial response to the scheme appears to be encouraging and by the end of 1995 all courts in England and Wales should have been operating the revised procedure.

Its most important provisions are as follows:

1. At the PDH, pleas would be taken, and, in contested cases, the prosecution and defence would be expected to assist the judge in identifying the key issues and to provide any additional information required for the proper listing of the case.
2. In every case, other than serious fraud cases in relation to which a notice of transfer to the Crown Court was given under s4 Criminal Justice Act 1987, and child abuse cases under transferred under s53 Criminal Justice Act 1991, the magistrates' court had to commit the defendant to appear in the Crown Court on a specific date fixed in liaison with the Crown Court listing officer for an initial plea and a directions hearing (PDH).
3. The purpose of the PDH was to ensure that all necessary steps had been taken in preparation for trial to provide sufficient information for a trial date to be arranged. It was expected that the advocate briefed in the case would appear at the PDH wherever practicable.
4. At least 14 days' notice of the PDH should be given unless the parties agree to a shorter period of notice. The PDH should be within six weeks of committal in cases where the defendant was on bail and four weeks where the defendant was in custody.
5. Where the defendant intended to plead guilty to all or part of the indictment, the defence had to notify the probation service, the prosecution and the court as soon as that was known.
6. The defence had to supply the court and the prosecution with a full list of prosecution witnesses they required to attend at the trial.
7. For all class 1 offences and lengthy and complex cases a case summary should be prepared by the prosecution for use by the judge at the PDH. All class 2 cases should be scrutinised by the prosecution to determine whether the provision of a summary was appropriate in any particular case.
8. The PDH should normally be held, and orders made, in open court and all defendants should be present except with leave of the court.
9. At the PDH the arraignment would take place.
10. If the defendant pleaded guilty the judge should proceed to sentencing whenever possible.
11. Following a not guilty plea, and where part or alternative pleas had not been accepted, the prosecution and the defence would be expected to inform the court of the following:
    a) the issues in the case;
    b) issues, if any, as to the mental or medical condition of any of the witnesses;
    c) the number of witnesses whose evidence would be placed before the court either orally or in writing;
    d) the defence witnesses in (c) above whose evidence had been served and whose evidence the prosecution would agree and accept in writing;

e) any additional witnesses who might be called by the prosecution and the evidence they were expected to give;
f) facts which were to be admitted and which could be reduced into writing in accordance with s10(2)(b) Criminal Justice Act 1967, and of the witnesses whose attendance would not be required at the trial;
g) exhibits and schedules which were to be admitted;
h) order and pagination of the papers to be used;
i) any alibi which should already have been disclosed in accordance with the Criminal Justice Act 1967;
j) any point of law anticipated to arise at the trial, any questions as to the admissibility of evidence, and of any authority upon which the party intended to rely;
k) any applications which were to be made for evidence to be given through live television links;
l) any applications to submit for pre-recorded interviews with a child witness as evidence-in-chief;
m) any applications for screens, video, tape recorders to be used in the trial;
n) any other significant matter which might affect the proper and convenient trial of the case;
o) the estimated length of the trial;
p) witness availability and the approximate length of witness evidence;
q) availability of advocate;
r) whether there was a need for further directions.

27.4 Arraignment

The trial starts with the accused being 'put up' in the dock, that is, brought up from the cells or entering the dock from the well of the court. The clerk of the court reads the charge against the accused, usually from the indictment. The accused is asked to plead to each charge in turn, and the plea is entered. The process of arraignment is then complete. Problems arise if the accused either says nothing in answer to the charges, or says something which is not clearly a plea of 'guilty' or 'not guilty'.

27.5 Standing mute

Where an accused says nothing whatever in answer to the charge put to him by the clerk, he is said to 'stand mute'. The judge must direct that a jury be empanelled to discover the reason for his silence. That jury consists of 12 people, and hears evidence from the prosecution as to the case of the muteness. There are two possible verdicts:

1. *Mute by visitation of God* – the accused is unable to speak in answer to the charge, even if he wished to. The jury must give its reasons for this, which may be that the accused is deaf and dumb, or does not speak English, or is of too weak a mind to understand what the proceedings are about. If the problem is one of language, the court adjourns to find the correct interpreter. If the problem is one of mental capability, the court determines that question as soon as it arises by a separate jury who, after hearing the evidence of two or more medical practitioners, decides whether the person is under a disability or not. If they decide that the defendant is under a disability, the trial must proceed no further. Then a special verdict of not guilty by reason of insanity is returned and the court may admit the defendant to hospital, make a supervision order, a guardianship order (MHA 1983), or an absolute discharge.
2. *Mute of malice* – the accused could answer if he wanted to do so, but has made a conscious decision to remain silent, in full knowledge of the nature of the proceedings. This is thus a wilful refusal to plead to the indictment. If the prosecution prove beyond reasonable doubt that malice is the cause, the court deems the accused to have entered a plea of not guilty, and the trial proceeds in the normal way: s6 CLA 1967.

27.6 Answers less than proper pleas

In almost all cases the accused will say something in answer to the charges. He may however make a statement rather than say anything which can be seen as a plea. For example, the accused terrorist who says 'I refuse to recognise the authority of this court'. In this case a plea of not guilty will be deemed to have been made, as if the accused were mute of malice. If the accused's reply is so far away from sense that the court suspects he is unfit to plead to the charge, the judge may consider empanelling a jury to decide that issue before proceeding to trial.

27.7 Equivocal plea

The accused may make a reply which is neither guilty nor not guilty, but of the type 'guilty, but I did not intend to do it' or the like. This problem has been discussed in relation to summary trial (see Chapter 24, section 24.10) and the duty of the court is the same: it must try to discover the true nature of the plea. If it remains equivocal, the judge should treat it as a plea of not guilty. The problem is unlikely to arise where the accused is represented by counsel or has a solicitor acting for him.

27.8 Not guilty plea

A clear and unambiguous plea of not guilty, made by the accused himself in answer to the charge, puts the whole of the prosecution case in issue and compels them to prove every element of the offence charged. The prosecution may decide to 'offer no evidence' on the charge, in which case the judge will ordinarily direct that a verdict of not guilty be returned. Unless a jury has already been empanelled, this verdict is returned by the judge himself: s17 CJA 1967. The decision to offer no evidence on a charge frequently occurs where the accused has been arraigned on several counts, has indicated his desire to plead guilty to some but not all of them, and the prosecution has, with the judge's consent, accepted the guilty pleas. A plea of not guilty given by the accused's counsel on his behalf is improper but does not render the trial a nullity: *R v Williams* [1977] 2 WLR 400.

27.9 Guilty plea

If the accused is to plead guilty to the charge against him, he must do so personally. A plea given by his counsel is liable to render the trial null and void so that a retrial will be ordered at which the accused must answer personally: *R v Ellis* (1973) 57 Cr App R 571. The trial judge has a discretion to refuse to accept a guilty plea tendered by the accused, but will rarely do so unless the plea is clearly mistaken or is of the equivocal type. The judge has power to allow a change of plea even though it is returned by the jury after the beginning of the trial and following a direction by the judge in consequence of the accused's expressed desire to plead guilty, so long as sentence has not yet been passed. Nonetheless, his exercise of that discretion will rarely be overturned on appeal, since he is in the best position to assess the strength of the reasons for requesting the change: *R v Drew* [1985] 2 All ER 1061.

The plea of guilty will be void unless it is made 'voluntarily', that is, without pressure from the judge or which appears to originate from the judge. If the judge informs the accused that there is no point in his pleading not guilty, and that he will be better off to plead guilty, the plea is void: *R v Barnes* (1970) 55 Cr App R 100. Similarly, if the judge makes it known through the accused's counsel that the sentence following a not guilty plea is likely to be custodial, while a guilty plea will bring a non-custodial penalty, the resultant guilty plea cannot be seen as safely voluntary and will be void: *R v Turner* [1970] 2 QB 321. Even if the pressure in fact comes from the accused's counsel, the plea will remain involuntary if it reasonably appears to the accused that it has emanated from the judge: for example, after the counsel has seen the judge in private, and counsel says that a plea of guilty will be treated more leniently, and leads the accused to infer that counsel is repeating the judge's words.

The line between informing the accused that a plea of guilty normally attracts a lower sentence than conviction following a plea of not guilty (which is a well-known fact), and informing the accused that in the particular case a plea of guilty will lead to a particular result, is a fine one, and must depend upon the facts of each case. The following principles have been established:

1. Private discussions between judge and defence counsel should be kept to a minimum. If possible, any discussion should take place in open court in the presence of the accused: *R v Coward* [1980] Crim LR 117; *R v Cullen* [1985] Crim LR 107.
2. If counsel does see the judge privately, the judge may indicate the level of sentence he is minded to impose for pleas of guilty and on conviction following not guilty plea, but counsel should not inform the accused of what the judge has said, or give the impression that he is repeating the judge's words when advising on plea: *R v Cain* [1976] Crim LR 464.
3. There is no objection to the judge telling counsel, and counsel informing the accused, that in general pleas of guilty lead to lower sentences than conviction following not guilty plea.
4. The accused must be left free to choose his plea. Counsel may give advice on what the plea should be, but must emphasise that if the accused is innocent he should plead not guilty, nor should the judge place counsel or defendant under undue pressure: *R v Pitman* [1991] 1 All ER 468.

A guilty plea which is obtained by pressure and is not voluntary may make the trial a nullity, in which case the Court of Appeal on appeal can order that the accused be arraigned once more and stand trial again: *R v Jones* [1990] Crim LR 815. This will happen if the accused has been so overwhelmed by the pressure as to be deprived of the free choice of plea. If the plea follows advice from counsel then, however reluctantly it may be made, it is a valid plea: *R v Peace* [1976] Crim LR 119, and the conviction will stand. But see *R v Lee* [1984] 1 All ER 1080 and *R v Clinton* (1993) The Independent 18 March.

27.10 Plea bargaining

It is in cases where the accused is charged with more than one offence, or with a serious offence to which there is a lesser charge (for example, murder, to which manslaughter is a less serious alternative) that the danger of involuntary pleas of guilty is greatest. The accused will probably know that if he is willing to plead guilty to some of the charges, others will not be proceeded with, or that if he pleads guilty to a less serious offence the more serious will be dropped. This may lead to negotiation with the prosecution upon whether they are willing to accept the lesser pleas in return for discontinuing the more serious, or will take a plea of guilty to one or more offences and drop the remainder – the latter being the equivalent of getting 'a bird in the hand better than two in the bush'. The negotiations are known as 'plea bargaining', and bring to English law some of the commercial traits which have invested the United States legal system.

It has been repeatedly stated that plea bargaining is unknown to English law. Nonetheless, it is impliedly sanctioned subject to strict rules, the principal of which are the following:

1. The judge should not allow the accused to plead guilty to some only of the charges in the indictment, and allow the prosecution to offer no evidence on the remainder, simply because the prosecution are prepared to accept that course.
2. The judge should not allow the accused to tender a plea of guilty to a lesser offence, and direct an acquittal on the more serious one charged, simply because the prosecution are willing for that to happen. Prosecuting counsel should satisfy himself that the proposed pleas in (1) or (2) are a 'fair way of dealing with the case', having in mind the strength of the evidence, the estimated length of the trial, the difference in sentence that continuing to trial on all or the most serious offence(s) is likely to make, and other matters such as the public interest.

It is for prosecuting counsel to persuade the judge that acceptance of the tendered plea, and discontinuance of other charges, is the proper course to take. In practice, judges assume that counsel has weighed all the relevant factors, and accept the 'bargain' without inquiring into the merits of the case. To give an example of a case in the Central Criminal Court, the accused was charged on an indictment charging six counts. The first was of conspiracy to rob building societies, the second, third, fourth and fifth were of participating in the robberies as a getaway driver, and the sixth was of using a firearm in the course of the robberies. The accused indicated that he remembered conspiring, and was willing to plead guilty to that charge. He also remembered taking part in some robberies, but could not remember in which of those charged he has actually driven the car; he had been on holiday at some time, and another driver had been involved. He said he knew nothing about the firearm, which must have been used by his co-accused, who was the one who in fact entered the offices to get the money, while he waited outside in the car. The prosecution had firm evidence of the co-accused's activities in the offices, but none of the accused's presence outside on any of the occasions. They accepted that he was not the user of the firearm, but only a secondary offender. The prosecution case in respect of the last five counts was therefore rather weak. The accused's plea of guilty to the count of conspiracy was accepted, and the other counts ordered to 'remain on the file, not to be proceeded with without leave of the court'. This effectively meant that he would never be tried on the robbery or firearm counts, although he was not formally acquitted of them. The 'bargain' had advantages for both prosecution and defence; the prosecution were assured of a conviction for conspiracy, without having to conduct a possibly totally unsuccessful trial on all counts; the defence obtained a sentence for conspiracy only, rather than risking conviction for the more serious charge of robbery with firearm. The judge accepted the proposed plea without inquiry.

27.11 Other pleas on arraignment

On rare occasions the accused may escape trial completely by making one of three pleas other than 'guilty' or 'not guilty'. These are the 'pleas in bar' of *autrefois convict* or *autrefois acquit*, and the plea of *pardon*. The third is self-explanatory, and consists of proof that, in respect of the offence charged, a pardon has been granted to the accused in the exercise of the royal prerogative. Since most pardons are granted after trial, rather than before, it is only in the most exceptional cases that the plea will be made. It is now for the trial judge, and no longer for a jury, to determine whether a plea of autrefois convict or autrefois acquit is proven by the defendant on a balance of probabilities: s122 Criminal Justice Act 1988.

Autrefois convict (or acquit) are separate pleas, made in writing at or before the start of the trial, and allege that on a previous occasion the accused has been tried for the offence with which he is now charged and has been convicted or acquitted of it. The rule lies in the principle that no man should be put at risk of conviction for the same offence more than once – the so-called 'double jeopardy' concept. They will succeed if the accused can prove on a balance of probabilities one of the following things:

1. that he has already been convicted or acquitted on trial on indictment or in summary proceedings of the precise offence charged (this is a mere matter of examining the indictment and the facts alleged); or
2. that in previous proceedings summary or on indictment he *could have been* convicted of the offence charged, even though the instant charge was not the one made against him in those proceedings. This is broadly the equivalent of saying that the offence now charged could have been the subject of a verdict of 'guilty of a lesser offence' in the first trial (see Chapter 28, section 28.31), or was charged as an alternative count in those proceedings and the jury impliedly acquitted him of it by finding him guilty of the count to which it was alternative; or
3. that, although the offence now charged was not charged in previous proceedings, and although the accused could not on the previous trial have been convicted of it, nevertheless the previous trial was for a 'substantially similar' offence which involved the prosecution in proof of all the facts and elements of the offence now charged.

The pleas of autrefois acquit and autrefois convict cannot be raised at a summary trial, but the principles of *Connelly* v *DPP* [1964] AC 1254 seem to apply as a plea in bar and the court has a discretion to dismiss an information as an abuse of the process of the court if the accused is being prosecuted for an offence which is 'substantially similar' to one for which he has already been pursued to trial: *DPP* v *Porthouse* [1989] Crim LR 224 QBD.

For the avoidance of doubt, it should be made clear that the following cannot be the foundation of a successful plea of autrefois convict or acquit:

1. unsuccessful committal proceedings: see Chapter 25, section 25.15;

2. the 'taking into consideration' of an offence for the purposes of sentence: see Chapter 30, section 30.22;
3. that at a previous trial for the offence, a jury has disagreed and has been discharged without returning a verdict: see Chapter 28, section 28.27;
4. 'penalties' imposed in disciplinary proceedings for the facts of the offence, if those proceedings were not truly criminal proceedings before a recognised court: *R v Hogan* [1960] 2 QB 513;
5. convictions quashed on appeal on the ground that the proceedings in which they were made were a complete nullity; here there is no risk of 'double jeopardy', for the accused was never truly in danger of conviction at the first trial;
6. charges dismissed before the defendant has pleaded: *Williams v DPP* (1991) The Times 26 March.

27.12 Presence of the accused

From the process described, it will be seen that the accused must be present at arraignment to plead personally to the indictment. There are various means of ensuring his attendance. No trial can proceed until the accused has entered a plea, so that, unlike summary proceedings, the court has no jurisdiction to begin to try him in his absence (though it has power to continue a trial in his absence provided he was present at arraignment: see Chapter 28, section 28.2 and Chapter 24, section 24.8). The means of ensuring attendance are as follows:

1. If the accused is in custody awaiting trial, by *warrant of commitment*, issued at the close of the committal proceedings, and addressed to the governor of the prison to which he was remanded in custody or to which he has been transferred pending trial.
2. If the accused is in custody for some other reason (for example, on charges other than the one for which he is to be tried, or for failure to pay a maintenance order), by a Writ of *Habeas Corpus ad Respondandum* or, more commonly, a written order of the Crown Court, addressed to the prison governor.
3. If the accused is on bail, by his answering to bail ('surrendering') at the time and place fixed for trial. Failure to appear will lead to the adjournment of the case and, usually, the issue of a bench warrant for the accused's arrest.
4. If the accused is abroad, by the institution of extradition proceedings under the Extradition Act 1989 or, if he is in a Commonwealth country, proceedings for the return of the accused under the Fugitive Offenders Act 1967. If he is outside England and Wales, but within the United Kingdom, no extradition proceedings are needed, and a warrant for his arrest can be issued forthwith: s38 CLA 1977.

28

Trial by Jury

28.1 Introduction
28.2 Absence of the accused
28.3 Choosing the jury panel
28.4 Choosing from the panel
28.5 Excusing jurors
28.6 Challenging individual jurors
28.7 Peremptory challenges
28.8 Challenges for cause
28.9 Challenges to the array
28.10 'Challenges' by the prosecution
28.11 Praying a tales
28.12 Time for making challenges
28.13 Interfering with the process of selection
28.14 Questioning potential jurors
28.15 Providing a 'balanced' jury
28.16 Investigating the background of jurors
28.17 Swearing in the jury
28.18 Appeals on the ground of improperly constituted juries
28.19 Course of the trial
28.20 Prosecution case
28.21 Defence case
28.22 Closing speeches
28.23 Summing-up

28.24 Other procedural points

28.25 Considering the verdict

28.26 Returning the verdict

28.27 Failure to agree on a verdict

28.28 Judicial pressure on the jury

28.29 Rejecting the verdict

28.30 Alternative offences and verdicts

28.31 Lesser offences under s6(3) Criminal Law Act 1967

28.32 Sentencing

28.1 Introduction

If on being arraigned the accused pleads guilty to all or some of the charges in the indictment, the judge will usually sentence him at once, though he may well postpone sentence until any outstanding counts have been disposed of by full trial. Where there is a plea or deemed plea of not guilty to any count, then a jury must be chosen and sworn in ('empanelled') and the accused put in their charge. The trial proceeds, sometimes in the absence of the accused, and the evidence is presented. The judge rules on points of law, evidence and procedure as they arise, often in the absence of the jury, and sums up the case to them. The jury consider and announce their verdict. The accused is released or sentenced according to the result. It is with all these things that this chapter is concerned.

28.2 Absence of the accused

In certain circumstances, a trial may proceed in the absence of the accused, that is, without him being physically present in the dock of the court. The general rule is that he should be present throughout, from arraignment to verdict, but the trial may continue in his absence in 'exceptional circumstances', a test created by case law and comprising, apparently, the following three principal occasions:

1. Where the accused, through his conduct in court, such as continual interruption, or noisiness, or other disruptive behaviour, makes it impossible or very difficult to continue with him present. The judge may have him removed to the cells below the court until he is fit to bring back into the dock, and the trial may proceed in his absence.

2. Where the accused absconds during his trial voluntarily. The trial may be going badly for him, so that he fears a custodial sentence and decides to 'make a run for it' while the court is adjourned for lunch or overnight. Provided the judge thinks it proper to continue, rather than to dicharge and issue a warrant for the accused's arrest, any resulting conviction and sentence will be valid. The judge therefore has a discretion, but not a duty or an unqualified right, to continue the trial: *R v Jones, Platter and Pengelly* [1991] Crim LR 856 CA.
3. If the accused consents to trial in his absence. There is it seems no reported authority on this point, but if a trial can proceed where the accused does not consent to it (as in (2) above) then a fortiori it should be lawful to continue if he gives his agreement. Examples may perhaps arise where the accused is taken ill during the trial and unable to travel to court. It would follow that the judge retains his discretion to adjourn the trial despite the accused's consent to its proceeding.

28.3 Choosing the jury panel

The jury which tries the accused consists of 12 men and women. Before the 12 are sworn in, however, two selection processes occur. Firstly, from the list of those eligible for jury service the clerk of the court selects a 'panel' of 'jurors in waiting'. Secondly, on the day of the trial 12 of that panel are chosen, after objection by defence and sometimes by prosecution, to form the trial jury. It falls first to discuss who is eligible to sit on a jury, and secondly how the panel is selected.

The general rule is that anyone between the ages of 18 and 69 inclusive may sit on a criminal jury provided:

1. he or she has been resident in the UK for any period of at least five years since attaining the age of 13; and
2. his or her name appears on the register of electors for local or national governmental elections: s1 Juries Act 1974; and
3. he or she is not disqualified at the time of serving on the jury; see below.

The following are disqualified from serving as jurors, and are liable to a fine if they serve knowing of their disqualification:

1. those who have at any time in the past been sentenced to imprisonment for life or to imprisonment for a term of five years or more, or have been ordered to be detained during Her Majesty's pleasure;
2. those who, during the ten years immediately preceding the date on which they serve, have served any sentence of imprisonment, youth custody or detention, or any period of Borstal training, or have had passed upon them any order for community service, or a suspended sentence; and those who during the preceding five years have been placed on probation in the United Kingdom: s1 Juries

(Disqualification) Act 1984, amending Part II of Schedule 1 to the Juries Act 1974. Also, those who are on police or court bail (s40 CJPOA 1994).

The following are ineligible for jury service, and are liable to a fine if they serve knowing of their ineligibility:

1. ministers of the church or of any recognised religious faith;
2. persons resident in mental institutions or under regular medical treatment for mental disorder;
3. judges and magistrates of all types: High Court, circuit, lay, stipendiary, recorders and Law Lords. They remain ineligible for life;
4. those concerned in the administration of justice, other than members of class (3) above. Solicitors, barristers, their clerks, court officers, police officers, probation officers and many others on the fringe of the legal system fall within this category. Ineligibility continues for ten years after the person has ceased to hold the position which rendered him ineligible.

From the list of eligible jurors the Lord Chancellor's Department selects a panel. The selection should be made at random, and not with any view to balance the panel as to age, sex, colour or background. The essence of jury selection is that it be a representative cross-section of society, but that no conscious attempt be made to provide such a cross-section, at least at the stage of selecting the panel. The panel is then summoned to attend court on the stated date. Refusal to attend lays the juror liable to prosecution and fine, unless the refusal is based upon disqualification, ineligibility, or perhaps, illness or other urgent necessity. In many cases one or more members of the panel is in some way prohibited from sitting on the jury; the register of potential jurors (marked with a capital 'J') by their names in the electoral register) is not always up-to-date. Such mistakes are often pointed out by the juror before he arrives at court. If not, they should become apparent before the jury is sworn.

28.4 Choosing from the panel

The panel of potential jurors usually comprises far more than 12 persons, to allow for some of them being ineligible or disqualified or otherwise not chosen to serve. Thirty-six is not an unusual number for a panel. On assembling at court they become the 'jury in waiting', and go to sit at the back of the court, often after the arraignment of the accused. A ballot has already been taken to decide in what order they will step forward to take their place in the jury box. In very many cases the first 12 names in that ballot will form the trial jury, but mention must now be made of the ways in which either prosecution or defence may object to particular jurors, and in which the judge may excuse them from service at their own request.

28.5 Excusing jurors

Even where neither side takes objection to a particular potential juror, that juror may be reluctant to exercise his constitutional right to sit in judgment. The judge has power to excuse otherwise eligible jurors in the following cases:

1. Peers and peeresses, members of the House of Commons, officers of the Commons and Lords, full-time serving members of the armed forces, and members of the medical profession (including nurses). These classes are *entitled* to be excused, so that if they ask to be excused the judge must grant their request: Sch 1 JA 1974.
2. Those who have previously served on a jury and were at the previous trial excused from jury service for a period which has not yet expired. They are similarly excusable as of right.
3. Persons who have some personal knowledge of the case or of any party or witness in it. The judge has a discretion to excuse them, and will invariably do so to ensure a fair trial by an open-minded jury.
4. Persons who have served on a jury within the two years preceding the trial for which they are now summoned. In practice they are excusable as of right: s8 JA 1974.
5. Persons who can show some good cause why they should be excused. The judge has a discretion to excuse anyone under this head, but the most common reasons seem to be hardship caused to a sole trader by having to give up his time, and other commitments or arrangements which it would be unjust to require the person summoned to abandon. The guiding principle remains however that those who are eligible and who are summoned should serve, as a public duty.
6. Persons who appear to the court to be incapable of acting as jurors because of some physical or mental disability eg deafness, or deficient knowledge of English: s10 JA 1974. This is a matter for the judge's discretion.
7. Persons aged between 65 and 69 inclusive, under the provisions of s119 Criminal Justice Act 1988.

It should be noted that persons summoned for jury service may ask to be excused before they assemble at court. This is usually done at the time the Summons is received, by endorsing on it a claim for excuse (or a statement of disqualification or ineligibility, if that is the reason for objecting to the Summons), and returning it to the court. If the court officer refuses to excuse, the potential juror may appeal to the judge against the refusal. The power of the judge to excuse jurors after the trial has started is considered at section 28.24.

The Crown Court further possesses power to defer jury service, that is, to postpone the date upon which a person summoned to serve on a jury shall perform his duty to serve, on proof of a good reason for deferral: s9A Juries Act 1974 as inserted by s120 Criminal Justice Act 1988.

28.6 Challenging individual jurors

The process of selecting the jury panel aims to produce a complement of eligible jurors representing a fair cross-section of the public. On the whole it achieves that aim, though concern continues to be expressed at the number of young people who are chosen for service; the average age of jurors falls year by year. Mistakes are however made. People who are disqualified or ineligible sometimes slip through the checks made by the Lord Chancellor's Department and are included in the panel. Unknown to the selecting officer, a potential juror may know the accused or a witness, or have personal interest in the outcome of the case. Perhaps the potential juror just does not 'look right' to the defence. The defendant is given a right of objection to the panel to cover these and other circumstances in which he does not wish one or more of the panel to serve on his trial jury. The right of objection is called *challenge for cause*.

28.7 Peremptory challenges

The accused no longer holds the right to object to jurors without proving some valid ground for his objection. This right, termed the 'peremptory challenge' was abolished altogether by s118 Criminal Justice Act 1988, its existence and exercise thought no longer appropriate. The accused now possesses only the right to challenge potential jurors for 'cause'.

28.8 Challenges for cause

The accused can object successfully to a potential juror only if there is some good reason why that juror should not serve. The burden of showing 'cause' why the juror should be discharged lies upon the defendant, and the following are the most common types of successful objection:

1. that the juror is ineligible or disqualified;
2. that the juror is acquainted with the defendant or a witness in the case;
3. where there is a suspicion, supported by some evidence, that the juror has been bribed or intimidated;
4. that the juror is likely to be biased, for example, a juror who, on walking to the jury box, glances sideways at the accused and mutters 'Damned rascals': *R* v *O'Coigley* (1798) 26 St Tr 1191.

It should be noted that a challenge for cause is most unlikely to succeed merely on the ground that a juror is female (for instance, in a rape case) or on the ground of his colour or religion. In these circumstances it seems that the judge does have a very limited discretion to 'adjust' the ballot of the panel and to provide the necessary cross-section of jurors, but that the discretion is rarely exercised: see further section 28.13.

28.9 Challenges to the array

Challenges to individual jurors are termed challenges 'to the polls'. There is in addition a right, most infrequently used, to challenge the entire panel of jurors as a block. This is the challenge 'to the array', but will only succeed where the defendant can show some bias or likelihood of bias in the selection of the panel by the officer responsible for summoning the jurors. For example, if the summoning officer is the prosecutor in the case, or the victim of the offence charged, or adopted in his selection some irrelevant consideration such as the age, colour or creed of the jurors.

28.10 'Challenges' by the prosecution

The prosecution has no right to challenge jurors. It can however achieve the same effect as challenge by requiring that any juror 'stand by'. This means that the juror objected to stands to one side while the process of selection continues from the remainder of the panel. If a complete jury is formed from the panel without the juror 'stood by', the prosecution need give no reason for their objection and have in effect gained a peremptory challenge. If, however, through challenges by the defence, the juror stood by is needed to make up the number to 12, he will serve on the jury unless the prosecution can show cause why he should not serve. The only common cause which succeeds is that the juror is ineligible or disqualified. The effect of standing by is that the juror goes to the end of the queue of the panel, to reappear for service if all the other jurors are called and there is still not a full jury. Since a panel usually consists of some two dozen potential jurors, and it is unlikely that more than half a dozen will be objected to by the defence either peremptorily or for cause, the prosecution has a right of peremptory challenge in all but name. The abolition of the accused's right of peremptory challenge by the Criminal Justice Act 1988 created a potential imbalance in favour of the prosecution between the rights of the parties to object to potential jurors. In efforts to redress that balance, the Attorney-General has issued guidelines restricting the exercise of the right to 'stand by': *Practice Note* [1988] 3 All ER 1086. These provide, in summary, that:

1. the prosecution should not exercise the right in order to influence the overall composition of the jury or with a view to tactical advantage;
2. the right should be exercised only sparingly and where the reason for its exercise is one of the following:
    a) that the potential juror to whom objection is taken is 'ineligible' or 'disqualified' according to the provisions of the 1974 Act (see section 28.3); or

b) where an authorised 'jury check' (see section 28.16) persuades the Attorney-General in person that the juror might be a security risk, be susceptible to improper approaches, or be influenced in arriving at a verdict because of his extreme sectarian views; or
c) where the defence agree that the potential juror is manifestly unsuitable, perhaps because he is illiterate and the case will involve understanding of complex documents.

28.11 Praying a tales

In very rare cases the entire panel is used up without producing a full jury of 12. Either because of a challenge to the array, or combinations of peremptory challenges and challenges for cause and objections by the prosecution, the number summoned for service is insufficient to form a jury. There is thus a residual power in s6 Juries Act 1974 to 'impress' jurors in the vicinity of the court. This consists in the court officers searching the court precincts and surrounding streets for persons eligible for jury service. Such are required to serve, even though they have received no formal Summons. The only occasion on which the power has been used in recent times is where the court clerk had by mistake discharged a jury-in-waiting in the belief that they would not be needed for the trial; by the time it became clear that the defendant would be pleading not guilty, the panel had gone home. Rather than use this power to 'pray a tales', the judge is very likely to adjourn the trial to allow a fresh panel to be summoned.

28.12 Time for making challenges

In the cases of challenges to the polls and standing by, the objection must be made before the juryman takes the oath. It is commonly made as he walks to the jury box, by a cry of 'challenge' from defence counsel, or 'stand by' from the prosecution. If the challenge is for cause, the argument follows at once as to the reason for the objection. In the case of a challenge to the array, it is usually made before the process of selection begins in court. It should also be noted that a juror can challenge himself on the ground of disqualification or ineligibility, even if the court or the parties are unaware of it.

28.13 Interfering with the process of selection

The fundamental principle of selecting juries is that the choice should be at random. The only recognised exceptions to this principle lie in the right of challenge and of standing by. In recent years however there have been attempts by defendants and prosecutors, and indeed with judicial support, to engraft additional rights of objection and interference onto the existing rules. The matter has three main aspects: allowing jurors to be questioned before being objected to, achieving a 'balanced' jury and investigating the background of jurors before their arrival at court.

28.14 Questioning potential jurors

In the United States, all potential jurors are liable to be examined at length by both prosecution and defence before being sworn. They are examined and cross-examined as to their political and religious beliefs, their knowledge of the case, what they have read of it, their employment and social habits, and so forth. This takes an inordinate amount of time, and seems to produce no better a jury than a wholly random process of selection.

In the United Kingdom, it is only on rare occasions that such pre-trial interrogation will be allowed. It seems that it is only where a case had been widely publicised, with newspaper articles highly prejudicial to the accused, that a judge will allow jurors to be asked whether they have read such articles, or seen television reports of the case, and will uphold a challenge for cause to those jurors who admit to having done so: *R v Kray* (1969) 53 Cr App R 412. There may also be a power to allow questioning where evidence of actual or reasonably inferrable bias has been first adduced, but in general no 'fishing expendition' will be allowed in the hope that something useful will emerge from the answers.

28.15 Providing a 'balanced' jury

Particularly in cases with a racial or sexual element, the defendant will be anxious to secure a jury containing members, or a certain proportion of members, of his/her race or sex. Despite earlier dicta, the Court of Appeal has now come down against this kind of interference with the principle of the random jury. Taken in conjunction with the abolition of the right of peremptory challenge (see section 28.7), this may have swung too much against 'perceived fairness'.

28.16 Investigating the background of jurors

In the late 1970s a practice arose in trials for serious offences or of public importance of the police investigating the backgrounds of those summoned for jury service and who would form the panel from which the trial jury would be chosen. The ostensible purpose of this investigation was said to be to discover which of the jurors might be biased or unreliable, and to allow the prosecution to exercise its power to 'stand by' at trial: see section 28.10. The practice has however one very great defect: it is available only to the prosecution. There must inevitably arise a suspicion that objection will be taken to jurors on the ground of actual or suspected political belief. If the juror is 'stood by', and the jury made up of others from the panel, the prosecution will never be required to state or prove the reason for its objection, and the supposedly random process of selection is being undermined. The practice acquired the name of 'jury vetting', implying a sinister meaning, ie that it was the prosecution who were passing jurors fit for service.

The permissibility of jury vetting, in the sense of prosecution's checks upon criminal convictions insufficiently serious to disqualify a potential juror, was in a state of confusion following two conflicting decisions of the Court of Appeal. The first in time, *Ex parte Brownlow* [1980] 2 WLR 892, contained statements by Lord Denning MR to the effect that jury vetting was illegal and unconstitutional, since it was not expressly permitted by the Juries Act 1974, and that jury selection should be at random. The second, *R v Mason* [1980] 3 WLR 617, upheld the right of the prosecution to inquire into the previous convictions of members of a jury panel for the purpose of ascertaining which if any were disqualified, and to stand by jurors who have convictions which do not disqualify. No ruling was given upon the legality of inquiries going beyond simple checks for convictions. The conflict appears now to have been resolved by *R v Bettaney* [1985] Crim LR 104, in which the Court of Appeal upheld as 'well-established' the Crown's right to stand by jurors, even though it is not recognised in the 1974 Act, and approved *Mason* so far as concerns checks for criminal convictions of panel members,

The present law appears to be that the prosecution may, with the consent of the Director of Public Prosecutions or of a chief officer of police, inquire into the criminal records of potential jurors, and ask to 'stand by' those whom that inquiry shows to be disqualified: *Practice Note* [1988] 3 All ER 1086.

So far as concerns inquiries going beyond checking criminal records, the Attorney-General has issued a revised set of guidelines on 'jury checks': *Practice Note* [1988] 3 All ER 1086. In the following types of case the prosecution may, in addition to searching for previous convictions, consult the records of Special Branch for any information held on the jurors' political activities, even if no proceedings have been brought in respect of them:

1. Cases involving national security (for example, prosecutions under the Official Secrets Acts) where evidence is likely to be so sensitive as to require its being received with the court in closed session in camera. This is to prevent leaks of official secrets through unreliable jurors.
2. Trials for terrorist offences. This aims at keeping off the jury persons who may be sympathetic to the defendant's cause.

On the effect of inquiries about a juror by the defence, see *R v K* (1995) The Times 14 April in section 28.18 and Chapter 36, section 36.6, for further details.

28.17 Swearing in the jury

Once the jury has been chosen, it must be sworn in and the defendant put in its charge. Each juror is sworn separately, taking the oath to 'faithfully try the defendant and give a true verdict according to the evidence': *Practice Direction (Crime: Jury Oath)* [1984] 1 WLR 1217. Once they are sworn, the clerk informs them of the charge in the indictment, and tells them that the accused has pleaded not guilty to it, and that their job is 'to say whether he be guilty or not'. The formal part of the trial then begins.

28.18 Appeals on the ground of improperly constituted juries

It is appropriate to mention at this stage the grounds upon which an appeal will lie from a jury which contained disqualified or ineligible persons, or which was improperly summoned or sworn. The general rule is that no appeal against conviction will succeed solely on the ground that the jury was improperly summoned, or that any member of it was not entitled to serve, or that the judge should have discharged any member of it during the trial, unless the irregularity is such that, either on its own or in combination with other factors, it makes the conviction in all the circumstances of the case unsafe (see further Chapter 33, section 33.12). Thus disqualification or ineligibility alone are not enough, nor is deafness, or inability to understand English, or mental defectiveness; there must be added features which show that the juror complained of actually had some effect upon the verdict which renders it unsafe: *R v Chapman* (1976) 63 Cr App R 75.

To this general rule (created by s18 JA 1974) there are the following principal exceptions:

1. the fact that a juror was impersonated, and that the impostor was disqualified or ineligible is a good ground of appeal in itself;
2. that the provisions for summoning or empanelling the jurors were not complied with, and that the defence took objection as soon as practicable, but the court refused to correct the mistakes. This too is a good ground of appeal in itself.

There are recent examples of appeals having been allowed where there was a real danger of bias on the part of a juror. Firstly, where a defence witness had alleged that one of the jurors was known to her: *R v K* (1995) The Times 14 April; and secondly, where a juror was the wife of a prison officer who had come into close contact with the defendants: *R v Wilson; R v Sproson* (1995) The Times 24 February. See Chapter 36, section 36.6, for further details.

28.19 Course of the trial

The jury being sworn, and the defendant put in their charge, the trial proper starts. It follows a more or less set course, much more so than a civil trial (see Part I, Chapter 16, section 16.7) and its main features will now be discussed. It should be remembered however throughout what follows that the judge has discretion to alter the order of witnesses, and to allow witnesses to be recalled or interposed as he thinks fit, but not so as to cause injustice to the defendant. The power to adjourn the trial at any stage should also be noted.

28.20 Prosecution case

Prosecuting counsel makes an opening speech, outlining the nature of the case and the evidence the jury will hear. If counsel is aware that the defence proposes to make objection to a particular item of evidence (for example, a confession), counsel will omit reference to it in his opening. The prosecution witnesses are called, examined, cross-examined and re-examined, and documentary evidence is put in as exhibits. The prosecution has a discretion whether to call or tender a witness, but this discretion must be exercised in the interests of justice: *R v Russell-Jones* [1995] 3 All ER 239. However, where a witness statement has been served, there is a duty on the prosecution to call that witness, unless that witness could not be believed: *R v Armstrong* [1995] Crim LR 831. For further details on these two cases, see Chapter 36, section 36.6. Statements of witnesses who were conditionally bound to attend the trial are read as evidence of the truth of the facts stated in them provided the defence has not required the prosecution to call them to give oral evidence (see Chapter 25, section 25.8). The judge may ask his own questions of the witnesses, giving counsel a right to reopen examination or cross-examination to deal with matters arising from the answers. If there are objections to the admissibility of evidence, they will be dealt with by the judge on the *voir dire* in the absence of the jury.

28.21 Defence case

Following the close of the prosecution evidence, the defence may submit that there is no case to answer. This submission is identical to that made at committal proceedings or summary trial, and the reader is referred to Chapter 25, section 25.3 for a full explanation. If the submission fails or is not made, the defence present their case. If the defendant is to be called to give evidence, he should be the first witness, s79 PACE 1984. Similar issues as to the admissibility of evidence may arise, and so may judicial questioning of the defence witnesses. When the defence case is closed after the last evidence has been given, it is only in very rare cases that the prosecution will be allowed to call further evidence. This may be in the nature of rebuttal evidence, to counter allegations raised by the defence which could not have been reasonably foreseen by the prosecution. If necessary, the judge may grant an adjournment before such evidence is adduced, to allow the defence time to prepare their case to meet it.

28.22 Closing speeches

The judge has power to call witnesses of his own, even in the face of objection by the parties, but very rarely does so in view of the adversarial nature of English criminal trials. The concluding part of the trial is therefore a closing speech by each side, by the prosecution first, then by the defence, pointing out to the jury the strength of that side's case and the weakness of the other's. There may be a right of reply for the prosecution if the defence raises points of law in its speech which were not canvassed by the prosecution. Prosecuting counsel will rarely make a closing speech if the defence calls no evidence at all (see *R v Francis* [1988] Crim LR 250), and in exceptional circumstances the judge has power to deprive the defendant of the right to a closing speech as, for instance, where the defendant has discharged his counsel, conducted his own defence in an unreasonable manner, and disregarded the judge's warnings to confine himself to the issues: *R v Morley* [1988] 2 WLR 963.

28.23 Summing-up

The judge summarises the facts for the benefit of the jury, and directs them on the relevant law. He must put the defence case fairly, and fully explain any difficult points of evidence or law, such as the burden of proof, the difficulties of identification evidence, confessions, previous convictions of the defendant, similar fact evidence and the like. The contents of the summing-up vary according to the facts of each case. A summing-up in a long and complex trial can occupy several days. Finally, the judge instructs the jury to retire to consider their verdict, and return a unanimous verdict if possible.

28.24 Other procedural points

The following, less frequently occurring, matters should be noted:
1. The judge can discharge a juror at any time during the trial on the ground of 'evident necessity': *R v Hamberry* [1977] QB 924 and s16 JA 1974. In practice, the judge has a very wide discretion to discharge jurors and his decision is almost never interfered with on appeal. And even though a former juror may have talked to remaining jurors after his own discharge, the conviction will stand if the Court

of Appeal is satisfied that the conviction was not affected and that a sufficiently strong warning was issued by the judge against taking such discussion into account: *R v Spencer* [1986] 2 All ER 928.
2. The judge may discharge the whole jury and order the trial begin over again. If there has been some evidence of attempts to interfere with the jury, he may think it best to restart the trial than to continue. The discretion is once more a wide one, and it appears that the Court of Appeal has no power to review its exercise if the judge decides to order discharge and to restart the trial with a fresh jury: *R v Gorman* [1987] 1 WLR 545.
3. The judge may order that a jury be given protection while away from court and throughout the trial, if there is some evidence to suggest it is necessary: *R v Dodd* (1982) 74 Cr App R 50.
4. If the trial is adjourned for lunch, or overnight, the defendant will usually be granted bail for the adjournment if he was on bail before the trial, except where the adjournment occurs upon the jury's retiring to consider its verdict. In the latter case the temptation to abscond may be too great, but the judge may grant bail in an appropriate case.

28.25 Considering the verdict

The jury are put in charge of the jury bailiff, a court officer, who swears to stay with them, and not to have any communication with them unless it be to ask them whether they have reached a verdict, or to take notes to the judge. The jury must not be allowed to separate from the time they retire until the time they return the verdict: s13 JA 1974. If they have not reached one within a reasonable time, the judge may order that the jury reside in some convenient hotel. Appeals have succeeded in cases where jurors have left the custody of the bailiff for such a time or in such a place that there is a chance that they have come into contact with outside influence, but momentary separation or in circumstances where the court can be confident that no possibility exists of such interference have not led to convictions being quashed. If the jury wishes further guidance upon the law or the evidence, they must send a written note to the judge, through the bailiff; the judge should read out in open court the substance of the note, and give his ruling upon it. In some cases he will call the jury back into court to give them the further directions. Directions given in writing by the judge without informing counsel that they have been asked for are a good ground of appeal, for justice must not be done secretly: *R v Rose* [1982] 3 WLR 192 and *R v Flack* (1984) The Times 20 October.

Where the jury wishes further guidance upon the law or the evidence, the procedure to be followed is strict, and a departure from it by the judge very likely to result in the quashing of a conviction. The relevant rules are to be found in *Gorman* [1987] 2 All ER 435:

1. If a communication from jury to judge raises some matter unconnected with the trial, such as a request by a juror to have a relative of his informed that the trial is lasting longer than expected and that a social engagement must therefore be postponed, the judge can answer the communication without needing to refer to counsel for either party and without calling the jury back into court.
2. In all other cases the judge should state in open court the nature and content of the communication he has received, and should, before recalling the jury to the courtroom, seek the assistance of counsel if he considers it helpful so to do. All the jurors should normally be present in court when the judge delivers his reply to their communication, and he should not call into court only the one or ones who sent him the note: *R v Woods* [1988] Crim LR 52.
3. If the communication contains an indication of the voting figures which a divided jury currently holds, that indication should not be made known, save that the judge may state that the jury is deadlocked.

28.26 Returning the verdict

The jury must make every effort to return a unanimous verdict, all agreeing to it. The court is not concerned to inquire how the verdict has been reached, and will not listen to appeals based upon alleged bias of jurors in the course of considering their verdict. It should be remembered that by reason of death or discharge, the number of jurors may have been reduced below 12. A verdict can be taken from a jury so long as it comprises at least nine jurors, all of whom have sat throughout the trial: s16 JA 1974.

The court has power to receive a majority verdict from a jury in certain circumstances. 'Majority' means:

1. in the case of 12 jurors, at last ten agree on the verdict;
2. in the case of eleven or ten jurors, at least nine agree on it. If there are only nine jurors, the verdict must be unanimous: s17 JA 1974.

The circumstances in which majority verdicts are acceptable are as follows:

1. the jury has deliberated for at least two hours without being able to reach a unanimous verdict. A *Practice Direction* suggests that an additional ten minutes be allowed so that the jury can get to the jury room and settle in before starting their deliberations: [1967] 1 WLR 1198;
2. the jury has had a direction from the judge on the nature of majority verdicts. In practice, a judge will urge them once more to try to be unanimous, but will direct them on majority verdicts all the same.

There is some confusion as to whether the judge may mention to the jury the subject of majority verdicts in his summing-up, or before the two hours have elapsed. To mention it may discourage the jury from attempting seriously to reach a unanimous verdict, but in modern times most jurors will know about majority verdicts even before they come to sit on a jury, thus the judge is not really called to keep them in ignorance. It seems that if he merely reads s17 Juries Act to them he acts properly (*R v Thomas* (1983) The Times 19 August), but no time should be mentioned after which a majority verdict can be accepted. Section 17 however mentions a time of two hours, thus it is difficult to see how a judge can read s17 without also infringing the Court of Appeal's statements that he must not say 'two hours'. It is probably better if the judge says simply 'You may be aware that there is such a thing as a majority verdict. The time for me to direct you upon that has not yet arisen. If it does so, I will give you a further direction. You must try your best to reach a unanimous verdict.'

On returning the verdict, the foreman of the jury (elected by the jury from among their number when they first retired to consider the verdict) rises and is asked whether they have reached a verdict upon which they are all agreed. If the answer is in the negative the judge asks them to retire once more to attempt to reach one, or gives them the majority verdict direction if appropriate. If the answer is negative, but the jury have already had a majority verdict direction, the clerk asks whether they have reached a verdict upon which at least ten (or nine, as appropriate) have agreed. If the answer remains in the negative, again the judge may ask them to retire for further consideration. If in any case the answer is in the affirmative, the clerk asks the foreman for the verdict on each of the counts charged and against each defendant separately. If the verdict is guilty by a majority, the numbers for and against must be stated; a failure to state the numbers against will not however be fatal to conviction, if they can easily be inferred: *R v Pigg* [1983] 1 WLR 6. If not guilty is the verdict, the clerk does not ask for the size of the majority, or even if there is one; it is not in the interests of justice that it should be known that some jurors thought an acquitted accused guilty.

No evidence of the jury's deliberations will generally be received on appeal for fear that jurors may be bribed or intimidated after conviction. In exceptional circumstances such evidence might be admitted to show that the verdict was returned in error, for instance where a juror was not present at its delivery and subsequently swears that he disagreed with it: *Nanan v The State* [1986] 3 All ER 248 PC.

28.27 Failure to agree on a verdict

Where, after long deliberation, and majority verdict directions, the jury is unable to agree a verdict one way or the other, the judge will usually discharge them from giving one. There is no time set after which this can be done, and all lies in the judge's impression of the case. The jury in notes to the judge may inform him that they are completely dead-locked and cannot possibly get a majority. The judge may call them into court for one further encouragement to agree, but is not obliged to do so. If the jury is discharged without returning a verdict, the accused may be retried, for the result of the case is neither conviction nor acquittal, and no pleas of *autrefois* will lie (see Chapter 27, section 27.11). Where the judge misunderstands a jury's note to him and discharges them from returning a verdict even though they had in fact reached one, that jury is *functus officio* and can no longer give any valid verdict at all: *R v Russell* (1984) The Times 25 March.

28.28 Judicial pressure on the jury

Judges often become irritated that juries are unable to reach rapid agreement upon the accused's guilt or innocence in a case which seems to be clear and straightforward. They must not however do anything which can be construed as the application of pressure upon the jury, except to urge them to reach a verdict. No threat or intimidation may be applied. A judge's threat that he would lock the jury up for the night without food and water unless they reached a verdict quickly could stand in 1500 but not in modern times: *R v McKenna* [1960] 1 QB 411. Similarly, a judge's refusal to allow the jury to retire to consider the verdict, coupled with an insistence that they remain in the jury box and deliberate under his watchful eye would, it is thought, lead equally to a conviction being quashed.

Where a jury fails to agree upon a verdict, even after a majority verdict direction has been given, the judge is strictly limited in the degree of 'encouragement' he may give to procure a positive result to the trial without need for the jury to be discharged. The classic form of direction which until very recently was acceptable had been formulated in *R v Walhein* (1952) 36 Cr App R 167, but that case pre-dates the introduction, in 1967, of the majority verdict provisions, and the judge is now enjoined to direct in terms complying with the decision of the five-judge Court of Appeal in *R v Watson* [1988] 1 All ER 897. His direction should, if he decides in his discretion to give one at all, resemble the following:

> 'Each of you has taken an oath to return a true verdict according to the evidence. No one must be false to that oath, but you have a duty not only as individuals but collectively. That is the strength of the jury system. Each of you takes into the jury box with you your individual experience and wisdom. Your task is to pool that experience and wisdom. You do that by giving your views and listening to the views of others. There must necessarily be discussion, argument and give and take within the scope of your oath. That is the way in which agreement is reached. If, unhappily, [ten of] you cannot reach agreement you must say so.'

28.29 Rejecting the verdict

The judge is by convention bound to accept the jury's verdict however much he may disagree with it, unless it is wrong in law (in which case he should explain the law and require them to reconsider it; the problem is only likely to arise where on multiple charges the jury purport to return inconsistent verdicts), or equivocal (in which case he should ask questions to clarify its meaning). Provided all the jurors were present when the verdict was given, and none then objects to it when the clerk asks whether that is the verdict of all (or a majority, as the case may be), no appeal will lie on the ground that some one or more jurors objected to it. Where the verdict of not guilty to one offence has been returned and the jury discharged, they may yet be recalled to return a valid verdict of guilty upon some other charge (perhaps a lesser offence contained by implication in that appearing in the indictment (see section 28.30)) if they intended to return such a verdict but through a misunderstanding failed to do so at once. The prejudice to the accused must be considered, but if the delay between discharge and recall is very short the conviction will stand: *R v Andrews* (1985) The Times 11 October. However, although there is no fixed rule that once the jury has been discharged it cannot reconsider its verdicts, it could not be considered safe for a jury to reconsider after hearing evidence of the defendants' antecedents: *R v Bills* (1995) The Times 1 March. For further details see Chapter 36, section 36.6.

28.30 Alternative offences and verdicts

The primary task of the jury is to consider the evidence upon the offences actually charged in the indictment. It is open to them however to return a verdict of not guilty of any or all of those offences but guilty of some other offence not expressly charged, even though the indictment has not been amended to include that other offence. The following are the principal circumstances in which this can occur:

1. Whenever a count charges a full offence, the jury may acquit of the full offence and instead return a verdict of guilty of an attempt to commit the offence charged. Every allegation of a completed offence implies an allegation of an attempt: s6(4) CLA 1967. Contrast the position in summary trials, where attempt must be expressly charged (see Chapter 24, section 24.16).
2. On a murder charge, the jury may convict instead of manslaughter, attempted murder, causing GBH with intent or (if appropriate) infanticide: s6(2).
3. On a charge of any arrestable offence (see Chapter 23, section 23.3) the jury may convict of assisting an offender after the commission of the offence by some third party: s4 CLA 1967.
4. Where the offence charged includes expressly or impliedly an allegation of some lesser offence (see section 28.31).

28.31 Lesser offences under s6(3) Criminal Law Act 1967

By s6(3) the jury may convict of an alternative, lesser offence if the allegations in the indictment amount to or include, expressly or impliedly, an allegation of that lesser offence. In many cases this causes no difficulty. On a charge of robbery the jury may convict of theft, since proof of theft is a necessary pre-condition to proof that force was threatened or used so as to convert it to robbery. Similarly, a verdict of guilty of indecent assault can be returned on a charge of unlawful sexual intercourse or rape, since proof of the greater offence involves proof of the lesser.

By contrast, there are cases where no conviction of a lesser offence can be sustained under s6(3). These are cases where the greater offence cannot, on the facts of the case or the allegations in the indictment, involve the lesser. For instance, on a charge of theft no conviction can be returned for handling stolen goods, for the elements of the offences are substantially different; if handling is to be the verdict there must be a specific count charging it.

The greatest problems have occurred around the words 'impliedly include' in s6(3). After more than a decade of uncertainty, the House of Lords has now settled the proper test, in *R v Wilson* [1983] 3 All ER 448. It seems that whether a lesser offence is impliedly included in a greater one which is specifically charged depends upon whether the lesser *may* be included in the greater, not whether it *must* in every case be so included. For example, a charge of inflicting grievous bodily harm under s20 OAPA 1861 can be committed by an assault, but may in some cases not include a verdict of guilty of assault occasioning actual bodily harm if, on the facts of the case there is no proof of an assault in the strict sense of the word. The jury may however return a verdict of guilty of common assault if on the facts of the case as charged, an assault is disclosed. The words 'impliedly include' seem therefore to mean 'may include, according to the facts of the case'. Thus, on charge of burglary under s9(1)(b) Theft Act 1968, of having entered a building as a trespasser and stolen therein, the jury may instead convict the accused of burglary under s9(1)(a), entering as a trespasser with intent to steal therein, if the prosecution evidence discloses the existence of such an intent at the moment of entry: *R v Whitting* (1987) The Independent 2 February CA.

28.32 Sentencing

The powers of the Crown Court to sentence following conviction on indictment, and the procedure on sentence, are discussed in Chapter 30.

29

Offences Triable Either Way

29.1 Introduction

29.2 Summary offences

29.3 Indictable offences

29.4 Triable either way offences

29.5 Beginning the prosecution

29.6 Determining the mode of trial

29.7 Absence of the accused

29.8 Change to and from summary trial

29.9 Criminal damage charges

29.10 Committal for sentence to the Crown Court

29.11 Committing on offences triable either way

29.12 Committing with summary offences

29.13 Committing for other offences or orders

29.14 Breach of orders made by the Crown Court

29.1 Introduction

The preceding chapters have been concerned with the two modes of criminal trial: summary and on indictment. All trials must be of the one type or the other, and in many cases statute directs which it shall be. In the case of purely summary offences, trial must be in the magistrates' court. In the case of offences triable only on indictment, trial must be in the Crown Court after a preliminary investigation (usually committal proceedings). There is however one class of offence where the mode of trial is not clearly known until after the accused's first court appearance, but depends upon a decision taken by him or by the magistrates before whom he is brought. This is the class of offences 'triable either way', and their trial forms the subject of this chapter. The most common of all triable either way offences is theft.

29.2 Summary offences

The major offences which can be tried only summarily have already been mentioned (see Chapter 24, section 24.2) and no further discussion is called for. Their place in the scheme of offences triable either way is relevant only to the magistrates' powers of committing to the Crown Court for sentence (see section 29.11).

29.3 Indictable offences

In strict theory, offences triable either way are a type of indictable offence, so that indictable offences fall into two categories: those triable only on indictment, and those triable either way. In practice they are considered as a separate class, and will be so considered in what follows. Offences triable only on indictment include all the most serious offences, for example, murder, manslaughter, rape, robbery, and all other common law offences. An offence created by statute is triable on indictment solely if the statute provides no penalty for summary conviction.

29.4 Triable either way offences

Recognising a triable either way offence is comparatively easy. The following guide will assist:

1. Inspect the statute which creates the offence. If it provides for penalties on conviction on indictment *and* summarily, the offence is triable either way.
2. If (1) gives no firm answer, go to Schedule 1 MCA 1980. This contains a list of offences triable either way.

29.5 Beginning the prosecution

There is no material difference between offences triable either way and those triable only on indictment in the way the proceedings are begun. It may be by arrest, if the offence carries such a power or the police act under a warrant, or by Summons to appear before the magistrate following the laying of an information. Reference should be made to Chapter 23 and Chapter 24, section 24.3 for a full description. It is not until the accused's appearance before the magistrates that the mode of trial will be known, and it is only at that hearing that the procedure begins to differ.

29.6 Determining the mode of trial

Since an alleged offence which is triable either way may be tried either in the magistrates' court or the Crown Court, it must be determined at the outset which it will be. The procedure is governed by ss18–21 and 23 MCA 1980. Briefly stated, the effect of these provisions is that if the magistrates think jury trial more appropriate, or if the accused wishes to be tried by jury, the case will be committed to the Crown Court. If is only if *both* the magistrates *and* the defendant agree that the case be tried summarily that the trial will be of the summary type. Where there is more than one co-defendant, each must choose his own mode of trial individually: *R* v *Brentwood Justices, ex parte Nichols* [1992] 1 AC 1. In deciding whether a case involving a co-accused is suitable for summary trial, justices must not base their decision on a wish to avoid separate trials: *R* v *Ipswich Justices, ex parte Callaghan* (1995) The Times 3 April; for further details see Chapter 36, section 36.7.

The amended National Mode of Trial Guidelines, revised by the Secretariat of the Criminal Justice Consultative Council, are now operable, replacing the earlier guidelines issued in 1990. When determining the appropriate mode of trial, the bench is required not only to take into account those factors provided for by s19(3) Magistrates' Courts Act 1990 but also by the revised guidelines. The guidelines make the following important observations:

1. The prosecution's version of the facts should be presumed to be correct.
2. Where cases involve complex questions of fact or law, transfer for trial should be considered.
3. By s39(1) Criminal Justice Act (CJA) 1991, the defendant's previous convictions can be taken into account aggravating the seriousness of the offence, making it more unsuitable for summary trial.
4. By s28 CJA 1991 the personal circumstances of the defendant may be accounted for when assessing the severity of the sentence, making it more suitable for summary trial.
5. The guidelines confirm the presumption in favour of summary trial but also identify certain features of 'either way' offences which may make summary trial unsuitable.

The procedure begins with the charge being taken down and read to the accused. The prosecutor outlines the facts of the case, then makes representations as to which mode of trial he thinks appropriate. In general he says simply 'summary trial' if that is desired, or points out the seriousness of the charge if he is applying for trial in the Crown Court. The magistrates then consider whether, in the light of those representations, and their powers of sentencing for the offence if they agree to try it, the case is a proper one for summary trial. If they think it is, the following steps are taken:

1. The accused is told of the magistrates' opinion that summary trial is appropriate: s21.
2. The accused is informed that he may be tried by the magistrates if he consents, but that he may be committed for sentence to the Crown Court if, having heard all about the case, they think their powers of sentencing are inadequate (see section 29.11).
3. The accused is then asked whether he consents. If he does so, the magistrates proceed to hear the case summarily as if it were a summary offence, and the procedure is thereafter identical to that described in Chapter 24, section 24.6. If he does not consent, the magistrates must hold committal proceedings, and from that moment the procedure is identical to that described in Chapter 25; the case proceeds as if the case were triable on indictment only.

In the following cases, the choice of mode of trial does not lie with the accused:

1. Where the magistrates are of the opinion that trial on indictment is more appropriate than summary trial. The proceedings turn into committal proceedings even if the accused objects.
2. If the prosecutor is the Attorney-General, Solicitor-General or Director of Public Prosecutions (see Chapter 23, sections 23.7 and 23.8). In these cases, the prosecutor can insist on trial in the Crown Court even if the magistrates and the accused want summary trial: s19(4) MCA.

It should be remembered that a decision not to hear the case summarily does not mean that the accused will be committed for trial to the Crown Court. The magistrates must, as in the case of an offence triable only on indictment, be satisfied that there is a case to answer. The diagram which follows may help to explain the sequence of events and the options open to the court.

Offences Triable Either Way

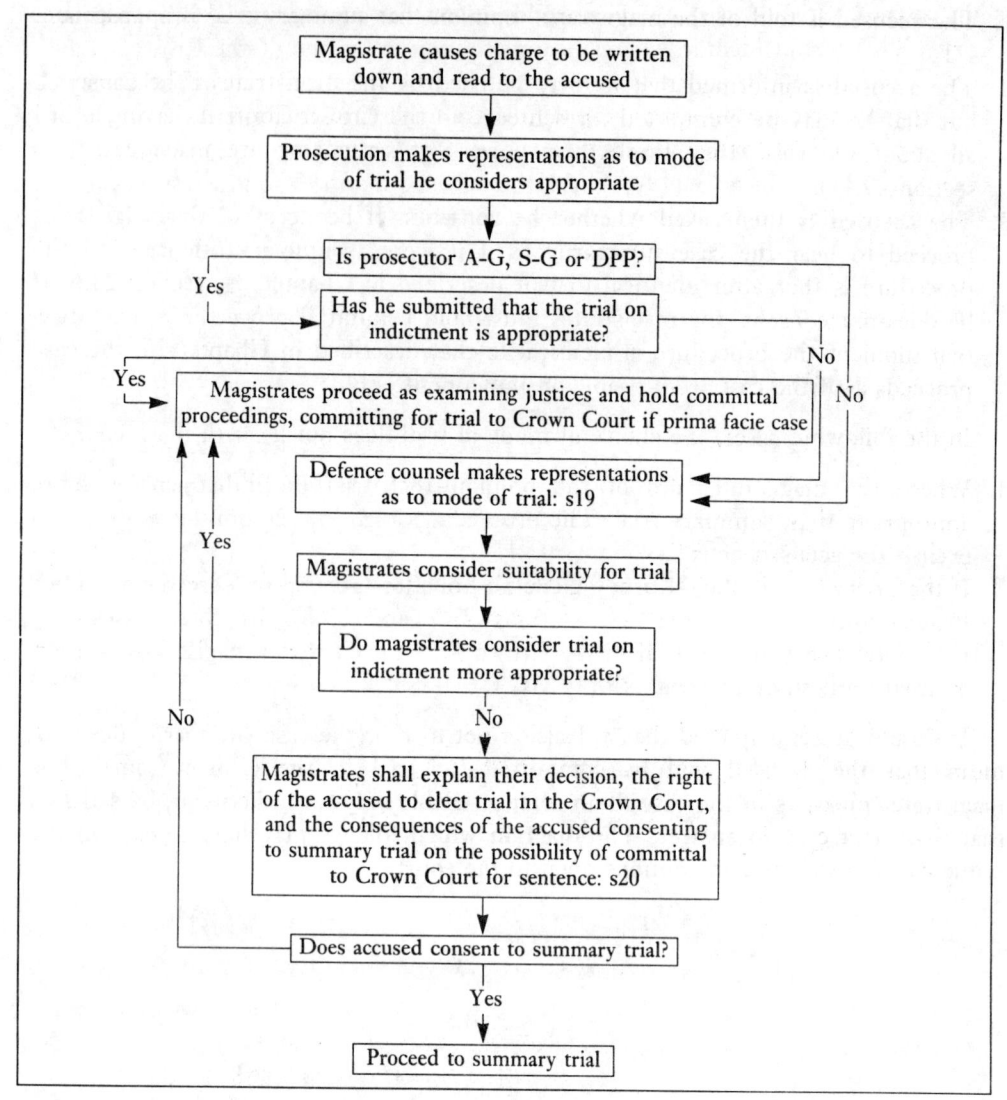

```
┌─────────────────────────────────────────┐
│ Magistrate causes charge to be written  │
│        down and read to the accused     │
└─────────────────────────────────────────┘
                    ↓
┌─────────────────────────────────────────┐
│ Prosecution makes representations as to │
│    mode of trial he considers appropriate│
└─────────────────────────────────────────┘
                    ↓
        Is prosecutor A-G, S-G or DPP?
         Yes ↓                    No
        Has he submitted that the trial on
              indictment is appropriate?
         Yes ↓                    No

 Magistrates proceed as examining justices and hold committal
 proceedings, committing for trial to Crown Court if prima facie case

        Defence counsel makes representations
              as to mode of trial: s19

         Magistrates consider suitability for trial

         Do magistrates consider trial on
              indictment more appropriate?
         No ↓                   Yes (back up)

 Magistrates shall explain their decision, the right
 of the accused to elect trial in the Crown Court,
 and the consequences of the accused consenting
 to summary trial on the possibility of committal
 to Crown Court for sentence: s20

         Does accused consent to summary trial?
                    Yes ↓   No (back up)
              Proceed to summary trial
```

29.7 Absence of the accused

In general, an accused should be physically present in court while the mode of trial of an either way offence is being determined: s18(2) MCA 1980. If the following conditions are met, the proceedings may continue in his absence:

1. the accused is represented in court by counsel or solicitor who in his absence signifies the accused's consent to the proceedings being conducted in his absence; and

2. the court is satisfied that there is good reason for proceeding in his absence: s23(1). This would include where the prosecution is by one of the Crown's Law Officers, or the DPP, and it is known that he will insist on trial on indictment, or where the accused does not intend to make any representations as to mode of trial except to elect for Crown Court trial; or
3. when (1) and (2) do not apply, where the accused makes it impracticable by his behaviour for the proceedings to continue with him present in the court: s18(3).

29.8 Change to and from summary trial

Even after the accused has elected for jury trial, or the magistrates have decided that jury trial is appropriate, the committal proceedings then held may be discontinued, and the matter be dealt with summarily, if representations are made: s25(3). Where however magistrates have convicted an accused after summary trial, and upon hearing of his character and antecedents consider that the case ought really to have been tried on indictment, they cannot invoke the power in s25(2), and instead have only the option of committing him for sentence by the Crown Court under s38 (see section 29.11): *Ex parte Gillard* [1985] 3 All ER 634. Similarly, where the magistrates have decided that summary trial is appropriate, but have remanded the accused to be tried by them at a later date, it is open to them to reverse their original decision before his trial in fact begins and to commit him for trial in the Crown Court under s24: *R v Newham Juvenile Court, ex parte F* [1986] 3 All ER 17 DC. Where a magistrate allows a plea of guilty to be changed, it is inescapable that the accused should be given the right to elect mode of trial afresh: *R v Bow Street Magistrates' Court, ex parte Welcombe* (1992) The Times 7 May.

29.9 Criminal damage charges

With the exception of arson with intent to endanger life, all offences under the Criminal Damage Act 1971 (as amended by s46 CJPOA 1994) are *prima facie* triable either way. In the case of criminal damage where the value of the damage (which is usually the cost of repairing it) done on any charge is clearly under £5,000 for the purposes of trial such offences become summary offences and neither the magistrates nor the accused may choose trial in the Crown Court. The procedure for determining mode of trial is governed by s22 MCA 1980.

The mode of determining trial of criminal damage charges is shown in the following diagram.

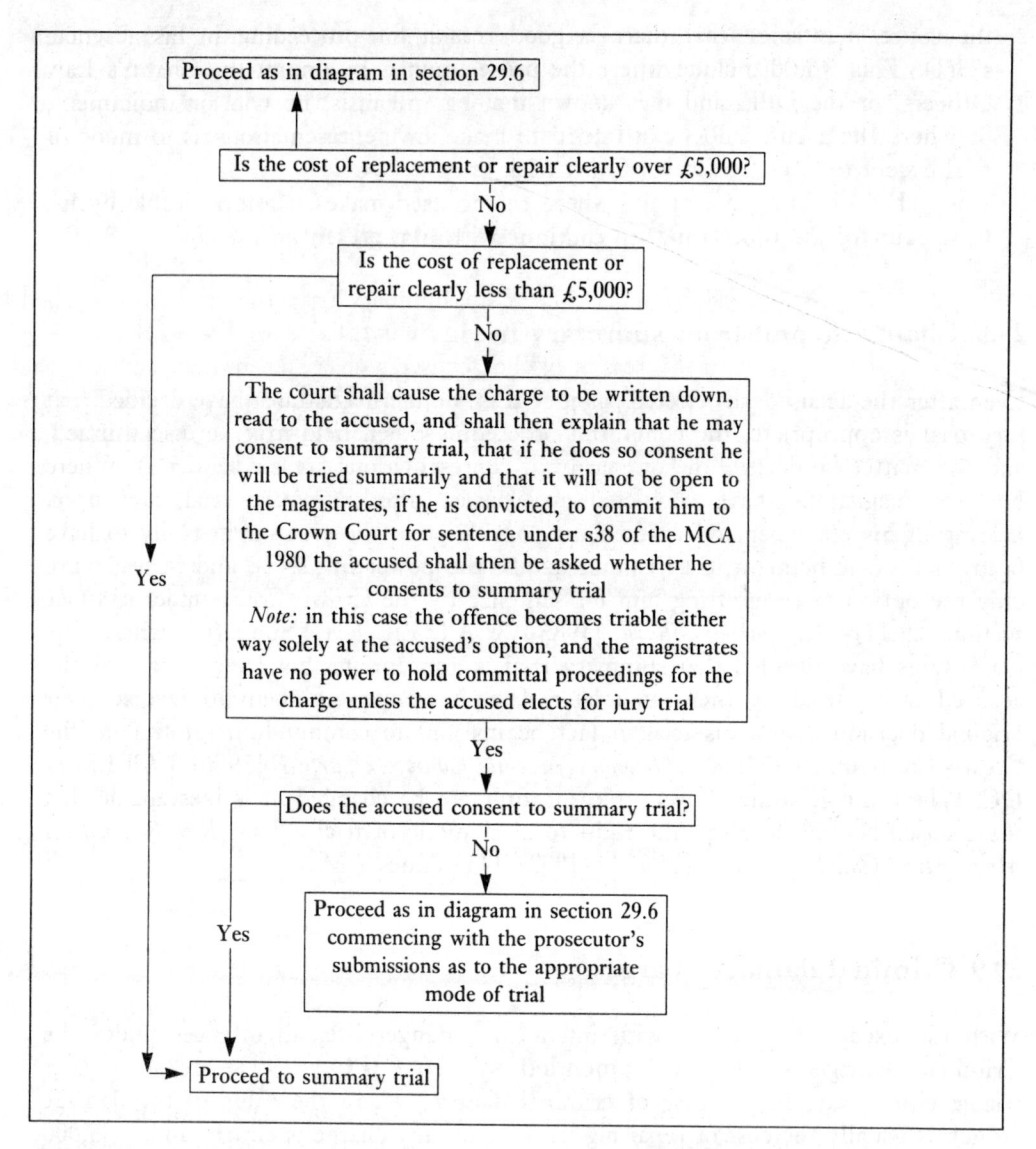

```
                    ┌─────────────────────────────────────┐
                    │ Proceed as in diagram in section 29.6│
                    └─────────────────────────────────────┘
                                    ▲
                                    │
                    ┌─────────────────────────────────────┐
                    │ Is the cost of replacement or repair │
                    │       clearly over £5,000?          │
                    └─────────────────────────────────────┘
                                    │ No
                                    ▼
                    ┌─────────────────────────────────────┐
                    │ Is the cost of replacement or       │
                    │ repair clearly less than £5,000?    │
                    └─────────────────────────────────────┘
                                    │ No
                                    ▼
         ┌───────────────────────────────────────────────────┐
         │ The court shall cause the charge to be written   │
         │ down, read to the accused, and shall then explain │
         │ that he may consent to summary trial, that if he  │
         │ does so consent he will be tried summarily and    │
         │ that it will not be open to the magistrates, if   │
         │ he is convicted, to commit him to the Crown Court │
  Yes    │ for sentence under s38 of the MCA 1980 the        │
         │ accused shall then be asked whether he            │
         │ consents to summary trial                         │
         │ Note: in this case the offence becomes triable    │
         │ either way solely at the accused's option, and    │
         │ the magistrates have no power to hold committal   │
         │ proceedings for the charge unless the accused     │
         │ elects for jury trial                             │
         └───────────────────────────────────────────────────┘
                                    │ Yes
                                    ▼
                    ┌─────────────────────────────────────┐
                    │ Does the accused consent to summary trial? │
                    └─────────────────────────────────────┘
                                    │ No
                                    ▼
                    ┌─────────────────────────────────────┐
         Yes        │ Proceed as in diagram in section 29.6│
                    │ commencing with the prosecutor's    │
                    │ submissions as to the appropriate   │
                    │ mode of trial                       │
                    └─────────────────────────────────────┘
                                    │
                                    ▼
                    ┌─────────────────────────────────────┐
                    │ Proceed to summary trial            │
                    └─────────────────────────────────────┘
```

29.10 Committal for sentence to the Crown Court

The underlying principle of offences triable either way is that they are triable summarily or on indictment, but remain indictable offences for the purpose of sentence. When deciding that summary trial is appropriate, the magistrates know little of the details of the offence and nothing of the accused's previous convictions and background. They may decide that their powers of sentencing seem adequate, in ignorance of factors which would call for a far more severe sentence than they have power to impose. Upon conviction for a single offence triable either way, the magistrates may sentence the accused to a maximum of six months' imprisonment and a fine of £2,000, depending of course upon the maximum provided by statute (if that is lower). Section 38 MCA therefore permits the court to commit the convicted accused to the Crown Court for sentence in certain circumstances.

29.11 Committing on offences triable either way

At the time of being asked for his consent to summary trial, the accused is warned that he may be committed for sentence if found guilty of an either way offence. The power to commit arises if, by reason of the accused's character and antecedents, the magistrates consider that their powers of sentencing are inadequate. This in fact means that if, by reason of fact emerging after the decision for summary trial has been taken, the court takes a more serious view of the case, the offender is sentenced by the Crown Court as if he had been convicted on indictment. If the facts upon which the court purports to act were known to the magistrates at the time that they were considering the suitability of summary trial, there is no power to commit, since, by virtue of their actual knowledge of matters making the offence unsuitable for trial (and therefore sentence), their decision to have summary trial is deemed to be an implied acceptance that their powers of sentence were adequate.

It follows that the most common occasions when committal for sentence will be allowed are the following:

1. where the accused has a bad criminal record which becomes known to the court only following his conviction;
2. where the accused pleads guilty, after a very brief inquiry into the suitability of summary trial, and the full facts of the offence only then become apparent.

If the convicted person is committed for sentence, committal is usually to the local Crown Court. The court comprises a judge sitting with two lay magistrates who must not themselves have sat to try the accused in the summary proceedings. The Crown Court can deal with the offender as if he had just been convicted by jury after trial on indictment, and can impose any penalty open to it. It may even impose a sentence which the magistrates themselves could have passed; it is not bound to give a higher sentence simply because the magistrates were of opinion that the offender should receive one greater than they could have imposed: s42 PCCA 1973. In general, however, the Crown Court will pass a more severe sentence.

29.12 Committing with summary offences

Magistrates have no general power to commit for sentence an offender who has been convicted solely of one or more summary offences. However, if they have convicted him of at least one offence triable either way, and have decided to commit him for sentence to the Crown Court on that offence, they may commit also for any summary offences of which they have convicted on the same occasion: s56 CJA 1967. This allows the Crown Court to deal with all the offences at once, rather than sentencing being split between different courts which may impose inconsistent sentences. It must be noted that in respect of any summary offences so committed the Crown Court only has the powers of sentencing open to the magistrates: s56(5) CJA 1967.

29.13 Committing for other offences or orders

In addition to the power to commit a summary offence conviction to the Crown Court for sentence under s56, along with a conviction for an offence triable either way, the following types of offence may also be the subject of a committal jointly with triable either way convictions:

1. breach of a probation order, imposed in respect of an earlier offence, by the court making the committal;
2. breach of a suspended sentence imposed by the court;
3. breach of a conditional discharge they imposed on a previous occasion: s56 CJA 1967.

When any of these additional matters is 'sent up' to be dealt with by the Crown Court, that court can only deal with the offence in a way which would have been available to the magistrates' court, that is, only with their limited powers of sentencing.

29.14 Breach of orders made by the Crown Court

Conviction by the magistrates of an offence (whether summary or triable either way) may put the offender in breach of a sentence imposed by the Crown Court on some previous occasion. Magistrates have no power to deal with any such breach, and should instead commit the offender for sentence in respect of the breach and of the offence of which they have just convicted him. In the following cases, therefore, there is an additional power to commit an offender for sentence following summary conviction, and whether or not the conviction is of a summary offence, that is, where the conviction puts the offender in breach of a Crown Court:

1. suspended sentence;
2. probation order;
3. conditional discharge;
4. community service order.

Once again, the Crown Court can deal with the offence of which the magistrates have convicted only on the basis of their own sentencing powers, but can deal with the breach of its own order in all cases (except suspended sentence order breaches) as if the offender had just been convicted on indictment of the offence in respect of which the order was made.

30

Sentencing of Adult Offenders

30.1 Introduction

30.2 Sentencing procedure

30.3 Deferring sentence

30.4 Absolute discharge

30.5 Conditional discharge

30.6 Community sentences

30.7 Probation orders

30.8 Effect of and breach of probation and revocation of community orders

30.9 Community service orders

30.10 Combination orders

30.11 Curfew orders

30.12 Fines

30.13 Young offender institutions

30.14 Imprisonment

30.15 Justifying the imposition of custody

30.16 Suspended sentences

30.17 Breach of the suspended sentence

30.18 Detention in a young offender institution

30.19 Life imprisonment

30.20 Early release and parole

30.21 Determining the length of the sentence.

30.22 Offences taken into consideration

30.23 Other orders

30.1 Introduction

Once the accused has been tried and convicted, whether by magistrates or by jury, the court proceeds to sentence him. A very wide range of sentences is available to each court in respect of any offence of which they convict, except murder, for which offence the accused must be sentenced to life imprisonment if he is 21 or over, or to custody for life if between 18 and 20 years old. This chapter considers the range of sentences, and the policy under which they are imposed, available to both Crown Court and magistrates' court on conviction or committal for sentence. Sentences for offenders under the age of 17 years are dealt with in Chapter 31. The Criminal Justice Act 1991, as amended by the Criminal Justice Act 1993, radically changed the provisions for sentencing both adult and young offenders. The latter are dealt with in Chapter 31.

Note: It is unlawful to sentence a defendant without legal representation, but the situation can be remedied by the sentence being imposed on appeal: *R* v *Wilson* [1995] Crim LR 510. See Chapter 36, section 36.8, for further details.

30.2 Sentencing procedure

The court must have before it materials upon which sentence can be properly assessed. The facts of the offence will have been established, but information about the offender's past is always useful. The following are the principal steps taken. There is no material difference between the magistrates' court and Crown Court in this area:

1. If the offender pleaded guilty, the prosecution outlines the facts of the offence. The offender may challenge the details of this, and in appropriate cases the court should reject the plea of guilty and order the prosecution to prove its allegations by evidence. Thus, where the dispute of fact between defendant and prosecution is material to the level of sentence, the judge should direct that the Crown's witnesses be called to testify to what they allege, and be subjected to cross-examination unless the defendant's allegations are 'manifestly false': *R* v *Newton* (1982) 4 Cr App R (S) 388 and *R* v *Mudd* [1988] Crim LR 326. Where however the dispute centres upon some issue which would not influence sentence, the judge ought not to waste time and money upon a 'quasi-trial', and should accept the version of events most favourable to the defendant: *R* v *Sweeting* [1988] Crim LR 131. Usually however the offender will accept the substance of what is said against him.
2. Prosecuting counsel gives evidence of the offender's previous convictions, where these are agreed, by reading from a list of known convictions, which has already been supplied to the judge and to the defence. Convictions which are 'spent' under the Rehabilitation of Offenders Act 1974 are normally not referred to and do not influence the sentence.

3. Evidence is given of other things known about the offender. His age, address, occupation, family circumstances and earnings are the most common ingredients of these 'antecedents'.
4. The defence may then call witnesses to the offender's character. His employer, for example, may testify to his good work record. The value of character witnesses is usually slight, and in most cases none are called unless they can show something out of the ordinary which will influence the judge to mollify the penalty. The witnesses are liable to be cross-examined by the prosecution and the judge.
5. The defence may then present a plea in mitigation, arguing for a lesser penalty than the court seems minded to impose. The low value of goods stolen, or the absence of violence, are good mitigation, as is a plea of guilty (unless the evidence against the offender was overwhelming) and the absence of previous convictions. It is also common for counsel to express the offender's remorse at his crime, and intention to 'go straight' if the court gives him the opportunity, and to compensate the victim of the offence. Judges listen patiently to and look with a degree of circumspection on such statements of good intention.
6. The judge considers any reports prepared upon the offender by the probation service or, in some cases, by psychiatrists. In some cases a pre-sentence report must be obtained before sentence is passed.

30.3 Deferring sentence

Although in most cases the court will pass sentence immediately after conviction or after an adjournment to allow preparation of reports, it is not obliged to do so. In appropriate cases it may be better to allow the offender time to mend his ways, and to postpone sentence for a period. If he leads a trouble-free existence during the period of postponement, the sentence imposed is unlikely to be a custodial one, and may even be a discharge. Under s1 PCCA 1973, a court may postpone ('defer') sentence in the following circumstances and with the following consequences:

1. The period of deferment must be six months or less.
2. The offender must give his consent to it: the court cannot defer against his will; and he must be told why sentence is being deferred, and that it is for him to improve his behaviour and so avoid the custodial sentence the court has in mind on conviction: *R v George* [1984] 1 WLR 1082.
3. Deferment is possible only if the court considers it in the interests of justice, having regard to the nature of the offence and the character and circumstances of the offender. It is unthinkable that someone convicted of armed robbery would have his sentence deferred and be allowed free from custody for up to six months.
4. If the offender is convicted of another offence committed and tried during the period of deferment, the court should curtail the period of deferment and

sentence him for the original offence at the same time as the second one: *Practice Direction* [1974] 1 WLR 441.
5. If the period of deferment expires without the offender getting into trouble again, the magistrates consider the appropriate sentence, but may commit the offender to the Crown Court for sentence. If the Crown Court deferred sentence (and it may do so for an offender committed to it for sentence), it may pass any sentence it could have done on his conviction before it.
6. Sentence should be passed by the same bench of magistrates, or the same judge, who deferred it. If this is not possible, the sentencing court should be told what sentence the convicting court had in mind.

30.4 Absolute discharge

This is available to both magistrates and Crown Courts. It is a complete exemption from punishment, and is very rarely given. The only common occasions are where the offender, although technically guilty, is free from moral blame. In some cases it may be given as an expression of the court's disapproval of the prosecution's insistence on bringing the charges at all, where the prosecution is oppressive or futile: *Ex parte Lamb* [1983] 3 All ER 29. An absolute discharge does not count as a 'conviction' or as a 'sentence' so that it cannot be combined with any other form of sentence except an order for costs, compensation, restitution, or recommendation for deportation. The only exception to its being deemed a 'non-conviction' is that the offender may appeal against it (s66 CJA 1982), and against conviction likewise. Such an order can however be taken into account in police disciplinary tribunals as a ground for punishing a police officer made subject to it: *R v Secretary of State for the Home Department, ex parte Thornton* [1986] 2 All ER 641 CA.

30.5 Conditional discharge

This is available to both courts, and has very similar effects to an absolute discharge. The material difference is that the offender is free from punishment on condition that he commit no offence during the prescribed period following discharge. This period may be not more than three years, and one year is the most commonly imposed period. If another offence is committed within the period of discharge, the offender is liable to be sentenced for the discharged offence as if he had just been convicted of it by the court which gave the discharge; if the discharge was given by the Crown Court, and the offender is tried in a magistrates' court for the second offence, both matters should be committed to the Crown Court to be dealt with on sentence (see Chapter 29, section 29.14).

30.6 Community sentences

The CJA 1991 provides for a sentence not involving custody to be passed by magistrates' court or Crown Court comprising one or more 'community orders', the latter term encompassing each of the following orders (s6(1) and (4)):

1. a probation order;
2. a community service order;
3. a combination order;
4. a curfew order;
5. a supervision order;
6. an attendance centre order.

Under s6 CJA 1991, a court shall not pass a community sentence unless it is of the opinion that the offence, or the combination of the offence and one other offence associated with it, was serious enough to warrant such a sentence. Section 6(2) also imposes a requirement that the community sentence should be suitable for that offender. For the requirements under s6 the court must take into account all factors relating to the seriousness of the offence and may take into account any information about the offender which is before it.

For some of the community sentences, a pre-sentence report (replacing social enquiry reports) is necessary. These include a probation order with additional requirements (but not without) and a community service order, but not, for instance, a curfew order or an attendance centre order.

30.7 Probation orders

The imposition of a probation order has two objectives: the rehabilitation of the offender and the protection of the public. The sentence is now available to courts considering 16 year olds.

This is available to both types of court, under s2 PCCA 1973. It is an order that the offender be put under the supervision of a probation officer who gives him guidance for a period of not less than six months and not more than three years. Before it can be made, the court must explain to the offender the effect of the order and the consequences of his failing to comply with it or of his committing further offences during its currency.

Conditions, or requirements, may be included in the probation order. These may include:

1. general requirements – good behaviour, staying in touch with the probation officer, complying with the probation officer's instructions regarding reporting;
2. residence requirements – the offender may be required to stay in an 'approved hostel';

3. activities requirements – the offender may be required to attend a probation centre where non-residential facilities are available to aid the rehabilitation of offenders;
4. requirements for sexual offenders – offenders convicted of sexual offences may be required to attend probation centres for a specified number of days but with no upper limit on that number;
5. mental condition treatment – an offender may be required, if evidence shows the necessity, to receive psychiatric treatment;
6. drug or alcohol dependency conditions – the offender with 'a propensity towards the misuse of drugs or alcohol' may be required to receive treatment at a specified place where the court is satisfied that the offence was in some way related to the dependency.

30.8 Effect of and breach of probation and revocation of community orders

Unlike a discharge, probation is a 'sentence' passed on 'conviction'.

Breaches of a community order (including a probation order) enable the offender to be summonsed or arrested and brought before the relevant magistrates' court. If it is there found that the offender has failed without reasonable excuse to comply with the requirement(s) of the order, the court may:

1. impose a fine of up to £1,000 (see section 30.12);
2. make a community service order of up to 60 hours;
3. make an attendance centre order (if appropriate) for breach of probation orders;
4. revoke the order and deal with the offender as if he had just been convicted (this applies where the order was made up by a magistrates' court);
5. commit to the Crown Court if the order was made there.

If the offender re-offends during the period of the order, he will not necessarily be in breach of the order, but the order may nevertheless be revoked.

A probation order may be revoked on the basis of the probationer's good conduct.

Community orders may also be amended on the basis of a change of circumstances (for example, no longer requiring mental treatment).

30.9 Community service orders

These are available to both types of court, under s14 PCCA 1973. They can only be imposed if the following conditions are met:

1. the offence in respect of which the order is to be made is punishable with imprisonment;

2. the court has considered a pre-sentence report;
3. the court considers the order appropriate for the offender and the offence;
4. the effect and the consequences of breach of the order have been explained to the offender;
5. the offender has consented to the order being made.

The order obliges the offender to perform unpaid work as specified in it, for a total period not less than 40 hours and not more than 240 hours, usually spread over a period of 12 months and in the offender's own time. The most common work ordered is helping aged persons, or gardening, or some other useful social service. The work is supervised by a probation or other appointed officer.

The order may be combined with a probation order (see section 30.10) or with a fine.

For breaches of community service orders, see section 30.8.

30.10 Combination orders

Section 11 CJA 1991 enables courts to impose, in effect, the combination of a probation order and a community service order. Before doing so, a pre-sentence report and the consent of the offender must be obtained. The offence must be punishable by imprisonment (murder is excepted).

30.11 Curfew orders

Section 12 CJA 1991 enables courts (after obtaining a pre-sentence report) to impose a curfew on any offender aged 16 or over. The curfew must be imposed for not less than two hours nor more than 12 hours duration in any one day. They may not last for more than six months.

Curfew orders may be imposed with other community orders and financial penalties or alone as a community sentence.

Electronic monitoring ('tagging') may be an additional requirement of a curfew, where provisions have been made locally for the implementation of a scheme.

This requirement has attracted much controversy, being largely regarded as an infringement on civil liberties and a humiliating and degrading form of punishment. Furthermore, where it has been tried out as an alternative to remanding in custody, it has met with widespread machine failure and a low take-up rate. As a result, curfew orders are not currently used.

30.12 Fines

Fines in the magistrates' court

Section 18 CJA 1991 (as substituted by the CJA 1993) states that, before imposing a fine, the court must inquire into the financial circumstances of the offender. The court then fixes the amount appropriate (within the statutory limits), reflecting the seriousness of the offence. The maximum amount is £5000 for the more serious offences within the magistrates' jurisdiction.

Fines in the Crown Court

These are 'tariff fines', not calculated according to units, although the court must take into account the offender's means as well as the seriousness of the offence.

30.13 Young offender institutions

Young offenders under 21 may be sentenced to detention in a young offender institution if a person of or over 21 could have been imprisoned for the same offence.

30.14 Imprisonment

It is only offenders aged 21 and over who can be sentenced to imprisonment, and then only if the offence carries such a power. The equivalent powers to send young offenders to 'youth custody' are considered at section 30.18. Indictable offences are all punishable with imprisonment. If they are created by statute, a maximum term is usually prescribed, but if none is mentioned the maximum is two years. Common law offences carry a maximum of life imprisonment unless statute provides to the contrary. The powers of the courts are, briefly, as follows:

1. The Crown Court may impose a sentence of imprisonment of any period up to the maximum provided for, on convicting an offender on indictment or sentencing for a triable either way offence committed to it under s38 MCA 1980 (see Chapter 29, section 29.10).
2. The magistrates' court may impose a period of imprisonment up to the maximum provided for by statute on summary conviction, but must not give a total period of greater than:
   a) in the case of two or more summary offences, six months on any one occasion;
   b) in the case of two or more offences triable either way, 12 months on any one occasion.

The maxima referred to in (2) above are the maxima which the magistrates can order be served at any one time. It is therefore open to them (subject to anything in the statute creating the offence which restricts the power of sentencing) to sentence to a number of consecutive or concurrent terms of imprisonment provided that the total which the offender is ordered to serve at any one time does not exceed six or 12 months, as the case may be. For example, on conviction for three offences of theft the maximum terms available to the magistrates in respect of each is six months, but they must not sentence to a total of more than 12 months to be served at any one time. Thus the following combinations are lawful:

1. three consecutive sentences of four months each;
2. two concurrent sentences of six months followed by a consecutive sentence of six months.

The following would be unlawful:

1. three consecutive sentences of six months;
2. three consecutive sentences of five months.

When a magistrates' court imposes imprisonment, it may not give a sentence of less than five days: s132 MCA 1980. Shorter periods of detention can only be given by exercising the power conferred by s134 to order detention in police cells for periods not exceeding four days. There is no restriction on the minimum period to which the Crown Court may sentence to imprisonment.

30.15 Justifying the imposition of custody

Before a court can send an offender to custody, it must be of the opinion that:

1. the offence, or the combination of the offence and one other offence associated with it, was so serious that only such a sentence can be justified for the offence; or
2. where the offence is a violent or sexual offence, that only such a sentence would be adequate to protect the public from serious harm from him: s1(2) CJA 1991.

The above provisions apply to all custodial sentences, including detention in a young offender institution, suspended sentences and immediate imprisonment (except in a committal for contempt of court). The criteria do not, however, apply where the sentence is fixed by law (for example, murder).

Where an offender refuses to give his consent to a community sentence for which it is necessary, the above criteria do not apply in relation to then imposing a custodial sentence on that offender.

Offences 'taken into consideration' (see section 30.22) are relevant for this section in that *one* of the 'TIC's' will form an offence 'associated with' the material offence. The 'TIC's' and the material offence cannot be all totted up to justify imprisonment where the material offence and one of the 'TIC's' would not (unless the 'serious harm' criterion apply, of course).

When imposing a custodial sentence, the court must give in open court its reasons for justifying such a sentence and must give this explanation 'in ordinary language'.

Except where the offence is indictable only, in which case the court has a discretion, a pre-sentence report must be obtained, including the offender's background and attitude to offending but not containing (necessarily) a recommendation as to sentence.

As well as hearing about the offender by means of the pre-sentence report, the court must (s3(3)(a)) take into account all such information about the circumstances of the offence (including any aggravating or mitigating factors) as is available to it.

30.16 Suspended sentences

A court which passes a sentence of imprisonment for a term of not more than two years may order that the sentence shall not take effect (that is, the offender should serve no part of the sentence) unless during a period specified in the order, which period may be not less than one nor more than two years, the offender commits another offence punishable with imprisonment: s22 PCCA 1973, as amended by s5 CJA 1991. This is the power to 'suspend' a sentence of imprisonment so that, if the offender keeps out of trouble for the period of suspension (termed the 'operational period') he will never have to serve it. The following points must be noted:

1. If the offender has not previously been sentenced to imprisonment, the court cannot impose a sentence of imprisonment, and cannot therefore impose a suspended sentence, unless there is no other appropriate method of dealing with him (see section 30.14).
2. The period of imprisonment specified must not exceed two years, but there is no statutory minimum.
3. The operational period must be not less than one nor more than two years.
4. A suspended sentence cannot be combined with a probation order for another offence (s22(3)).
5. It should not be combined with a sentence of immediate imprisonment.
6. The sentence should only be passed if, but for the power to suspend, the court would have considered a sentence of immediate imprisonment appropriate but, due to exceptional circumstances, it is possible to suspend it. Since the CJA 1991 it is much more unusual to get a suspended sentence; showing these 'exceptional' circumstances is much more difficult than before.
7. Two or more suspended sentences may be imposed on the same occasion, so long as the total period of any term the offender may have to serve under them does not exceed two years, that is, four concurrent sentences of two years suspended on each charge are lawful.
8. Suspended sentences may be combined with fines or compensation orders.

If the offender stays out of trouble for the duration of the operational period, the suspended sentence lapses, and he will never serve any of it, even though he is later convicted of offences committed after the end of the operational period (although the fact that he has been given a suspended sentence may lead to a greater sentence for the later offence). It is only if he *commits* a further offence during the operational period that he is at risk of having to serve any or all of the suspended term. It must therefore be remembered that, in deciding whether an offender is in breach of a suspended sentence, it is the date of the commission of the further offence which is material, not the date that offence comes to trial.

30.17 Breach of the suspended sentence

If an offender is convicted of a further offence committed during the operational period, the convicting court has a number of options open to it. It should be noted that the Crown Court may deal with a breach of a suspended sentence passed by any court, but that the magistrates' court cannot deal with a breach of a Crown Court suspended sentence (it must instead commit the offender to the Crown Court or deal with him for the further offence and notify the Crown Court of the breach of its sentence). The magistrates can deal with a breach of any suspended sentence passed by their own or another magistrates' court.

The options open to the court having jurisdiction to deal with the breach are as provided by s23 PCCA 1973:

1. 'Activate' the suspended sentence in whole, and order that the offender serve the whole of the term suspended either concurrently with or consecutively to any sentence of imprisonment imposed for the offence which put the offender in breach of it. This is the usual order, and the court should make it unless of the opinion that it would be unjust to do so in all the circumstances. Reasons for not activating the sentence must be given in the judgment. Among those that have been upheld are that the subsequent offence was trivial (*R v Smithers* [1973] Crim LR 65), and that it was of a totally different nature to that for which the suspended sentence was imposed: *R v Moylan* [1970] 1 QB 43.
2. 'Activate' the suspended sentence in part. This destroys the sentence so that the unactivated parts cannot later be revived and ordered to be served. Once again, the order may be that the sentence be served concurrently or consecutively. In this case and in (1) above, the normal order is that the sentence run consecutively.
3. Extend the operational period of the suspended sentence by up to two years, but without activating any part of it. The offender gets a second chance, and time is extended.
4. Make no order on the suspended sentence. The operational period continues to run unaltered, and none of the term suspended is served unless the offender offends once more within the operational period and is on that future occasion ordered to serve it.

In addition, the following should be noted:

1. It is only if the further offence *is itself punishable with imprisonment* that the power to make any order on the suspended sentence arises.
2. It is not unlawful, but is unusual, for the offender to be sentenced to a non-custodial penalty for the further offence but to be ordered to serve the whole or part of the suspended term.
3. The offender may appeal against the activation of a suspended sentence, or against any extension of the operational period (s23(9) PCCA 1973), and against the imposition of the suspended sentence on its first being passed.

30.18 Detention in a young offender institution

No person under the age of 21 years at the date of sentence may be sentenced to imprisonment (s1(2) CJA 1982), except when remanded in custody before trial or committed to custody between conviction and sentence: s1(2). Instead, there is a roughly similar sentence termed 'detention in a young offender institution', which consists of detention in a 'young offender institution'; this is sometimes a part of a prison set aside to receive and detain offenders between the ages of 15 and 20 inclusive. The regime of 'detention in a young offender institution' probably differs little from that of imprisonment, but the offender is kept away from the corrupting influence of more experienced villains in the adult prison.

The criteria for justifying custody for young offenders is the same as for adults (see section 30.15).

The following points should also be noted:

1. there is no power to pass a suspended sentence of detention in a young offender institution;
2. the minimum term of detention in a young offender institution is 21 days for offenders between 18 and 20 inclusive and two months if under 18;
3. detention in a young offender institution attracts the rights to early release and to have time spent in custody before sentence count towards sentence which apply to prison terms;
4. where a young offender under 18 is sentenced to 12 months exactly, he will be released after six months, unconditionally;
5. consecutive and concurrent 'detention in a young offender institution' terms may be imposed upon adult offenders: s7(2);
6. the offender must be represented by counsel or solicitor, or have been refused legal aid on the ground that his means appeared sufficient for him to afford his own defence, or have declined to apply for legal aid when informed of his right to do so: s3(1) CJA 1982;
7. special provisions apply to convert a sentence of detention in a young offender

institution to a sentence of imprisonment when the offender attains the age of 21 during his sentence: s13;
8. magistrates have a power to impose a total of six months detention in a young offender institution on any one or more summary offences, 12 months on two or more offences triable either way, subject to the maximum created for the particular offence(s).

30.19 Life imprisonment

An offender who is convicted of murder must be sentenced to imprisonment for life if he is 21 years or over, to custody for life if between 18 and 20: s1 Murder (Abolition of Death Penalty) Act 1965 and s8 CJA 1982. If 17 or under, he is ordered detained during Her Majesty's Pleasure: s53 CYPA 1933. The sentence cannot be suspended or combined with any other form of sentence except, perhaps, an order for costs. Other offences which have power to imprison for life include robbery, manslaughter, grievous bodily harm, rape and arson. In these cases, an offender under the age of 21 but at least 17 years old cannot be given life imprisonment but instead receives custody for life under s8 if the court thinks life detention appropriate: s8(2). The death penalty is now available only for high treason (Treason Act 1351) and piracy with violence. The latter is never charged under English law, but instead under international law, so that the penalty is in effect redundant.

30.20 Early release and parole

Early release is where a prisoner is released unconditionally or on licence before serving the whole sentence. For offenders sentenced to less than four years custody, the early release date will be after they have served half the sentence. For those sentenced to four years or more, the relevant period is one third of the sentence. For 'short-term' prisoners the release will be 'unconditional' if the sentence was for under 12 months and 'on licence' if 12 months or over.

Where an offender commits another imprisonable offence within the currency of the original sentence, he may be returned to prison to serve the rest of that term as well as whatever else is imposed.

Where an offender breaches the term of his licence conditions, he commits an offence and may be recalled to prison for up to six months or the remaining term of the licence, whichever is the shorter.

Parole (the mechanism by which prisoners could be released on licence before their earliest release date) has been merged with the old remission (automatic lessening of a sentence if the prisoner was of good behaviour). However, the Parole Board may recommend release at the half way point to the Home Secretary for long-term prisoners. For sentences up to seven years, the Parole Board's decision is binding – over seven years the Home Secretary has discretion.

30.21 Determining the length of the sentence

Section 2 CJA 1991 lays down certain specific criteria for the determination of the length of custodial sentences:

1. s2(2)(a) for such term (not exceeding the permitted maximum) as in the opinion of the court is commensurate with the seriousness of the offence, or the combination of the offence and other offences associated with it; or
2. s2(2)(b) where the offence is a violent or sexual one, for such longer term (not exceeding that maximum) as in the opinion of the court is necessary to protect the public from serious harm from the offender.

It is still open to the court to take into account matters such as a guilty plea as mitigation.

Where several offences are involved, s28(2)(b) makes reference to the principle where offenders should not receive an overall sentence which is disproportionate to the overall seriousness of the offence.

Where the offence is a violent or sexual one, s2(3) requires that the court must explain in open court that s2(2)(b) applies and why and do so in ordinary language.

Under s48 CJPOA 1994, the court must, when determining what sentence to pass on an offender who has pleaded guilty, take into account (a) the stage in the proceedings at which the defendant indicated his intention to plead guilty, and (b) the circumstances in which this indication was given. If, as a result, a less severe sentence is passed, the court must openly state that this has happened.

30.22 Offences taken into consideration

At the time of being convicted of an offence, the offender may wish to admit to one or more other offences (usually of a type similar to that charged) which have not been charged. In doing so all outstanding matters are dealt with on one occasion. The other offences are listed and submitted for the offender's approval, and the trial judge confirms that the offender wishes him to take those other offences into consideration in assessing sentence. No formal verdict of guilty is taken in respect of any of them. In general, the sentence will be little affected by the extra offences, but may be slightly increased above what the court would have given for the offence charged. No sentence may be passed on any of the 'TIC' offences, but only on the offence charged. The police are able to close their files on the previously unsolved 'TIC' crimes, and the offender in effect escapes the possibility of those offences being specifically charged and attracting their own (possibly consecutive and higher) penalties. An offence taken into consideration does not have the effect of a conviction for that offence, so that in theory charges could later be brought for it; in practice this never happens, and if charges were brought it is very likely that the Attorney-General would intervene to stop them proceeding (see Chapter 23, section 23.8 and Chapter 27, section 27.11).

30.23 Other orders

Orders for costs, compensation, restitution and binding-over are considered in Chapter 32. The contributions payable toward legal aid costs fall for discussion in Chapter 34.

31

Trial and Sentence of Juveniles

31.1   Introduction

31.2   Mode of trial

31.3   Trial on indictment

31.4   Summary trial in the magistrates' court

31.5   Critical date for determining the mode of trial

31.6   Trial procedure on indictment or trial in the magistrates' court

31.7   Trial procedure in the youth court

31.8   Sentencing of juveniles tried in the magistrates' court

31.9   Sentencing following conviction on indictment

31.10 Sentencing in the youth court

31.11 Attendance centre order

31.12 Detention in a young offender institution

31.13 Community sentences

31.14 Supervision orders

31.15 Recognisance by parent or guardian

31.16 Sentencing policy

31.17 Table of orders and sentences with age limits

31.1 Introduction

The mode of trial and the powers to sentence persons under the age of 18 differ in material respects from those applicable to adult offenders. This chapter highlights the most importance differences. For these purposes, a juvenile is anyone between the ages of 10 and 17 years inclusive, and is either:

1. a *child* between the ages of 10 and 13 inclusive; or
2. a *young person* between the ages of 14 and 17 inclusive.

The distinction is for the main part relevant only to powers of sentencing, and the two classes will be considered together in discussion of the mode of and procedure at trial.

31.2 Mode of trial

The general rule is that all juveniles are tried in the youth court, a court similar to the magistrates' court but which sits usually in a different building or at different times from the adult magistrates' court, and the judges of which are drawn from a panel specially qualified in youth court work. Usually there are three magistrates, and at least one of them must be male and another female unless that is not reasonably possible and the court does not adjourn to allow a properly constituted bench to be formed; it is only in the interests of justice that the general rule will be broken, and only very rarely. The court does not sit in public, and the press are allowed to report only the outcome of the proceedings and not the name of the offender: s47 CYPA 1933. If the hearing is held in a building or court used by an adult magistrates' court, the youth court must not sit earlier than one hour after the conclusion of its so being used, and at least one hour must elapse after conclusion of the juvenile proceedings before it can be used again for adult trials.

31.3 Trial on indictment

In the following cases, a juvenile may be tried on indictment in the Crown Court:

1. Where he is charged with homicide. In this case, he must be tried by jury.
2. Where he is charged with an offence which, in the case of an adult, carries a maximum sentence of 14 years or more imprisonment (for example, rape, robbery, handling stolen goods). Trial will be on indictment if the juvenile is 14 or over (that is, a 'young person') and the magistrates before whom he first appears consider the offence so serious that an order for his long term detention under s53 CYPA 1933 is likely.
3. He is charged jointly with an adult and the magistrates before whom he appears, whether or not actually with the adult (*R* v *Coventry City Magistrates, ex parte M* (1992) The Times 13 April), consider that the adult should be tried on indictment and that the juvenile should, in the interests of justice, be tried jointly with him; or where the adult elects for trial (if the offence is triable either way) and the magistrates consider likewise: s6 CYPA 1969. In this case, the juvenile may be tried on indictment at the same time for any indictable offence with which he is solely charged if that other offence arises out of circumstances which

are the same as or connected with those giving rise to the offence jointly charged: s35 CLA 1977. For instance, if adult and juvenile are charged jointly with theft of jewellery, and the juvenile alone with burglary of the premises from which the jewellery was taken, both offences may be tried on indictment since they arise out of the same incident.

31.4 Summary trial in the magistrates' court

In the following principal cases, the juvenile will be tried by the magistrates' court rather than the juvenile or crown courts:

1. where he is charged jointly with an adult. He *must* be tried jointly with the adult unless the adult pleads guilty and the juvenile not guilty, in which case the juvenile is usually remitted for trial in the youth court: s34 CLA 1977. If both plead guilty, the magistrates will deal with them, jointly, but may well remit the juvenile to the youth court for sentence (see section 31.8); or
2. if he is charged with an adult and the charge is that he aided or abetted the adult, or vice versa, on the offence charged. The magistrates have in this case a discretion to remit him to the youth court for trial if they think it just and convenient; or
3. he is charged with an offence arising out of the same or connected circumstances which give rise to the offence charged against the adult. In this case also, the magistrates have a discretion to remit the juvenile for separate trial in the youth court.

It must be remembered that if the offence is triable either way, trial may be on indictment if the magistrates or the adult so choose (see section 31.3).

31.5 Critical date for determining the mode of trial

A juvenile may attain the age of 18 between the commission of the offence and the date he is tried or sentenced. This problem has given rise to considerable difficulty, but the main principles appear to be as follows:

1. If proceedings are commenced before he attains 18, the youth court may try the whole case if, and only if, he makes his first appearance in court before attaining that age: s29 CYPA 1963.
2. If proceedings are commenced after he has attained 18, he may be tried only in the adult magistrates' court or Crown Court.
3. If proceedings are commenced before he reaches 18, but he makes his first court appearance after attaining that age, he can only be tried in the adult magistrates' court.

4. For the purpose of sentence, it is the age at the date of conviction that determines the court's powers, but if the offender has attained 18 during the proceedings, the court may deal with him as if he were still 16. The court's powers of sentencing are fixed by reference to the offender's age at the date of conviction, even if he is tried on indictment: *R v Danga* (1991) The Times 1 November.
5. If the offence charged would be triable either way in the case of an adult, and the court has determined mode and place of trial before the accused attains 18, he cannot on reaching that age claim to elect jury trial: *Ex parte T* (1984) The Times 28 July.

31.6 Trial procedure on indictment or trial in the magistrates' court

If the juvenile is to be tried on indictment, committal proceedings are held in the adult magistrates' court if he is charged jointly with an adult, and in the youth court if he appears charged alone. Procedure at committal and at trial is very similar to that in the case of adults, but with the following principal differences:

1. At the committal proceedings the court is cleared of everyone except the parties and their legal representatives, court officials and members of the press. The juvenile's name is not published unless the Home Secretary so directs: s47 CYPA 1933.
2. Once committed for trial, the juvenile is remanded to the care of the local authority or, if he is very unruly, to a remand centre or prison: s23 CYPA 1969.
3. At the trial the juvenile is kept apart from any adults with whom he appears charged, and his name may not normally be published outside the courtroom.
4. If the trial takes place in the magistrates' court, similar restrictions apply upon publicity and segregation.

31.7 Trial procedure in the youth court

The marked difference between trial of adults and juveniles is the absence of formality in court in the latter case. The proceedings in the youth court are low key, everyone remains seated, and the accused is called by his first name. The principal steps are these:

1. The court explains the charge to the juvenile in clear language, and he is asked whether he 'admits' it. There is no formal arraignment or plea.
2. The trial proceeds as if it were that of an adult, with witnesses and evidence, prosecution and defence case, and closing speech. The juvenile may represent himself, or appear by solicitor or counsel.
3. The magistrates make their decision. Instead of a verdict of guilty, they make a 'finding of guilt'. They then proceed to impose the penalty after hearing evidence

of character and antecedents, and plea in mitigation. They do not however pass sentence, but instead 'make an order consequent upon a finding of guilt'.
4. Section 34A CYPA 1933 provides that the parent or guardian of all persons under 16 brought before a court for any reason must attend, unless it would be unreasonable in all the circumstances. Where the person is 16 or over, the court *may* require the parent or guardian's attendance.

31.8 Sentencing of juveniles tried in the magistrates' court

Where a juvenile is tried in the adult magistrates' court, that court has very limited sentencing powers. It may make only the following orders:

1. an absolute or conditional discharge; or
2. a fine, limited to a maximum of £250 in the case of an offender under 14 and £1,000 in the case of an offender under 18 years; or
3. an order that the juvenile's parent or guardian enter into a recognisance (see section 31.15); and in any case
4. disqualify from driving, order payment of costs or compensation, or restitution.

If the magistrates wish to impose any form of sentence or order greater than or of a type different from these four, their only option is to remit the juvenile to the youth court for it to exercise its wider powers of sentence: s7 CYPA 1969.

31.9 Sentencing following conviction on indictment

The Crown Court on sentence following trial and conviction of a juvenile on indictment has the following principal powers:

1. remittal to the Youth Court for sentence;
2. detention in accordance with the Children and Young Persons' Act 1933, s53(2);
3. detention in a young offender institution (for 15, 16, 17-year-olds) for a maximum of 12 months. When s17 CJPOA 1994 comes into force, this will increase to 24 months.

31.10 Sentencing in the youth court

Upon a finding of guilt in the youth court, or upon the offender being remitted to it by the magistrates or Crown Court, the youth court has a wide range of sentences and orders open to it. These are illustrated in the diagram at section 31.17, but the principal features of each must be known.

31.11 Attendance centre order

This is available for offenders aged between 10 and 20 inclusive. It can therefore be imposed upon adult offenders and not merely upon juveniles. This order is a 'community order' for which the offender's consent is not required (see Chapter 30). The criteria applying for the imposition of community sentences for adults apply equally to these orders.

The order is also available for a breach of probation order or any other community order where consent was necessary.

31.12 Detention in a young offender institution

The criteria for imposing a custodial sentence on a young offender are the same as for someone over 21. Subject to the maximum power of imprisonment provided for in the case of an offender aged 21 and over, the youth court may impose a maximum sentence of six months detention in a young offender institution upon a juvenile aged 15, 16 or 17.

1. The maximum term of detention in a young offender institution that may be imposed on a 15, 16 or 17 year old is 12 months (or the maximum for the offence, whichever is the lesser), whether for one offence or more than one.
2. The minimum term is now 21 days for an offender who is aged 18–20 inclusive and two months for under 18 year olds.
3. An offender of 18 or over may be committed to the Crown Court for sentence if, because of the seriousness of the offence, the magistrates feel it warrants greater punishment.
4. Where an offender aged 15, 16 or 17 years old has committed an offence for which the punishment (for those over 21) could be 14 years or more, or a 16 or 17 year old has committed an indecent assault upon a woman, the offender may be detained at Her Majesty's Pleasure: s53 CYPA as amended by CJA 1991. The CJA 1991 provides that this does not apply to non-domestic burglaries, where the maximum term of imprisonment is now ten years.

CJPOA 1994 section 1 (not in force at present) has introduced secure training orders for 12, 13 and 14-year-olds for periods of six months to two years. This amounts to a period of detention followed by a period of supervision.

31.13 Community sentences

Subject to various age limits, the availability of and criteria for the imposition of community sentences is the same as for adults over 21. However, a person of up to and including the age of 17 may receive a supervision order.

31.14 Supervision orders

The principal features of this order are:

1. The offender is placed under the supervision of a local authority (and the supervisor will usually be a social worker) or a probation officer.
2. The order may contain conditions, for example, as to residence, attendance on the supervisor, restriction on certain types of activity or (in appropriate cases) submission to psychiatric treatment.
3. The order lasts for three years unless it is specified to be for a shorter period, or is discharged earlier: s17.
4. It may be discharged on application to the court by the offender or his supervisor.
5. If the offender breaches the conditions of the order and is under 18 years old, the court may impose a fine or an attendance centre order. If the breach occurs after the offender reaches 18 years, the court may discharge the order and impose any sentence which it may have imposed at the time of sentencing *except* for detention in a young offender institution unless the original sentencing court stated that the supervision order was an alternative to custody.
6. The order can continue beyond the juvenile's 18th birthday.

31.15 Recognisance by parent or guardian

Section 58 CJA 1991 empowers the court to bind over the parents or guardians of a young offender under 16 to enter into a recognisance to a maximum of £1,000 to ensure that the offender stays out of trouble. The period of recognisance must not exceed three years or last beyond the minor's 18th birthday (whichever is sooner). The court does not have to do this if it is unreasonable in all the circumstances. If the parent/guardian refuses without reasonable grounds, the court may impose a fine of up to £1,000 on the parent/guardian.

31.16 Sentencing policy

Sentencing policy for young persons and children is the same as for adults over 21.

31.17 Table of orders and sentences with age limits

Order/sentence	Age limits
Imprisonment Suspended sentence	21 or over
Detention in a young offender institution	15, 16 and 17 – maximum 12 months, minimum 2 months 18, 19 and 21 – minimum 21 days
Probation order	16 or over
Community service order	16 or over
Curfew order (not in force at present)	16 or over
Combination order	16 or over
Attendance centre order	16–20 – maximum 36 hours, minimum 12 hours; under 14, no minimum
Supervision order	16 and 17, may continue past 18th birthday Breach – under 18 court may fine or make attendance centre order Breach – over 18 court may impose any punishment it may have made at sentencing except young offender institution unless original court said order was an alternative to custody
Discharge	All eligible
Fines	All eligible, subject to differing maximums

32

Orders Other Than Sentences

32.1 Introduction

32.2 Binding over

32.3 Compensation orders

32.4 Restitution orders

32.5 Costs

32.6 Forfeiture orders

32.7 Recommendation for deportation

32.8 Criminal bankruptcy orders

32.9 Criminal Injuries Compensation Board

32.1 Introduction

At the close of proceedings either summary or on indictment the court has power to make orders additional to or in lieu of penalties imposed on sentence, and to adjust the parties' position as to costs. This chapter outlines the process of binding over, compensation, costs, forfeiture, restitution, deportation and bankruptcy. In some cases the court may make one or more of these orders even though the charge has been dismissed or the defendant acquitted. None of the orders to be discussed are properly called 'sentences'.

32.2 Binding over

On conviction of an offence, any court may, instead of passing sentence at once, require that the defendant 'guarantee' his later appearance by entering into a recognisance (a set sum of money rather like a bond) to come back for judgment at some later date. The following are its principal features:

1. the court may require sureties for the recognisance ie persons other than the offender who put up their own money to guarantee his later appearance;
2. it is in effect a means of postponing sentence, though the power to defer sentence under s1 PCCA 1973 is more widely used (see Chapter 30, section 30.3);
3. it cannot be used when the sentence is fixed by law, that is, murder, treason or genocide.

The power to bind over the offender to keep the peace for some stated period can also be used as an alternative to sentence, and with effects similar to a conditional discharge. Both the magistrates' court and Crown Court may make the order on convicting the accused, and the power extends much further, to allow the order to be made even where the accused has been acquitted, and even against someone other than the accused, for example, a witness in the case, or the prosecutor himself. In general, the order will be made only in the following circumstances:

1. the intended subject of the order must be warned of the court's intention to make it;
2. where the court fears that, unless the order is made, there will be a breach of the peace in the near future either by or as a result of the conduct of the intended subject of it;
3. where the subject of the order has been allowed to object to it;
4. where the amount of recognisance to be taken from the subject has been determined (unless it is a trivial sum) after investigating the subject's ability to pay it should it be forfeited: *Ex parte Boulding* [1984] 2 WLR 321.

Where the person to be bound over has just been convicted of an offence by the court, the practice is to combine it with some other order in the nature of a sentence, rather than to make the binding over order alone; usually that sentence will be a fine. If the person to be bound over is not already on trial before the court, a formal complaint must be made to the court that further breaches of the peace are feared unless an order is made. Where the order is made by a High Court judge, he makes it in his capacity as a justice of the peace for the county where he is sitting. The making of the order is governed by s115 MCA 1980 and s1 Justices of the Peace Act 1968. In *Percy* v *DPP* (1994) The Times 13 December the Divisional Court held that violence or the threat of violence was required before justices could exercise their powers under MCA 1980 s115; a civil trespass would be insufficient.

Binding over orders are used most frequently to prevent disruptive political or industrial demonstrations. The principal leaders of the march or rally are bound over to keep the peace, without being convicted of any offence. If they refuse to be bound over, after the justices have been persuaded that an order is called for, they may be committed to prison for up to six months or until they accept the order, whichever is the sooner: s115(3). If they accept the order but are later found to have caused a breach of the peace, they (and any sureties bound with them) are liable to forfeiture of the amount of the recognisances. A person who is bound over by a magistrates' court has a right of appeal against the order to the Crown Court: s1 Magistrates' Courts (Appeal from Binding Over Orders) Act 1956. If the order was imposed following conviction of the subject of it, and he later breaches the peace by doing something the order was intended to prevent, the court which made the order can order forfeiture of the recognisance. Binding over orders normally last three or six months, and are intended as 'cooling-off' periods to stop disputes escalating into more serious disorder.

32.3 Compensation orders

By s35 PCCA 1973, any court which convicts an accused of an offence may order that he pay compensation to the victim of the offence to cover all or some part of any personal injury, loss or damage resulting from the offence. The order in effect relieves the victim from having to bring proceedings in the civil courts to recover the amount of the damage, or part of it at least. The following matters should be noted:

1. It can be made, to compensate for bereavement and funeral expenses, in favour of the dependants of a person who has died as a result of being the victim of the offence in respect of which compensation is ordered, unless the death arises out of a road accident: s104(1) CJA 1988.
2. A compensation order can be made in respect of personal injury, loss and damage (but not death) arising out of a road accident, but only if either the offender is uninsured and the victim would have no right to recover his loss from the Motor Insurers' Bureau or the offence arises out of an offence under the Theft Act 1968 (for example, in cases where the vehicle causing the loss has been stolen or taken without authority).
3. The order can be made without any application for it by the victim.
4. The order can be combined with any other sentence, and with a discharge or probation, but not with a criminal bankruptcy order (see section 32.8).
5. The order can be made in lieu of any other sentence or order: s67 CJA 1982.
6. The Crown Court has no limit upon the amount of compensation it can order, but the magistrates' and youth courts may not make orders exceeding £5,000 on any one occasion; the youth court should order the parent to pay under the order.
7. Where the means of the offender are such as to give the court the choice between imposing a fine and ordering compensation, it should give preference to compensation (s67 CJA 1982), though it may impose a fine as well.
8. Where more than one victim claims compensation against the same offender in the same proceedings, the court is under no duty to make orders in respect of each, either for equal amounts or equal shares, but has a discretion to select which of the victims it will aid by an order if the offender's means are inadequate fully to compensate all: *R v Amey* (1982) The Times 21 December.

9. The amount of the order should be 'such ... as the court considers appropriate, having regard to any evidence and to any representations made by or on behalf of the prosecutor': s67 CJA 1982. It is not therefore necessary to prove the amount of the injury, loss or damage by evidence of sufficient weight to establish the claim in civil proceedings; the court can act on the basis of the materials before it (but will be hesitant to make heavy orders if there is a risk that, because of the paucity of evidence, the victim might be over-compensated). Nonetheless, if the accused disputes the value of the property stolen or damaged, or of the injury done the court should make no order unless clear evidence of such value is produced: *Ex parte Richards* [1985] 2 All ER 1114.
10. The victim must give credit in later civil proceedings for the amount received under the order (or due under it, if he expects to receive them), and the court can order repayment of sums paid, or reduction of sums due under the order, if in the civil proceedings the amount of the injury, loss or damage is held to be less than the amount of the order.
11. If the order was made in respect of stolen or unrecovered property, the offender can apply to the court to reduce the amount payable, or discharge the order, or recover payments made, if the victim subsequently recovers the property: s37 PCCA 1973.
12. The refusal to make an order does not deprive the victim of his right to sue the offender in the civil courts for the amount of the damage.
13. The court can make an order in respect of an offence taken into consideration.
14. An offender may appeal to the Crown Court against the making and/or amount of the order, or the time given to comply with it by instalment payment.
15. It seems that a compensation order can be made in favour of the 'victim' of an offence even though that victim would have *no* right to sue in civil courts to recover the amount of his loss: *R v Chappell* (1984) The Times 26 May.

Section 24 CJA 1991 allows for deductions to be made from income support for fines and compensation orders made in the magistrates' court (not those made in the Crown Court).

32.4 Restitution orders

If the title to goods stolen is as a matter of law still vested in the original owner and has not passed to a third party, an offender convicted of an offence 'with reference to the theft' of the property, or who has such an offence taken into consideration in sentencing, can be ordered to hand them over to the owner, or the court can order the person in possession of them, even though not himself guilty of any offence, to restore them: s28 Theft Act 1968. 'Stolen goods' includes goods obtained by deception or blackmail as well as theft, and the offence of which the offender has been convicted may include not only theft but handling also. Apart from ordering restitution of the goods themselves, the court has the following alternative powers:

1. Order that the offender pay to the owner, out of money proved to belong to him (though not necessarily the proceeds of sale of the goods), a sum not exceeding the value of the goods, from money in his possession at the time of his arrest.
2. Order that goods representing the stolen goods directly or indirectly (for example, goods exchanged for the stolen goods, or bought with the proceeds of their sale) be transferred to the owner of the goods stolen.

If there is any doubt as to the true owner of goods stolen, or money found in the offender's posssession, or as to the link between the stolen goods and the goods to be ordered transferred as representing the stolen goods, the restitution order should not be made. If recovered stolen goods have been damaged by the offender, the court may make both a restitution and a compensation order (and in this case it is presumed that the damage has been caused by the offender, while the goods are out of the owner's possession).

32.5 Costs

The award of costs at the conclusion of a criminal trial is governed primarily by ss16–21 Prosecution of Offences Act 1985. In summary, the court's powers are as follows:

1. If the accused is found not guilty, an order for payment of his costs out of 'public funds', that is, money set aside by the state from central government revenue, may be made if and in so far as those costs are not to be paid by the legal aid fund, and the power exists whether the case was tried summarily or on indictment. Interest cannot be awarded on these costs: *Westminster City Council* v *Wingrove* (1990) The Times 13 August. No order may however be made in most cases for payment of defence costs by the prosecution.
2. If the accused is found guilty, the prosecution cannot recover its costs from central funds if it was conducted by the Crown Prosecution Service or by a local authority or government department, but the court may order the convicted accused to pay or contribute towards those costs in all cases.

32.6 Forfeiture orders

Where an offender is convicted of any offence, the convicting court may order the forfeiture of any property which has been lawfully seized from him or which was in his possession or control at the time he was apprehended for the offence or a

Summons issued in respect of that offence, if it is satisfied either that the property has been used for the purpose of facilitating the commission of an offence or was intended by the offender to be used for that purpose, or the offence consisted in the unlawful possession of the property: s43 PCCA 1973 as amended by s69 CJA 1988. The following should be noted:

1. 'Facilitating' includes steps taken after commission of the offence as well as before.
2. The court must have regard to the value of the property, and to the likely financial effect on the offender of making the order, before it commands forfeiture.
3. The property is taken into police possession and kept for six months. If no one comes forward to claim it during that time the accused is by reason of the order deprived of all rights in it, and the police sell it or otherwise dispose of it, the proceeds being dealt with as if they were a fine: s140 MCA 1980.
4. The forfeiture order should not be made in respect of property owned by someone other than the accused unless firm evidence is produced that such owner knew that it was to be used in criminal activities: *R v Maidstone Crown Court, ex parte Gill* [1987] 1 All ER 129 DC.

Special powers of forfeiture apply, under the appropriate legislation, to obscene publications, vehicles on which excise duty has not been paid, property used for poaching, property used for illegal gaming, beer and liquor held for sale without a licence, counterfeit coinage and notes, prohibited drugs, and illegally-based wireless equipment.

32.7 Recommendation for deportation

A person who has no right of abode in the United Kingdom may, on being convicted of an offence punishable with imprisonment in the case of a person aged 21 or over, be recommended for deportation provided he is at least 17 years old. The recommendation is made by the convicting or sentencing court, and the offender must be given seven days' written notice of the court's intention to make it. Although not in theory a 'sentence', the recommendation may be appealed against to the Court of Appeal. The decision to deport lies with the Home Secretary.

32.8 Criminal bankruptcy orders

The power to make a criminal bankruptcy order was abolished by s101 Criminal Justice Act 1988, following the enactment of powers to freeze, charge, confiscate and sell an offender's property.

32.9 Criminal Injuries Compensation Board

Injured victims of crime rarely have any prospect of recovering damages from their assailant; lack of money is usually the motive for the offence, especially of theft and robbery. Even if the court makes a compensation order in the victim's favour, it is most often a hollow remedy, and civil proceedings have the same effect. In 1964 the government set up a fund to compensate the victims of crime who suffer injury and loss through criminal activities. Applicants need not show that the offender has or even could be brought to trial, or that he has insufficient means to pay damages, and the principles of assessment are broadly similar to those of other personal injuries in civil cases. There is however no entitlement to compensation, and the Board reserves the right to refuse or reduce it having regard to the applicant's character and way of life. For example, a persistent offender, even if injured in the course of an offence in which he was taking no part but was an innocent bystander, may have his claim rejected or the amount of the compensation cut. The fund only covers injuries sustained through crimes of violence, and only if the offender has been tried or the offence was reported to the police without delay. The fund pays out some £35,000,000 per year, with a minimum of £400 in any case. Thus most injuries of a trivial nature fall outside the scheme and go uncompensated. The administration and powers of the Board have been put on a statutory footing in ss108–117 Criminal Justice Act 1988.

33

Appeals

33.1 Introduction
33.2 'Appeal' from committal proceedings
33.3 Appeal from acquittal on indictment
33.4 Appeal against conviction on indictment
33.5 Appeal against sentence on indictment
33.6 Procedure on appeal to the Court of Appeal
33.7 Grounds of appeal
33.8 Application for leave to appeal
33.9 Direction for loss of time
33.10 Hearing appeals against conviction
33.11 Powers of the Court of Appeal
33.12 The conviction is 'unsafe'
33.13 Powers of the Court of Appeal in determining appeals
33.14 Fresh evidence
33.15 Additional powers of the Court of Appeal
33.16 Appeals against sentence
33.17 Composition and judgment
33.18 Other hearings by the Court of Appeal from trial on indictment
33.19 Appeal to the House of Lords
33.20 Judicial review of the Crown Court
33.21 Appeal from summary trial in the magistrates' court
33.22 Appeal to the Crown Court
33.23 Appeal from the Crown Court to the Court of Appeal

33.24 Appeal from the magistrates' court to the Divisional Court

33.25 Appeal from the Divisional Court to the House of Lords

33.26 Appeal from the Crown Court to the Divisional Court

33.27 Judicial review of the magistrates' court and Crown Court

33.28 Appeals from youth courts

33.29 Appeal to the European Court of Justice

33.30 Criminal Cases Review Commission

33.31 Diagram of appeals in criminal cases

33.1 Introduction

From decisions of magistrates, judges and juries, appeals lie in most cases to a superior court. This chapter concerns appeals from convictions and acquittals, and against sentence. Appeal against particular decisions (for example bail, legal aid orders) is dealt with in appropriate places in the text of the chapter relating to each. The rights of appeal differ according to the nature of the proceedings, the court in which they are held, the outcome, and the identity of the appellant.

The Criminal Appeal Act (CAA) 1995 received Royal Assent on 19 July 1995. The Commencement (No 1 and Transitional Provisions) Order 1995 (SI 3061/1995) brought into effect ss1, 4, 6, and 7 (the powers and functions of the Court of Appeal); ss26 and 27 (powers of magistrates to rectify mistakes); s28 (criteria for payment of compensation for wrongful conviction; ss29–34 (supplementary provisions); and Schedules 2 and 3.

One of the main recommendations of the Royal Commission on Criminal Justice, the establishment of the Criminal Cases Review Commission (which is in Part II of the Act), is unlikely to be implemented before the middle of 1996 at the earliest. The implemented provisions of the 1995 Act are noted where relevant in this chapter.

33.2 'Appeal' from committal proceedings

Against the refusal of magistrates to commit an accused for trial on indictment there is no right of appeal. Instead, an aggrieved prosecutor must start fresh proceedings before (usually) a different bench of magistrates, or apply to a High Court judge for a voluntary bill of indictment (see Chapter 25, section 25.15). An accused who has been committed for trial may challenge the committal only on the basis of a very serious defect in the procedure followed or the test of '*prima facie* case' applied: in effect, that the proceedings were so fundamentally flawed that his committal for trial is null and void. Such cases will be rare. If made, the challenge is by way of judicial review (see section 33.37).

33.3 Appeal from acquittal on indictment

An accused who has been acquitted by jury cannot be retried unless, perhaps, his first trial was itself a nullity (for example, because the judge was an impostor). Provided he was at risk of conviction at trial, as will be the case in all but the most exceptional circumstances, the general rule that no man should be at risk of conviction for the same charge twice (the so-called 'double jeopardy' rule), means there can be no appeal from the decision of a jury to find the accused not guilty. To all intents and purposes, therefore, the prosecution has no right of appeal from an acquittal following jury trial. If a person was accused of something for which he had been acquitted, he would plead '*autrefois acquit*'.

33.4 Appeal against conviction on indictment

A person convicted on indictment may appeal against his conviction to the Court of Appeal on the following grounds:

1. with leave of the Court of Appeal, or
2. if the judge of the court of trial grants a certificate that the case is fit for appeal: s1 Criminal Appeal Act 1968 as amended by s1(2)(a) and (b) Criminal Appeal Act 1995.

Section 1 of the 1995 Act is an important amendment to the 1968 Act. Appeals on a question of law alone are brought into line with appeals against conviction on a mixed question of law and facts or law alone, and appeals against sentence. In all cases the leave of the Court of Appeal is required or the trial judge must certify that the case is fit for appeal.

33.5 Appeal against sentence on indictment

A person sentenced by the Crown Court following his conviction on indictment has no right of appeal against sentence. Instead, he has a right to apply for leave to appeal against it. This is so even if the sentence was unlawful and one which the court had no power to pass: s9 CAA 1968. There can be no appeal where the sentence is fixed by law (murder, genocide, treason), and even where appeal lies the leave of the Court of Appeal is required in all cases. It should be remembered that discharges and probation, although not 'sentences' (or indeed 'convictions') for most purposes, are treated as sentences for the purposes of appeal, so that an appeal lies against the 'conviction' and the discharge or probation order which resulted from it: s66 CJA 1982. A reference may be made by the Attorney-General to the Court of Appeal to consider a sentence if it is considered too lenient.

33.6 Procedure on appeal to the Court of Appeal

It is quite rare that a ground of appeal against conviction involves a question of pure law and therefore lies without leave. Almost all mistakes in the course of the trial involve elements of fact. For example, the credibility of witnesses is a question of fact, and may be relevant to a finding by the trial judge on the sufficiency or admissibility of evidence; although his ruling on admissibility is a matter of law, the ruling is based upon a finding of fact by him, and the ground of appeal is in such a case mixed fact and law. Instances of grounds which qualify as law alone include misdirection to the jury upon the elements of an offence, the nature of corroboration, the form of verdict and the effect of an accused's previous convictions. When law alone is the ground of appeal, the appellant must serve *notice of appeal* on the Crown Court centre at which he was convicted, within 28 days of conviction. The Crown Court then sends the notice, together with the relevant case papers, to the Registrar: *Practice Note* [1988] 1 All ER 244.

The same procedure applies where the appeal is brought without leave by reason of a trial judge's certificate that the case is fit for appeal. Where the ground of appeal is fact or mixed law and fact, the appellant serves an *application for leave to appeal* within 28 days of conviction, on the Crown Court centre which dealt with him. There is power to extend the time limit, but it is exercised only in rare cases; the appellant must show why he did not think the conviction worth taking to appeal within the month following it: *R v Towers* (1984) The Times 16 October.

33.7 Grounds of appeal

Rather like the parties to civil cases, the appellants from criminal cases must identify the issues and show where the trial judge went wrong or the trial contained irregularities. This is normally done in two stages. The first stage will involve counsel attaching his longhand notes of the trial to the application for leave to appeal. The second stage occurs after receipt of the relevant parts of trial transcript. Counsel will then perfect the grounds of appeal by the drafting and service of detailed grounds of appeal, a type of criminal 'pleading', which must be sufficiently detailed to allow the appeal court to understand at once the thrust of the appellant's complaint. For example if the ground is misdirection in the summing-up, the relevant parts of the summing-up should be recited. Any relevant case law should also be cited. See generally 77 Cr App R 223 for the requirements.

33.8 Application for leave to appeal

Where the ground of appeal is made under a trial judge's certificate, the appeal is listed for hearing by the full court and the case proceeds directly to a hearing. Where leave is required to appeal against conviction under the 1995 Act, and in all cases of appeal against sentence, the application and the proposed grounds of appeal are sent by the Registrar to a single judge of the Court of Appeal (Criminal Division) who considers the merits of the appeal and decides whether to grant leave for it and deal with ancillary issues such as legal aid and bail. The single judge also reviews the cases in private, and the appellant has no right to present argument to him except in the grounds of the appeal themselves.

If he grants leave, the case is listed for hearing. If he refuses leave, the appellant has 14 days to apply to renew his application before the full court (consisting usually of three judges) sitting in open court, but should consider, in deciding to do so, the powers of the court to order loss of time under s29 CAA 1968 (see section 33.9). In exceptional cases, where it seems to the Registrar that leave is likely to be given or that the case is of public importance, the case will be listed immediately for hearing before the full court of three judges instead of the single judge.

If leave is granted by the court, the appeal is heard at once; this is summary determination of the application. A similar procedure can be employed to dispose of an application for leave which appears to be frivolous or vexatious: the application can be listed for determination by the full court, which, if satisfied that it has no prospect of success, may dismiss it without hearing argument from either the accused or the Crown: s20 Criminal Appeal Act 1968 as substituted by s157 Criminal Justice Act 1988.

33.9 Direction for loss of time

Many appeals have not the slightest prospect of success. In refusing leave to appeal, the court has power to order that any time spent by the appellant in custody between the date of lodging his application and the date leave is refused shall not count towards his sentence (so that he serves that time again). This power to order 'loss of time' arises under s29 CAA 1968 and is intended to discourage meritless appeals which are persisted in after it becomes crystal clear that they musst fail. The principles governing its making appear in *Practice Note* [1980] 1 All ER 555 and *R v Wanklyn* (1984) The Times 14 November:

1. If leave is refused by the single judge, the appellant can expect a direction for loss of time 'if the grounds of appeal were not signed by counsel and not

supported by counsel's written advice. If counsel has not advised an appeal, or has advised specifically against it succeeding, the appellant makes the application at his own risk. In *R v Morley* (1995) The Times 25 January, the Court of Appeal held that the power under s29 CAA 1968 would be used very rarely where counsel had argued there were arguable grounds of appeal.
2. If, after having leave refused by the single judge, the appellant renews his application before the full court which itself refuses leave, a loss of time direction will usually be made even if the renewed application was supported by counsel. Counsel's advice does not protect the appellant in such a case, since the single judge's decision was sufficient warning to him that the appeal had no merit.
3. If either the single judge or the full court grants leave, no direction for loss of time will be made even if the appeal fails, for there was clearly sufficient merit in it at least to warrant full argument.

33.10 Hearing appeals against conviction

If the appellant is granted leave to appeal, or is able to bring the appeal without leave by reason of the trial judge granting a certificate, the appeal is heard by three judges of the Court of Appeal (Criminal Division) sitting in open court. Except where the appeal is against sentence, the prosecution are usually represented. The appeal takes the form of legal argument based upon the transcript of the trial and the judge's notes of it, and it is very rare for the court to allow oral evidence to be given before it. No ground of appeal may normally be raised that has not gained leave from the single judge. An appellant in custody has a right to be present at the hearing unless the ground of appeal is pure law (s22 CAA 1968), and even in this case may be given leave to attend by the single judge. The proceedings take place in public unless, perhaps, evidence of a sensitive nature is to be discussed.

33.11 Powers of the Court of Appeal

Section 2(1) CAA 1995 has amended s2 CAA 1968 and now provides that the Court of Appeal:

1. shall allow an appeal against conviction if they think that the conviction is unsafe; and
2. shall dismiss such an appeal in any other case: s2(1)(a) and (b) CAA 1995.

The single ground, that the conviction is 'unsafe', replaces the three former grounds under the CAA 1968.

33.12 The conviction is 'unsafe'

At first sight, s2(1)(a) CAA 1995 appears to reduce significantly the grounds upon which the Court of Appeal can allow an appeal against conviction. Two of the former grounds under the 1968 Act, 'error of law' (s2(b)) and 'material irregularity' (s2(c)), are repealed by the 1995 Act. The third ground, that 'the conviction is unsafe and unsatisfactory' (s2(a)), has been replaced by the single ground that the conviction is 'unsafe'. There is no definition of what amounts to 'unsafe' in the new legislation.

How is the Court of Appeal likely to exercise its new powers in deciding whether a conviction is 'unsafe'? The Court may resort to the rules of statutory interpretation. The Oxford English Dictionary defines 'unsafe' as something which is 'exposed to danger or risk'. This surely finds echo with a familiar phrase widely applied under the previous grounds, that an appeal might be successful where the Court considered there to be a 'lurking doubt' about the safety of the conviction.

Although repealed with the legislation, it would be surprising if the Court was not influenced by its previous decisions on what constituted an 'unsafe' conviction under the 1968 Act. There is a mass of case law on this point for guidance.

The Court will also be permitted to take a purposive approach of what Parliament intended the CAA 1995 to achieve. Perhaps of special assistance will be the travaux preparatoires to the new legislation. During the passage of the Bill through Parliament, the Home Secretary suggested that the new Act would '... restate the existing practice of the Court of Appeal'. In the Standing Committee the Minister of State suggested: 'The Lord Chief Justice and members of the senior judiciary have given the test a great deal of thought and they believe the new test re-states the existing practice of the Court of Appeal'. The practice of referring to parliamentary speeches to ascertain the general purpose of the legislation has recently been approved in *Three Rivers District Council and Others* v *Governor and Company of the Bank of England (No 2)* (1996) The Times 8 January.

It is to be hoped that in spite of the perplexing situation of Parliament literally reducing the grounds upon which the Court of Appeal can act to overturn miscarriages of justice, the Court will abandon its previous restrictive practices and approach its new task with renewed vigour and effectiveness, making full use of the wide discretion that Parliament has given it.

33.13 Powers of the Court of Appeal in determining appeals

In determining appeals, the Court of Appeal has the following principal powers:

1. To allow the appeal and quash the conviction: s2(1) CAA 1968.
2. To dismiss the appeal: s2(1) CAA 1968.
3. To substitute a verdict of guilty of some other offence of which the jury could

have found the accused guilty at trial (but not an offence for which he has been acquitted, even if the acquittal was wrong in law): s3 CAA 1968.
4. To order a retrial of the accused if his conviction was quashed because it was 'unsafe' and the interests of justice so require: s7 CAA 1968.
5. To order a retrial under the common law power of venire de novo if the trial was a complete nullity (for example the accused's plea of guilty was obtained by pressure) or had not been validly commenced (for example the committal proceedings were null and void), or had come to an end without a valid verdict. Such cases will be rare: *R v Rose* [1982] 3 WLR 192.
6. Make various orders where the appellant was found unfit to plead, or not guilty by reason of insanity in the Crown Court: ss12 to 15 CAA 1968.

33.14 Fresh evidence

Appeals against conviction invariably take the form of arguments presented by counsel for the appellant and prosecution. Appellants may sometimes wish that the Court of Appeal could listen to new witnesses, or look at fresh evidence, in the hope that the appeal court will view it favourably. The following must be considered:

1. the general discretion of the Court of Appeal to receive fresh evidence;
2. the grounds upon which the Court of Appeal exercises its discretion to admit fresh evidence which is 'likely to be credible'.

The Court of Appeal has discretion to hear and look at evidence (that is the testimony of witnesses and real evidence) in all cases without restriction: s23(1) CAA 1968. There is no requirement that it should not have been either available or used at trial, so that there is power to rehear trial evidence as well as fresh evidence not previously used. Wide though this discretion is, the occasions of its exercise are few. The credibility of witnesses is a matter for the trial jury, so that it will be very rare indeed that witnesses called at trial will be reheard unless they are to give new evidence. The decision not to call a witness or piece of evidence at trial is a matter for counsel, and a mistake by him will hardly ever be alleviated by the appeal court hearing the evidence itself. Nonetheless, instances of the reception of evidence under this general power do arise, the most recent being *R v Lee* [1984] 1 All ER 1080 and *R v Foster* [1984] 3 WLR 401.

Section 4 CAA 1995 has replaced s23(2) CAA 1968 with the following:

'The Court of Appeal shall, in considering whether to receive any evidence, have regard in particular to –
(a) whether the evidence appears to the Court to be capable of belief;
(b) whether it appears to the Court that the evidence may afford any ground for allowing the appeal;
(c) whether the evidence would have been admissible in the proceedings from which the appeal lies on an issue which is the subject of the appeal; and

(d) whether there is a reasonable explanation for the failure to adduce the evidence in those proceedings.'

Section 4 outlines the considerations to be taken into account by the Court in deciding whether to exercise its power under s23(1) CAA 1968. The most significant effect of s4 CAA 1995 appears to be that the Court of Appeal is no longer under a duty to hear fresh evidence in certain cases. Also, the basis for the admission of that evidence is that it should be 'capable of belief'. It remains to be seen whether this new test allows the Court to exercise a greater discretion in admitting fresh evidence under s2(1) or whether the discretion is curtailed.

Where the Court of Appeal receives the evidence tendered, it applies the test: 'In the light of the evidence, does the conviction seem "unsafe"? Taking all the evidence into consideration: is the Court persuaded that there is a lurking doubt about the safety of the conviction?' If the answer is in the affirmative, it must quash the conviction, but may order the accused to be retried on indictment: s7 CAA 1968. If ordered, the new trial takes place without committal proceedings, and a voluntary bill of indictment is preferred. It is not incumbent on the court to order retrial. Since there is no strict time limit during which the appeal on the ground of fresh evidence needs to be brought, the court may feel that the case is so 'stale' that memories of witnesses have failed and that it would be unjust, in view of the lapse of time, to put the accused in danger of conviction once more.

The issue of the reception of fresh evidence (among other issues) was considered by the Court of Appeal in the cases of the 'Tottenham Three' (where three men had been convicted of the killing of a police officer during a public disturbance). Regarding the obtaining of fresh evidence it was held that counsel's opinion should be obtained as to the propriety of granting legal aid to obtain new expert's reports and that while 'expert shopping' was to be discouraged, the interests of justice should prevail: *R v Silcott, R v Braithwaite, R v Raghip* (1991) The Times 9 December.

33.15 Additional powers of the Court of Appeal

In addition to the powers mentioned in sections 33.11 and 33.13, the Court of Appeal has the following principal powers:

1. To substitute a verdict of guilty of some other offence of which the jury could have found the accused guilty at trial (but not of an offence of which he has been acquitted, even if the acquittal was wrong in law): s3 CAA 1968.
2. To order a retrial of the accused if his conviction is quashed because of some error of law or material irregularity, or because it was unsafe or unsatisfactory: s7 CAA 1968 as amended by s43 CJA 1988.
3. To order a retrial under the common law power of *venire de novo* if the trial was a complete nullity (for example, the accused's plea of guilty was obtained by pressure) or had not been validly commenced (for example, the committal

proceedings were null and void), or had come to an end without a valid verdict. Such cases will be rare: *Rose* [1982] 3 WLR 192.
4. To direct the Criminal Cases Review Commission to carry out investigations and report to the court. See section 33.30.

33.16 Appeals against sentence

If a conviction is quashed on appeal, any sentence or order made on the conviction is automatically quashed as well. If the appeal against conviction is not made, or is dismissed, the Court of Appeal will only interfere with a sentence on one of the following grounds:

1. that it was unlawful, that is, that the court had no power to pass it, or that some necessary procedure was not carried out; or
2. that it was wrong in principle. This includes sentences which, although not in themselves unlawful, have been wrongly combined (for example, a combination of immediate imprisonment and community service) and the use of a tariff sentence where the case clearly called for an individualised sentence, and other mistakes such as imposing consecutive sentences when concurrent ones should have been given. It should however be remembered that principles of sentencing can be departed from in appropriate cases, so that this is not a conclusively good ground of appeal; or
3. that it was 'manifestly excessive'. The trial judge is given a rather wide discretion in his choice of type and severity of sentence, so that it is only sentences clearly above the tariff for the seriousness of the particular offence, or out of proportion to those given to co-accused for the same offence, which are commonly disturbed.

If the appeal court finds one of the conditions satisfied, it must quash the sentence and replace it with a sentence of its own. It can award any sentence or order (eg probation, discharge) which would have been open to the trial court, but must not deal with the offender *more* severely than he was dealt with by the trial court: s11 CAA 1968. This does not mean that there is no power to increase sentence, but that that power can only be used to 'adjust' sentences on multiple charges so that, taken as a whole, the aggregate term or amount the accused will serve in prison, or on probation, or subject to some other penalty or order, is not increased. Finally, it should be mentioned that the prosecution has no right of appeal against sentence or to apply for leave to appeal; however, the Attorney-General has (see section 33.18).

33.17 Composition and judgment

For the hearing of appeals against conviction and/or sentence, the Court of Appeal (Criminal Division) must consist of an uneven number of judges, with a minimum of three. It has been proposed that a two-judge court be able to hear appeals against sentence, but there is presently no power for this to be done. The same court hears both types of appeal if they were lodged together or consolidated. Lords Justices of Appeal and any judge of the High Court may sit on the court, but the trial judge may not: s3 CAA 1968. The Lord Chief Justice sits in many appeals, and is head of the Court of Appeal. In giving judgment, it is the practice that only one judgment (usually that of the presiding judge) is delivered, unless that judge considers that individual judgments on questions of law are called for. The court is not as strictly bound by precedent as its civil counterpart, and has power to depart from its own previous decisions when not to do so would cause injustice to the appellant: *R v Gould* [1968] 2 QB 65, and *R v Spencer* [1985] 2 WLR 197.

33.18 Other hearings by the Court of Appeal from trial on indictment

Apart from appeals by the convicted defendant, there are three principal ways in which the result of a jury trial can come for review by the Court of Appeal:

1. Where the case is referred to the court by the Home Secretary. This is done rarely, and usually where the Home Secretary responds to public disquiet about the correctness of a conviction, but the Court of Appeal has refused leave to appeal or has dismissed an appeal. The reference is made under s17 CAA 1968, and the 'whole case' is referred to the court, to be heard as if it were a normal appeal against conviction. If the Home Secretary makes a reference, the defendant can add his own grounds of appeal to the points on which the case has been referred, and argue those without leave of the court: *R v Chard* [1983] 3 All ER 637. Even where (as in the case of Judith Ward and the 'Tottenham Three') the Crown ceases to dispute an appeal on the basis of the referral, the Court of Appeal must hear the entire appeal. The practice in these cases now appears to be to bail the appellants until the judgment.

    Section 3 Criminal Appeal Act 1995, when it comes into force, will abolish the s17 CAA 1968 procedure for references to the Court of Appeal by the Home Secretary. The Criminal Cases Review Commission has been established to take over this role. See section 33.30.

2. Where the Attorney-General refers a case to the Court of Appeal for its decision on a point of law alone, following an *acquittal* on indictment, under s36 CJA 1972. The power is used to prevent wrong decisions on law becoming generally accepted, and to obtain a binding ruling on them. Only points of law which have actually arisen may be referred, and not hypothetical points of law, however interesting and important they may be. The case is referred to by a number and not by the name of the defendant. The appeal court's decision has no effect upon the acquittal but, somewhat curiously, the defendant has the right to appear in person or by counsel to argue at the hearing of the reference. Only a half dozen

or so cases are referred each year under this power. The prosecution has no right to insist upon a reference.
3. Where the Attorney-General refers a case to the Court of Appeal, with that court's leave, for the review of and possible increase in a sentence imposed by the Crown Court and which he considers 'unduly lenient': s36 and Sch 3 Criminal Justice Act 1988.

33.19 Appeal to the House of Lords

From a decision of the Court of Appeal on the hearing of an appeal against conviction and/or sentence an appeal lies to the House of Lords by either prosecution *or* defence provided either the Court of Appeal or the Appeals Committee of the House gives leave *and* the Court of Appeal has granted a certificate that a point of law of general public importance is involved. Against the refusal of the Court of Appeal to grant such a certificate there is no appeal at all, so that in theory the Court of Appeal can stifle appeals to the Lords and in that way circumvent binding House of Lords decisions. On hearing the appeal, the House applies the same tests, and has the same powers to quash the conviction, apply the proviso, and substitute alternative convictions, as the Court of Appeal: s33 CAA 1968. It should be noted that no appeal lies to the Lords in the following principal cases:

1. against the refusal by the Court of Appeal of leave to appeal to that court against conviction or sentence;
2. against the refusal by the Court of Appeal or High Court to grant leave for judicial review to a person aggrieved by the outcome of proceedings (see section 33.22): *Re Poh* [1983] 1 WLR 2.

Application for leave to appeal to the Lords (if refused by the Court of Appeal) must be lodged within 14 days from the Court of Appeal's judgment in the case.

Pursuant to a grant of leave to appeal to the House, documents relating to the case, such as transcripts of the trial evidence and of the summing up, and lists of authorities to be cited at the hearing of the appeal, must be lodged with the House: *Procedure Directions* [1988] 2 All ER 819 and 831.

33.20 Judicial review of the Crown Court

In rare cases, a defendant may apply for judicial review of the Crown Court's proceedings instead of applying for leave to appeal. Such review is not, however, allowed upon any matter relating to trial or indictment, though the Divisional Court has held in *R v Central Criminal Court, ex parte Randle and Pottle* (1991) 92 Cr App R 323 that the Crown Court judge's exercise of his discretion whether to halt a prosecution as oppressive is not 'a matter relating to trial or indictment', and can be the subject of judicial review. The availability of judicial review from the Crown Court's decisions on appeal from or committal to it by the magistrates' court is considered at section 33.27.

33.21 Appeal from summary trial in the magistrates' court

The structure of appeals from summary proceedings is far more complicated than that of appeal from trial on indictment. There are appeals to the Crown Court, to the Court of Appeal, to the Divisional Court of Queen's Bench, to the High Court for judicial review, and to the House of Lords. They will be examined in turn, but it may be convenient to refer at each stage to the diagram at section 33.31.

33.22 Appeal to the Crown Court

From summary conviction the defendant has a right of appeal to the Crown Court on any ground of fact or mixed law and fact: s108 MCA 1980. It is not necessary that the offence charged should have been triable on indictment, but the rights of appeal are restricted thus:

1. if the accused pleaded not guilty, appeal may be against both conviction *and* sentence;
2. if he pleaded guilty, appeal lies *only* against sentence unless the plea was equivocal and the magistrates should have taken steps to clarify it before treating it as a guilty plea (see Chapter 24, section 24.10). See also *Ex parte Sharma* [1988] Crim LR 741 QBD.

It should be remembered that a discharge or probation rank as 'convictions' and 'sentences' so that both may be appealed against in this case. The appellant must give notice of appeal within 21 days of the magistrates' decision appealed against, to the clerk to the justices and to the prosecution. The notice of appeal should be in prescribed form, but the grounds contained in it are usually less detailed than those in a notice of appeal to the Court of Appeal. The Crown Court may extend the time for service of the notice if good reason is shown.

The appeal is in the form of a complete rehearing before the Crown Court, with oral evidence from witnesses, and the appellant may in most cases call evidence additional to that used before the magistrates. If against sentence alone, no evidence of liability is of course adduced. The hearing is before a circuit judge or recorder sitting with at least two lay magistrates other than those who sat to hear the case at first instance; there is no jury. Decision is by a simple majority, and the judge has no casting vote; the justices must accept his opinion on the law. There is no need for the appellant to be personally present at the hearing of his appeal though his presence of course increases his chances of success should there be a conflict of evidence which he can resolve by his own testimony: *R v Croydon Crown Court, ex parte Clair* [1986] 2 All ER 716 DC.

The Crown Court may confirm, reverse or vary any finding or sentence imposed by the justices, but only has their powers of sentencing, even if the offence is triable either way (cf committal for sentence). It can *increase* sentence up to the maximum the magistrates could have given, and defendants think carefully before exercising this right of appeal. It has power also to remit the case to the magistrates with direction on how they should proceed, and will do this often where it becomes clear that there should be a retrial as to liability; for instance, where the plea of guilty at first instance was equivocal, or the court thinks that there should for some other reason be a rehearing on evidence. The court may also make ancillary orders for costs and other matters as the magistrates could have done, or vary existing orders.

It should be remembered that the judge on hearing the appeal may only convict the appellant of an offence which it was open to the magistrates to find him guilty of upon the basis of the Summons as served upon him before summary trial. Thus, if the Summons charged a full offence, and the magistrates convict of it, the Crown Court on appeal may not substitute a conviction for an attempt if the Summons did not charge it: *Ex parte Hill* (1984) The Times 2 November.

33.23 Appeal from the Crown Court to the Court of Appeal

There is only one circumstance in which a case tried summarily can come before the Court of Appeal, and concerns appeal against sentence; where the offender was committed to the Crown Court, under s38 MCA 1980 after summary conviction, and the ground of appeal is one of the following:

1. that the sentence was for six months or more imprisonment or youth custody; or
2. the sentence was one which the magistrates could not have passed. This is not now material, since there are very few sentences which are available only to the Crown Court on committal which were not available to the magistrates other than (1) except a fine in excess of £5,000;
3. the sentence was or included a recommendation for deportation or disqualification from driving, or concerned the activation of a suspended sentence, or sentencing for a breach of probation or conditional discharge imposed by the Crown Court on a previous occasion: s10 CAA 1968.

Where any of the above applies, the procedure on appeal is the same as that against sentence following conviction on indictment, and the offender requires the leave of the Court of Appeal in all cases. Further appeal lies to the House of Lords against sentence if the Court of Appeal certifies a point of law of general public importance and either the Court of Appeal or the House gives leave.

33.24 Appeal from the magistrates' court to the Divisional Court

If the ground of complaint against a magistrates' court decision in a summary trial is that the magistrates acted outside their jurisdiction or made a wrong decision in law alone (but not in fact or mixed law and fact) appeal lies to the Divisional Court of Queen's Bench of the High Court by way of 'case stated' under s111 MCA 1980. The following points should be noted:

1. The appeal is open to both prosecution and defence.
2. It applies to mistakes in sentencing as well as to those in convicting or acquitting, but does not lie to quash a committal for sentence to the Crown Court.
3. The issue must relate to pure law or jurisdiction – questions of fact (for example, the credibility of witnesses) are excluded unless the court's findings are so unreasonable as to amount to errors of law.
4. The appeal can be brought by any party and any person 'aggrieved' by the decision. This includes anyone whose financial interests are affected by the decision, for example, the owner of stolen goods in whose favour the court has refused to make a restitution order.
5. The magistrates can, under s114 MCA 1980, require the appellant to give some financial security for the court's costs should the appeal fail, by imposing a condition that no case will be stated by them unless and until the appellant enters into a recognisance, but the appellant's means and ability to meet the recognisance should first be carefully assessed: *R v Newcastle Justices, ex parte Skinner* [1987] 1 All ER 349.

Procedure entails the aggrieved person applying to the magistrates, within 21 days of the decision complained of, to state a case for the opinion of the Divisional Court. The case is in prescribed form and details the findings of fact made by the magistrates, the principles of law they applied, any authority they were referred to, and the question upon whch the court's opinion is sought. If the magistrates refuse to state a case (and they may lawfully to so only where they regard the application as frivolous), the aggrieved person may apply to the High Court for judicial review and an order of mandamus to compel the case to be stated. If the appellant chooses to appeal to the Divisional Court, he cannot at the same time also appeal to the Crown Court: s111(4) MCA 1980. The case stated is drafted and submitted to the appellant and respondent for comments and amendments are made as necessary; it is finally filed in its agreed form at the Crown Office.

The hearing is before the Divisional Court of Queen's Bench, sitting as a court of two or three judges. Although it is the magistrates' decision that is being challenged, argument takes place in practice between the appellant and respondent, though the justices are sometimes represented and allowed to present argument as an aid to the court. The court can confirm, reverse or vary the magistrates' decision, including substituting its own sentence, but will usually remit to the magistrates with its opinion on what principles the magistrates should apply. Thus, if the prosecution has appeal by case stated on the ground that the justices took a wrong view of the law, the Divisional Court will, if it agrees, remit the case to the justices with a direction (which they must obey) to convict the accused and sentence him. The court may also make ancillary orders such as those for costs, compensation or restitution.

33.25 Appeal from the Divisional Court to the House of Lords

From the Divisional Court's opinion on a case stated appeal lies direct to the House of Lords (*not* the Court of Appeal), subject to the same conditions as to a certificate of a point of law of general public importance, and the leave of either the court or the House, as apply to appeals from the Court of Appeal (see section 33.19).

33.26 Appeal from the Crown Court to the Divisional Court

Appeal lies from the decision of the Crown Court to the Divisional Court by way of case stated in the following cases:

1. on a ground of pure law or jurisdiction following an appeal to the Crown Court from conviction by the magistrates' court; or
2. on a ground of pure law or jurisdiction following committal for sentence to the Crown Court.

Either party may appeal in this way, but other persons cannot, even if their interests are affected by the decision. In all other material respects, the procedure is identical to case stated appeals from the magistrates' court. Since an accused cannot have appeal by way of case stated from the magistrates' court as well as appeal to the Crown Court, he is better advised to appeal first to the Crown Court, and then later to the Divisional Court if there is an error of law by the magistrates' court which is repeated by the Crown Court. From the Divisional Court appeal lies to the House of Lords in the circumstances described above.

33.27 Judicial review of the magistrates' court and Crown Court

The High Court exercises a supervisory jurisdiction over inferior tribunals, of which both the magistrates' court and the Crown Court are examples. However the jurisdiction of the High Court only extends to the Crown Court where it is dealing with matters other than indictments. Control is over the workings of those tribunals, to prevent or remedy breaches of natural justice or acts in excess of jurisdiction. The three orders provided for are:

1. Certiorari – the High Court quashes the proceedings in inferior tribunals and, if necessary, orders a complete rehearing of the case.
2. Mandamus – the tribunal is ordered to do a particular act (for example, try an information, or state a case).
3. Prohibition – the tribunal is ordered to refrain from doing something, before its decision has become final ie before judgment.

In some cases a party to proceedings may have concurrent remedies by judicial review and case stated; the precise limits of each procedure have never been clearly defined. However, the following examples of its use will illustrate the type of complaint it issues to uphold:

1. Where the police take statements from witnesses but do not inform the defendant of the existence of the witnesses. This is a denial of natural justice, and the magistrates' decision is liable to be quashed: *R v Leyland JJ, ex parte Hawthorn* [1978] Crim LR 627.
2. Where the magistrates dismiss an information without giving the prosecutor opportunity to proceed with it on the day fixed for hearing: *R v Dorking JJ, ex parte Harrington* [1984] 3 WLR 142.
3. Where the magistrates purport to dismiss an information, without hearing evidence, because they think the prosecution unfair or oppressive: *R v Birmingham JJ, ex parte Lamb* [1983] 3 All ER 29.
4. Where the Defendant is not given a reasonable opportunity to prepare his case: *R v Thames Magistrates' Court, ex parte Polemis* [1974] 2 All ER 1219.
5. Where proceedings are begun outside any relevant time limit for their issue (see Chapter 23, section 23.12): *Ex parte Tesco Stores* [1981] 2 WLR 419.
6. Where the magistrates have wrongly committed a convicted accused for sentence: *Ex parte Osman* [1971] 1 WLR 1109.
7. Where a private prosecutor who is the principal prosecution witness fails to disclose to the defence that he has been convicted in the recent past of an offence which seriously undermines his credibility: *R v Knightsbridge Crown Court, ex parte Goonatilleke* [1985] 2 All ER 498.

Where the court quashes a sentence imposed by the magistrates' court on the ground that it is wrong in law and in excess of jurisdiction, it may substitute its own sentence rather than having to remit the case: s43 SCA 1981. In other cases where the conviction is also quashed, there is usually power to order the case heard or reheard if the accused was never in danger of being convicted at the first hearing for example, because the magistrates refused to try the case, or because the proceedings were so fundamentally flawed as to be null and void.

Procedure for application for judicial review is substantially the same in criminal as in civil cases, and reference should be made to Chapter 19, section 19.6. If leave is granted, the hearing takes place in the Divisional Court of Queen's Bench before two or three *puisne* judges or, during legal vacations, before a single judge in chambers.

33.28 Appeals from youth courts

In all material respects, the youth court is a part of the magistrates' court, and juveniles have the same rights of appeal to the Crown Court, High Court, Court of Appeal and House of Lords as are held by adults tried in the adult magistrates' court. Additionally, there are rights of appeal to the Crown Court against care and supervision orders: ss3 and 16 CYPA 1969.

33.29 Appeal to the European Court of Justice

It is possible, though rare, that a criminal case could be considered by the Court of Justice of the European Communities established under the Treaty of Rome. Appeal lies only on questions of the interpretation and application of Community legislation. Although any court has a discretion to refer a case to the European Court, it is only where all local remedies have been exhausted (eg all rights of appeal in England have been used) that the case *must* be referred. To all intents and purposes, therefore, it will only be from the House of Lords that references will commonly be made, and the diagram of appeals accordingly omits the possibility of reference at an earlier stage. Those wishing to know the guidelines applicable to references from lower courts should consult *Bulmer* v *Bollinger* [1974] 1 WLR 1107 and RSC O.114 and *An Bord Bainne* v *Milk Marketing Board* (1984) The Times 26 May.

33.30 The Criminal Cases Review Commission

The establishment of the Criminal Cases Review Commission was one of the main recommendations of the Royal Commission on Criminal Justice. An important reason for setting up the Review Commission has been the failure of successive Home Secretaries to make full use of their powers under s17 Criminal Appeal Act 1968 to refer cases back to the Court of Appeal. On a practical level there is likely to be a greater commitment to the resourcing of criminal appeals. At present 17 staff are employed by the Home Office compared with up to 60 people staffing the Review Commission, although it is envisaged that in the early years of its existence the Commission will be dealing with approximately 1,460 cases, twice the number currently handled by the Home Office. The important provisions relating to the Review Commission are:

1. Section 5(1) CAA 1995 inserts in the CAA 1968 a new s23A which provides the Court of Appeal with power to direct the Commission to carry out investigations and report to the court.
2. Section 8 and Schedule 1 include provisions relating to the constitution of the Commission.
3. Section 9 provides the Commission with power to refer to the Court of Appeal

convictions and/or sentences in Crown Court trials, verdicts of not guilty by reason of insanity and findings regarding people under a disability.
4. Section 11 provides the Commission with the power at any time to refer to the Crown Court a conviction in the magistrates' court and/or a sentence imposed by the magistrates' court, and such reference will be treated as if it were an appeal pursuant to s108(1) Magistrates' Courts Act 1980. The Crown Court has no power to increase the sentence.
5. Section 15 sets out the procedure for the carrying out of investigations by the Commission.
6. Section 16 allows assistance to be given by the Commission to the Home Secretary in connection with the exercise of the prerogative of mercy.
7. Section 17 empowers the Commission to require a person serving a public body to produce documents and other material to the Commission.

33.31 Diagram of appeals in criminal cases

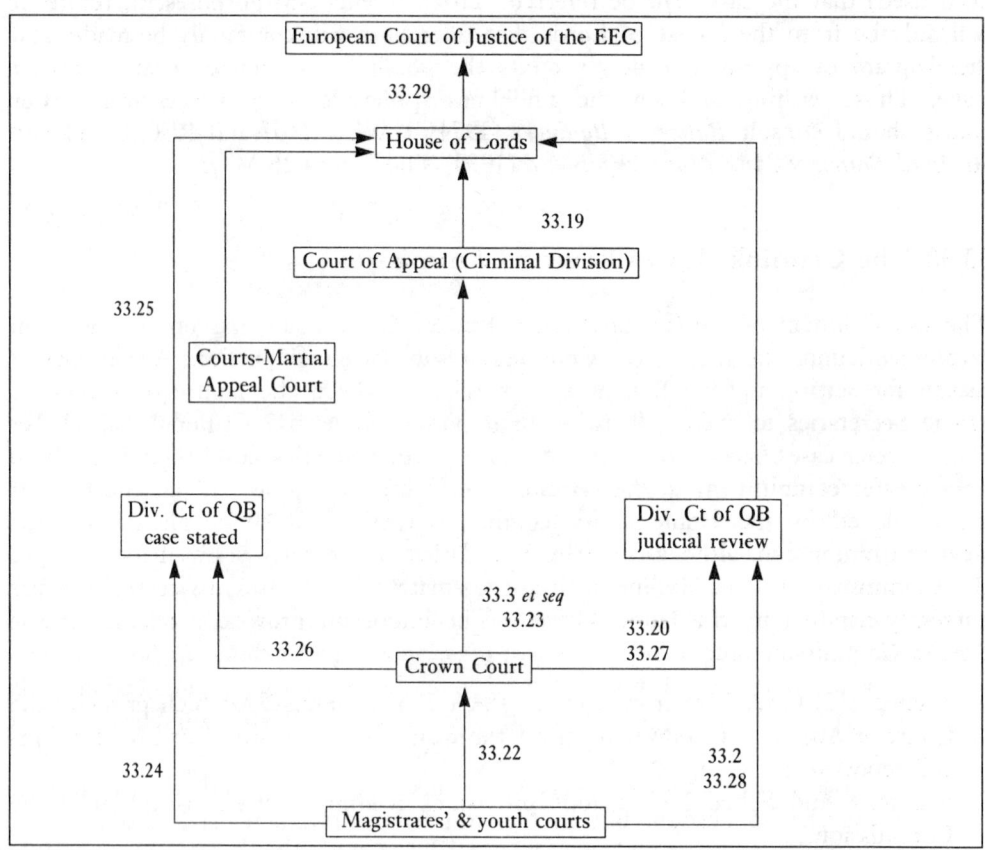

```
                    European Court of Justice of the EEC
                                    ▲
                                  33.29
                            House of Lords
                                    ▲
                                  33.19
                    Court of Appeal (Criminal Division)
          33.25              ▲
                    Courts-Martial
                    Appeal Court

    Div. Ct of QB                           Div. Ct of QB
    case stated                             judicial review
         ▲                                       ▲
                          33.3 et seq
                          33.23         33.20
              33.26                     33.27
                          Crown Court
                               ▲
                             33.22              33.2
         33.24                                  33.28
                    Magistrates' & youth courts
```

Note: matters on indictment in the Crown Court may only go to the Court of Appeal.

34

Miscellaneous Proceedings

34.1 Introduction

34.2 Legal aid

34.3 Legal aid as of right

34.4 Legal aid in the court's discretion

34.5 Application for legal aid

34.6 Amount of aid and contributions

34.7 Choice of representative

34.8 Remands

34.9 The duty of counsel

34.1 Introduction

This chapter contains proceedings and procedures which do not fit easily into any category already discussed. They are: the process of legal aid, the rules for remand and bail pending trial and appeal, and the duty of counsel.

34.2 Legal aid

The system of assistance, through funds provided by the state, to a person accused of a criminal offence, differs in some material respects from the system which applies in civil law. The accused has the benefit of the 'Green Form' scheme for preliminary advice, but if he wishes assistance in the presentation of his defence or mitigation in court, he must apply directly to the court having jurisdiction in his case and not, as in civil proceedings, to the Legal Aid Board: s20 Legal Aid Act 1988.

There is, in civil and criminal cases alike, a 'means and merits' test for determining the application, but in the criminal courts there is a separate set of regulations which determine whether he is eligible for legal aid: s21(5) Legal Aid Act

1988. Instead, the court is given a wide discretion in ruling upon the sufficiency of his means to pay for his defence, and takes into account the seriousness and complexity of the charge in its determination of the costs he is likely to incur.

34.3 Legal aid as of right

In very few instances does an accused have an indefeasible right to state aid. In the great majority of cases the grant of criminal legal aid is a matter for the discretion of the court before which he is brought. In three principal circumstances, however, a magistrates' court has a duty, under s21(3) Legal Aid Act 1988, to make an order granting aid in the first instance, if it appears that the accused's means (his disposable income and disposable capital) are such that he requires assistance to meet his costs of the proceedings:

1. where the accused is committed for trial on a charge of murder; or
2. where a person charged with an offence before a magistrates' court is brought before the court in pursuance of a remand in custody on an occasion when he may again be remanded in custody and is not (but wishes to be) legally represented before the court, not having been legally represented before the court when he was so remanded; or
3. where a person who is to be sentenced or dealt with for an offence by a magistrates' court or the Crown Court is to be kept in custody to enable inquiries or a report to be made to assist the court in sentencing or dealing with him for the offence.

34.4 Legal aid in the court's discretion

Where the accused cannot bring himself within any of the principal exceptions described at section 34.3, he has no entitlement to legal aid, and must instead hope that the magistrates will exercise in his favour the general discretion given them by s21(2) of the 1988 Act to make a legal aid order in respect of the whole or of some part or parts of the proceedings, if it appears to them 'in the interests of justice' so to do. This discretion is, as will be seen below, rather difficult to define, and its exercise somewhat difficult to challenge.

Whether it is 'in the interests of justice' that legal aid be granted to the accused for the purpose of his trial is in all cases a question of fact or degree. The court is directed to consider, in the exercise of its discretion, the factors listed in s22 of the 1988 Act (which may be varied or added to by order of the Lord Chancellor), and should grant aid if any of the following conditions is met:

1. the offence is such that if proved it is likely that the court would impose a sentence which would deprive the accused of his liberty or lead to the loss of his livelihood or serious damage to his reputation; or

2. the determination of the case may involve consideration of a substantial question of law; or
3. the accused may be unable to understand the proceedings or to state his case because of his inadequate knowledge of English, mental illness or other mental or physical disability; or
4. the nature of the defence is such as to involve the tracing and interviewing of witnesses or expert cross-examination of a witness for the prosecution; or
5. it is in the interests of someone other than the accused that the accused be represented.

There is no set class of cases in which any presumption arises that aid will be granted, though the more serious is the charge the greater the prospects of a successful application. It is recognised that courts in different areas exercise their discretion in different ways, and previous experience of the bench before whom an application is made is particularly valuable. Statistics show that about 90 per cent of applications succeed when made before magistrates where the offence is triable either way, and some 60 per cent where the offence is triable only summarily, provided that in either instance the accused's means justify his need for assistance.

34.5 Application for legal aid

In the magistrates' court, application for legal aid can be made wholly or partly in writing and by oral argument. It is governed by the Legal Aid in Criminal and Care Proceedings (General) Regulations 1989. If it is anticipated that the accused will be remanded, perhaps on several occasions, before trial, it is usual to make a formal application in writing to the magistrates' clerk, which gives:

1 the name and address of the applicant;
2. the date on which the applicant is next due to appear before the court;
3. a short description of the charge or charges laid;
4. a statement of which (if any) of the s22 considerations applies;
5. details of any sentence or order of a criminal court to which the applicant is subject, and which may render the penalty he receives on conviction for the current offence more severe than might otherwise be imposed, or expose him to additional punishment. For instance, if it is alleged that he committed the offence charged within the operational period of a suspended sentence or while subject to a conditional discharge or probation order (see Chapter 30 above), that fact should be stated in the application.

The application must, whether made orally or in writing, be accompanied by a detailed written statement of the applicant's means, including his disposable capital and disposable income, so as to establish that he requires assistance in his defence. If that statement is not submitted, no legal aid order can be made.

An oral application for aid will always be considered by the magistrates themselves, though a single magistrate has power to hear and determine that application alone. A written application is assessed first by the court clerk, who may make the order sought, refuse it (if his decision can be made subject to review by a Criminal Legal Aid Committee under (2) below), or refer it to a magistrate or a full bench for decision. The determination of the applicant's contribution, if any, is considered at section 34.6.

If magistrates refuse an application for legal aid, the accused may have one or more of three possible remedies to challenge that refusal. The availability of these remedies depends upon the nature of the offence charged and the stage which the proceedings in respect of it have reached by the time the challenge is made. In summary, the following rules apply:

1. The accused may apply to a Criminal Legal Aid Committee for review of the magistrates' decision, if:
    a) the offence charged is triable only on indictment or is triable either way; and
    b) the magistrates' reason for refusing legal aid was not the sufficiency of means; and
    c) application for the review is served on the Committee within 21 days of the refusal.
2. Application may be made (usually in writing) to the Crown Court which will try the accused if legal aid was refused to him on the occasion of his being committed to that court for trial or sentence. This is in effect a fresh application for aid and not strictly speaking an 'appeal' against the magistrates' decision.
3. Application might be made in any case to the High Court for judicial review of the magistrates' decision, and for an order to compel them either to reconsider their decision or to grant aid, if they have failed to take account of relevant factors, or have taken account of irrelevant factors, or have exercised their discretion in a clearly unreasonable way. Such an application is both expensive and difficult to maintain.

It can therefore be seen that, if the accused is to be tried summarily, for instance, for careless driving, or on a charge of theft for which he has elected summary trial, he has no entitlement to legal aid in respect of the preparation of his defence and its presentation at trial, and can challenge the magistrates' denial of it to him only by application for judicial review or (if the offence is triable either way) to the Criminal Legal Aid Committee. Having in mind the complexity, delay and expense of the former remedy, it is the latter which in almost all cases the accused should be advised to choose provided he satisfies the conditions which give the Committee jurisdiction.

34.6 Amount of aid and contributions

If legal aid is granted to the accused, he may be ordered to pay a contribution towards the costs of his defence. This will most usually be calculated by reference to his means as they appear from the written statement he is obliged to submit on application. If the accused is receiving supplementary benefit, he cannot be ordered to make any contribution at all, but otherwise the court assesses the contribution in accordance with scales laid down by the Treasury.

The contribution can be ordered paid immediately and in full upon the grant of aid being made, if the court thinks it should come from the disposable capital of the accused. If it is instead ordered paid from his disposable income, it is usual to order payment by weekly instalments over a period of six months (termed the 'contribution period') following the date the grant was made. Payments are made into the court which granted aid.

If the accused fails to pay the contribution assessed upon him, the magistrates may take one of two courses once it is proved to them that the failure is deliberate, and that the accused has the means to make the required payments:

1. the grant of legal aid may be revoked if the proceedings have not yet been concluded;
2. the accused may be sued in the civil courts for debt if the proceedings have been concluded or following revocation of the grant of aid.

If the accused is found not guilty at trial, the court which tries him usually has the power to order that his costs paid from central funds, and if he is in receipt of legal aid it may reduce or even revoke the contribution order made against him while the proceedings were still going on, and may repay to him all or some of the instalments he has already paid in compliance with the order.

34.7 Choice of representative

Where legal aid is granted for criminal proceedings, the court can give aid for representation by counsel if the case is to be tried on indictment or, if tried summarily, is an offence triable either way and the court considers that the retention of counsel is justified by the seriousness or difficulty of the case. Orders that the co-accused be represented by the same counsel may be made where no conflict of interest seems likely to arise between defendants. The order for aid almost always allows for the retention of a solicitor both for preparation of the case and its presentation. Mention should also be made of the newly-created duty solicitor schemes which provide instant legal advice and representation in selected magistrates' courts without the need for a formal application for legal aid; thus far such schemes are not widespread. The grantee has a free choice of representative insofar as solicitors are willing to accept legally-aided work and counsel is not 'too busy' to deal with the case; no counsel or solicitor ever made his fortune from the legal aid fund, since bills of costs and fee notes are invariably 'taxed down' by the court on assessing payments due from the fund, to a level far below what could be charged to a client who pays privately.

34.8 Remands

A remand is the dealing with the accused on an adjournment of the case either before, during or after his trial. Whenever a court has proceedings before it, and wishes to adjourn those proceedings to a later fixed day or time, it must remand the accused to appear before it at the resumed hearing. The remand may be in custody or on bail, and the following points must be noted:

1. Where an accused is brought before the magistrates after his arrest for an indictable offence which is to be tried on indictment, and the magistrates will hold committal proceedings at some later date, they must remand the accused to a fixed time and place: s5 MCA 1980.
2. If the magistrates have before them an accused who is charged with a summary offence, or with an indictable offence which is to be tried summarily, they *may* remand the accused either before or during the hearing, fixing a date for the resumed hearing, and *must* remand him if the trial has begun, he is 17 or over, the offence is triable either way, and he came first before the court in custody or has been remanded at an earlier hearing: s10 MCA 1980.
3. If the accused is remanded on bail, the remand can be for an unlimited period unless he has been convicted, in which case it must be not more than four weeks at a time: s10(3) MCA 1980.
4. If remanded in custody before conviction, the remand must normally not exceed eight days: ss128 and 128A MCA 1980 as inserted by s155 CJA 1988. Following conviction, a remand in custody before sentence must not exceed three weeks: s10(3) MCA 1980.
5. A person remanded in custody must be brought before the court at the end of the period of remand unless either he is too ill to attend, or is legally represented and consents to the further remand being made in his absence: s10(3) as amended by s59 and Schedule 9 CJA 1982.
6. On the occasion of his appearance before the court on the day fixed in the remand (or with his consent, in his absence) the court considers whether to remand him further, and whether to change the remand from bail to custody or vice versa. There is no limit to the number of times an accused may be remanded in the course of proceedings against him, but if there are many remands in custody the High Court may grant bail on the ground that they are excessive.
7. The decision to remand can be challenged by application for judicial review, or, if in custody, by application for bail to the Crown Court or High Court or Court of Appeal as appropriate.

8. Remand is the process of fixing a time and place for a resumed hearing. Where the magistrates are under no duty to remand, they may instead simply adjourn the case to a date to be notified to the accused.
9. The purpose of remand is to ensure the accused's attendance at court on the date fixed for resumption of the hearing or further remand. A failure to appear on the due date may be a breach of bail if the accused was remanded on bail.
10. An accused may lawfully be remanded by one magistrates' court to appear later before another such court within the same petty sessional division. It is not necessary that the remand require him to return to the very court which gave it: *R v Avon Magistrates' Courts Committee, ex parte Bath Law Society* [1988] 2 WLR 137.

34.9 The duty of counsel

There is no compulsion upon an accused to engage representatives to act for him. He may conduct his own defence in any court if he so chooses. Where he retains counsel, counsel is under a general duty to ensure that the accused is not left unrepresented at any stage of the trial, unless he is dismissed by the accused. This includes a duty to appear at the due time to act for the client (and a court which proceeds in the absence of counsel, knowing that the accused wishes him to be present, risks having its decision quashed), and a duty not to absent himself from the trial except in circumstances which could not reasonably have been foreseen, and only then if the client and solicitor have given their consent, and a competent replacement is found who is cognisant with the case. If the client tells counsel before the trial that he is guilty, but wishes to plead not guilty, counsel must withdraw from the case. If the accused informs counsel of his guilt during the trial, but makes no application to change his plea, counsel has a discretion to withdraw or to continue to act but, if he chooses the latter course, he must not assert his client's innocence to the court and is restricted to arguing that the prosecution have failed to prove his guilt. These and other duties of defending (and prosecuting) counsel can be found in the General Council of the Bar's *Code of Conduct for the Bar of England and Wales* .

35

Bail

35.1 Introduction

35.2 The presumption of bail

35.3 Grounds for denial of bail

35.4 Factors material to a bail application

35.5 Procedure at a bail hearing

35.6 Renewed applications to the magistrates

35.7 Application to the Crown Court

35.8 Application to the High Court

35.9 Bail conditions

35.10 Bail following conviction

35.11 The prosecution's right of appeal

35.1 Introduction

Bail is the release of a person from lawful custody subject to a condition that he surrender once more to custody at a stated time and place, and subject also to such other conditions as are necessary to secure his subsequent surrender and to prevent his obstructing justice or causing harm to persons or property pending that surrender. The grant of bail by a magistrates' court falls for consideration in this chapter, together with the courses open to an accused person to whom bail is denied by magistrates or is granted subject to conditions he considers unduly restrictive.

There are more than a dozen different circumstances in which applications for bail may be made, but the discussion which follows centres upon applications made before a defendant has been convicted by magistrates or committed by them for trial in the Crown Court. Mention will be made also of bail applications following conviction by magistrates.

35.2 The presumption of bail

An accused person who appears before magistrates has no 'right' to be released from custody pending trial. It is common to speak of a 'right to bail', but in truth there is merely a presumption that bail will be granted to someone charged with an offence. In effect, the prosecution bears the burden of proving to the magistrates' satisfaction that there are good reasons for remanding the accused in custody.

Section 4 Bail Act 1976:

> '(1) A person to whom this section applies shall be granted bail except as provided in Schedule 1 to this Act.
> (2) This section applies to a person who is accused of an offence when:
> (a) he appears or is brought before a magistrates' court or the Crown Court in the course of or in connection with proceedings for the offence, or
> (b) he applies to a court for bail in connection with the proceedings, but this subsection does not apply as respects proceedings on or after a person's conviction of the offence.'

Section 26 CJPOA 1994 removes the right to bail for persons accused or convicted of committing an offence while on bail. Under s25 CJPOA, no bail will be given to defendants charged with or convicted of homicice or rape, including attempted homicide or rape, if they have a previous conviction for such an offence.

35.3 Grounds for denial of bail

The presumption created by s4 of the 1976 Act can be rebutted only in a limited number of circumstances. The most common grounds for denying bail relate to the dangers of the accused's absconding, reoffending or interfering with witnesses while awaiting trial.

Schedule 1 para 2 Bail Act 1976:

> 'The defendant need not be granted bail if the court is satisfied that there are substantial grounds for believing that the defendant, if released on bail (whether subject to conditions or not) would:
> (a) fail to surrender to custody, or
> (b) commit an offence while on bail, or
> (c) interfere with witnesses or otherwise obstruct the course of justice, whether in relation to himself or any other person.'

There are other, less commonly invoked, grounds of refusal, and these, taken together with the grounds contained in para 2 of Sch 1 of the 1976 Act, comprise the complete and exclusive reasons for which a court may lawfully deny bail to an accused person.

Schedule 1 paras 3 and 5 Bail Act 1976.

> '3. The defendant need not be granted bail if the court is satisfied that the defendant should be kept in custody for his own protection or, if he is a child or young person, for his own welfare.

5. The defendant need not be granted bail where the court is satisfied that it has not been practicable to obtain sufficient information for the purposes of taking the decisions required by this part of this Schedule for want of time since the institution of the proceedings against him.'

35.4 Factors material to a bail application

When an accused appears before a magistrates' court and applies for bail, the court must consider whether any of the grounds stated above is made out by the prosecution. In deciding that question, the court must have regard to prescribed matters. The list of relevant factors contained in Sch 1 to the Bail Act is very nearly exhaustive, though the inclusion of 'other things which appear to be relevant' among them indicates that the court should look for any special features in the offence charged or the accused before it.

Schedule 1 para 9 Bail Act 1976:

> 'In taking the decisions required by paragraph 2 ... the court shall have regard to such of the following considerations as appear to it to be relevant, that is to say:
> (a) the nature and seriousness of the offence (and the probable method of dealing with the defendant for it),
> (b) the character, antecedents, associations and community ties of the defendant,
> (c) the defendant's record as respects the fulfilment of his obligations under previous grants of bail in criminal proceedings,
> (d) except in the case of a defendant whose case is adjourned for inquiries or a report, the strength of the evidence of his having committed the offence,
> as well as to any other things which appear to be relevant.'

In preparing an application for bail, a defending solicitor must review carefully the state of the evidence against the client (though at an early stage of the proceedings detailed statements of prosecution witnesses might not be available from the CPS), take full instructions from the client upon his previous criminal record and record of bail (if any), his home circumstances, his employment, the availability of sureties (see section 35.9) and the client's willingness to submit to a curfew, or to report regularly to the police, should conditions be attached to a grant of bail. It is important to anticipate objections the CPS will take to bail being granted, and to have the evidence ready at court to meet those objections.

35.5 Procedure at a bail hearing

In the magistrates' court, bail applications are made orally in open court. Only rarely do they last more than a few minutes. In the great majority of cases the CPS will not object to bail and it will be granted without conditions. In cases where objection is however made, and a remand in custody requested by the prosecution, the proceedings will usually follow a conventional course:

1. The court clerk asks the CPS representative whether a grant of unconditional bail is opposed.
2. The defence representative formally requests that bail be granted.
3. The CPS outlines the basis of its objection and identifies which of the grounds in Sch 1 of the 1976 Act it believes satisfied (see section 35.3).
4. A police officer nominated by the CPS, and usually attached to the police station responsible for collecting evidence of the offence, enters the witness box, takes the oath and testifies in support of the objections. He will refer, if appropriate, to printed records of the accused's previous convictions (though these should not be read out, the magistrates being supplied instead with a copy of them) and of his compliance with bail on earlier occasions, and will give details of the grounds upon which he believes that the accused will abscond, commit further offences, or interfere with witnesses, if granted bail.
5. The officer is cross-examined by the defence representative as to the basis and strength of his objections. Matters such as the time lapse since the accused last committed an offence, a stable home life, family and employment ties should, if appropriate, all be raised in an attempt to undermine the risk that the magistrates will too readily be persuaded that the officer's fears are justified.
6. The defence representative addresses the court, pointing out features about the case and about the accused which argue in favour of bail being granted. The prosecution objections should be taken one by one and the court referred to the Sch 1 matters stated at section 35.4. The accused's ability and willingness to abide by conditions imposed, such as sureties, a curfew or reporting requirements, should be mentioned.
7. The magistrates reach their decision. It is unusual for them to retire from the court, and most often they stay on the bench, confer very briefly and declare their ruling at once.
8. If bail is granted, the clerk explains to the accused the nature of the obligation he has to surrender to the court's custody at the time fixed for further consideration of his case, the consequences of his failure to appear at that time, and the effect of any conditions the magistrates have thought it necessary to attach to the bail.
9. Where the charge against the accused is one of murder, attempted murder, manslaughter, rape or attempted rape, and the court decides to grant bail, it must usually state the reasons for its decision and cause those reasons to be entered in the record of the proceedings: s9A BA 1976 as inserted by s153 Criminal Justice Act 1988.

35.6 Renewed applications to the magistrates

If bail is denied to an accused on his first appearance, and he is remanded in custody after a full or briefly argued bail application, he must normally be brought again before the court before the expiry of eight days following that remand. On that second appearance, the magistrates must allow him to make and must consider afresh a further full application for bail, even though there has been no change of circumstances since his first appearance and the further application is based upon precisely the same factual and legal argument as was advanced on his first appearance: Sch II Part I Bail Act 1976 as inserted by s154 CJA 1988. If bail is once more denied, the court need not, on subsequent remand hearings, hear argument on bail unless some fresh issue of fact or law can be raised in support of it.

It is therefore very difficult to obtain bail for a client from a magistrates' court once a bench has ruled against his first and second applications after a full hearing. For most practical purposes, the only courses open to the accused to overturn the magistrates' decision will be application to the Crown Court or the High Court, as outlined in sections 35.7 and 35.8.

35.7 Application to the Crown Court

The Crown Court has jurisdiction, under s81 Supreme Court Act 1981, to grant bail to an accused to whom it was denied by magistrates, and to vary a grant they made so as to remove or mollify conditions they imposed and to which the accused objects. The jurisdiction is 'original', in the sense that the Crown Court rehears fully the question of bail, and is not truly acting in the role of an appellate tribunal: it is not necessary that a change of circumstances be proven such as would require a magistrates' court to reopen the matter of bail. Thus an accused who fails to procure magistrates' bail is usually best advised to pursue his application before a Crown Court judge.

The application is most often made in writing on a standard form, the original of which is served on the CPS and a copy delivered to the Crown Court which is to hear the application. The form contains the following information:

1. the accused's name and address;
2. the name and address of the defending solicitor;
3. the name of the prison in which the accused is detained (if he was remanded in custody);
4. the date of his last remand;
5. the stage the proceedings have reached;
6. the name of the offence with which the accused is charged;
7. the accused's previous convictions;
8. brief grounds upon which the decision of the magistrates is challenged;
9. the names of proposed sureties and the amounts they are prepared to offer.

The copy sent to the Crown Court must, if the application relates to a refusal of bail, be accompanied by a certificate, issued by the magistrates who refused it, stating that they made their refusal only after hearing full argument on the question of bail. The certificate must be issued to the defence on request, and if the defence does not bother to obtain it the Crown Court has no power to grant bail. It should therefore be asked for at once on the conclusion of the unsuccessful application to the magistrates.

35.8 Application to the High Court

The High Court has power under s22 Criminal Justice Act 1967 to grant bail to an accused to whom it has been refused by magistrates, and to vary to the advantage of the accused the conditions of bail which has been given. It is now quite rare for this jurisdiction to be invoked, because the alternative route of application to the Crown Court described at section 35.7 is simpler. Legal aid for applications to a High Court judge is not available under the criminal legal aid scheme, so a separate legal aid application would have to be made. In practice, an accused who fails to obtain bail from a magistrates' court, or who is granted bail but thinks the conditions attached too onerous, will first apply to the Crown Court and only if unsuccessful in that application will consider asking the High Court's assistance.

The procedure for High Court bail hearings is contained in RSC O.79 r9 and is briefly as follows:

1. the accused takes out an *inter partes* Summons returnable before a judge in chambers;
2. an affidavit is sworn detailing the grounds of the application;
3. the Summons and affidavit are served on the CPS;
4. an oral hearing takes place at which both parties may appear and present evidence;
5. there is no appeal from the judge's decision, and the accused cannot make further application to a different High Court judge.

35.9 Bail conditions

Whenever bail is granted, a court can make the grant 'unconditional', in which case the accused's sole obligation will be to surrender to custody at a time and place notified to him, or 'conditional', in which case additional requirements are imposed upon him under s3(6) Bail Act 1976 to guarantee that he complies with that obligation and does not commit further offences or interfere with witnesses in the meantime. There is no closed list of the types of condition which can be imposed, but the court must be satisfied that the ones it has in mind are reasonably necessary to the case before it because there is a 'real and not a fanciful risk' that the accused will abscond, re-offend or interfere with evidence. A defendant complies with his obligation to surrender to bail by reporting in person to the court official responsible for keeping records of his attendance. He is however liable to be arrested if he subsequently leaves the court precincts without permission: *DPP* v *Richards* [1988] 3 All ER 406.

The conditions most commonly attached include a condition of residence, whereby the accused must live and sleep at a specified address; a condition of reporting to the local police station on a regular basis (for example, three times a week); a curfew to keep the accused indoors between certain hours; a condition preventing the accused from entering a particular area or place; a condition preventing contact with specified persons, such as the alleged victim; the surrender of travel documents.

The provision of sureties may also be required before release on bail (s3(4) Bail Act 1976). A surety's obligation is to ensure that the accused attends court and he promises an amount of money which will be forfeited if the accused fails to attend. There is a strong presumption that the surety will forfeit the full amount he has promised: see *R* v *Southampton Justices, ex parte Green* [1976] QB 11 and, most recently, *R* v *Maidstone County Court, ex parte Lever* (1994) The Times 7 November.

35.10 Bail following conviction

Once an accused has been convicted by magistrates of the offence charged, he has no 'right' to bail and there is no presumption that bail will be granted pending the imposition of sentence or the hearing of an appeal. The court which convicts him has a discretion to grant bail in these circumstances, but usually denies bail unless:

1. it is unlikely that a custodial sentence will be imposed; or
2. there is little prospect of the accused's absconding before sentence is passed upon him or his appeal to the High Court or Divisional Court against conviction or sentence is heard.

A convicted accused may make a further application for bail, if it is denied him by magistrates, in the following manner:

1. To the Crown Court, if the magistrates have remanded him in custody pending sentence by themselves or by the Crown Court on committal for sentence, or if the accused has given notice of appeal to the Crown Court against conviction or sentence.
2. To the High Court, if the accused has given notice of his intention to appeal to that court by way of case stated or judicial review against conviction or sentence by the magistrates, or against the determination of any appeal he may have brought to the Crown Court against the magistrates' findings.

35.11 The prosecution's right of appeal

The Bail (Amendment) Act 1993 allows the prosecution a right of appeal against decisions to allow bail. It is only available against a decision by the magistrates' court and where the offence is one punishable by a term of imprisonment of five years or more or s12 and 12A Theft Act 1968. The appeal is to the Crown Court and oral notice must be given at the conclusion of the proceedings in which bail was granted, with written notice within two hours of the conclusion. The prosecution must already have requested during the proceedings that bail be denied. The defendant is remanded in custody until the appeal is heard, which must be within 48 hours (excluding weekends and public holidays).

In order to ensure that custody time limits under ss128 and 129 MCA 1980 are complied with, a Crown Court judge, hearing an appeal by the prosecution, should stipulate a time limit if the person is remanded in custody and has not as yet been committed for trial: *R v Governor of Pentonville Prison, ex parte Bone* (1994) The Times 15 November.

36

Recent Cases

36.1 Service of proceedings

36.2 Discovery and inspection of documents

36.3 The effect of delay

36.4 County court procedure

36.5 Prosecuting a summary trial

36.6 Trial by jury

36.7 Offences triable either way

36.8 Sentencing of adult offenders

PART I: CIVIL PROCEDURE

36.1 Service of proceedings

Forward v *West Sussex County Council and Others* [1995] 1 WLR 1469 Court of Appeal (Sir Thomas Bingham MR, Rose and Hobhouse LJJ)

Service of the writ by post at the defendant's last known address – defendant not living at the address and having no notice of the proceedings – whether service valid

Facts
By a writ issued in 1988 the plaintiff commenced proceedings against a number of defendants claiming damages for personal injuries. In 1989, within the period for service, the writ was purportedly served on the fourth defendant by sending a copy by ordinary first class post to the defendant's last known postal address. The defendant had left the neighbourhood in 1989. No acknowledgement of service was entered but the writ was not returned undelivered to the plaintiff's solicitors.

Held
On a true construction of RSC O.10 r1(2) service was effected when the proceedings

were brought to the attention of the defendant and not on the delivery of the writ to his last known address.

Sir Thomas Bingham MR:

'The issue which we now have to resolve arises on the construction of RSC O.10, r1(2)(a). Is service duly effected if the proceedings are duly sent by ordinary first class post to the defendant at his usual or last known address? The plaintiff argued that it is. If judgment were entered in default following such service and the defendant were able to show that he had never received the proceedings and so had no opportunity to defend, he would have strong grounds for asking that the judgment should be set aside. But that would not impugn the validity of the service as service, only the fairness of allowing the judgment to stand. Counsel for the fourth defendant challenged this approach. It was a cardinal rule of procedure that a party should not in ordinary circumstances be answerable to a claim of which he had no notice. If he could show that the proceedings, although sent to and delivered to his last address known to the plaintiff, had not in fact come to his notice then, good service had not been effected.'

Commentary
For further consideration of the issue see *The Supreme Court Practice* 1995, paragraphs 10/1/1 and 10/1/4.

Trade Indemnity plc and Others v *Forsakringsaktiebolaget Njord (in liq)* [1995] 1 All ER 796 Queen's Bench Division (Commercial Court) (Rix J)

Forum conveniens

Facts
The plaintiffs obtained ex parte leave under RSC O.11, r1(1) for service out of the jurisdiction of a writ against the defendant Swedish company on the ground that the contracts between the parties had been made within the English jurisdiction and, by implication, were governed by English law. The defendant company issued a summons to set aside the writ and its service, disputing the jurisdiction of the English court on the principal ground that Sweden was the natural and appropriate jurisdiction.

Held
Allowing the appeal the court held that the plaintiffs were unable to establish that England was the appropriate forum since the real focus of dispute was the conduct of the defendant's business in Sweden. The Swedish courts were far better placed to hear and determine issues as to Swedish business practices. Sweden was clearly the most convenient forum.

Commentary
The decision encompasses the general principle that the system of law most suited to hearing the action has the closest and most real connection with the issues under

dispute. On the principles to be applied in contract cases see Lord Denning's comments in *Coast Lines Ltd* v *Hudig Chartering* [1972] 1 All ER 451 Court of Appeal.

36.2 Discovery and inspection of documents

Liddell* v *Middleton (1995) The Times 17 July Court of Appeal (Stuart-Smith, Peter Gibson and Hutchinson LJJ)

Limiting expert witnesses

Facts
The defendant appealed against the decision of Steel J giving judgment for the plaintiff against the defendant subject to a 25 per cent deduction in respect of the plaintiff's contributory negligence in a road traffic accident on 5 May 1990.

Held
The appeal was allowed to the extent that each party was equally to blame and the court made an apportionment of 50:50. It was of the opinion that whilst it could not order the restriction of the evidence of expert witnesses in a particular case on the grounds of its relevancy or admissibility, the opinion of such witnesses could not consist of conclusions in respect of findings of fact, which were strictly matters for the trial judge to determine.

Stuart-Smith LJ:

> 'There was no trial by experts in the English courts; they contributed to the expense of trials. There was a regrettable tendency in personal injury cases involving road accidents to have a large number of experts. They added to the costs of litigation and the length of the trial.'

Commentary
The comments of the Court of Appeal in *Rawlinson* v *Westbrook* and *Liddell* v *Middleton* provides judicial support for the concerns expressed in Lord Woolf's interim report and the Lord Chief Justice's *Practice Direction (Civil Litigation: Case Management)* [1995] 1 WLR 262.

Rawlinson* v *Westbrook and Another (1995) The Times 25 January Court of Appeal (Staughton, Nourse and Leggatt LJJ)

Too many experts

Facts
The plaintiff appealed against the dismissal by Morritt J of his claim to entitlement of fees on a quantum meruit basis for providing his services to the defendant's practice as surveyors, known as Frank Westbrook.

Held
Dismissing the appeal, the court was of the opinion that to save litigants from their own folly, the Rules of the Supreme Court should be amended to so as to make provision to enable judges and masters to refuse to allow expert evidence to be given at the trial of the action.

Staughton LJ:

> 'RSC O.38, r4 allowed a judge to limit the number of experts but not to exclude such evidence altogether. As a result judges and masters were frequently forced to observe the spectacle of litigants, like lemmings, rushing to their own doom by engaging too many and unnecessary experts. There had been no need for any expert evidence to be called at all: both parties were chartered surveyors who could have given the relevant evidence themselves. But every litigant thought, or at least his solicitor did, that he had to have at least one expert called to give evidence for him. It was high time that the courts were given power to refuse to allow such evidence to be called.'

36.3 The effect of delay

Owen (trading as Max Owen Associates) v *Pugh; Beamish and Another* v *Owen (trading as Max Owen Associates)* [1995] 3 All ER 345 Queen's Bench Division (Otton J)

Dismissal of counterclaim for want of prosecution

Facts
The defendants engaged the plaintiff to supervise building work on a property they owned. The plaintiff finished the work in September 1987 and in June 1988 commenced proceedings in the county court to recover £774.48 in professional fees. The defendants served a defence and set-off and counterclaimed £69,548 in damages for breach of duty. Orders were made for discovery and inspection and in December 1988 the action was transferred to the High Court. After agreeing various extensions of time the plaintiff heard nothing further from the defendants until November 1993 when they served a notice of intention to proceed. The plaintiff applied for and obtained an order dismissing the defendant's counterclaim for want of prosecution. The defendants appealed.

Held
Dismissing the appeal the court held that it had jurisdiction to dismiss a counterclaim for want of prosecution both under its inherent jurisdiction to control

litigation and on an interpretation of the RSC which made it clear that a counterclaim was equivalent to a separate action. Therefore, the rules which applied to a plaintiff in a main action applied to a counterclaim in that neither could remain unprosecuted without a sanction applied.

Rowe v *Glenister and Others* (1995) The Times 7 August Court of Appeal (Beldam, Waite LJJ and Sir Christopher Slade)

Defendant's application to strike out

Facts
The plaintiff appealed against an order of Millett J on 20 June 1991 striking out for want of prosecution her action against the second and fourth defendants, Graham and Margaret Glenister.

Held
Allowing the appeal, the court held that a defendant who sought the striking out of an action on the ground of delay had to establish that he had suffered additional prejudice since the writ was issued.

Waite LJ:

> '... it was not enough for the defendant to show merely that memories must have grown fainter during the period of the post-writ delay. He had to establish that in some specific respect particular witnesses had become disabled, by reason of lapse of time during the period of culpable delay, from giving evidence as cogent and complete as they would have been in a position to give had the trial been held without the delay.'

Yorkshire Regional Health Authority v *Fairclough Building Ltd* (1995) The Times 16 November Court of Appeal (Neill, Evans and Millett LJJ)

Section 35 Limitation Act 1980 – 'new claims'

Facts
The plaintiffs, a regional health authority, brought proceedings against the defendant architect for breach of contract in respect of works carried out at one of the plaintiffs' hospitals. Before issue of the writ, a National Health Service Trust was established to own and manage the hospital. On the plaintiffs' application under O.15 r7 the Official Referee allowed the trust to be made a party to the proceedings. The defendants appealed on two grounds. Firstly, the substitution of the trust was a 'new claim' within s35 Limitation Act 1980. Secondly, does O.15 r7 allow the substitution after the expiry of the limitation period?

Held
Dismissing the appeal the court considered the words 'the addition or substitution of a new party' in s35(2)(b) do not include claims, which although involving a new or

substituted party, do not involve a new cause of action. The court therefore had jurisdiction under r7 to make the substitution. Second the substitution of the trust under O.15, r7 did not amount to a 'new claim' within the meaning of s35(2). The trust could therefore be made a party to the action even though the limitation period had expired.

36.4 County court procedure

Heer v *Tutton and Another* (1995) The Times 5 June Court of Appeal (Sir Thomas Bingham MR, Gibson and Saville LJJ)

Extension of time for the service of the summons in the county court

Facts
The plaintiff had begun an action in the county court by default summons claiming damages for personal injuries and had reached an agreement with the defendants to extend time generally for the service of the defence. In consequence of the agreement 12 months had expired from the date of the service of the summons without delivery of admission, defence or counterclaim. The plaintiff appealed against an order by Heald J at Nottingham County Court, who had refused his application to enter a default judgment against the defendants, following their submission that the action had been struck out under CCR O.9, r10.

Held
Allowing the appeal the court held that where parties to a county court action begun by default summons agreed to extend time for the delivery of the defence with the result that a period of 12 months elapsed from the service of the summons, the effect of the agreement was to oust CCR O.9, r10 as the agreement supersedes provisions of the rules, so that the action could not be struck out under that rule.

Commentary
The parties' agreement superseded the operation of the rules. For further reference see the County Court Rules Supplement, paras C9/10 and C13/14.

Taylor v *Remploy* [1995] 3 CL 434 Cardiff County Court (Norman Francis sitting as a Deputy County Court Judge)

Exchange of witness statements after agreed time – oral evidence

Facts
The plaintiff's and defendant's solicitors in a personal injuries action had agreed a date for the exchange of witness statements. The defendant's solicitors had exchanged one witness statement in compliance with the agreement but three

months after the agreed date served five more witness statements. All were witnesses still in the employment of the defendant and whose existence and importance to the action should have been appreciated prior to the date for the exchange of witness statements. The deputy district judge refused the defendant's application for leave to adduce oral evidence from the five witnesses whose statements had been disclosed late. No affidavit evidence was adduced by the defendant's solicitors on the appeal from the deputy district judge's order. The defendant appealed.

Held
Dismissing the appeal, the court held that a party failing to comply with CCR O.20 r12A and O.17 r11(4) requiring the simultaneous exchange of witness statements and disclosing witness statements late must explain his/her default on affidavit if seeking the exercise of the court's discretion to allow him to adduce oral evidence at trial from witnesses whose statements had been disclosed late. Otherwise a late witness cannot be called.

PART II: CRIMINAL PROCEDURE

36.5 Prosecuting a summary offence

R v Birmingham Magistrates' Court, ex parte Ahmed [1995] Crim LR 503 Queen's Bench Division (McCowan LJ and Buxton J)

The magistrates' clerk

Facts
The applicant sought an order for certiorari quashing convictions for receiving stolen goods and deception. He argued that the Justices' Clerk had retired with the magistrates, without having been invited to do so in open court. It had been the practice of the chairman for 20 years to invite the clerk to join them in the retiring room to learn the court's findings.

Held
In quashing the conviction the court held it had been wrong for the clerk to join the magistrates in the retiring room unless invited to do so in open court. To do this arouses suspicion that he/she is participating in deciding the verdict, which was particularly undesirable as there was no point of law arising. The fact that this had been the regular practice of the chairman for 20 years was no justification and ran contrary to *Practice Direction* [1953] 1 WLR 1416 and *R v Eccles Justices, ex parte Fitzpatrick* (1989) 89 Cr App R 324.

Commentary
The decision confirms the previously-held practice that the clerk should retire with the magistrates only when it is plainly necessary and the clerk's conduct should not give rise to a reasonable inference of their involvement in the decision-making process.

36.6 Trial by jury

R v *Armstrong* [1995] Crim LR 831 Court of Appeal (Criminal Division) (Hirst LJ, Hidden and Mitchell JJ)

Witness – statement served with committal bundle – prosecutor's duty to call

Facts
The defendant was convicted of robbery and possession of a firearm arising out of an armed robbery. The defence was alibi. A statement was taken by the police from the defendant's girlfriend in which she said that he was with her two-and-a-half hours before the offence, but could not remember if he had then gone out. The statement was included in the committal bundle and her name was given by the defence in the alibi notice. At the trial defence counsel requested that prosecution counsel should read the statement. Prosecution counsel declined, relying on *R* v *Nugent* [1977] 1 WLR 789. The judge ruled against the defence submission that prosecuting counsel was bound to do so.

Held
Dismissing the appeal, it was clear from *R* v *Oliva* [1965] 3 All ER 116 that there was a duty on the prosecution to call or tender a witness whose statement had been served, if required to do so, unless that witness could not be believed. The judge should have allowed the submission that the prosecution should read the statement, but the irregularity was not material in the light of the other evidence.

Commentary
Both the judgments in *R* v *Armstrong* and *R* v *Russell-Jones* (below) agree on the substance of the prosecutor's duty in that it is the prosecutor who has the primary responsibility for deciding whether a witness is incredible or unworthy of belief. *Russell-Jones*, however, appears to give the prosecutor a wider discretion when deciding whether to call peripheral witnesses not essential, in the view of the prosecutor, to 'the unfolding of the narratives on which the prosecution is based' (per Lord Roche in *Seneviratne* v *R* [1936] 3 All ER 36).

R v Bills (1995) The Times 1 March Court of Appeal (Russell LJJ, Turner and Hooper JJ)

Jury changed verdict after hearing antecedents

Facts
The defendant had been charged with an offence of wounding with intent to cause grievous bodily harm contrary to s18 Offences Against the Person Act 1861. The jury acquitted him of that offence and convicted him of the lesser offence of unlawful wounding contrary to s20. After the trial judge had accepted the verdict, and while the jury remained in the jury box, prosecuting counsel dealt with the defendant's antecedents which included other offences of violence. The jury were then discharged. Immediately upon leaving the court a juror spoke the court usher and told him the jury foreman had given the wrong verdict. The judge was informed who decided to reconvene the jury and invited them to explain themselves. They indicated the wrong verdict had been returned. The judge clarified three possible verdicts and the most serious verdict was given and recorded. The defendant appealed against his conviction for wounding with intent to cause grievous bodily harm contrary to s18 of the 1861 Act.

Held
In allowing the appeal the court stated that although there was no fixed rule of principle or of law that once the jury had been discharged it could not reconsider its verdicts, it could not be considered safe for them to reconsider when they had heard evidence of the defendant's antecedents.

R v K (1995) The Times 14 April Court of Appeal (Hutchinson LJ, Alliot and Curtis JJ)

Solicitor should not have had juror followed – bias

Facts
A defence witness claimed at the conclusion of the trial on one count of indecent assault and two counts of rape that a juror was known to her and to two other witnesses, including the complainant. The defendant's solicitors instructed inquiry agents to follow the juror and to establish that she was the person the witness claimed her to be. The defendant appealed against his conviction.

Held
Allowing the defendant's appeal and ordering a retrial the court stated that at no stage of the trial had the juror indicated that she knew any of the witnesses, although, as was well known, jurors should give such an indication. The case was a highly sensitive one, and the fact that two of the witnesses were known to the juror

was vital. There was a real danger of bias in the sense that the juror might have unfairly regarded the appellant's case. That was the test posited in *R* v *Gough* [1993] AC 646.

Curtis J:

'Their Lordships wished to observe that the conduct of defence solicitors, who, when they became aware of what had been said by the witness, took steps themselves to follow the juror and instructed an inquiry agent to follow he, was most ill advised and should never be repeated.

It was perfectly permissible for them to take steps to clarify the position concerning their client but not without leave of the Court of Appeal. The principle had been made quite clear in *R* v *McCluskey* (1993) 98 Cr App R 216.'

R v *Russell-Jones* [1995] 3 All ER 239 Court of Appeal (Kennedy LJ, Owen and Laws JJ)

Witness not called by prosecution – whether court should have required calling or tendering of witness

Facts

On 26 October 1993 at Swansea Crown Court, on a retrial, the appellant was convicted of arson and attempting to obtain property by deception. He appealed against the conviction on the ground that at the start of the retrial the trial judge wrongly rejected the defence submission that the prosecution should either call or tender PC Parsons, a witness who had given evidence at the first trial. The defendant appealed.

Held

Dismissing the appeal the court held that generally the prosecution must have at court all witnesses whose statements have been served as witnesses on whom the prosecution intends to rely, if the defence want those witnesses to attend. In deciding which statements to serve, the prosecution has an unfettered discretion, but must normally disclose material statements not served. The prosecution enjoys a discretion whether to call, or tender, any witness it requires to attend, but the discretion is not unfettered and must be exercised in the interests of justice, so as to promote a fair trial (see *R* v *Viola* [1965] 3 All ER 116). In practice, the prosecution ought normally to call or offer to call all the witnesses who can give direct evidence of the primary facts of the case, unless for good reason the prosecutor regards the witness's evidence as incredible or unbelievable, but he cannot regard a witness as incredible merely because his account is not favourable to the prosecution case. However, a prosecutor will not be obliged to proffer a witness merely in order to give the defence material with which to attack the credit of other witnesses on whom the Crown relies. Because the judgment to be made is primarily that of the prosecutor, in general the court will only interfere with it if he has erred in principle.

R v Wilson; R v Sproson (1995) The Times 24 February Court of Appeal (Russell LJ, Turner and Hooper JJ)

Where wife of prison officer employed at prison where defendants on remand served on jury at their trial – real danger of bias

Facts
The appellants were arrested and held on remand at Exeter prison pending their trial for robbery. A Mr Roberts, a prison officer, came into close contact with the defendants whilst each was employed in the prison kitchens. Mr Roberts' wife received a summons for jury service and returned the form asking to be excused attendance on the basis that her husband was a serving prison officer. She was told that she could not be excused and was required to attend. Mrs Roberts was called to serve on the jury in the trial of the two appellants who were both convicted on one count of robbery.

Held
Allowing both appeals against conviction there was a real danger arising from the relationship of Mr and Mrs Roberts that in carrying out the duties of a juror Mrs Roberts might have consciously or unconsciously been guilty of bias. The court was referred to *R v Gough* [1993] AC 646, 670 where Lord Goff of Chieveley said: 'Finally, for the avoidance of doubt, I prefer to state the test in terms of real danger rather than real likelihood, to ensure the court is thinking in terms of possibility rather than probability of bias'.

Commentary
The decisions in *R v K* and *R v Wilson* indicate the increasingly difficult and sensitive issue that jurors should not have their deliberations affected by external factors and the strict application of the principles relating to biased jurors (actual or suspected) by the courts.

36.7 Offences triable either way

R v Ipswich Justices, ex parte Callaghan (1995) The Times 3 April Queen's Bench Division (Pill LJ and Keene J)

Accused's right of election for mode of trial

Facts
Mr Callaghan was jointly charged with two co-defendants with offences of attempted theft and burglary. At the mode of trial hearing, where all the parties were legally represented, the prosecution stated the case was suitable for summary trial. Mr Callaghan's solicitor concurred. His co-defendants made no representations. Before

the justices were formally asked to consider mode of trial, the clerk asked if any of the defendants were electing Crown Court trial. The two co-defendants indicated they were. The justices were advised that because two defendants were electing Crown Court trial, that was a matter for consideration in the interests of justice being served by all defendants being tried together. They stated the matter was not suitable for summary trial.

Held
Where justices were to decide whether a case involving a co-accused was suitable for summary trial it was not permissible for them to base their decision on a wish to avoid separate trials, since that would defeat the right of election given to each accused.

36.8 Sentencing of adult offenders

R v Wilson [1995] Crim LR 510 Court of Appeal (Criminal Division) (Lord Taylor CJ, Owen J and the Recorder of London)

Legal representation for the purposes of sentence

Facts
The appellant pleaded guilty to arson. She was granted legal aid for the proceedings in the magistrates' court but dismissed her solicitors after appearing in the magistrates' court. A second firm was assigned to represent her under an amended legal aid order. When she appeared at the Crown Court and pleaded guilty she was represented by counsel instructed by the second firm of solicitors, and the matter was adjourned for reports. Before she next appeared at the Crown Court, the second firm of solicitors and counsel informed the court they could no longer appear for the appellant because she no longer wanted them to act for her. At the next hearing different counsel attended to appear for her but she indicated to the court that she wished to speak for herself and did not wish to be represented. After the prosecution addressed the court the appellant spoke at length and requested that another firm of solicitors be assigned under an amended legal aid order. The judge declined to adjourn the case further and imposed seven years' imprisonment. The appellant argued the sentence was unlawful by reason of the s21(1) Powers of the Criminal Courts Act 1973.

Held
Upholding the appeal the court held that to sentence her without legal representation was unlawful. However, deciding on the merits of the case, seven years' imprisonment was the proper sentence and this would be imposed.

Commentary
The case shows the dramatic effect of the court failing to comply with the provisions requiring legal representation although, as in this case, the situation can be salvaged by the sentence being imposed on appeal. It also highlights the problematical situation of where the defendant dismisses her advocate between conviction and sentence.

Special Offer!

Would you find a revision guide, summarising the major legal developments during the previous academic year useful?

Law Update 1996 could be yours for only
£2.50 reduced from the RRP of £6.95.

Simply fill in the following questionnaire and return it to:
Andrea Dowsett, Publisher, HLT Publications, 200 Greyhound Road, London W14 9RY

If you return your questionnaire before 31st January 1997, you will be entitled to a copy of our Law Update 1996 at the reduced price of £2.50.

Student Questionnaire

Which course are you studying?

Course: _____

Institution: _____

Address: _____

Which HLT title have you bought? _____

Did you buy it:

a) at the beginning of the academic year ☐

b) half way through the academic year ☐

c) before your exams ☐

Did you buy it because:

a) you have used HLT books before ☐

b) it was recommended by your lecturer ☐

c) it was recommended by a friend ☐

d) you chose it from the bookshop ☐

Is the coverage in the book:

a) too detailed ☐

b) not detailed enough ☐

c) just right ☐

Would you describe the book as good value for money compared to other textbooks in the area?

Yes ☐   No ☐

How many HLT titles have you bought in the past? ☐

Which ones?
_____

Are there any subject areas you would like to see an HLT book on?
_____

_____

Any other comments?
_____

_____

_____

Do you own or have easy access to a PC? If so what kind of PC (hardware/software) do you use?
_____

Simply fill out your name and address below and send it with your questionnaire and a cheque made payable to 'HLT Publications' for £2.50. Address on previous page.

Name: _____

Address: _____

_____

_____

_____

LAW

UPDATE 1996

Administrative Law
Civil and Criminal Procedure
Commercial Law
Company Law
Conflict of Laws
Constitutional Law
Contract Law
Conveyancing
Criminal Law
Criminology
English Legal System
Equity and Trusts
European Union Law
Evidence
Family Law
Jurisprudence
Land Law
Law of International Trade
Public International Law
Revenue Law
Succession
Tort

HLT Publications

The HLT Law Series is planned and written to help you at every stage of your studies. Each of our range of Textbooks is brought up to date annually, and the companion volumes in the series are all designed to work together and are regularly revised and updated.

The series comprises a Textbook, a companion Casebook expanding on significant cases, a Revision WorkBook containing notes and answers to previous examination questions, the Suggested Solutions Pack of numerous previous examination questions with our suggested answers and finally the Single Paper 1996 with the paper and suggested solutions to the last London University examination paper.

We are also able to offer you Cracknell's Statutes which provide you with the relevant legislation for most of the subject areas listed below.

The HLT Law Series covers all that you need to pass your law examinations.

You can buy HLT books from your University bookshop or your local bookshop, or in case of difficulty, order direct using this form.

Here is the selection of modules covered by our series:

Administrative Law, Commercial Law, Company Law, Conflict of Laws (no Suggested Solutions Pack), Constitutional Law, Contract Law, Conveyancing (no Revision WorkBook), Criminology (no Casebook or Revision WorkBook), Criminal Law, English Legal System, Equity and Trusts, European Union Law, Evidence, Family Law, Jurisprudence (Sourcebook in place of a Casebook), Land Law, Law of International Trade, Legal Skills and System (Textbook only), Public International Law, Revenue Law (no Casebook), Succession, Tort.

Mail order prices:

Textbook £19, Casebook £19, Revision WorkBook £10, Suggested Solutions Pack (1991–1995) £7, Single Paper 1996 £3.

To complete your order, please fill in the form below:

Module	Books required	Quantity	Price	Cost
		Postage		
		TOTAL		

Prices include postage and packing in the UK.
For Europe, add 15% postage and packing (£20 maximum).
For the rest of the world, add 40% for airmail.

ORDERING

By telephone to **01892 724371**, with your credit card to hand.

By fax to **01892 724206** (giving your credit card details).

By post to:

HLT Publications, The Gatehouse, Ruck Lane, Horsmonden, TONBRIDGE, Kent TN12 8EA.

When ordering by post, please enclose full payment by cheque or banker's draft, or complete the credit card details below.

We aim to despatch your books within three working days of receiving your order.

Name:

Address:

Postcode: Telephone:

Total value of order, including postage: £

I enclose a cheque/banker's draft for the above sum, or

charge my   ☐ Access/Mastercard   ☐ Visa   ☐ American Express
Card number

☐☐☐☐ ☐☐☐☐ ☐☐☐☐ ☐☐☐☐

Expiry date ☐☐☐☐

Signature: .... Date: ....